THE EUROPEAN MONETARY
UNION AFTER THE CRISIS

This book provides a much-needed detailed analysis of the evolution of Europe over the last decade, as well as a discussion about the path of reform that has been trodden in the aftermath of the financial crisis. It offers a multidisciplinary view of the E(M)U and captures the main factors that induced the reform of the monetary union – a process that has not been linear and is far from being concluded.

The author examines the policy responses designed throughout the development of the crisis and assesses the scale of the crisis in Europe, in comparison to other parts of the world, as well as its prolonged effects both in economic and financial terms. An update on the current 'state of the art' in the conception of risk-sharing mechanisms is provided. With its innovative approach, the book analyses the financing issues which need to be taken into consideration in the design of these instruments and highlights the main categories of governmental risk-sharing mechanisms – in particular, the ones to be used as 'fiscal capacity'.

This is a timely and topical book and will be of interest to a broad audience, including experts, scholars and students of European affairs, particularly those with economic, financial, legal and political science backgrounds.

Nazaré da Costa Cabral is Associate Professor at Lisbon School of Law of the University of Lisbon and principal researcher at the Center for European, Economic, Fiscal and Tax Law Research (CIDEEFF) of the same University. She is also Chair of the Senior Board of the Portuguese Public Finance Council.

ROUTLEDGE STUDIES IN THE EUROPEAN ECONOMY

For more information about this series, please visit: www.routledge.com/series/SE0431

THE EUROPEAN MONETARY UNION AFTER THE CRISIS

From a Fiscal Union to a Fiscal Capacity

Nazaré da Costa Cabral

Routledge
Taylor & Francis Group

LONDON AND NEW YORK

First published 2021
by Routledge
2 Park Square, Milton Park, Abingdon, Oxon OX14 4RN

and by Routledge
52 Vanderbilt Avenue, New York, NY 10017

*Routledge is an imprint of the Taylor & Francis Group,
an informa business*

British Library Cataloguing-in-Publication Data
A catalogue record for this book is available from the British Library

Library of Congress Cataloging-in-Publication Data
Names: Cabral, Nazaré da Costa, author.
Title: The European Monetary Union after the crisis : from a fiscal
union to a fiscal capacity / Nazaré da Costa Cabral.
Description: Abingdon, Oxon ; New York, NY : Routledge,
2020. | Series: Routledge studies in the European economy |
Includes bibliographical references and index.
Identifiers: LCCN 2020011079 (print) | LCCN 2020011080
(ebook) | ISBN 9780367496616 (hardback) |
ISBN 9781003046929 (ebook)
Subjects: LCSH: Economic and Monetary Union. | Monetary
unions—European Union countries. | Financial crises—European
Union countries. | Global Financial Crisis, 2008–2009. | European
Union countries—Economic conditions.
Classification: LCC HG930.5 .C3185 2020 (print) | LCC HG930.5
(ebook) | DDC 332.4/94—dc23
LC record available at https://lccn.loc.gov/2020011079
LC ebook record available at https://lccn.loc.gov/2020011080

ISBN: 978-0-367-49661-6 (hbk)
ISBN: 978-0-367-49663-0 (pbk)
ISBN: 978-1-003-04692-9 (ebk)

Typeset in Sabon
by Apex CoVantage, LLC

CONTENTS

CONTENTS

CONTENTS

CONTENTS

ILLUSTRATIONS

Figures

Tables

1

INTRODUCTION

1.1. The Great Financial Crisis as a global and systemic crisis

Despite the varieties of crises and their dates,[1] the 'this time is different' syndrome, referred to by Reinhart and Rogoff (2009b) explains that the ingredients and steps that usually lead to a crisis once again occurred in the most recent and memorable one, the *subprime crisis*. Experiences and mistakes committed by others in the past did not provide good lessons, and similar mistakes, overconfidence and lack of precaution happened once more.[2]

This crisis was not only the most severe financial crisis after the 1930s crash but also a global and systemic crisis – henceforth labelled the *Great Financial Crisis (GFC)*. As recalled by Rixtel and Gasperini (2013, p. 4), the initial tension in the U.S. subprime mortgage markets spilled over to banks' short-term wholesale funding markets, causing liquidity shortcomings.

---

1 Reinhart and Rogoff (2009b, pp. 4–14) identify two major categories of financial crises. Firstly, crises defined by quantitative thresholds, including inflation crises (considered as a threshold of 20 percent per annum), currency crashes (taken as an annual depreciation in excess of 15 percent), currency debasement (in fact the predecessor of modern inflation and foreign exchange rate crises, when the means of exchange was metallic coins) and, finally, the bursting of asset price bubbles (equity or real estate). Secondly, crises defined by events, which include banking crises (which arise from a protracted deterioration in asset quality, either from a collapse in real estate prices or from increased bankruptcies in the nonfinancial sector), external (sovereign) debt crises (the failure of a government to meet a principal or interest payment on the due date vis-à-vis foreign lenders) and domestic debt crises. On this issue, for a historic panorama of financial crises in modern history, see the influential book by Kindleberger and Aliber (2005). See also Cooper (2008), Reinhart and Rogoff (2009a), Krugman (2009), Cabral (2010), Quelhas (2013) and Brunnermeier and Schnabel (2015).

2 This fatality was appropriately qualified as a 'hardy perennial' by Kindleberger and Aliber (2005, p. 1). A list of historically significant crises can be found in Bordo and Landon-Lane (2013): the South Sea bubble in the early eighteenth century; stock market crashes in the nineteenth century; the 1929 Wall Street crash; the UK housing boom-bust in 1973; the Nordic crisis of the 1980s; the Japanese housing and equity bubble and crash of 1990; the dotcom crisis; finally, the subprime crisis.

Contagion through the interconnectedness of major global banks and their funding models led to unprecedented increases in interbank spreads. Problems intensified in U.S. investment banks, but also in European banks – e.g. the failure of Northern Rock.[3] With solvency concerns on the rise, bank share prices tumbled across the globe (Rixtel and Gasperini, 2013).

To explain how a regional or local (financial) crisis transforms into a *global crisis*, it should first be noted that the transmission effects of a financial crisis can occur due to the occurrence of common financial shocks in different countries (e.g. the collapse of the dot-com bubble in 2001 and the collapse of housing prices in the crisis of the late 2000s) or due to mechanisms related to the cross-border contagion emanating from the epicentre of the crisis (which was mostly the case with the subprime crisis transmission effects) (in this regard, see Reinhart and Rogoff, 2009b, p. 240). Transmission effects can, in turn, be explained through the notions of *contagion* and *spillovers*. Again, in the words of Reinhart and Rogoff (2009b, p. 241), contagion is an episode in which there are significant immediate effects in a number of countries following an event – then the consequences are 'fast and furious' – whereas spillovers correspond to the emergence of gradual and protracted effects, which, notwithstanding this, may have major economic consequences.[4]

Reinhart and Rogoff (2009b, p. 260) then consider that for the crisis to be categorised as a global crisis, it has to present four main characteristics (*Idem*, p. 260): (i) one or more global financial centres are mired in a systemic or severe crisis of one form or another; (ii) the crisis involves two or more distinct regions; (iii) The number of countries in crisis in each region is therefore greater; (iv) the composite GDP-weighted[5] index average of global financial turbulence suggested by the authors is at least one standard deviation above normal. Applying these criteria, the authors then conclude that the 2008 crisis was clearly a global crisis (in fact, the only global crisis after World War II), because it started in two financial centres (the U.S. and the UK), involved all the regions of the world ('cross-country synchronicity') and affected several countries in each region (see particularly the case of Europe).

The crisis was furthermore a *systemic crisis*, and this description is used in a double sense: (i) a *narrow sense*, meaning that the effects of the crisis were felt in the traditional banking sector and in the shadow-banking sector as well, therefore spreading throughout the entire financial system; (ii) a *wider sense*, meaning that the financial crisis was simultaneously a financial and economic crisis – that is, a *broad spectrum* or *wide scope* crisis – due to its

---

3 More details in Lannoo (2015a).
4 Ozkan and Unsal (2012) develop this idea of transmission effects (from a foreign shock to a domestic economy), by identifying channels that involve both financial and trade linkages.
5 GDP – Gross Domestic Product.

effects on the financial system but also on overall economic activity, output and (un)employment.

Beginning with the first sense, a narrow sense for the systemic nature of the crisis, let me recall that standard Minsky moments (Minsky, 1986, 1992), of 'displacement-euphoria-manias-distress-panic' of financial crises, also took place with great intensity in the subprime crisis. The 'panic moment' in particular included massive 'runs' either on traditional banks or on shadow banking entities. The collapse thus hit the entire financial system. It should also be recalled that the moment of distress that gave rise to massive runs on banks, money market funds, markets for mortgage-backed securities and other similar markets was first determined by the exacerbation of depositor and investor informational asymmetry regarding the quality of assets involved and the condition of their bank or financial institution. An attitude of suspicion spread throughout the financial markets.

The financial crisis exhibited its systemic nature – affecting the overall financial system, including banking and shadow banking sectors – because the fulfilment of systemic risks, notably counterparty or default risks, increased dramatically. As mentioned by Bullard *et al.* (2009, p. 403), a "systemic risk refers to the possibility that a triggering event, such as the failure of an individual firm, will seriously impair other firms or markets and harm the broader economy."

1.2. The GFC, hysteresis and secular stagnation

The financial crisis was therefore also a systemic crisis in a wider sense. In fact, the subprime crisis caused the *Second Great Contraction* (the first being the 1930s Depression), in the appealing words of Reinhart and Rogoff (2009b, p. xlv). Note that the attempts to measure the impact of banking crisis (and to measure the respective magnitude) are not new. Reinhart and Rogoff (2009b, p. 224) considered the respective total average impact in terms of output and unemployment. Other economists have computed the impact of past banking crises into observed GDP growth rates (see, for example, Cerra and Saxena, 2008).[6]

A forward-looking approach consists of evaluating the effect of the crisis in output prospects, by confronting the realized GDP at each moment (in absolute terms or in terms of its growth rate) with the 'counterfactual' GDP – that is, what GDP would have been if the financial crisis had never occurred (Atkinson *et al.*, 2013). The counterfactual long-term trend can be a constant growth rate (Ollivaud and Turner, 2015) or the potential output.[7]

---

6 Similar attempts have been undertaken for the years after the subprime crisis to assess and to forecast its economic impacts, particularly in the U.S. and Europe (see Gros and Alcidi, 2010).

7 As noticed by Ollivaud and Turner (2015), the use of these different methodologies is not without their practical consequences. When comparing, for example, methodologies based

Furceri and Mourougane (2009, pp. 5–6) and Mourougane (2015, p. 5) detail these ideas by separating two types of effects on potential output resulting from a financial crisis. Direct effects are related to Solow's neoclassical production function (used to explain and measure economic growth), namely to labour, capital and total factor productivity (TFP). The indirect effects are exactly related to macroeconomic policies that are adopted to cushion the economic downturn (Mourougane, 2015, p. 6). Stabilization policies may indeed have long-term effects: on the one hand, investment in infrastructure can boost potential output; on the other hand, some policies adopted to fight high deficits and debts (which also tend to increase during the crisis) may have procyclical effects and prevent economic growth (see also Afonso and Furceri, 2008a).

The idea of *Great Contraction* or, more radically, the notion of *Secular Stagnation*, recovered by Summers (2016), can be used to capture precisely the impact of the 2007–2008 crisis in terms of potential output. This is so because factors that induce long-term growth – capital accumulation, labour participation and innovation – were significantly shrunk in the aftermath of the crisis.

It should also be noted that conventional models on business cycles (with financial frictions) would at first sight imply the return to normality once the crisis has ended (Hall, 2010, p. 3). However, in the case of the subprime crisis, and consistent with its severity and twofold nature (by hampering actual and potential output), GDP and employment failed to recover once it ended at the latest in 2011. Particularly in Europe, long-lasting effects upon output persisted.

This slow recovery is most likely related (Ball, 2014; Mourougane, 2015; Blanchard *et al.*, 2015) to the presence of *hysteresis*, i.e. the idea that recessions may have permanent effects on the level of output relative to the trend.[8] Furthermore, for some of the countries studied by Ball (2014), not only has

---

on growth rate evolution (recall Cerra and Saxena, 2008) and counterfactual methodologies, significant differences in the output gap assessment may arise (Biggs and Mayer, 2010). This explains, for example, why the results found in Furceri and Mourougane (2009) were not as pessimistic as those estimated by Cerra and Saxena (2008). In the former study, severe financial crises were estimated to lower potential output by nearly 4% (in high-income countries), whereas for the latter the reduction of total GDP was computed at 15%. See also Ball (2014).

8 Hysteresis is founded upon the idea from the physical sciences that systems have memory, which implies that a transitory shock may have permanent effects. The notion was notably first used in macroeconomics, by Blanchard and Summers (1986), to explain the persistence of unemployment levels after an economic bust, using the distinction between equilibrium and actual unemployment – the idea now was that the unemployment rate would depend on the history of the actual unemployment rate. For this reason, in strict terms, hysteresis should be used only in the case where there was path dependence of steady state equilibrium unemployment. But in broader terms – preferred by the authors in their article – hysteresis would refer to the situation where the actual unemployment rate would affect equilibrium unemployment for a long time.

potential output fallen significantly below its pre-crisis trend, but the current growth rates of potential output have also become much lower than past growth rates. This means that the crisis has also affected the current growth rate of potential output, an effect that is referred to as *super-hysteresis* (Ball, 2014; Blanchard *et al.*, 2015).

1.3. The metamorphosis of the crisis in Europe, misguiding policy signs and the EMU's vulnerability

In a rather unexpected fashion, the crisis evolved in Europe and transmuted into a deeper crisis: an economic and fiscal crisis. The causes for that metamorphosis are detailed further on, as well as the (delayed and inappropriate) way political leaders initially perceived the impact of the crisis in the EMU: misguiding policy signs were given, and the response was ineffective. Amongst such action were the signs and direction of monetary policy. It is now commonly agreed that the reaction to adopt more intensive action – notably within non-conventional monetary policy – was protracted in Europe unlike that which had happened with central banks, the Fed and even more conservative banks such as the Bank of England. The ECB – safeguarded by the no-bailout clause of the Treaty on the Functioning of the European Union (TFEU) – awoke late to the (possible) benefits of quantitative easing. Additionally, one can throughout the crisis identify an evolution in the discourse about the main causes of the crisis: it started with the fiscal profligacy of certain EMU countries and ended up with acknowledging E(M)U[9] flaws.

As will be shown in Part I, what is nowadays certainly consensual is the recognition that the European Economic and Monetary Union (EMU) has not only been able to cope adequately with the effects of the GFC, but it has also proved to be much more exposed and vulnerable to those effects than other developed economies. The vulnerability of the EMU to the effects of the GFC resulted first and foremost from its basic flaws as a currency union (Stiglitz, 2016, 2017), an original sin in its basic foundation: a union lacking elements of fiscal and political integration usually found in other currency unions. Indeed, unlike successful and long-lasting currency unions, the EMU is not politically embedded (McNamara, 2015).

On economic grounds, the reasons for these basic vulnerabilities have also been identified. Firstly, when countries joined the single currency, they gave up two vital tools for managing their economies: firstly, the power to create money and set interest rates (monetary policy), and secondly, the freedom to allow their exchange rates to fluctuate in order to adjust to internal

---

9 The acronym E(M)U is used throughout the Book as referring not only to the EMU but also eventually to the EU itself.

imbalances or external shocks (exchange rate policy) (Matziorinis, 2011). The crisis showed that a single monetary policy was inadequate for different countries, with different macroeconomic fundamentals. 'One size did not fit all': the single monetary policy had possibly been too lenient for one group of countries (peripheral countries) and too strict for others (core countries). For the former, it fostered easy access to credit and increasing debt, while for the latter it limited consumption and investment. This same single monetary policy has, in turn, helped to mask the surge of significant (external) imbalances between those same groups of EMU countries, with the former experiencing increasing deficits and the latter benefiting from chronicle surpluses.

Secondly, EMU member states became more vulnerable than advanced economies with their own currency, after large fiscal deteriorations (Gilbert *et al.*, 2013). During the sovereign crisis, government bond yields showed signs of persistent overshooting (Gilbert *et al.*, 2013), and this was furthermore aggravated by economic fundamentals, such as current accounts (De Grauwe and Ji, 2012), potential growth, private debt, and indicators of financial sector problems (see Gilbert *et al.*, 2013). Moreover, the single currency increased the elasticity of capital flows (*Idem*, 2013), explaining the reaction of the markets to signs of distress, with a movement of 'flight to quality' that ultimately froze access to funding by countries with worse macroeconomic outlooks. It is not by hazard that the EMU crisis has been characterized as a 'sudden stop' in capital flows and in external financing (Baldwin *et al.*, 2015) that mostly affected countries of the periphery of the euro area. Ultimately, the fundamental argument relies on the fact that EMU member states issue debt in a currency that they no longer control (because the task was assigned to a European Central Bank). Due to this 'original sin' – which resembles that of emerging markets that decide to peg their currencies to a foreign and more credible one – they became vulnerable to multiple equilibria in the sovereign debt market, where market loss of confidence can trigger interest rate increases and a self-fulfilling solvency crisis (De Grauwe, 2011b)

Thirdly, EMU countries showed themselves to be more vulnerable to a negative interaction between government and the banking sector than other economies (in particular, the U.S.). In the same way, significant bailouts to the banking sector (e.g., Ireland and Spain) worsened the fiscal position of the respective governments, and most European banks also held large quantities of domestic government debt on their balance sheets: the funding problems of the sovereign ultimately exposed banks to significant losses with the deterioration of the respective assets. The 'doom-looping' between sovereigns and bank debt was indeed a major feature of the EMU crisis. Curiously, this unwarranted outcome was favoured by regulatory rules themselves. Following the Basel II Accord in 2004, the EU Capital Requirements Directive on the application of capital adequacy rules allowed Eurozone banks to assign a risk weighting of 0% to member states' sovereign debt exposure in domestic currency; therefore, euro area banks buying euro area sovereign bonds denominated in euros did not have to post any capital against them, since they were treated as risk free (Matziorinis, 2011). The implications of this incentive were significant: banks were not properly capitalized to face exposure to sovereign debt.[10]

Finally, the latter vulnerability resulted in the difficulties faced by the EMU in its crisis management, as a consequence of the legal design of its main pillars – ultimately they had become impossible to maintain as they were originally conceived. In this regard, Bénassy-Quéré (2015, pp. 78–79) highlighted the 'trilemma' faced during the Eurozone crisis management. Since the Treaty excludes both debt monetization and a bailout to member states, the reluctance of the Europeans to proceed with debt restructuring led to one of the 'impossible trinities' widespread in economic literature. As such, in this case, the impossible trinity (in fact, an internal contradiction of the crisis management) relied on the coexistence of these three vertices: (i) no monetization; (ii) no bailout clause; (iii) no debt restructuring. The ultimate paradox is that one of these vertices had to be given up, and yet we are still far from a political agreement on which of these vertices – and how – should be abandoned (or relaxed).

1.4. Monetary policy exhaustion, economic slowdown and 'foggy' times in Europe

Even if delayed, the ECB action embodied in Mario Draghi's 2012 statement – "to do whatever it takes to preserve the euro" – was effective by ensuring

---

10 Despite the significant changes introduced after Basel III (in 2010), especially in Europe with the new rules on capital requirements for the banking sector (see *infra*, when addressing the Banking Union), the fact is that the treatment of sovereign risk has not met with significant changes in recent years. Sovereign exposures *de facto* receive a zero risk weight in EU legislation and are exempt from limitations on concentration risk; indeed, regulation treats sovereigns as risk-free (Lenarcic *et al.*, 2016). Sovereign exposure is usually less costly than other assets: since it is considered to be low-risk, it can be used to de-risk the balance sheet and lower bank funding costs (Lenarcic *et al.*, 2016). Moreover, the fact that some sovereign bonds can be used as collateral to accede to central bank liquidity may render these bonds especially attractive to banks. As one can see, the different treatment given to sovereign risk exposure is inherent to the banking system, but it is also promoted by regulation itself (*Idem*, 2016). The authors consider that the *status quo* should be challenged and a different treatment of sovereign risk should be given, alternatively adopting two regulatory modifications: (i) assigning positive risk weights to sovereign exposure, which would require higher capital buffers; (ii) putting limits on exposures to sovereigns (e.g. a large exposure limit), which would lead to greater diversification (*Ibidem*). From a systemic risk perspective, as noted in turn by Goves *et al.* (2016), 0% risk weights to sovereign exposure should be challenged due to: (i) large exposure risk; (ii) systemic risk for the financial system in the probable case of realisation of sovereign risks (e.g. the doom loop); (iii) crowding out of the private sector.

a reduction in the sovereign yield spreads in peripheral countries and by reducing the domestic bank-sovereign loop (Acharya *et al.*, 2016). The consequence was a reversal of the 'flight-to-quality' to 'core' countries' banks, even though peripheral banks did not immediately benefit from that reversal. Through portfolio balancing, bank lending and signalling effect channels, several analysts (to be referred to further on) investigated and confirmed the effectiveness of the monetary policy toolkit adopted by the ECB, and how it helped to reduce interest rates and improve market access conditions to funding notably for those same peripheral countries.

However, despite the positive results obtained through the ECB's monetary policy, signs of concern remain, especially concerning two aspects. Firstly, the case for the plausible exhaustion of the monetary policy toolkit, that is, a situation where the 'zero lower bound' of monetary policy is reached and this becomes ineffective.[11] Secondly, the question 'Has the lesson of the subprime crisis been learnt?', that is, the issue of knowing whether an expansionist monetary policy, despite its non-overall inflationary effects, may determine partial inflationary effects in certain (financial) assets, thereby leading to the surge of a new financial bubble similar to the subprime one.

As for the former aspect – that which for the time being should deserve more attention – it can be said that certain E(M)U countries have not entirely recovered from the effects of the crisis, economic recovery seems fragile and weak, and so the monetary policy (including quantitative easing) followed by the ECB appears to be exhausted, or at least not as effective as it was in the beginning. This (in)effectiveness is explained on the basis of two contrasting arguments: on the one hand, the situation is associated with the excess of savings (in comparison to investment) verified in certain European countries (first and foremost in the case of Germany) and the resistance in those countries to seize the benefits of such a favourable policy (e.g. low interest rates) and promote more public and private investment; on the other hand, the outcome is attributed to the inadequacy of the expansionist monetary policy itself (in particular, through non-conventional programmes of asset purchases) in a context where the risk of deflation was already impaired. From a long-term perspective, according to this latter view, expansionist monetary policy will encounter the risk of inflationary tensions and the financial erosion of pension funds and other forms of savings needed to address ageing problems in the near future.

In turn, monetary policy cannot by itself fully control price developments (and hence economic growth). Exogenous factors can interfere and prevent the expected transmission of monetary policy to the 'real' economy,

---

11 A situation resembling the 'liquidity trap' faced since the 1990s by the Bank of Japan: despite the expansionist monetary policy, the action was not able to stop economic recession.

distorting the action of its main channels (e.g. credit channel, trade channel, expectations channel). In fact, in the E(M)U, exogenous signs of uncertainty remain. Together with the global tension involving trade and currency relationships between the U.S. and other regional blocks (in particular China), the economic slowdown in some EMU core countries should be highlighted – with Germany at the head – and most of all the chaotic political situation being experienced in the United Kingdom (UK) surrounding Brexit. (A hard or soft Brexit? With a deal or no-deal Brexit?) Such a puzzling and foggy climate has already affected the UK's economic and financial performance and will propagate in a more or less intensive way – completely depending on the type and nature of the withdrawal itself – to the EU as well.[12]

Above all, one can say that several European countries still today face the protracted, unresolved effects of recent crises. The EU faces the effects of 'secular stagnation', which also partially explains this (long-term) cycle of ultra-low interest rates. Structural causes – amongst which the insufficient supply of safe assets and increasing demand for them (aggravated by the financial crisis) – may eventually force a policy shift from the predominance of monetary policy to a new role for fiscal policy both at the national and at the E(M)U level. The appeal for fiscal union – or at least (in a mitigated version), for fiscal capacity – has gained momentum in the European agenda.

1.5. A new policy agenda for the EMU: risk-sharing mechanisms as a panacea to save the euro

In recent years, especially under the Juncker presidency, a profusion of roadmaps and policy initiatives has been announced, with the ambitious goal of undertaking an in-depth reform of the EMU. The promotion of the so-called 'risk-sharing mechanisms' has definitely entered the political agenda. In an initial moment, besides the new and more active role assigned to monetary policy, attention was given to 'typical' private risk-sharing mechanisms – e.g. the banking union and the capital markets union.

Progressively, the plausible exhaustion of an expansionist monetary policy – in the face of the zero lower bound effect and economic slowdown[13] – and the alleged incompleteness of the banking and capital market unions have

---

12 On the several implications of 'Brexit' both to the EU and the UK, see Cabral *et al.* (eds.) (2017).

13 In a moment of transition for the ECB's governing council (the replacement of Mario Draghi by Christine Lagarde) the question is to know if and how monetary stimulus will be maintained. Market expectations for the medium term are that (ultra-) low interest rates will be kept and quantitative easing (QE) will be phased out only gradually. However, as noted before, the critique of this policy direction is increasing in the euro area, with the so-called 'ECB hawks' pleading against QE and cutting interest rates more deeply (to negative values). Once again, the political correlation of forces in the composition of the

led to the recognition that fiscal policy should be given a new opportunity.[14] The E(M)U, within the legal limitations of the Treaty (i.e. the non-bailout clause) and the Stability and Growth Pact (i.e. the compliance with strict fiscal rules), should develop new financial instruments in order to promote growth and, above all, to ensure the absorption of macroeconomic shocks. At the same time, new fiscal-type instruments should be developed in order to backstop the existing private risk-sharing mechanisms – especially the banking union – thereby ensuring its completeness and conclusion.

However, a new role for fiscal policy should not be confused with the creation of a full-fledged fiscal union: the risk-sharing instrument for the EMU intends only to mimic a fiscal federal setup, so it will not be a central budget with typical allocation, inter-individual and regional redistribution and stabilization functions, but rather a 'micro-budget', a small, precise and direct fiscal instrument – in short, it will be a 'fiscal capacity'.

In the current political scenario that prevails in the E(M)U (and now inherited by the new Commission led by Ursula von der Leyden), the acceptance of such an instrument will have to balance some antagonistic objectives: firstly, the need to combine solidarity with the prevention of moral hazard; secondly, the need to reconcile some governmental risk-sharing action with (the reinforcement of) market mechanisms within the E(M)U territory.

Moreover, on technical grounds, the exact design, nature and effects of this new fiscal capacity is yet to be perceived.

A crucial task of the new Commission will precisely be to define the model behind the instrument. In Part II, I propose a taxonomy of fiscal capacity modalities seeking to classify the proposals presented (and which can also frame others to be presented in the near future). Then, in order to describe the modality of fiscal capacity to be chosen, two main intersecting questions should be answered. Firstly, to verify whether the governmental risk-sharing mechanism is an insurance device (*stricto sensu*), or a stabilizer instrument (*lato sensu*) but with no specific features of an insurance mechanism. Secondly, the question of knowing whether the fiscal capacity is primarily and mostly present for macro stabilizing purposes – a direct and visible stabilization device – or whether it is instead an instrument where the stabilizing effect is only indirect – that is, a collateral effect of other policy goals, e.g. allocation of resources. A remaining question, no less important, is to verify whether the fiscal capacity will effectively be a 'fiscal' (governmental) instrument or mainly an instrument to promote the internal market,

---

ECB's governing council – on the one side Draghi's inheritors (the doves), on the other its opponents (the hawks) – will dictate the direction of this same policy for the years to come.

14 In this regard, Corsetti *et al.* (2019) stress that at a time when the central bank's policy rates are expected to stay at or close to the lower bound for an extended period of time, monetary and fiscal policy *together* can have a sizeable impact on the economy.

notably by supporting private risk-sharing mechanisms ultimately acting as a 'market-maker'.

It should be noted that the model chosen may combine several of these dimensions, and it can in the end be a mixed model. The result will precisely express the way the aforementioned antagonistic ideological objectives will be resolved in the complex EU political arena.

Part I

THE GREAT FINANCIAL CRISIS AND THE ECONOMIC AND MONETARY UNION

2

FROM THE FINANCIAL CRISIS
TO THE EURO CRISIS

2.1. The 'twin and triple crisis' theoretical framework

2.1.1. Twin and triple crisis

Banking/financial crises are often accompanied by other kinds of crises – including exchange rate crises, inflation outbursts and debt crises (Reinhart and Rogoff, 2009b, p. 145 and p. 249).

Reinhart and Rogoff present the *prototype for the sequencing of the 2008 crisis* (*Idem*, pp. 249–250). Such an event occurs when financial liberalization facilitates the access of banks to external credit and riskier lending practices at home. After a while, following a boom in lending and asset prices, weaknesses in the balance sheets of banks become evident and the first problems in the banking sector arise: a banking crisis breaks out. In these cases, the central bank must intervene to support distressed financial institutions. If the exchange rate is managed (and ultimately pegged), policy inconsistency may arise between the need to support the exchange rate and the need to act as a 'lender of last resort'. Usually the latter tends to prevail, either directly, or indirectly through a greater reluctance to use monetary policy to shore up the depreciating/devaluing domestic currency. A currency crash then occurs. The depreciation/devaluation of the currency worsens, in turn, the situation of the financial sector, notably by exacerbating the situation of banks that have borrowed in foreign currency, by boosting inflation, and by increasing the odds of external and domestic government default (if the government has foreign-currency denominated debt). Finally, at this stage, the banking crisis either peaks following a currency crash or becomes even worse, leading the country to a sovereign domestic or external default.

Seminal studies on this issue have basically focused on the relationship between the banking crisis and the currency crisis ('*twin crises*'), intending to identify whether one caused the other, or whether they could instead be explained through common causation. Kaminsky and Reinhart (1999, p. 15) considered that both crises tended to be preceded by common recessionary conditions: the weakening of the export sector, the deterioration of terms of trade, the rise in real interest rates and the fall in foreign exchange reserves. In the same study, Kaminsky and Reinhart (1999) highlighted that during the 1970s, no apparent link existed between these two crises, partially because financial markets were then deeply regulated. On the contrary, in the 1980s and 1990s, banking crises proliferated (preceding balance-to-payments crises), and this change of pattern could be thus explained by the deregulation and liberalization of financial markets.

Additionally, Kaminsky and Reinhart (1999) associated balance-of-payments crises with currency crises. As a note of caution, however, I should add that balance-to-payments crises and currency crises may not be entirely synonymous in their respective meaning. Indeed, balance-to-payment imbalances may not necessarily generate a process of major depreciation/devaluation of the domestic currency (as I will discuss further on with respect to the EMU crisis), whereas in certain other cases, certainly minor, currency attacks may not be strictly related to a real external imbalance or to a problem of competitiveness.

However, most of the time, currency crises are effectively associated with *pure* balance-to-payments crises: they are two sides of the same coin. Pressures for the depreciation/devaluation of the domestic currency usually reflect economic fundamentals – e.g. weak competitiveness – or other idiosyncratic features of the country, notably of a political nature – e.g. political (in)stability, a (corrupt) political regime, (poor) quality of public institutions, (fragile) democracy. The links between real economic and political factors and speculative attacks have been given attention, since the seminal contribution of Krugman (1979), under the so-called 'speculative attack model'. As noted by Frankel and Rose (1996, p. 5), this model delivers several important factors in the prediction of currency crashes: monetary and fiscal expansions (as in Krugman's model), declining competitiveness, current account deficits and losses in international reserves.[1]

---

1 Also see, on this issue, Eichengreen *et al.* (1995). For these authors, the variability of causes of speculative attacks with respect to a currency are varied and can occur within fixed (more often) and floating exchange rate regimes; this was the case with the Italian lira and British pound in 1992, the French franc in 1993, the Mexican peso in 1994 and the Spanish peseta in 1995, but also the process of depreciation of the American dollar vis-à-vis the Japanese yen, in 1994–1995. As the causes are diverse (e.g. too much restrictive monetary policy – the case with the British pound in 1992 – or, on the contrary, an inflationist environment – the case with Mexico) the proper policy menu is also of a different type. Indeed, a clear-cut solution fitting well with all types of situations does not seem to exist. This is certainly one of the major dilemmas in the field of macroeconomic policy. As noted precisely by the same authors (Eichengreen *et al.*, 1995, p. 2), "many observers have derived an impossibility theorem: neither pegging like Sweden, nor occasionally realigning like Mexico and the EMS countries, nor floating like the United States is a tolerable option. Policymakers seem to retain no acceptable international monetary alternative."

The concept of 'twin crises' has evolved over time. More recently, Laeven and Valencia (2008, 2012) extended this concept and, at the same time, developed the notion of 'triple crises'. For these authors, 'twin crises' involve not only the simultaneous occurrence of currency (or balance-to-payment) crises and banking crises (as in the Kaminsky-Reinhart framework), but also the simultaneous occurrence of currency and sovereign crises, and banking and sovereign debt crises. As for the concept of 'triple crises', it refers to the simultaneous occurrence of banking, currency and sovereign debt crises.

As for the sequencing of the crises, as in the Reinhart-Rogoff prototype, Laeven and Valencia (2012) specify that banking crises usually precede both currency and sovereign debt crises. More recently, Balteanu and Erce (2017, p. 6), relating banking mostly with sovereign debt crisis (without, however, ignoring external sector channels) have identified four types of situations: (i) single bank crises, i.e. bank crises not followed by sovereign distress; (ii) single sovereign debt crises, i.e. sovereign defaults that are not followed by a banking sector crisis; (iii) twin bank-debt crises that start with a bank crisis and are followed by a sovereign debt episode within three years; (iv) twin debt-bank crises, where a sovereign crisis is followed by a banking one within three years.[2] In their research, the authors show that there are significant differences between single and twin debt crises, with respect to the interplay between the balance sheets of domestic banks and the relevant central bank and the government, the level and dynamics of financial inter-mediation, public finances, public openness and real growth. In particular, certain effects tend to occur *only* in twin crises: notably, this is the case with deposit runs and credit crunches.

Additionally, the authors (Balteanu and Erce, 2017) analysed transmission channels both from banking to sovereign crises and from debt crises to the banking sector. As for twin bank-debt crises, the transmission occurs either through direct or indirect channels. The former refers to the fiscal costs the government incurs to bail out the banking sector, and the latter is related to the way a banking crisis can affect the entire economy and market senti-ment. As for twin debt-bank crises, the effects of a sovereign default on the economy can occur through the domestic financial system, in addition to direct balance-sheet channels (bank sovereign exposures may lead assets to be written off or rescheduled, ultimately leading to large capital losses that may threaten bank solvency).

Finally, the same authors (*Idem*, p. 5) address the external sector channels both of banking and sovereign debt crises. A banking crisis can ignite a cur-rency crash, making the sovereign debt unable to repay its foreign currency

---

2 From a sample of 104 emerging and developing countries, for the period from 1975 to 2007, Balteanu and Erce (2017) identify 100 sovereign debt crises and 81 bank crises. Of these, 34 are twin events: according to the sequence, 18 are twin bank-debt crises and 16 are twin debt-bank crises.

debt. Additionally, such crises may impair external financing and involve massive capital flows (see *infra*). In turn, sovereign defaults also tend to trigger capital outflows and foreign credit crunches, which can ultimately be the cause of a 'sudden stop'.[3]

Note, in turn, that the definitions of *banking crisis* and *currency crisis* are not straightforward. Haan *et al.* (2012, p. 40) qualifies as a banking crisis the situation in which part of a country's banking sector becomes insolvent after heavy investment losses, banking losses, banking panics, etc. Reinhart and Rogoff (2009b, p. 249) use a financial turbulence index aiming to measure the severity of the crisis with respect to its basic components (including banking and currency crashes).

A distinction is sometimes made between systemic and non-systemic banking crises. For example, Laeven and Valencia (2008) consider that a systemic banking crisis occurs whenever a country's corporate and financial sectors experience a large number of defaults and financial institutions, and corporations face great difficulties in repaying contracts on time. As a result, non-performing loans increase sharply, and all or most of the aggregate banking system capital is exhausted.

Later on, Laeven and Valencia (2012) provided more details to this definition, considering that a (systemic) banking crisis occurs whenever two conditions are met: (i) significant signs of financial distress in the banking system (as indicated by significant bank runs, losses in the banking system, and/or liquidations); (ii) significant banking policy intervention measures in response to significant losses in the banking system.[4] The year where both conditions are met is considered the year when the crisis becomes systemic.[5]

---

3 These cascade effects will be detailed further on when addressing the sequence of the EMU financial-sovereign debt crisis.

4 In particular, Laeven and Valencia (2012) consider that intervention is significant if at least three out of these six measures are used: (i) extensive liquidity support (5% of deposits and liabilities to non-residents); (ii) bank restructuring gross costs (at least 3% of GDP); (iii) significant bank nationalizations; (iv) significant guarantees granted to banks; (v) significant assets purchased (at least 5% of GDP); (vi) deposit freezes and/or bank holidays.

5 Recall, in turn, that from a theoretical perspective, and considering bank balance sheets, a banking crisis can be explained using two lines of arguments (Haan *et al.*, 2012, pp. 45–47). The first line of argumentation (the Diamond–Dybvig-Rajan model) relies on the asset side of bank balance sheets: banks are fragile structures subject to bank runs – if everyone expects a problem and acts as if one is about to occur, then the run becomes a self-fulfilling prophecy. Conversely, if no one expects the crisis to take place, the expectation is also self-fulfilling and the run does not occur. Indeed, this is a typical of multiple equilibria, where the run is the consequence of a shock of confidence that moves a good to a bad equilibrium. Under the second line (the Bernanke-Gertler-Gilchrist model), banking problems arise mostly from the asset side of bank balance sheets – a crisis is due to the protracted deterioration in asset quality due to poor fundamentals arising from the business cycle, like a collapse in real estate prices or increased bankruptcies in the non-financial sector (Bernanke, 1983; Bernanke and Gertler, 1987, 1995; Bernanke and Blinder, 1990; Bernanke *et al.*, 1999).

As for the notion of currency crisis, Frankel and Rose (1996) refer to a currency crash as a large change in the nominal exchange rate. In particular, they define a currency crash as a depreciation of the nominal exchange rate of at least 25% that is also at least a 10% increase in the rate of nominal depreciation. In a similar vein, Laeven and Valencia (2008 and 2012), refer to a currency crash as a nominal depreciation of the currency vis-à-vis the U.S. dollar of at least 30% that is also at least ten percentage points higher than the rate of depreciation in the year before. Others adopt a broader definition of currency crisis that may not coincide with the occurrence of a crash: for example, Eichengreen *et al.* (1995) include in this definition not only major cases of currency depreciation/devaluation, but also speculative attacks that are successfully warded off by the authorities (attacks driven by a sudden fall in reserves and/or interest rate increases).

Finally, as for the notion of *sovereign debt crisis*, this is usually related to an episode of domestic or external debt default (Reinhart and Rogoff, 2009b). However, the definition of debt default is not unequivocal. Paoli *et al.* (2011, p. 25), for example, define a debt default episode when either: (i) sovereign arrears on principal are 15% or more of the total of outstanding debt owed to the external private sector; (ii) arrears on interest payments are 5% or more; or (iii) a rescheduling agreement is reached with foreign private sector creditors.

Conventional wisdom stresses that *countries do not go bankrupt*, or do so only in rare cases. Unlike companies, countries do not usually go out of business, and bankruptcy is often the result of a complex cost-benefit calculus involving political and social considerations, not just economic and financial ones (Reinhart and Rogoff, 2009b, p. 51). Usually, debt is manageable, not only because, in general, the present value of the future stream of (tax) revenues allows us to believe that debt will be sustainable in the long run, but also because the sovereign can make use of different strategies in order to make debt payable and to ensure its permanent rollover. Eventually, countries manage to achieve debt reduction or better conditions to carry on with debt charges (see, on this issue, Reinhart and Rogoff, 2013, p. 9).

Amongst measures that throughout economic history have been used by sovereigns to tackle debts, it is possible to classify them in the following way: (i) *macroeconomic measures*, either through economic growth (higher economic growth implies the reduction of the debt to GDP ratio) or through inflation (that in turn can be of a different magnitude); (ii) *fiscal measures*, for example fiscal austerity, aiming not only to improve the primary budget balance, and therefore to reduce net financing needs on a short-run basis, but also to increase countries' creditworthiness and improve the respective fiscal outlook, on a long-run basis; (iii) *financial measures* which are directly targeted to lenders – these can involve a negotiated process of debt restructuring or an implicit debt reduction strategy, which is the case with so-called financial repression, detailed later on.

Note that the mix of measures that can be used by the sovereign in order to ensure effective debt management greatly depends on the type of debt involved: usually debt management strategies aim at long-term debt (short-term debt is not 'manageable' in this sense, precisely because it is short term); the strategic mix is different whether the debt is domestic or external; finally, the mix also varies according to types of lenders – particular strategies have been used in the case of bank lending to sovereigns, a matter that has regained attention in recent literature, notably in the aftermath of the European sovereign debt crisis and with the surge in the so-called 'doom-looping' between sovereign debt and banking debt (I will return to this further on). In short, prior to *de jure* and explicit default, many other strategies can be and have been recurrently used by sovereigns in different historical moments, and these strategies may not necessarily imply a default – a *de facto* default. Besides, even when this is the case, the default tends mostly to be of a partial nature.

In any event, explicit default (a 'declared bankruptcy') should then be viewed as a solution of last resort: this is why governments show reluctance to use it. At this point, the question is no longer about the government's ability to pay, but about its willingness to pay (Reinhart and Rogoff, 2009b, p. 54). An important strand of literature has been devoted to this matter: it aims to model and analyse the incentives governments have to default or not, and the incentives vary according to the type of indebted countries (advanced or emerging economies), lenders (domestic or external) and the current outlook of the country.

2.1.2. Twin crises and capital flows

Banking crises and currency crises (and ultimately, sovereign debt crises) have also been explained from the *capital flow perspective*.

For example, Reinhart and Rogoff (2009b, pp. 157–158) relate banking crises with capital inflows. They present evidence that the majority of countries where financial crises occurred register a higher propensity to experience those crises (notably banking crises) around a certain type of good economic moments, in fact capital inflow bonanza periods. There is also evidence that in many countries, credit booms are often preceded by surges in capital inflows. Taylor (2013), in contrast, challenges this view, presenting evidence that the credit booms explanation is the most plausible predictor of banking crises since the late nineteenth century. In contrast, the external imbalance indicator has only a weak correlation with financial distress compared to other indicators drawn from the financial sector itself. This is partially explained by the fact that external imbalances (i.e. capital inflows) can come from a variety of forms – foreign direct investment, private portfolio securities, sovereign loans – which have nothing to do with the destination country's banking sector.

In a similar manner, there is the analytical option of relating balance-to-payments/currency crises (and ultimately, sovereign debt crises) to capital flows. According to this perspective, preceding the crisis, countries tend to benefit from massive capital inflows; when the crisis erupts, the sudden stop occurs.

This perspective has become more significant in recent years, as today there is a broadening consensus amongst economists that the EMU crisis was mostly a 'sudden stop' crisis, a 'sudden stop' in capital flows vis-à-vis the peripheral countries (Baldwin *et al.*, 2015, and Baldwin and Gros, 2015). As explained by these authors, in 2007 the Eurozone (EZ) was a crisis waiting to happen. During the early 'good years' of the euro, massive imbalances built up (mostly related to large current account deficits), although largely unnoticed (or neglected). Big capital flows from EZ core countries such as Germany, France and the Netherlands to peripheral countries (such as Ireland, Portugal, Spain and Greece) were viewed as a real convergence dynamic, thus hindering the imbalances that were being created. The problem became evident when it was perceived that the periphery was relying on foreign lenders to cover the respective savings-investment gap. Then, in the aftermath of the subprime crisis, investors become reluctant to lend and ultimately stopped lending across borders (Baldwin *et al.*, 2015).

In the opinion of Baldwin *et al.* (2015), the sudden stop in the EZ had, in turn, specific features – it was a *monetary union sudden stop*. Indeed, the special features of the monetary union (addressed further on) meant that the sudden stop was not precipitous (as in the case of Iceland). Rather, they led to the increasing rise in national (sovereign) risk-premium; the abrupt end of capital flows raised concerns about the future viability of banks and governments in nations dependent on foreign lending (Baldwin *et al.*, 2015, p. 2).

Within this perspective are the seminal contributions of Calvo (1998) and Kaminsky *et al.* (2004). The former relates the current account position to capital flows (the two sides of the balance-to-payments structure), explaining that financial and balance-to-payments crises ('sudden stops in international credit flows') occur in the persistence of current account deficits, regardless of the way these deficits are financed: e.g. securities, (external) debt and even foreign direct investment (FDI). Calvo (1998) also explains that in the context of a monetary economy, a slowdown in capital inflows can eventually be met by a loss of foreign reserves, albeit at the cost of rising interest rates (also recall, on this matter, Kaminsky and Reinhart, 1996).[6]

---

6 Kaminsky *et al.* (2004), in turn, present some stylized facts regarding the interaction between capital flows, fiscal policy and monetary policy. It should be said, looking at the evolution in the EZ countries (notably regarding peripheral countries), before and after the crisis, that capital flow behaviour here was clearly pro-cyclical: inflows in good times, outflows in bad ones. See also, more recently, Reinhart *et al.* (2017).

Prior to the financial crisis, the world (and particularly advanced economies), taking advantage of financial globalization and liberalization, experienced a process of significant financial interconnection, which in turn helped to explain the growth in international financial flows. Besides this, the main driver for the massive growth in capital flows was the increase in the fraction of wealth invested abroad (the 'portfolio reallocation' channel of capital flows) (Milesi-Ferretti and Tille, 2011, p. 4). Within the process, financial globalization and liberalization led to the *polarization of net external positions and flows,* with some countries posting large current account deficits and others experiencing large surpluses (*Idem,* p. 4). External imbalances indeed became a mark of the globalized financial world.

At the deepest roots of such global imbalances (and an extreme example of them), can be, first and foremost, the case with the U.S. dollar and the American balance-of-payments position, after the collapse of the Bretton Woods monetary system (in the late 1970s). The dollar then obtained the privileged status of core currency in the world (replacing the role that before had been played by gold). As a consequence, the U.S. was given the capacity to issue debt instruments denominated in their currency, therefore the ability to take on unprecedented levels of debt with no risk of default (Wonders, 2010, pp. 76–77). Increasing U.S. current account deficits (today one of the largest in the world) are met because foreign exporters (as was, in the 1980s, the case with Japan and as is now the case with China) have either been accumulating reserves in dollars or investing them in dollar-denominated assets (e.g. precisely dollar-denominated debt instruments) (*Idem,* pp. 78–79).

In a famous lecture, Bernanke (2005) addressed this issue, stressing that the rapid increase in the external account deficit in the U.S. was fuelled to a significant extent both by a *global saving glut* (notably, in developed economies compelled to meet the long-term challenges of their ageing societies) and a greater interest on the part of foreigners in investing in the U.S., starting with investors from developing economies (the case precisely of China).

Moreover, the polarization of these external imbalances (and capital flows) can itself help to explain the surge of complex and in-depth financial bubbles and, what is more, explain them regardless of whether they are created through a trade surplus (e.g. the Japanese bubble burst in the 1990s) or a financial account surplus (e.g. the case of the U.S. on the eve of the subprime crisis) (Wonders, 2010, pp. 86–87).

Milesi-Ferretti and Tille (2011, p. 2) argue that the central feature of the recent financial crisis was a shock to risk aversion and that the impact of this shock on a specific country became dependent on the extent and nature of its international financial links, its macroeconomic conditions, and its dependence on world trade. Countries with large net external liabilities particularly in the form of debt, countries whose external portfolio was more exposed to liquidity risk, or countries more dependent on trade were likely to be more affected.

2.2. Metamorphosis of the crisis in the EMU: from the financial crisis to the euro crisis

2.2.1. Causal events that determined the mutation of the crisis

Bearing in mind what was said in the previous subsection, I will now try to explain how the 'twin and triple crises' framework can be transposed to the recent crisis in the EMU, proceeding to identify the main causes why it evolved from a banking to a debt crisis, and eventually to a currency crisis (to be discussed).[7]

The crisis in the EMU was determined by two main subsequent causes or events: an outstanding event and an immediate trigger.

2.2.1.1. An outstanding event: the EMU crisis as an extension/expression of the subprime bubble

The extension of the subprime bubble burst effects in the EMU was related to two main sources: firstly, by contagion effects from the U.S. banking sector in European banks, due to the global interconnectedness of banking and financial markets (as seen before); secondly, because many European countries had in the precedent years faced a similar 'boom-bust' cycle in the mortgage loans market and banks had increased their exposure to the emerging bubble, using similar business models and innovative financial instruments to those used in the U.S. to finance those types of mortgages, mostly based on securitization.

The case with the British bank Northern Rock is elucidative. A few months before the crisis bust in the middle of 2007, Northern Rock exhibited record profits, and this was due – as explained at that time in a chronicle of *The Economist* (18 October 2007) – to a business model relying "on wholesale markets rather than on retail deposits to finance most of its lending. More than any other big British lender, it relied on 'securitising' its mortgages."[8] In August 2007, as a prescient signal of the market drain in the money market to finance securitized mortgages, the bank became unable to repay those loans, and immediately afterwards, in September 2007, the bank was forced to require a liquidity support facility from the Bank of England. This ultimately led to a bank run from panicking depositors, fearing that Northern Rock could no longer meet its commitments.

The second case is the destruction of a significant part of the Irish banking sector: apparently, an astonishing and unpredictable outcome, if one looked solely at the Irish economic performance at the beginning of 2007 and

---

7 For a summary of the main stages of the crisis, see also Baldwin and Giavazzi (2015b, pp. 18–60).
8 Available at: www.economist.com/node/9988865.

ignored the financial risks hidden by that strong economic growth. Indeed, one should inquire, with Kelly (2010):

> How did an economy where employment doubled and real GNP quadrupled during the 'Celtic Tiger' era from 1990 to 2007, come to have GNP contract by 17% by late-2009 (with further falls forecast for 2010), the deepest and swiftest contraction suffered by a western economy since the Great Depression?

Together with the economic boom in the aforementioned period, the Irish economy also experienced an unprecedented housing boom, and with it construction and credit (demand and supply) booms (Whelan, 2013, p. 6). The leading bank in this leveraging process was the Anglo Irish Bank, but other big banks – like the Bank of Ireland – were also involved in the boom. When markets came under stress – due to the sudden collapse in the housing market –

> these banks found it increasingly difficult to raise funds on bond markets and on September 29, 2008, two weeks after the collapse of Lehman Brothers, the senior management of the largest Irish banks turned up at government buildings looking for help. Anglo Irish was losing funds and running out of eligible collateral to be used to borrow from the ECB.
>
> (Idem, p. 13)

Indeed, it was then possible to realize the scale of the exposure of the Irish banks to the real estate sector and how they were facing not just a liquidity difficulty, but a real solvency problem.[9]

In the case of Ireland, the bailing out of the Irish private banks was due not to the earlier intervention of the Central Bank of Ireland (in its role of 'lender of last resort') – as happened in the U.S. and in the UK – but mostly due to the intervention of the Irish government (starting in 2008 and 2009), through the approval of financial assistance programmes (e.g. the Eligible Liabilities Guarantee Scheme) that also involved the recapitalization of the banks receiving assistance. New legislation came into force increasing the intervention sphere of the Irish government with respect to management of banks and the injection of money to cope with losses,[10] which *de facto* meant a nationalization of those same banks.

The massive financial support provided by the Irish government to the banking sector, in addition to the economic downturn resulting from the

---

9 Regarding boom and the bust in the Irish banking sector, see also Stancil (2010b, pp. 43–49).
10 Information available at: www.irishtimes.com/news/government-to-nationalise-aib-1.869303.

housing bubble burst and along with a jump in unemployment, resulted in a huge loss in income tax revenues and a large increase in social welfare payments. This in turn led to the budget deficit and eventually to the significant rise in the Irish government debt (Whelan, 2013, p. 10).

Finally, mention should be made of the case of Spain. As noted by Akin *et al.*, (2014, pp. 7–8), the Spanish banking sector had, in the 2000s, a higher regulatory perimeter for its banks than U.S. banks, and therefore this did not foster the creation of shadow banking activities. In fact, the mechanism did not rely on the lack of incentive for monitoring the quality of mortgages – as in the U.S. – but the ability of financial institutions to influence the valuations of properties by appraisal companies.

Despite this, Spain also experienced a housing bubble and a credit boom-bust cycle. Indeed, Spain, during the 2000s, experienced one of the most important housing booms among developed countries, and this boom was also one of the main engines for the respective economic growth (Akin *et al.*, 2014, p. 8). The mortgage business – mostly involving savings banks (*cajas de ahorro*) – also prompted this massive increase: the average Spanish mortgage rate of 3.71% was the lowest in the EU, which averaged 4.51%. In addition, the business model associated with credit provision was permissive (low credit standards): real estate appraisal firms were encouraged to introduce upward bias in appraisal prices to satisfy their owners or most important clients (banks), shaping recommendations from the Bank of Spain (with respect to granting credit), according to which credit over 80% of the value of the property should not be granted (Akin *et al.*, 2014, p. 6).

In the middle of 2007, the first signs of distress were felt in the real estate and mortgage markets, and in 2009, major difficulties erupted. Gradually, the Spanish government and regulatory institutions were confronted with the real financial situation of the *Cajas*: the list of undercapitalized institutions (low solvency ratios) included the four giants Bancaja, Catalunya, Caja del Mediterráneo and Caixa Galicia, which a year later would be bailed out by the FROB (*Fondo para la Reestructuración Ordenada Bancaria*),[11] a restructuring fund that had been created in July 2009 (see Martin-Aceña, 2013, p. 92).

This process for the resolution of the banking sector was destructive and costly: the Bank of Spain and the FROB bailed out seven savings banks or groups of savings banks, and four of them were nationalized. Moreover, in June 2012, the Spanish government was forced to request external assistance from the European Financial Stability Facility (EFSF), under a Memorandum of Understanding signed on July 20, including financial aid of €100 billion to cover losses and to capitalize all of Spain's viable banking institutions still in need of restructuring.

---

11 Fund for the Orderly Restructuring of the Banking Sector.

In short, by December 2012, the funds channelled to the banking sector amounted to the staggering figure of €61.2 billion, or about 5.8% of GDP; 36.5% of these funds came from the FROB, and the rest, 63.5%, from the EFSF.[12] The amount of help received by the Spanish banks in terms of GDP was the second largest in the European Union and the United States, preceded only by the assistance granted to the Irish financial system (*Idem*, p. 85).

As a parenthesis, I would like to introduce an aspect to be developed later. As we have seen, the first government initiatives to support the financial system (particularly to support banks) were justifiably adopted in this initial moment. The *government bailout* of the banking system was indeed one of the first inevitable consequences of the financial crisis in Europe, as it was in the U.S. The rationale for the government bailout is straightforward: it is intended to avoid bank runs, to assure the functioning of the payment system, to prevent a credit crunch and to limit the social costs (externalities) and the negative effects on the real economy that a bank default might entail (Gerhardt and Vennet, 2016). On the other hand, many of these governmental initiatives were coupled with the intervention of central banks, in the context of conventional or non-conventional monetary policy, therefore performing their (usual) role as 'lenders-of-last-resort'. I will return to this issue further on.

As noted, in turn, by Fernandes *et al.* (2016), government bailout measures can be of a different nature, such as: (i) direct equity injections, providing liquidity to support banks; (ii) government-guaranteed debt issuance programmes and the issuance of guarantees to reassure depositors; (iii) purchases of distressed assets by the government or, more generally, provision of mechanisms to relieve financial institutions from impaired or 'toxic' assets.

While the U.S. adopted a balanced mix of equity injections in financial institutions with distressed asset purchases, in the EU, liability guarantees (typically an insurance against default on bank debt) were preferred to other measures. Indeed, the outstanding amount of liability guarantees in the EU reached its peak in 2009 with €835.8 billion outstanding. As for direct capital injection for the capitalization of banks, the amount reported for

---

12 The Bankia-BFA holding company (which includes the old Caja de Madrid) alone has taken the astronomical figure of €22.4 billion (Martin-Aceña, 2013, p. 94). Note that the process of creation and further restructuring involving Bankia also revealed cases of mismanagement, political promiscuity and corruption. Some of these cases date back to the past, when regional *cajas* were an interface for 'influence-peddling' between political parties (at national, regional and local levels), construction companies and, of course, financial institutions. The judicial and criminal affair involving Rodrigo Rato (leader of the *Partido Popular* Spanish party and former Managing Director of the IMF, appointed in 2010 as President of the Caja Madrid), in which he was condemned for embezzlement, demonstrates these kinds of inappropriate connections.

the period between 2009 and 2012 was smaller, but even so significant, at €413.2 billion (Gerhardt and Vennet, 2016, p. 6).

2.2.1.2. The immediate trigger: the revelation of the Greek deficit in 2009

If, until 2009, the European crisis had been an extension/expression of the financial crisis that had hit the U.S., exhibiting a similar pattern, from this date onwards the crisis transmuted into a different being. In October 2009, the newly elected Greek government announced that the previous government had masked the size of the budget deficit, and that the true deficit – at 12.5% – was twice as large as previously announced (Baldwin and Giavazzi, 2015b, p. 37; and Baldwin *et al.*, 2015).

In the words of Stancil (2010a, p. 25), Greece was soon perceived as a scenario with a 'proliferation of problems', the history of which was well established, beginning before the adoption of the euro. As summarized,

> prior to the establishment of the euro, Greece was among the worst economic performers of eventual Euro area members. Annual inflation was one of the highest in the region; the Greek government paid the highest borrowing premium; and GDP growth was the slowest in Europe.
>
> (*Idem*, p. 25)

The introduction of the euro was unable to solve these problems; on the contrary, it had masked the problems and to a large extent helped to magnify them. Massive capital inflows and a panorama of low interest rates (fostered by the euro) fuelled domestic demand growth, increasing domestic labour costs and eroding Greek competitiveness. These conditions also led to an increase in government demand (and with it in public deficits), and ultimately to the rise in sovereign debt. Problems in the public sector were furthermore aggravated by high levels of tax inefficiency, with the high level of the informal sector of the economy (mostly explained by tax evasion) and to inadequate, engineered statistics that helped to hide the real fiscal situation of the country (Stancil, 2010a, p. 29).

From 2009 onwards, the Sovereign 10-Year Swap Spreads in Greece started to rise significantly, increasing the respective borrowing costs from 1.5% to 5%, as credit rating agencies repeatedly downgraded Greek government debt (Baldwin *et al.*, 2015, p. 7).[13] *Sovereign risk premia* widened across the euro area, reflecting increasing concerns in financial markets about certain

---

13 Rating agencies use a combination of several quantitative and qualitative variables (economic, social and political), which include: per capita income; GDP growth; inflation rate; economic development; current account; foreign debt/GDP; real exchange rate; default

governments' capacity to meet their future debt obligations. In particular, the widening of sovereign bond yield spreads vis-à-vis Germany was interpreted by many observers as a welcome reassessment and differentiation of country-specific risks (Attinasi *et al.*, 2011, p. 408).

Also, as the EZ crisis evolved, global risk factors (that had been very present in the beginning) were thus progressively replaced by concerns about national outlooks, either with respect to the liquidity and solvency of the domestic financial sectors (the default risk), or with respect to each country's fiscal sustainability (Sgherri and Zoli, 2011, p. 421). Therefore, concerns about *long-run debt sustainability* with respect to certain EZ countries were raised,[14] and the idea that a *sovereign default episode* might happen started to echo (particularly in the case of Greece). Political and academic discussion about debt restructuring and its legal, financial and reputational effects multiplied in this moment.[15]

This triggering event – in October 2009 – corresponded to the date when the euro "ceased to be boring": investors, who had already been awakened from their indolence by the global finance crisis, reran their calculations and concluded that Greek debt was more risky than German debt (Pisani-Ferry, 2011, p. 8). The spread between Greek and German bond rates doubled, to 4%, in April 2010.

Even worse, the disease seemed contagious because spreads between 'good' and 'bad' borrowers started to widen throughout the EZ – Ireland was the first victim, followed by Portugal, where the absence of growth fuelled doubts about the country's capacity to repay its debts (*Idem*, p. 8). Contagion was indeed about to happen to other European countries, notably after the failed attempt to rescue Greece with the first bailout programme from the 'Troika' – the European Commission (EC), the European Central Bank (ECB) and the International Monetary Fund (IMF) – formed in early 2010.[16] Firstly, peripheral countries (Ireland and Portugal) were dramatically affected with increasing borrowing costs; and this was the beginning of the so-called 'sudden stop' in capital flows, addressed further on. Secondly, immediately afterwards, core countries also became under stress, notably the ones with historically high government debt levels – which was the case with Belgium. Most of all, the high exposure of core European banks to Greek debt was a new source of anxiety: in October 2011, the Franco-Belgium bank Dexia was brought into the bank-debt vortex due to its exposure to the Greek debt – in a radical response, the bank

---

history; debt ratio to GDP; ratio reserves/imports; corruption index; aggregate governance indicators.

14 Further on, I will detail the criteria/factors found in literature regarding debt sustainability.
15 I will also come back to this point.
16 See *infra*, more details on this fiscal stimulus programme.

was nationalized by Belgium at the end of that same month (Baldwin *et al.*, 2015, p. 10).

In this period – it is claimed – financial markets, in association with credit rating agencies, seemed to have regained power (Pisani-Ferry, 2011, p. 70). Suddenly, the main causers of the 2007–2008 financial crisis with its (alleged) anti-ethical and greedy actions of financial engineering and toxic product creation were now unashamedly making judgements about each country's outlook and past fiscal behaviour in the most rigorous manner. With hindsight, there is today a broadening consensus that the EZ crisis should not be considered a government debt crisis in terms of its origin, and that, apart from Greece, countries that ended up with bailouts were not those with highest debt-to-GDP ratios (Baldwin *et al.*, 2015, p. 2). However, by that time, when fundamentals stepped onto the stage, the formerly accused (financial markets and rating agencies) had become the accusers, regaining power to decide who should have 'access to the market' and under which conditions – *dura realitas, sed realitas*.

As noted again by Pisani-Ferry (2011, pp. 70–71), sovereign debt markets are relatively simple and homogenous: the market is determined by one variable, the rate of interest on government bonds. In normal times, predicting its evolution is mostly a macroeconomic exercise. However, forecasts become difficult when solvency problems arise and the question of whether government debt will ever be repaid has to be considered along with future economic developments. Furthermore, in the case of the euro area, the nature of this forecasting exercise was changed due to three main factors (Pisani-Ferry, 2011). Firstly, markets started to scrutinize countries individually, whereas macroeconomic forecasts had been designed for the area as a whole. Secondly, insolvency raised the stakes – macroeconomic fundamentals that usually explained negligible differences in spreads amongst European countries started to be significantly relevant. Thirdly, insolvency turned credit default swaps (CDSs) – financial products aimed to insure against the risk of the default of a borrower – into powerful speculation tools.

The action from European institutions and political leaders was not successful: the first Greek bailout failed because it was weak, and because the prevalent attitude from public actors was, at the time, a resigned and naïve 'washing of hands', as if private sector involvement would suffice: private holders should bear the losses of the Greek debt write-down, and this was supposed to stop there. For this reason, some authors argue that contagion from Greece to the rest of the EZ (peripheral and certain core countries) was caused primarily by policy mistakes and blurriness that switched a 'good equilibrium', where government debt could be financed at a reasonable cost, to a 'bad equilibrium', where financing costs became unbearable – the case for a 'self-fulfilling prophecy' (Baldwin *et al.*, 2015, p. 10). As a matter of fact, the more profound weaknesses of the European institutional and legal build-ing blocks had started to be exposed at that time.

2.2.1.3. The causal complexity of the metamorphosis of the crisis

According to Caceres *et al.* (2011, pp. 395–396), the transformation of the crisis in Europe, from a typical financial crisis to a sovereign debt crisis, took place between 2007 and the end of 2009. Furthermore, the factors that contributed to the (gradual) transformation over this period were basically three: (i) global risk aversion; (ii) contagion (measured by the so-called spill-over coefficient); (iii) country-specific fundamentals (stock of public debt and budget deficit as a share of GDP). Note that the authors use these crite-ria to assess and interpret the evolution of 10-year government bond yields and of swap yields.

Each factor was more intense in each of the different phases that Cace-res *et al.* (2011) disentangle within this *metamorphosis period*. In the first phase – named the 'financial crisis build-up' (July 2007–September 2008) – securities from Germany and other core countries of the EMU benefited from 'flight-to-quality' flows, whereas bonds from peripheral countries saw their yields rising versus swap yields as global risk aversion was weighing adversely on these lower-rated issuers.

In the second phase – 'the systemic outbreak phase' (October 2008–March 2009) – which was characterized by sovereign interventions concerning sup-port for banks (recall the case of Ireland), government bond yields gener-ally rose relative to swap yields, on contagion from countries more directly involved in the financial crisis and from fundamentals, which started to deteriorate. In this phase, contagion was then the predominant factor.

During the third phase – the 'systemic response phase' (April 2009–September 2009) – all government bond yields fell back towards swap yields, as the lower probability of distress in some countries was favourably affecting others. In this phase, weaker contagion was nevertheless offsetting further deteriorations in fundamentals.

Finally, the 'sovereign risk phase' (that started precisely on the aforemen-tioned trigger date of October 2009) meant that the process of metamorpho-sis had finally been concluded: in this phase, swap spreads started to increase due to country-specific risks, directly from worsening fundamentals, or indi-rectly from spillovers originating in other sovereigns (*Idem*, pp. 396–397). *Fundamentals* that could be already foreseen in the precedent phases defi-nitely took the lead.

It should be noted that government debt did not, in general terms, become a problematic issue until the 2007–2008 financial crisis. Figure 2.1 shows that, with few exceptions (e.g. Portugal), government debt had not risen significantly in the years after the adoption of the euro (for some of the

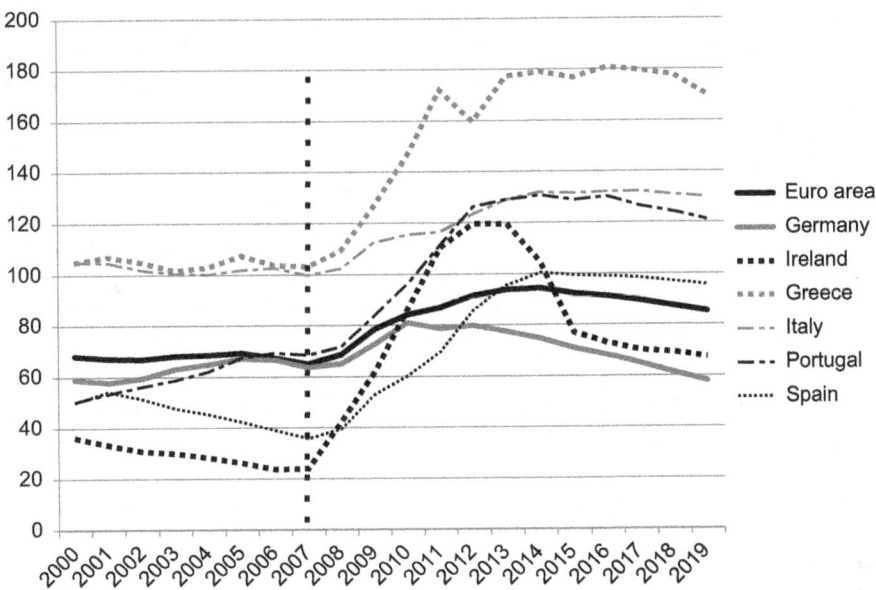

Figure 2.1 General government consolidated gross debt, as a percentage of GDP (based on ESA 2010)

Source: The Author

Data Source: AMECO online database

countries, it had even been reduced).[17] Figure 2.1 also clearly denotes a split into two distinctive periods with respect to government debt levels, namely before and after the eruption of the crisis.[18] It should also be noted that before the crisis, the average debt level for the EZ (as a ratio of GDP) was

17 It can be seen that the economic growth model of many of these (southern) countries was a 'bad' model of economic growth, explained by structural handicaps that had not been solved, but also fuelled by the environment created immediately before and after the euro that helped to magnify those pre-existing imbalances. Recall what happened with Greece (Stancil, 2010b). As for the case of Portugal, the path of growth was similar. As noted by Ali (2010, p. 63), Portugal, with the euro, "could have taken the opportunity presented by the boom to move into higher value-added and faster growth sectors and toward a more outward-oriented production structure. Instead, its export structure was weighted too heavily toward traditional sectors. In addition, the government missed the opportunity to build a budgetary surplus – which would not only have balanced the budget, but would have also moderated the domestic demand boom and the excessive concentration in non-tradable activities. In hindsight, a tax structure weighted toward discouraging consumption and investments in non-tradables (e.g. housing) could also have been imposed."

18 Note that at least for peripheral countries, the deterioration of government debt levels with respect to GDP (after the 2007–2008 crisis) was both related to the increase in the global debt stock and to the decrease in GDP, particularly between 2011 and 2013. The presence of these two effects is intuitive, although it is not captured by the figure.

slightly above the reference value of the EU Treaty, of 60% of GDP; but after that, it clearly became an 'excessive' debt.

Two preliminary (while important) factors can help to explain the rupture in sovereign debt after 2008. Firstly, the banking sector bailout programmes adopted from 2008 onwards by some of the peripheral countries (in particular, Ireland), which meant, as seen previously, a strong financial pressure on public budgets. Secondly, the fiscal stimuli packages adopted in 2009–2010 by different European countries as an immediate response to the financial crisis, under the so-called 'European Economic Recovery Plan – EERP' (detailed further on). In several countries, these stimulus measures implied a significant increase in public expenditure (in particular investment expenditure) and public deficit (raising the net borrowing needs of the general government)[19] – and the institutional relaxation of the Stability and Growth Pact criteria during the applicability period of the EERP also contributed to this.

While significant, these two factors do not tell the whole story. The sovereign debt crisis was – since its origin – far more complex. In fact, further investigation on this matter shows that the sovereign debt crisis emerged due to a complex mix of causes that included (macro)economic, financial, fiscal and ultimately psychological factors. The territorial scope of these factors – global, regional or national – also evolved throughout the process of metamorphosis.

What is fundamentally at stake, then, is to identify what determined this unique mutation of the crisis, meaning that a financial/banking crisis gave rise to a fiscal and sovereign debt crisis, and ultimately to a currency or monetary crisis. The links between these three kinds of crises have been widely studied in economic literature, notably since the seminal article of Kaminsky and Reinhart (1999) referred to previously. Nevertheless, the mutation of the crisis in the euro area was of an uncommon nature, because while being a double and eventually a triple crisis, it lasted longer than usual and entailed more severe effects (when compared to other previous crises affecting developed countries). Furthermore, it exhibited the following precise and well-defined time sequence:

Banking crisis $\Rightarrow$ Debt crisis $\Rightarrow$ Currency crisis

De Paoli *et al.* (2011, p. 26) present the interaction of these three types of crises (banking, debt and currency crises) and the mechanism explaining why they all cause output losses (considering past crises and also anticipating what could happen in the EZ case). In a first round, a banking crisis

---

19 As an example, Portugal, which adopted significant stimulus measures in 2009–2010, saw its budget deficit (as a percentage when compared to GDP) move from 3.0% in 2007 to 9.8% in 2009, and then to 11.2% in 2011 (one of the highest levels in its history).

interacts with a debt crisis, mostly through the combined and reciprocal effects of the fiscal costs of recapitalization and the default on government bank loans. In a second round, the debt crisis interacts with a currency crisis, and they mutually reinforce each other through the refusal to roll over local currency debt and the increase in net foreign debts. It should also be noted that a banking crisis can also (directly) foster a currency crisis, notably when a run on local currency deposits takes place.

2.2.2. *The cascade effects driven by metamorphosis of the crisis*

2.2.2.1. *'Doom looping' between sovereign debt and bank debt; bailouts to the banking sector; bank debt nationalization issue*

2.2.2.1.1. 'DOOM LOOPING' BETWEEN SOVEREIGN DEBT AND BANK DEBT

At this time, the existence of doom looping between sovereign debt and bank debt became clear (Rixtel and Gasperini, 2013; Baldwin and Giavazzi, 2015a; Baldwin *et al.*, 2015). As mentioned by Schoenmaker (2015, p. 2), the sovereign-bank loop works in two ways. Firstly, banks carry large amounts of bonds of their own government on their balance sheet – thus, a deterioration of a government's credit standing automatically worsens the solvency of that country's banks. Secondly, a worsening of a country's banking system deteriorates the government's budget, because of a potential government-financed bank bailout.[20,21]

From these words, one could say that the origin of the looping was sovereign debt, and only afterwards, in a second round, did the deterioration of bank balance sheets occur (implying a government bailout). As we know

20 See also Cooper and Nikolov (2013, p. 2).

21 'Doom-looping' should not be confused with another relationship between EZ bank balance sheets (in general) with sovereign debt (in general). This relationship is explained through a carry-trade process. Acharya and Steffen (2013) explain that since mid-2008 government bond-yield (to 2012) spreads between pairs of European countries (e.g. German bunds and peripheral countries) have widened, mirroring the economic divergence between these countries. At the same time, the authors show that bank risk in this period can be understood as a *carry-trade behaviour*: after the outburst of the financial crisis, GIPSI and non-GIPSI banks focused on the survival of the Eurozone choosing to hold peripheral sovereign bonds and financing their investments in the short-term wholesale market. European banks were long GIPSI government bonds and short (long-term) German bunds, which suggests that they were financing long-term peripheral bonds with short-term debt in a carry trade. Consequently, German bunds appreciate whenever short-term funding dries up, due to the so-called 'flight-to-quality effect' (as detailed further on, this co-movement also confirms that the sovereign debt crisis has fostered both financial fragmentation within the Eurozone and a phenomenon of home bias in capital allocation).

from the transmutation process of the crisis in EMU, this was not (necessarily) the case.

In fact, as noted by Farhi and Tirole (2016), if it is true that in some cases the initial shock was effectively related to sovereign debt (the case of Greece), in others the shock started in bank balance sheets (the case of Ireland). In either case, the fact is that, at a certain moment (2009 onwards), the sovereign CDS spreads and bank CDS spreads started to co-move.

The mechanism described by Farhi and Tirole (2016) goes as follows. As banks use sovereign bonds as a store of liquidity, the solvency of the sovereign is reduced for two reasons when the economy suffers an adverse shock. Firstly, there is a direct negative effect on output and on revenue collection, worsening the fiscal stance of the government. Secondly, there is an indirect effect of the shock that operates through bank balance sheets – the initial fall in the price of public debt hurts the net worth of the banks and thus their investment; if the sovereign attaches high value to investment, it will bail out banks. The key point, then, is that these bailouts are financed by issuing additional debt, increasing the stock of debt and further decreasing its price. Basically, for every dollar of bailout that the sovereign provides to the banks, public debt must increase by more than a dollar: there is thus a 'doom loop' or a 'deadly embrace' between sovereign and financial balance sheets (Farhi and Tirole, 2016, p. 4).

In 2011, when doom-looping started to become more evident, Acharya *et al.* (2011) considered that financial sector bailouts were an integral factor in igniting the rise of sovereign debt risk in advanced economies, considering at the same time that the feedback going in the other direction – from the sovereign credit risk to the banking sector – was indeed present due to the financial sector's implicit and explicit guarantees and holdings of sovereign bonds. Furthermore, they concluded:

> The tests presented show that in the post-bailout period (2008–2010) an increase in sovereign credit risk is associated with a robust and statistically significant increase in the credit risk of that country's banks, even after controlling for market-wide shocks to credit risk, volatility, 'local' CDS-market conditions, common variation in bank CDS, and changes in bank-levels fundamentals.
>
> (*Idem*, p. 5)

In a similar vein, Rixtel and Gasperini (2013) note that the tension due to the increase in the sovereign debt risk arose before banks were able to fully purge their balance sheets of impaired assets from the 2007–2009 financial crisis. Therefore, sovereign concerns spilled over to banks, as reflected in marked increases in bank CDS spreads along with sovereign ones. The co-movement became more intense after the nationalization of the Allied Irish Bank in January 2009 (*supra*), and it intensified even more during the crisis

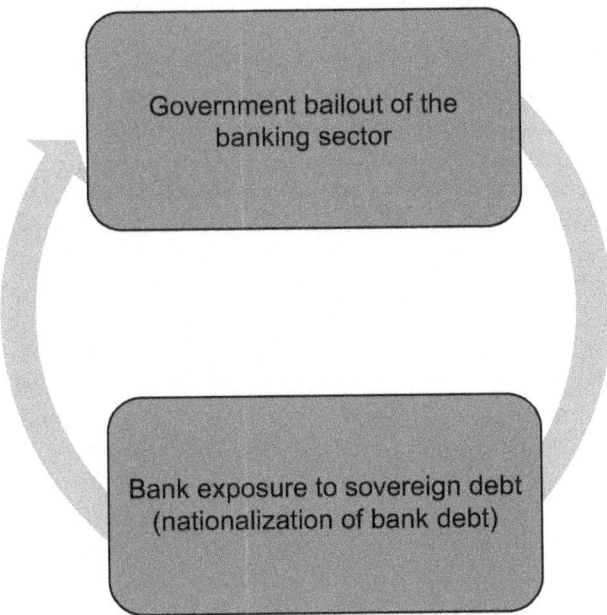

Figure 2.2 'Doom looping' between banks and sovereign debts
Source: The Author

periods involving peripheral countries (Greece, Ireland and Portugal, joined later by Italy and Spain) (Rixtel and Gasperini, 2013, p. 6).[22]

Figure 2.2 captures the basic elements making up doom looping. As can be seen, the loop is to a large extent explained both by government bailouts to distressed banks and by bank exposure to sovereign debt itself (due to nationalization of bank debt).

I will now detail these two sides of the looping.

2.2.2.1.2. GOVERNMENT BAILOUT OF THE (DOMESTIC) BANKING SECTOR

An important line of research seeks to analyse the sovereign's economic incentives to proceed with a bank bailout. Keister (2010) stresses that

---

22 As also noted by Rixtel and Gasperini (2013, p. 8), such correlations would only decline when these peripheral countries received financial assistance, under their respective bailout programmes (see *infra*), and particularly when the first initiatives involving non-conventional monetary policies were announced by the ECB – e.g. the re-activation of the Securities Markets Programme in 2011, for Italian and Spanish sovereign debt, and the announcement of Outright Monetary Transactions in 2012.

bailouts provide insurance to cope with financial risks and losses. For this reason, a commitment from the government to a no-bailout policy would be suboptimal because in an environment of bank fragility (see the seminal contribution of Diamond and Dybvig, 1983), a situation of stress would leave them illiquid and potentially susceptible to a self-fulfilling run. These bailout payments (diverting resources from public production to the private consumption of banking investors) aim to improve the allocation of the remaining resources in the economy, even if at a cost of negative *ex ante* incentives (e.g. moral hazard).

In turn, for Acharya and Steffen (2011), a bailout benefits the economy by ameliorating the under-investment problem of the financial sector. In practice, as also noticed (Acharya and Steffen, *Idem*, p. 4), government bailouts imply (new) government debt issuing that will be repaid by future taxation. However, there are two basic constraints to the bailout size: Firstly, the greater the legacy debt of the government, the lower the ability to undertake a bailout.[23] Secondly, the announcement of the bailout lowers the price of government debt due to the anticipated dilution from newly issued debt. Ultimately, this will result in a deterioration of the sovereign's creditworthiness, which can feed back into the financial sector, reducing the value of its guarantees and existing bond holdings and increasing its sensitivity to future sovereign shocks.[24]

On the other hand, Gaballo and Zetlin-Jones (2016) consider that in the presence of banks' *home bias*, the temptation of the sovereign to enact bailouts is reduced, and this is mostly justified with the banks' own interests. Domestic sovereign debt, in contrast to other assets, causes bank capital losses to be contingent on the bailout policy of the sovereign. Therefore, home bias is an optimal mechanism to discipline *ex post* public interventions. Indeed, as we have seen before when describing the outstanding events of the crisis, as home bias increased, bailouts were progressively deterred, with the exception of the Irish case. Spain provides a significant illustration of this. It became clear that a domestic bailout was difficult due to the high exposure of its banking sector to Spanish government debt: the cost of a bailout exceeded the benefits. This also explains the reason why bailouts, in Spain, were mostly supported by stability programmes implemented at the euro level (*Idem*, p. 35).

2.2.2.1.3. BANK EXPOSURE TO SOVEREIGN DEBT (NATIONALIZATION OF THE BANK DEBT)

Re-nationalization of financial markets serves to explain the incentives given to the sovereign to comply or not with domestic debt, that is, the possibilities of *default* on this type of debt.

---

23 This is because the Laffer curve of tax revenue leaves less room for the government to increase tax rates for repaying its bailout-related debt.

24 Also on this issue, see Cooper and Nikolov (2013).

Analysis of the re-nationalization of financial markets has been developed through three types of approaches (Farhi and Tirole, 2016, pp. 6–7). Firstly, *discrimination theories* rely on selective domestic sovereign defaults on foreign banks but not on domestic banks. This difference is higher in bad times when sovereign bond yields are high, leading to a re-nationalization of domestic sovereign debt. Secondly, *risk-shifting theories* rely on the assumption that domestic banks prefer the risk profiles of domestic sovereign bonds. This preference is stronger in bad times when sovereign bond yields are high, leading to a re-nationalization of domestic sovereign debt.[25] Thirdly, *financial repression theories* rely on the moral suasion by which the sovereign may coerce or incentivize domestic banks to buy domestic sovereign bonds at above market prices in order to reduce its financing costs. This incentive is stronger in bad times when sovereign bond yields are high, leading to a re-nationalization of domestic sovereign debt.

Let me detail the latter approach. The idea of *financial repression* can be found in Reinhart and Rogoff (2009b, 2013), Reinhart and Sbrancia (2011), Reinhart (2012) and Reinhart and Kirkegaard (2012). Under financial repression, banks are vehicles that allow governments to squeeze more indirect tax revenue from citizens by monopolizing currency and the entire savings (e.g. pension funds) and payment system. Governments force local residents to save in banks by giving them few alternative options. Then, they stuff debt into the banks via reserve requirements and other devices. This allows the government to finance a part of its debt at a very low interest rate; financial repression thus constitutes a form of taxation (Reinhart and Rogoff, 2009b, p. 143).

Note that financial repression, coupled with inflation, is a typical instrument of partial default on domestic debt (Reinhart and Sbrancia, 2011), a possibility not found in the case of external debt. Indeed, as added by Reinhart and Kirkegaard (2012), financial repression, combined with inflation, cuts debt burdens from two directions: (i) low nominal interest rates reduce debt servicing costs; (ii) negative real interest rates erode the debt-to-GDP ratio (it is a tax on savers). In short, financial repression is a form of redistribution of wealth between savers and borrowers by using monetary policy transmission channels (Reinhart and Rogoff, 2013, p. 6). Reinhart and Kirkegaard (2012) describe the recent movement of negative real interest rates (post-crisis) – a consequence of the 'aggressive expansionist monetary policy' adopted by the central banks – as a modern case of financial repression.

Also note, on the other hand, that financial repression can be channelled through regulation (Reinhart, 2012; Uhlig, 2013). In fact, regulators can force banks to hold sovereign bonds, perhaps in exchange for 'looking the

---

25 See Acharya and Rajan (2013) and Gennaioli *et al.* (2014)

other way' concerning the weak portfolios of commercial banks and mortgages, or simply as a 'favour' in a long, ongoing relationship. In particular, Basel III provides for the preferential treatment of government debt in bank balance sheets via substantial differentiation (in favour of government debt) in capital requirements (Reinhart and Kirkegaard, 2012).

2.2.2.2. Fiscal effects of the crisis

Declining revenues and higher expenditures, due to the combination of bailout costs and higher transfer payments and debt servicing costs, lead to a rapid and marked worsening of a government's fiscal balance (Reinhart and Rogoff, 2009b, p. 231).[26] As shown by Borio *et al.* (2016), the financial/sovereign debt crisis was no exception: first, there was a persistent increase in public deficits (around 2007–2008, the median fiscal balance fell by over five percentage points within three years, to about 6% of GDP, with a quarter of countries experiencing a much larger deterioration to over 10%); in addition, government debt to GDP soared (recall Figure 2.1 *supra*).

Borio *et al.* (2016) then present the main factors explaining the impact on fiscal stance: (i) The sovereign uses its fiscal space to repair bank balance sheets – the *bailout fiscal costs – and, in some cases, it also bails out companies and households*.[27] (ii) Output and employment collapse, shrinking revenues and boosting non-discretionary expenditures, to put in motion automatic stabilizers. Output losses are significant, ranging from 6% to 14% on average across countries, against only 2% in ordinary recessions (i.e. not accompanied by financial crises). (iii) For a given behaviour of output and income, compositional effects may further deteriorate the fiscal balance: the collapse in asset prices may indeed play a significant role. (iv) Furthermore, exchange rates are relevant: a financial and sovereign debt crisis usually coincide with a currency crisis (currency depreciation).[28] (v) Output losses may also translate into a decline in long-term or potential output. (vi) Finally, the policy response may lead to a further worsening in the fiscal position, when the option is either for fiscal stimulus measures (immediate increase in public current or capital expenditures), or for austerity measures, as austerity usually involves contractionary effects, negatively affecting both revenue collection and the GDP growth rate.

26 According to the estimations presented by the same authors considering a group of events that have occurred since the nineteen seventies onwards, the deterioration in government finances is striking, with an average debt increase of eighty six percent, within three years from the onset of the crisis (Reinhart and Rogoff, 2009b, p. 231).
27 Laeven and Valencia (2012) explain that the fiscal costs of a crisis can be mostly attributed to bank recapitalizations and asset purchases. These costs are higher for advanced countries, in contrast to emerging economies.
28 I will come back to this further on.

A specific fiscal effect of sovereign debt is related to debt-service costs. Bond yields imply higher debt-servicing costs and can significantly raise funding costs. This can also lead to an increase in roll-over risk, as debt might have to be refinanced at high cost or, in extreme cases, cannot be rolled over at all (Caceres *et al.*, 2011, p. 393; and Jalilvand and Switzer, 2011, p. 401). Additionally, the rise in sovereign yields tends to be accompanied by a widespread increase in long-term interest rates in the rest of the economy, affecting both investment and consumption decisions (Caceres *et al.*, 2011, p. 393).

The role of interest rates is, in fact, twofold. As noted by Borio *et al.* (2016, p. 6), interest rates may rise in the aftermath of a financial crisis, notably in countries with a weak financial position or with a large stock of debt denominated in foreign currency. The same may happen in countries with limited room for monetary policy manoeuvre – as in the case with the EMU: in these cases, interest rates may rise either as a way to defend the single currency and prevent inflationary pressures, or due to the increase in risk premia, as investors lose confidence in the sovereign's creditworthiness. When interest rates rise, this adds immediately to the deficit and debt burden, to an extent that depends on the size of the outstanding debt and its contractual features (e.g. maturity and interest rate sensitivity, more generally).[29]

On the other hand, though, central banks may intervene with an aggressive ('super-expansionist') monetary policy, thereby leading to a sharp decrease in the interest rate (in same cases pushing it down to zero). When interest rates sink persistently to exceptional low levels, fiscal positions may look stronger than they really are, with policymakers and investors overestimating debt sustainability and prospects for debt repayment (Borio *et al.*, 2016).

As will be seen further on, these two double-side effects occurred in the EMU: after the outbreak of the sovereign debt crisis, sovereign bond yields (of peripheral countries) rose sharply from 2009 onwards; with the fundamental change in the sense and intensity of the monetary policy led by the ECB (in particular with the 'Outright Monetary Transaction – OMT' announcement), the 'widening gap' between those yields vis-à-vis the Germany sovereign bond yields started to reverse.

2.2.2.3. The euro crisis and the fragmentation of the financial markets

The creation of the E(M)U had brought the conviction that risk premia should disappear within the area as markets believed the Maastricht Treaty's

---

29 Also see Corsetti (2015, p. 93). In his opinion, the charges are also borne by banks thus suffering the damages of the sovereign risk premia increase: losses on bank holdings of sovereign debt are transmitted to the real economy via a credit crunch, which in turn feeds back into lower taxes and these higher public deficits, raising sovereign risk even further.

promises of 'no devaluation', 'no default' and 'low inflation forever for all' (Baldwin and Giavazzi, 2015b, p. 22). The crisis has shown, on the contrary, that this was not the case because investors (*lato sensu*) started to negatively discriminate against sovereigns that presented poor fundamentals, exacerbating a 'flight to quality' effect that ultimately led to considerable divergences in the Eurozone for 10-year government bond yields. The crisis thus once again showed risk premiums and the idiosyncratic nature of sovereign risks.

A definition of financial integration can be found in Baele *et al.* (2004).[30] In their opinion, the market for a given set of financial instruments and/or services is fully integrated if all potential market participants with the same relevant characteristics (i) face a single set of rules when they decide to deal with those financial instruments and/or services; (ii) have equal access to the aforementioned set of financial instruments and/or services; and (iii) are treated equally when they are active in the market.

Agénor (2001), Kose *et al.* (2006) and Haan *et al.* (2012, p. 185) identify the main advantages of financial integration. Firstly, financial integration ensures more opportunities for risk sharing and diversification. Secondly, financial integration promotes a better allocation of capital (due to the elimination of barriers to trading, clearing and settlement platforms). Thirdly, it increases the potential for higher economic growth.

As for the potential costs and disadvantages of financial integration, Agénor (2001)[31] highlights: (i) the concentration of capital flows and the lack of access to financing small countries, either permanently or when it is more needed is highlighted; (ii) a domestic misallocation of capital flows (when capital is allocated for example to speculative domestic investments instead of growth-enhancement investments); (iii) undesirable macroeconomic effects, such as rapid monetary expansion, inflationary pressures, real exchange appreciation and widening current account deficits; (iv) procyclicality of short-term flows, which makes access to funding easy in 'good times' and difficult in 'bad times'; (v) herding, contagion and volatility of capital flows, which can make borrowers face costly 'liquidity runs' when certain events occur or due to distress in the markets.

Increasing financial integration in the EMU seems undisputable. Haan *et al.* (2012, pp. 178–184) show that with respect to the main financial markets (money market, government bond market, corporate bond market and equity market), after the EMU's creation a path of integration has been followed, even if not with the same intensity with respect to all of these markets.

---

30 When considering the notion of financial integration one should realize that it comprises financial assets *stricto sensu* (e.g. equity, bonds and derivatives), but also money, the latter including, in turn, cash, money market instruments (e.g. treasury bills, deposit certificates and repos) and foreign currencies.

31 See also in this regard Stiglitz (2000).

Indeed, significant evidence has been presented that the creation of the EMU has fostered financial integration amongst its constitutive members. As noted by Lane (2006, p. 52), "the single currency has reorganized and unified financial markets across the euro areas." The most immediate illustration of such integration was related to the integration of the euro-area bond market, as yield differentials across EMU members started to decrease and the volume of private bond issues increased rapidly. In particular, spreads across government bond yields have decreased to very low levels. Furthermore, a 'euro bias' has developed with respect to cross-border equity and bond holdings: there has been a much higher cross-border asset trade between member partners than with 'foreign' ones. The same happened with foreign direct investment (FDI), which has increased much more amongst euro-area members than with external countries (Lane, *Idem*, p. 53). Finally, as for the banking sector, the EMU has facilitated the development of interbank lending between member countries and, supported by the rising securitization of asset-backed loans, a narrowing in interest rate differentials concerning mortgage products. Nevertheless, as also noted, retail markets have continued to be highly segmented across the euro area and cross-border transactions have remained limited (*Idem*, p. 55).

The basic question is not if financial integration occurred in the EMU (which has indeed occurred), but whether financial integration – as was developed in the area – was able to ensure cross-border consumption smoothing (under the 'permanent income hypothesis'), that is, to ensure risk sharing amongst its members.[32]

As noted by Cabral (2017, p. 253), "the crisis has highlighted two effects that only apparently may be considered paradoxical." The first effect, resulting from free capital movement (in itself an essential element of the EMU) is the existence of large cross-border financial flows between financial institutions of the Eurozone, the strong interdependency of financial markets within the area and, because of this, the existence of the specific risk of contagion in situations of distress. The second effect, and as mentioned by Breuss *et al.* (2015, p. 3), the financial markets (notably the capital markets) in the EMU are not fully integrated and thus provide only limited risk sharing across countries. Adverse financial shocks (e.g. mortgage loan losses in countries like Ireland and Spain) therefore have effects, which are largely confined to countries from which they originate, or – one could add – countries that exhibit country-specific risks due to a deterioration in their fundamentals (see Caceres *et al. idem*, p. 397), as was the case with Greece and Portugal. Financial interdependency did not create full financial integration, in the sense that country-specific risks were not eliminated or reduced by the existence of risk-sharing mechanisms indirectly provided by the financial markets.

---

32 I will detail this issue in Part II, notably when analysing the Capital Markets Union.

As noted by the ECB (2016, p. 91), when financial markets are sufficiently integrated, members in a currency union can obtain insurance against idiosyncratic shocks, via cross-border holdings of productive assets, government bonds and/or other types of financial assets, the payoffs of which depend on those shocks. Furthermore, well-functioning credit markets can contribute to consumption smoothing against relative income fluctuations via intertemporal borrowing and lending. Finally, relative prices in goods markets can also help in hedging risk, helping to insulate income and wealth from those same idiosyncratic shocks.

Lane (2006) had precociously identified the main reasons why such a risk sharing effect was/is not conveniently ensured despite the EMU's progresses towards financial integration. Firstly, such integration has not happened evenly across countries: in particular, E(M)U countries exhibit significant geographical differences in their cross-border portfolios. Secondly, hedging against macroeconomic risks can be difficult, notably through international financial integration. Thirdly, most wealth remains domestically held (e.g. real estate). Fourthly – and most important – the single currency has actually reduced the scope for risk sharing between countries: the disappearance of individual national currencies means that the relative returns on the nominal bonds issued by member countries can no longer vary in line with shifts in bilateral nominal exchange rates – which would be a major source of risk sharing.[33]

On the other hand, when assessing if financial integration can be beneficial or not (from the point of view of risk sharing), one should consider three main general dimensions (ECB, 2016, pp. 81–86). Firstly, there is the type of cross-border financial instruments traded – debt or equity. Hence, one important element of the financial integration in the EMU (in contrast, for example, with the U.S.) is that it is biased towards debt finance, and especially towards intermediation by banks (ECB, 2016, p. 82), and this fact can help to magnify the impact of negative shocks on economic growth.[34] [35]

---

33 As noted in turn by Lane (2013), during the crisis, countries with independent currencies obtained net external wealth gains through currency depreciation, raising the (local currency) value of foreign-currency assets relative to domestic-currency liabilities. This possibility is excluded for EMU members. Here, national policymakers cannot deploy inflation and currency depreciation to alter the returns on local currency instruments relative to foreign-currency instruments.

34 Indeed – as also noted (ECB, 2016, p. 82) – debt tends to be more prone to runs than equity. Liquidity crises are often related to sudden stops in debt investment rather than in equity-type forms of finance. Two conceptual arguments can be added in this vein: (i) unlike equity finance, debt-finance lacks 'state contingency' considered as an insurance device: equity payoffs tend be lower in economic downturns; (ii) unlike equity (which is provided for an unlimited period), debt is provided for a limited period of time, therefore imposing roll-over risks on investors.

35 Milesi-Ferretti and Tille (2011) and Lane (2013) show that during the 1990s, the debt-equity ratio in capital flows had declined, while during 2002–2007, debt flows grew more

Secondly, capital instrument maturity, as short-term instruments are considered more volatile – short-term flows have a pro-cyclical nature, therefore increasing overall macroeconomic instability (financially integrated countries that rely more on short-term debt are more exposed to crisis).

Finally, the composition of the intra-euro-area foreign bank lending is considered as another crucial driver.

One of the structural biases of EMU financial integration is that it has most relied on the (secured) interbank market. As had been noted before by Fecht *et al.* (2007), secured interbank markets are an optimal risk-sharing mechanism when banks face true liquidity needs. However, free riding in liquidity provision in such a market restrains the capacity of the mechanism to ensure a risk-sharing effect. Thus, in large integrated areas, this moral hazard problem can require other alternative sources of cross-border bank funding, notably through unsecured interbank markets and mostly through retail markets. The fact is that, as shown by Lane (2006) and the ECB (2016), in the EMU, while interbank money markets integrated very quickly, the same did not happen with banking and retail financial services – cross-border direct lending to households and non-financial companies has played a minor role.

2.3. The euro area crisis as a balance-to-payments and a currency crisis[36]

As mentioned earlier, there exists today a broadening consensus amongst economists that the EMU crisis was mostly a 'sudden stop' crisis, a 'sudden stop' in capital flows vis-à-vis the peripheral countries (Baldwin *et al.*, 2015; Baldwin and Gros, 2015). It is also claimed that this phenomenon is related to structural imbalances – the polarization of external imbalances within the EMU – that moreover were fuelled by the respective (dysfunctional) building block, hence creating a pro-cyclical behaviour in capital flows (notably in the case of its peripheral countries): capital inflows in good times; outflows in bad ones (recall Kaminsky *et al.*, 2004).

The polarization of external imbalances was thus at the heart of the European sovereign debt crisis. Since the EMU's inception and until the crisis, the problem had clearly been minimized. But this does not mean that it was unknown. Lane (2006), while recognizing that the EMU had fostered financial integration in the area and had increased the so-called 'euro bias' in different segments of financial markets, also highlighted that this integration had not been the same for all EMU countries. As a sign of this bipolar financial integration, Lane (2006, p. 54) focused

---

than equity flows. The crisis put an end to this credit boom, as the sudden stop mainly affected bank-related debt flows.

36 This point will be detailed in Part II, when addressing the alleged flaws of the euro.

precisely on the increasing larger current account deficits in the poorer countries of the EMU (Greece, Portugal and Spain), since the enactment of the monetary union.

However, it was only after the crisis that the issue created more attention. Treichel (2012), Hale and Obstfeld (2014), and Ferra (2015) investigated whether unbalanced trade relationships and capital flows amongst EZ countries could be considered a dominant cause of the European crisis. Furthermore, they analysed in which way these relationships affected EZ trade and financial relationships with the rest of the world, in particular with other advanced economies.

Treichel (2012) found that the euro itself played a major role in the propagation of the crisis. In fact, the euro led to the integration of capital markets and to the gradual reduction of interest rates: these favoured cross-border capital flows, with claims by core countries on non-core countries' banking systems dominating the increase. Treichel (2012) then considers that "at the heart of the euro crisis is hence an intra-area balance of payment crisis caused by seriously unbalanced intra-area competitiveness positions and the – largely private – accompanying cross-border flows."

Hale and Obstfeld (2014, pp. 1–2) explain the large current account deficits in the periphery through the following mechanism (*the geography of international debt flows*): after the EMU launch, compression of bond spreads in the euro area periphery encouraged excessive borrowing by these countries, domestic lending booms, and asset price inflation; thus, the EMU contributed not only to large net deficits in the periphery, but also to inflated gross foreign debt liability and asset positions for core countries (Belgium, France, Germany and the Netherlands) – in fact, in 2008, net foreign assets of the core were mostly vis-à-vis the peripheral countries, and these assets were in turn matched by liabilities of the core vis-à-vis the rest of the world (*Idem*, p. 8).

Ferra (2015) develops these precise ideas, starting with detailing the polarization of external imbalances in the EMU. On the eve of the global financial crisis, the current account deficit was above 10% of GDP in Portugal and Greece and above 5% in Ireland and Spain, whereas in Germany the current account surplus amounted to 7% of GDP. The second aspect detailed is the financial linkage intermediation existing within the EMU and with respect to the rest of the world. Internally, Ferra (2015) describes the close interdependence between EZ economies: euro area core countries represented major financial partners for peripheral countries (gross liabilities of these latter countries held by the former ranged from 40% of GDP in the case of Italy to 69% in the case of Portugal). Externally, EMU relationships with the rest of the world presented two main features: (i) core euro area economies played the role of intermediary for international capital flows between peripheral countries and the rest of the world; (ii) the magnitude of gross external positions of the euro area with the rest of the world was large, highlighting its financial openness and close integration with world financial markets.

If today it seems obvious that the euro – as a common currency – played an important role in the surge of balance-to-payments imbalances within the Euro area, the severity of which was exacerbated by the crisis, we should now look to a different aspect of the problem (less focused on in the literature): the impact of the euro crisis on the exchange rate of the euro vis-à-vis other (international) currencies. Furthermore, one should verify if the crisis implied a loss of overall competitiveness of the euro area vis-à-vis external markets, that is, if it caused some disturbance in the E(M)U's global balance-to-payments position.

The depreciation of the euro in the aftermath of the crisis was anticipated by Wyplosz (2012, p. 74). As noted in this regard by the ECB (2017, p. 15), the euro's depreciation against the U.S. dollar accompanied movements in long-term interest rate differentials, suggesting that exchange rate developments mainly reflected changing expectations about the relative future path of monetary policy and term premia.[37] Apparently, this depreciation was able to bring some positive effects to sustain the euro area, increasing external competitiveness, even if this was certainly not the only reason. Interestingly, if it is true that the output gap of the euro area shrank with the financial-sovereign debt crisis, it is no less true that its external trade surplus has been growing continuously since 2009 (Landmann, 2017, p. 126). The author shows that most of this is due to the rise in external demand (instead, domestic demand remains behind GDP growth).

If this is so – a positive effect of the Euro's depreciation in the overall E(M)U balance-to-payments stance – one should not ignore, in contrast, the effects of the crisis on the international role of the euro. The euro, despite what some had feared at its inception, performed well in its first years: it became a strong, stable and well-accepted currency (Landmann, 2017, p. 127). However, the crisis seemed to have weakened the international role of the euro, that is, its acceptance as a currency in worldwide terms. In the study conducted by the ECB (2017), the main results were a decline in the international role of the euro across several indicators, notably in: (i) the euro in official holdings of foreign exchange reserves; (ii) its function as a payment currency (with a recovery in 2016); (iii) its usage as an international investment currency; (iv) its use in loan and debt markets.

---

37 The justification for this strong depreciation in November 2016 depended, in the ECB's (2017) view, on the results of the U.S. presidential election and growing market expectations of rising U.S. inflation and fiscal expansion, which led to a substantial increase in U.S. long-term interest rates and which further drove up U.S. equity prices. In 2017, the euro exchange rate recovered part of its earlier depreciation, allegedly because of a change in market participant expectations about the ECB's future monetary policy stance, and despite concerns about the prospective outcomes of national elections in some euro area countries.

3

MISGUIDING SIGNS IN THE POLICY RESPONSES TO THE EMU CRISIS

3.1. From market forces to public action

A policy shift, qualified by Brunnermeier *et al.* (2016a, p. 20) as a 'shift from Brussels to national capitals' meant to a large extent the idea of the 'privatization' of crisis responses (instead of a European governmental action). The first illustration of this initial strategy was related to the decision – taken at the Ecofin meeting of 16 March 2010 – of involving the IMF in the resolution of the sovereign debt crisis. The IMF had already intervened in Hungary and Latvia, in 2009, two countries that did not belong to the EMU. In January 2010, it became clear that Greece would also need financial assistance. The intervention of the IMF was considered desirable (notably from Germany) on the basis of two main arguments (Brunnermeier *et al.*, 2016a, p. 22): (i) the IMF's programmes follow well-established procedures, therefore reducing moral hazard and the idea of a permanent international rescue operation; (ii) the IMF intervention could, despite historical resistance, be politically less critical than an intervention stemming from an EU institutional framework. Germany – despite the opposition of the French president Nicolas Sarkozy – was determined to move the European Commission (EC) away from any bailout measures to be applied to Greece. For this reason, the first Greek assistance programme set up in May 2010 by the Eurogroup was supported by bilateral loans pooled by the EC, also including a financial participation from the IMF with €30 billion (see *infra* next subsection).

The second illustration of this shifting ('privatizing') strategy was the so-called *private sector involvement – PSI* strategy. This strategy was defined under the imposition of Germany in the Deauville meeting (18 October 2010) between Chancellor Merkel and President Sarkozy.

The PSI, being consistent with the no-bailout rule of the Treaty (see *infra*), meant that holders of bonds issued by non-euro-area governments would be asked to assume the losses if the issuing country needed support from other euro-area members – with this, markets should at least provide some *ex ante* discipline for fiscal excesses (Brunnermeier *et al.*, 2016a, p. 29). In hindsight, one can say this bail-in strategy underlying PSI ('making the banks pay for their mistakes') was a disaster: soon after its announcement, interest rates on peripheral countries' debt (as well as sovereign CDS) increased markedly; the probability of a default was perceived by investors as an inevitability (Brunnermeier *et al.*, 2016a, p. 31).

This attempt to avoid a bailout was also an attempt to avoid government intervention notably at the European level. If for the French, the PSI was seen with scepticism, for Germans in general, this strategy was most welcome. They were frustrated that European institutions had proved powerless in disciplining fiscal policies (*Idem*, p. 32).

The failure of this initial strategy was soon acknowledged. European leaders and institutions saw that only government action at the European level, even if involving some sort of bailout, had to be adopted. The assistance programmes under the Troika (*infra* next subsection) and the way they evolved – with the increasing involvement of European institutions and mechanisms in the financial assistance given to the most affected countries (*infra*) – showed this change of pattern: the resolution of the crisis could no longer rely solely on market forces.

The third illustration of the shift was related to the design and nature of the preliminary assistance mechanisms. It is not by chance that the first emergency mechanisms (aiming to provide financial assistance to countries hit by the sovereign debt crisis) – the *European Financial Stabilization Mechanism* (EFSM) and the *European Financial Stability Facility* (EFSF) – were created on an intergovernmental basis (Hinarejos, 2015, p. 24) and from the spectrum of European institutions. But what is more, the EFSF was conceived as a temporary loan vehicle (and not as a funding mechanism within the institutional background of the EMU), a company based in Luxembourg that could obtain financing by issuing debt on the financial markets backed by securities of the shareholder member states (Hinarejos, *Idem*, p. 24).[1] The initial programmes to distressed countries (e.g. the second programme to Greece and the assistance programmes to Ireland and Portugal) were financed under these two temporary financial instruments (see *infra*).

After the amendment was introduced (March 2011) to Article 136 of the Treaty on the Functioning of the European Union (TFUE) (allowing member states to create a permanent crisis mechanism to safeguard the stability of the euro), the *European Stability Mechanism* (ESM) was established in 2012. Even if the act of creation was an act of an intergovernmental nature (see Hinarejos, 2015, pp. 25–26), at least the ESM implied a return to the EMU institutional framework and a return to government action at the

---

1 The EFSF could hence borrow on financial markets (up to €440 billion) and lend the proceeds to countries that agreed on a reform programme. Moreover, it could also intervene in the primary and secondary bond markets, act on the basis of a precautionary programme, and finance recapitalizations of financial institutions in non-programme countries through loans to governments (Brunnermeier *et al.*, 2016a, p. 26).

European level. Above all, it meant the recognition that the previous strategy of relying on external private vehicles was no longer suitable as an adequate mechanism for financial support to EMU countries in crisis.

3.2. From fiscal stimulus to austerity; the magnitude of fiscal multipliers

3.2.1. The initial response: fiscal stimulus – the 'European Economic Recovery Plan' (EERP)

Between the two aforementioned events – the outstanding event and the Greek trigger moment – an intermediary period can be traced, running from the last quarter of 2008 to the beginning of 2010. Since this intermediary period can be seen as a very brief but enthusiastic Keynesian moment in the history of the E(M)U, therefore exhibiting remarkable features, I will call it the *intermezzo*. Indeed, the initial strategy defined by European institutions to cope with the effects of the financial crisis, and the risk that it might evolve into an economic downturn, was marked by the adoption of a surprising *fiscal stimulus* package.[2] Surprising, that is, if one considers the basic (orthodox) grounds which provided for the creation of the EMU, the display of nominal convergence criteria as an entrance condition, the disciplinarian device of the Stability and Growth Pact (SGP) framework – in short, the mainstream rationale for fiscal discipline in the context of the monetary union. Surprising, even if one considers the flexibility introduced by the 2005 revision in the SGP, and which allowed countries to slow down the movement towards fiscal consolidation and eventually to pass the deficit limits prescribed by the Pact, in exceptional negative circumstances notably vis-à-vis the business cycle.

On 26 November 2008, the European Commission (EC), in the Communication addressed to the European Council,[3] presented the *European Economic Recovery Plan* (EERP). The first words were quite emphatic – "The time to act is now" – because the current economic crisis was providing an "opportunity to show that Europe serves its citizens best when it makes concrete action the touchstone. Europe can make the difference."

The EC clarified the instruments through which the stimulus should be fulfilled. Proposing a 'mix' of revenue and expenditure instruments, the

---

2 As mentioned at the time by Pisani-Ferry *et al.* (2008), a budgetary stimulus can be characterized as a sudden and generalized dash for liquidity combined with an across-the-board heightening of the aversion to debt. As also noted, the fear of illiquidity was then becoming overwhelming and the general aversion to debt was leading to deleveraging, which implied a drop in demand for goods and spending on consumption and investment. Budgetary policy should, for these reasons, step in to boost aggregate demand. In short, for these authors, Keynesian policy was needed and could have been effective.

3 COM (2008), 800 final.

following measures were to be considered: public expenditure (e.g. temporary transfers to the unemployed or low-income households; public investment in projects that could benefit SMEs); guarantees and loan subsidies to compensate for the unusual risk premium in an environment of credit constraint; well-designed financial incentives; lower taxes and social security contributions; and temporary reductions in the level of the standard Value-Added Tax (VAT).

What really stood out in this Communication was the optimistic tone that through active public action, the major effects of the crisis could be quickly removed from the European economic scenario. Europe could rapidly reverse the business cycle. This was indeed a new Marshall Plan (Steinbach, 2012) designed to reconstruct Europe from the ashes of the financial turmoil.

3.2.2. The magnitude of fiscal multipliers: results of investigations regarding the ARRA

Different studies (using different methodologies) were made to compute the effects of the European fiscal stimulus packages, for the EU as a whole and for each of the component countries (see, for example, CESIFO, 2010, p. 61). Nevertheless, some contemporaneous studies highlighted the shortcomings of the package, either with respect to its short duration (in fact, it was meant to be implemented during 2009 and 2010) or with respect to its general amount, considered insufficient (1.5%–1.8% of the EU GDP) (Watt, 2009), and that these shortcomings could eventually limit the effectiveness of the programme.

Later on, other studies sought to analyse the economic effects of this programme, comparing it with the similar programme adopted in the U.S. during the Obama administration (February 2009) – the *American Recovery and Reinvestment Act* (ARRA). The ARRA envisaged the largest fiscal stimulus in American history, of approximately $800 billion, with its main objectives being to 'preserve and create jobs' and 'promote economic recovery' after the Great Recession (Klein and Staal, 2017, p. 396). This amount would correspond to over 5% of the U.S. GDP, in contrast with the aforementioned amount of 1.5% of GDP in the case of Europe (Wieland, 2009a).

As noted by Romer and Bernstein (2009), the considerable size of ARRA's effects on economic recovery was mostly justified through a high estimation of the expenditure multiplier, of 1.6. In this respect, Nakamura and Steinsson (2011) note that behind the estimation of the multiplier, there was not just one methodological approach or theoretical conception. In fact, the estimated magnitude of the multiplier varied according to different views about preferences, technology, government policy and various types of 'frictions'. For this reason, simple versions of the neoclassical model generally imply a small multiplier (smaller than 0.5), whereas in the light of the ('old') Keynesian view, the multiplier is much larger.[4]

The research carried out by Nakamura and Steinsson (2011) estimated the impact of ARRA on U.S. regions, bearing in mind the nature (accommodative or not) of monetary policy. Regarding this, the results are not straightforward, mostly depending precisely on the assumptions that lie behind the research. For example, in some New Keynesian models,[5] the size of the multiplier critically depends on the extent to which monetary policy 'leans against the wind'. For this reason, strong counter-cyclical policy (such as that used during the Volcker-Greenspan era) can generate low multipliers, comparable to those of the neoclassical model (Nakamura and Steinsson, 2011, p. 2). The only exception to this stance occurs when monetary policy becomes less responsive and even ineffective, e.g. at the zero lower bound. In this case, multipliers regain their strength and can even exceed 2 (Nakamura and Steinsson, 2011, p. 2).[6,7]

3.2.3. The enthronement of austerity and the ordoliberal justification

While temporary since its conception, one could not imagine that the EERP would be abandoned so precociously due to a profound policy change, such as that which took place from 2009 to 2010. One would even admit, as more likely, that the basic framework of the ERRP could be refurbished, allowing the maintenance for more months (or years) of fiscal stimuli packages in affected economies.

In contrast, what happened was one the most extraordinary changes in the conception and carrying out of fiscal policy since the launch of the EMU. Indeed, within a few months, the EMU put into motion a radical change from a tough Keynesian, stimulus-based plan to a neoclassical, orthodox

---

4 In this regard, under a New Keynesian approach, Cogan et al. (2009) (following Smets and Wouters, 2007) discover, in the case of ARRA, much smaller government spending multipliers than those used by Romer and Bernstein (2009), below 1. In other words, government spending should not induce additional private spending, but instead would quickly crowd out private consumption and investment (see also Wieland, 2009b).

5 As mentioned by Cogan et al. (2009), the term 'New Keynesian' is used to indicate that the models have forward-looking, or rational, expectations by individuals and firms, and some form of price rigidity, usually a staggered price or wage setting. The term is also used to contrast these models with 'old Keynesian' models without rational expectations of the kind used by Romer and Bernstein (2009).

6 Banerjee and Zampolli (2016) arrive at a different conclusion: they find that short-term fiscal multipliers remained lower than 1, during the crisis, for most of the countries (including 'bad countries'). In particular, they did not find evidence that fiscal multipliers should be above unity when the output gap is negative and monetary policy is tight.

7 Briefly, I will come back to this issue.

programme of 'muscled' fiscal consolidation. Indeed, at this stage, Keynesianism was outlawed (Ferreira, 2012, p. 27).

Some causes might explain this sudden policy change: (i) *abrupt fiscal deterioration* – notably from 2008 to 2009 (when the most significant variations took place, including, on average, for the whole euro area); (ii) *political pressure* – notably from core countries (e.g. Germany) which despite also suffering from a similar deterioration and of a similar magnitude, wished to rapidly restore the basic disciplinarian grounds of the EMU (the so-called 'ordoliberal' conception of the stabilization policy within the area), and notably to ensure the full applicability of the SGP, rapidly ending the (temporary) fiscal tolerance entailed in the EERP;[8] (iii) *financial pressure* – recall that from October 2009 (with the revelation of the true Greek deficit, considered as 'the triggering event' of the sovereign debt crisis), the Sovereign 10-Year Swap Spreads in Greece started to rise significantly. In the subsequent months, sovereign risk premia widened across the euro area, reflecting increasing concerns in financial markets about certain governments' capacity to meet their future debt obligation. In particular, the widening of sovereign bond yield spreads vis-à-vis Germany was interpreted by many observers as a welcome reassessment and differentiation of country-specific risks (Attinasi *et al.*, 2011, p. 408). Since (fiscal) *fundamentals* started to matter (first and foremost for investors, gradually more reluctantly in financing EMU distressed economies), this was taken by European policy leaders as a strong argument to overturn stimulus packages and to restore a disciplinarian path for fiscal management.[9]

Using the words of Blyth (2013, p. 2), one could define austerity as

> a form of voluntary deflation in which the economy adjusts through the reduction of wages, prices, and public spending to restore competitiveness, which is (supposedly) best achieved by cutting the state's budget, debts, and deficits. Doing so, its advocates believe,

8 In June 2010 – as noticed by the *Financial Times* – Wolfgang Schäuble, Germany's finance minister, launched a defence of his country's economic policy on the eve of the G20 summit in Toronto, addressing the criticisms made by several politicians and investors (such as George Soros) that the view of Germany not only would entail recession in Europe but also would delay global economic recovery. Schäuble claimed at that time that "the German government knows it has a responsibility to promote growth in Europe and the world." He stressed, in turn, that growth should be promoted "not by piling up public debt but by fulfilling our traditional role as an anchor of stability" (available at: www.ft.com/content/504fa87a-7eec-11df-8398-00144feabdc0). By the same token, a month later, the ECB's President Jean-Claude Trichet would proclaim: "Stimulate no more – it is now time for all to tighten" (see Blyth, 2013, p. 60). By the time of the G20 summit, these same European leaders – challenging the American policy of economic recovery undertaken by Obama – would advocate the need to evolve to a programme of 'growth friendly fiscal consolidation'.

9 See also Wolf (2014, pp. 17–44), explaining the shifts in the European economic policy from the EERP to the adoption of austerity measures.

will inspire 'business confidence' since the government will neither be 'crowding-out' the market for investment by sucking all the available capital through the issuance of debt, nor adding to the nation's 'too big' debt.

Immediately after the shift towards austerity,[10] criticisms started to be voiced: most of them anticipated the contractionary effects and the harmful social consequences that could accompany this.[11] Many of these criticisms were based on Keynesian-type economic arguments (e.g. the discussion about the magnitude of fiscal multipliers),[12] others on deeper, more political and ideological arguments (of a left-wing type) mostly confronting the E(M)U with its alleged perversion as being, from the beginning, an area made to host and to blank out the excesses of financial capitalism.[13] Conjuring up both types of arguments, Blyth (2013, p. 10) ascribes to austerity the most negative descriptors: firstly, he names it as a 'zombie economics idea' which has been disproven time and again, but always keeps coming back throughout history;[14] secondly, he considers it a 'dangerous idea' for three main reasons: (i) it does not work in practice; (ii) it relies on the poor paying for the mistakes of the rich; (iii) it rests upon the absence of a rather large fallacy of composition that is all too present in the modern world.

One of the most controversial issues, opposing the two lines of macroeconomic theory was – is – indeed the impact of austerity on private consumption (and on economic growth). Austerity is certainly not a recent event, as the previous historical examples given demonstrate. Austerity as a guiding principle of fiscal policy (and of macroeconomic policy) is the product of a long-lasting intellectual/ideological melting pot that includes the 'two faces of Juno', only at first sight contradictory: on the one hand, the *neoclassical and liberal conservative doctrines* mostly represented by the *Austrian*

---

10 Later on, I will indicate the main policy instruments that translate this shift towards the austerity framework.

11 Stiglitz (2016, pp. 164–165) shows and confirms the poor economic performance of the EZ since the euro's inception, a trend that has been reinforced by the crisis (notably in those countries most affected by the sovereign debt crisis and subject to severe austerity measures): Greece showed, between 2007 and 2015, a cumulative decline of its GDP of more than 25%, Portugal of more than 6% and Spain of more than 2%.

12 See *infra*.

13 See, for example, Varoufakis (2016) and Louçã (2017, pp. 95–107).

14 Blyth (2013, pp. 179–205) recalls austerity policies conducted in the interwar period (firstly, under the gold standard and then under the gold bullion standard). In his opinion, austerity exacerbated the effects of the 1930s economic depression and created a global deflationary environment that was surely at the origin of the subsequent world conflict. Examples of austerity moments during this period are: U.S. policy between 1921 and 1937; British austerity under the Treasury position between 1921 and 1939; German austerity between 1923 and 1933; Japanese austerity between 1921 and 1937; and the French austerity policies between 1919 and 1939.

School, *Monetarism* and *Public Choice* (including the so-called *Bocconi School*); and, on the other hand, the *ordoliberal doctrine* as it was conceived and as it evolved under German economic policy since the beginning of the twentieth century and how it embedded, in the end, the European integration process under the Maastricht set.

As explained in this regard by Young (2017, p. 32), "historically, the German concept of ordoliberalism originated in 1930s, in opposition to Anglo-Saxon *laissez-faire* liberalism and self-regulating markets and totalitarian alternatives in the form of fascism and communism." Eucken was responsible for the conceptual foundation of the idea of 'ordo-' as 'order in the economy' – as an alternative to the classical notion of 'economic order'. As a consequence, the market should be conceived as a synthesis of legal and economic ordering. Eucken not only contested private power in *laissez-faire*, but he also criticized state power and all forms of market (public or private) concentration. Thus, as concluded by Young (*Idem*, p. 33), Eucken "envisioned an ordo to consist of a competitive order (*Wettbewerbsordnung*) regulated by a constitutional order (*Ordnungspolitik*), intimately linked and regulated by the rule of Law (*Rechtsstaat*)."[15]

Additionally, as mentioned by Winkler (2017, p. 93), ordoliberalism is defined by its focus on order, concretely the order established by economic policies. The basic economic principles – due to Eucken construction – are thus the liability principle and the principle of the primacy of monetary order. Indeed, in his *Principles of Economic Policy* (*Grudsätze der Wirtschaftspoltik*), Eucken (1952) set the basis of the role of monetary policy that later on would be popularized by Milton Friedman. When Eucken mentioned the primacy of monetary policy, he was already considering price stability as the main condition for adequate functioning of the market economy (see Praet, 2017d).

Therefore, despite the major differences in the conception of economic policy – in liberal conservative doctrines we see the enthronement of the market and economic freedom, in ordoliberalism we find the legitimacy for government intervention in the economy (Table 3.1)[16] – there is a common element between them: the recognition of price stability as the primary macroeconomic goal, including within this the need to impair government budget deficits as they are seen as the major determinants for inflationary pressures.

On the other hand, the liberal conservative intellectual framework (notably monetarism and the theory of rational expectations) also resembles

---

15 On the historical bases of ordoliberalism, its evolution, and its influence on the European integration framework, notably in the conception of the E(M)U, see also Bento (2013) and Blyth (2013).
16 Concerning the differences between the 'laissez-faire doctrine' and ordoliberalism, see Zettelmeyer (2017).

Table 3.1 The intellectual framework of austerity (the 'two faces of Juno')

Neoclassical and Liberal Conservative Doctrines	Ordoliberal Doctrine
i) Austrian School: conservative liberalism; the negative conception of freedom; the apology for non-government economic intervention. ii) Monetarism and the theory of rational expectations: macroeconomic neoclassical-type models; macroeconomic policy, the long term and the role of expectations; the scope of monetary and fiscal policies; price stability as the main macroeconomic goal; rules rather than discretion. iii) The Public Choice: the Government-leviathan model (as opposed to the Government-benevolent model); the political economy of budget deficits; the internal factors of expenditure growth (political and electoral systems; bureaucracy; lobbying and logrolling).	The concept of 'social market economy': respect for economic freedoms and for basic market economy principles, though with a strong intervention from the government notably in the field of regulation (preventing market abuses, economic concentration and monopolies). A rules-based order; the liability principle. The primacy of monetary order: price stability as the main economic goal (based on the German fear of inflationary pressures related notably to budget deficits: the historical memory of the hyperinflation and the economic instability of the 1920s that would partially justify the rise of Nazi power).

Source: The Author

the firm 'rule-oriented approach' that Eucken personified. Indeed, the very idea of 'rules rather than discretion' underlying the construction of rational expectations, notably with respect to the definition of monetary policy (for example, in the seminal article from Kydland and Prescott, 1977), is not distant from Eucken's approach (on this issue, see Feld *et al.*, 2017, p. 44).

3.2.4. Economic reasoning for austerity

3.2.4.1. Expansionist fiscal adjustment

Having said this, one can better understand the vindication of 'austerity' in many political and intellectual sectors after the crisis, and the respective comprehension of the macroeconomic effects associated with monetary and fiscal policies. In particular, unlike the assumptions resulting from the basic Keynesian model – according to which a reduction in public expenditure involves, in principle, contractionary effects – the neoclassical-type arguments developed since the 1990s, notably by leading economists of the Bocconi School, stressed that austerity could – in certain cases and under certain conditions – involve expansionary effects. Departing from the seminal contributions of

Giavazzi and Pagano (1990), Alesina and Perotti (1994, 1995, 1996), Alesina and Ardagna (1998), Perotti (1998), and Alesina *et al.* (1998), the basic arguments of the 'expansionary austerity' doctrine goes as follows (in short):[17]

- 'Expansionary austerity' (successful long-lasting adjustment) relies mostly on expenditure cuts, notably cuts in transfer programmes and government wages and employment. Unsuccessful adjustments, in contrast, rely primarily on increase in taxes, leaving transfer programmes and government wages and employment untouched. Furthermore, only reductions in spending that are expected to persist can yield permanently lower taxes (Giavazzi and Pagano, 1990, p. 5). In fact, expectations matter.[18]

- On the revenue side, the most successful adjustments do not increase taxes on labour (that is, household income taxes and social security taxes), but instead rely on indirect taxes and taxes on business to increase revenue.

- Political and budgetary institutions matter: presidential governments are more likely to carry out successful fiscal consolations than representational governments (Alesina and Perotti, 1994); a coalition government is much less likely to succeed in consolidating the budget than a single party government (Alesina and Perotti, 1995 and Alesina *et al.*, 1998); the strength of the position of the Prime Minister's office and the Minister of Finance matters; the type and timing of parliamentary votes, and the limits to parliamentary amendments to the budget are relevant to a successful fiscal consolidation (Alesina and Perotti, 1994).

- Successful long-lasting adjustment (relating to persistent and credible deficit reduction) can come both through the demand and supply side:

    i)   On the *demand side*, two non-Keynesian type mechanisms operate, preferably in 'bad economic times' (Perotti, 1998): (a) wealth effects on consumption: spending cuts perceived as permanent; such a positive wealth-expectation effect should be even stronger when fiscal consolidation occurs in 'bad times' with a high and rapidly growing debt/GDP ratio; (b) credibility effects on interest rates: fiscal consolidation, if perceived as permanent and successful, can bring about a discrete reduction in real interest rates.

    ii) On the *supply side*, the analysis refers to the labour market structure and to the influence of the unit labour cost channel – related

17 Note that these authors do not use the word 'austerity'. They refer to 'fiscal adjustment' or 'fiscal consolidation'. The word 'austerity' started to be used in the aftermath of the sovereign debt crisis, with a common pejorative sense notably following Blyth's book (Blyth, 2013). Further on, I will address the *polysemic* nature of the concept of 'austerity' and explain the different meanings it may have.

18 The two illustrative examples of successful fiscal consolidation were the policies implemented in Denmark and Ireland during the 1980s.

to distortionary labour income taxation – on economic growth (through external competitiveness). According to this channel, tax increases affect unit labour costs for firms, influencing their competitiveness (Alesina and Perotti, 1996, p. 7).

The second generation of the 'expansionary austerity' doctrine was developed during the euro crisis (by most of its main original defendants), thus providing an important justification and support for the marked policy shift, from fiscal stimulus to the so-called 'growth friendly fiscal consolidation' (see the re-publication of the arguments in Alesina and Ardagna, 2009, 2012).[19] According to these more recent analyses (Alesina and Ardagna, 2009, pp. 8–9), the adjustment is considered to be successful and expansionary if: (i) the cyclically adjusted primary balance improves during one year by at least 1.5% of GDP; (ii) there has been a cumulative reduction in the debt to GDP ratio three years after the beginning of the adjustment greater than 4.5 percentage points; (iii) the average growth rate of GDP, in terms of the difference from the G7 average (weighted by GDP weights), in the first period of the occurrence and in the two years afterwards, is greater than the value of the 75th percentile of the same variable empirical density in all the periods of fiscal adjustment.

Moreover, in Alesina and Ardagna (2012, pp. 1–2), a new argument is added in favour of comprehensive processes of fiscal adjustment: the periods of expansionary austerity are more likely to occur "when they are accompanied by a growth oriented policy mix such as labour market and goods market liberalization." This was in all ways the timely and needed justification to combine fiscal consolidation with the so-called 'structural reforms' (as indeed happened with the adjustment programmes applied to the EMU assisted countries).[20]

More recently – and considering the effects of fiscal adjustment programmes adopted in the course of the crisis – Alesina et al. (2019) show that spending cuts can in certain conditions be associated with output gains and are much more successful than tax increases at reducing the growth of debt.

The IMF, in its *World Economic Outlook* (IMF, 2010), challenged some of the findings of Alesina and Ardagna (2009). By using a similar methodology to that used by Romer and Romer (2010), contrasting findings to the 'Bocconi explanation' were presented:[21] (i) Fiscal consolidation

---

19 In the first of the studies, Alesina and Ardagna (2009, pp. 12–13) show that in successful cases of fiscal adjustment, total primary spending as a percentage of GDP falls by about 2% of GDP. Total revenues actually decline by about half of one percentage point of GDP. Thus, successful fiscal adjustments are completely based on spending cuts accompanied by modest tax cuts. On the contrary, in unsuccessful adjustments, total revenue goes up by almost 1.5% of GDP and primary spending is cut by about 0.8% of GDP.

20 See *infra*.

21 Somehow, these different results were due to (alleged) errors contained in the cyclically adjusted primary balance (CAPB) measure used (notably by Alesina and Ardagna, 2009)

typically has a contractionary effect on output.[22] (ii) Reductions in interest rates usually support output during episodes of fiscal consolidation – central banks offset some of the contractionary pressures by cutting policy interest rates, and *longer-term rates also typically decline, cushioning the impact on consumption and investment*.[23] (iii) A decline in the real value of the domestic currency typically plays an important cushioning role by spurring net exports and is usually due to nominal depreciation or currency devaluation. (iv) Fiscal retrenchment in countries that face a higher perceived sovereign default risk tends to be less contractionary; however, even among such high-risk countries, expansionary effects are unusual. (v) In the long term, though, the IMF (2010, p. 111) acknowledges economic growth gains obtained from debt reduction (notably due to fiscal consolidation) – where these gains come from two main factors: firstly, lower real interest rates that in turn crowd in private investment; secondly, lower income taxes, made possible with savings from lower interest rates and lower debt principal.

These findings were passed as an alert to those defending the idea of 'expansionist austerity', an alert that was certainly perceived. Perotti (2011, p. 5), for example, was aware of the different environment and constraints created by the EMU that could jeopardize the positive outcomes of fiscal austerity: firstly, because previous conditions that had made consolidations expansionary (such as the previously mentioned consolidations in Denmark and Ireland in the 1980s) were no longer applicable in the current position of low interest rates and low wage inflation; secondly, because those countries had managed to depreciate their currencies prior to pegging and consolidation, an option no longer available to members of the EMU.

Appropriately, in this regard, Perotti (2011) also notes that finding the effects of fiscal consolidations is not different from estimating fiscal policy multipliers – already mentioned here[24] – in ascertaining the controversy regarding this matter over the last few years.

---

as the standard measure of fiscal consolidation. As noted by the IMF (2010), the standard approach based on the behaviour of the CAPB may create bias in the estimated consolidation effects. Perotti (2011) addresses this issue, recognizing there is value in the IMF's criticisms and yet pleading in favour of the standard approach: removing the 'cyclical adjustment bias' would only reinforce the main finding that spending-based consolidations tend to be expansionist, unlike tax-based consolidations (which are usually contractionary). See also, as a response to the IMF's approach, Alesina and Giavazzi (2012, pp. 11–15).

22 A fiscal consolidation equal to 1% of GDP typically reduces GDP by about 0.5% within two years and raises the unemployment rate by about 0.3 of a percentage point. Domestic demand – consumption and investment – falls by about 1%.

23 For each 1% of GDP of fiscal consolidation, interest rates usually fall by about 20 basis points after two years.

24 For a representation/formalization of the fiscal multiplier, see Buti and Pench (2012, pp. 45–54).

In particular, assuming the (new) environment of constrained monetary policy,[25] two lines can be disentangled: firstly, the 'neoclassical approach' – relying on the idea of 'expansionist austerity', the main arguments of which have just been focused on; secondly, the 'Keynesian approach' underlying the analyses conducted by DeLong and Summers (2012), Blanchard and Leigh (2013) and Fatás and Summers (2016).

DeLong and Summers (2012) advocate that the combination of low real U.S. Treasury borrowing rates, positive fiscal multiplier effects, and modest hysteresis effects are sufficient to render fiscal expansion self-financing. Conversely, for the same reasons, fiscal tightening can be self-defeating.

Blanchard and Leigh (2013) note that before the crisis, analyses were based predominantly on actual multipliers of roughly 0.5. Notably, in the aforementioned IMF Outlook (IMF, 2010), a multiplier for 15 advanced economies during 1979–2009 is presented, averaging 0.5 within two years. As noted in turn by Mota (2017, p. 121), the first adjustment programmes (under the so-called 'Troika')[26] were designed mostly assuming this value for fiscal multipliers. Blanchard and Leigh (2013) note that these pre-crisis (and immediate post-crisis) forecasts underestimated the value of fiscal multipliers. The underestimation occurred both with respect to tax multipliers and expenditure multipliers but was significantly larger in this latter case. Introducing a new methodology, Blanchard and Leigh (2013) then present evidence that these multipliers were clearly above 1.[27]

Finally, Fatás and Summers (2016) assess not only the short-term negative effects on growth (impact on actual output), due to fiscal shocks (austerity measures), but also their long-term effects (impact on potential output), mostly due to the presence of hysteresis. Fatás and Summers (2016) are, indeed, mainly focused on the permanent effects of fiscal consolidations. The estimates presented confirm that consolidation was *self-defeating*, as they "suggest that the fiscal contraction in European economies reduced output not only in the short term but also in the medium term and possibly on a

---

25 As noted by Corsetti (2012a, 2012b, p. 106), fiscal policy austerity can be self-defeating in an environment of both unemployment and underemployment (deflation) with a situation of a 'liquidity trap' (or similar) – which is a situation where monetary policy operates at the zero lower bound.

26 I will detail this further on.

27 Fatás and Summers (2016, p. 18) summarize the new methodology used by Blanchard and Leigh (2013), a methodology aiming to deal with endogeneity in order to measure the impact of the 2009–2010 fiscal consolidations in European economies: "Their methodology is in many ways similar to the identification assumptions of more complex econometric specification (such as a VAR) but in a much simpler framework. Their methodology relies on the fact that GDP forecast errors should be uncorrelated with fiscal policy if the model used to generate the forecasts has the right assumptions about fiscal policy multipliers. If we find that the correlation is negative and significant it means that the model is underestimating fiscal policy multipliers."

permanent basis." Consequently, "this reduction in output makes the goal of the fiscal consolidation harder as it raises the ratio of debt to GDP and it reduces tax revenues" (Fatás and Summers, *Idem*, p. 23).

By that time, some other different approaches can be identified (as a compromise between the neoclassical Bocconi approach and the Keynesian approach): it is the case with Gros (2011), Cottarelli and Jaramillo (2012), Corsetti (2012a, 2012b) and Eyraud and Weber (2013).

Gros (2011), when asking whether austerity can be self-defeating, shows that in the short term, a fiscal adjustment can be self-defeating if the product of the starting debt/GDP ratio and the multiplier (of fiscal policy on output) exceeds one. On the contrary, in the long term, any initial increase in debt/GDP will be reversed over time because the permanent deficit cut lowers the growth rate of debt.

Cottarelli and Jaramillo (2012), when considering only the short-term effects of fiscal consolidations, highlight their negative impact on economic growth (mostly through the Keynesian, aggregate demand channel) but also, the other way around, explain the way in which economic deceleration (negatively) impacts fiscal accounts.

In turn, as noted in addition by Cottarelli (2012, pp. 39–40) – in a similar vein as Blanchard and Leigh (2013) – driving the economy to operate below its potential also helps to magnify the value of those same multipliers. In fact, when output is near or above capacity, deficit cuts are likely to result in reduced inflationary or current accounts pressures rather than lower output, biasing down estimates of multipliers that do not control for cyclical positions. Two additional factors can help to explain why fiscal multipliers become larger: firstly, monetary authorities have little manoeuvring room to offset the deflationary impact of fiscal tightening; secondly, nominal exchange rate depreciation is no longer an option for EMU countries.

Despite the evidence presented for the short term, the same authors recognize the positive effects that fiscal consolidation may have in the long term, and these can be due to either macroeconomic or microeconomic channels. The macroeconomic channel is related to the negative effect of high public debt (beyond a threshold of 80%–90%) on potential growth. As for the microeconomic effects of fiscal policy on growth, they are related to the presence of the state itself in the economy (non-Keynesian effects): the overall tax pressure, the way taxes are levied and the way public spending affects economic incentives in the private sector.

Corsetti (2012a, 2012b), in turn, based on a standard new-Keynesian model, addresses the role of fiscal multipliers when markets charge a risk premium on government debt. The model seeks to encompass the possibility that markets price sovereign risk based on expectations of future deficits and debt, and that rising risk premia on sovereign debt create, in turn, a country risk, affecting all those involved in the economy, via a deterioration of the balance sheets of banks and corporates, increasing taxation risk and the costs of utilities, and falling internal demand.

Finally, Eyraud and Weber (2013) argue that with fiscal multipliers close to 1, fiscal consolidation can in the short term raise the debt ratio. Ultimately, debt targeting (through austerity) could be self-defeating: if authorities focus on the short-term behaviour of the nominal debt ratio, they may engage in repeated rounds of tightening in an effort to get the debt ratio to converge to the official target, undermining confidence and setting off a vicious circle of slow growth and further tightening.

In short, 'front-loaded austerity' – such as that followed in the adjustment programmes implemented by the 'Troika' in some of the GIPSI countries – can be associated with different, contrasting outcomes, and the outcomes depend mostly on the initial circumstances of the country. In particular, for highly indebted countries – as were/are several GIPSI countries – a situation of multiple equilibria resulting from the interaction between sovereigns and financial markets can indeed occur (and the risk of there being a bad equilibrium is strong). As noted by Cottarelli (2012, p. 40), if markets anticipate that (aggressive, front loaded) fiscal tightening will not slow growth, spreads could fall and growth could indeed be maintained (non-Keynesian, long-term effects predominate); if, on the contrary, markets anticipate that growth will slow, spreads can rise and growth will suffer (a Keynesian reaction prevails).

I agree that austerity has gone too far and too fast. It has had immediate (probably needless) dramatic social and economic consequences – greatly affecting the survival of firms and peoples' lives. It has also caused a long-term, possibly permanent economic backwardness (recall Fatás and Summers, 2016, about the impact on potential output). Peripheral countries, even if at a slow pace, have started to recover: time is needed to confirm the role austerity played in this economic recovery and if, in the end, the outcome was a good equilibrium. This also implies evaluating whether the ongoing recovery is sustainable or not (and countries are not alike). One should not, on the other hand, ignore the impact of other policy measures on this recovery, with evidence regarding the reorientation of ECB monetary policy, from a typical conventional policy to non-conventional interventions (I will go into detail regarding this further on). Finally, one should not ignore the actual nature of short-term cycles (mutable by nature): when the bottom is reached, some recovery must occur.

3.2.4.2. The relationship between (high) debt and economic growth

Behind the design of fiscal consolidation or austerity instruments was not only the argument driven by the 'expansionist austerity' doctrine. Another strong argument in favour of muscled fiscal consolidation was the alleged (negative) relationship between (high) debt and economic growth. These two strong arguments in turn provide strong support for the so-called 'TINA' doctrine (inspired by Margaret Thatcher's dictum) – that is, 'There Is No Alternative' to austerity.

As for this latter argument, its basic framework can be found in a most quoted (and also contested) study: that of Reinhart and Rogoff (2010). Here, the authors find that while the relationship between government debt and real GDP growth is weak for debt/GDP ratios below a threshold of 90% of GDP, above this threshold median growth rates fall by 1%, and average growth falls considerably more. Hence, fiscal consolidation is needed to reduce high debt levels that jeopardize economic growth. Amongst other critical arguments, with respect either to the construction of the regression (data collection and encoding errors)[28] or to the interpretation of the results (the traditional jargon in econometrics according to which 'correlation does not involve causality'), the IMF (2012, p. 109) considered:

> there is no simple relationship between debt and growth. In fact, our subsequent analysis emphasizes that there are many factors that matter for a country's growth and debt performance. Moreover, there is no single threshold for debt ratios that can delineate the 'bad' from the 'good'.

Despite the criticisms, 2012 was a crucial political moment in the implementation of most of the adjustment programmes (see *infra*). In particular, a recipe that could now serve the assisted GIPSI countries, a role model for a sound fiscal consolidation had by then been identified: the case of Belgium in the 1980s. Over the 10-year period from 1981 to 1991, Belgium managed to reduce its high level of government debt, improving its primary balance – the largest consolidation over any 10-year period among advanced economies since World War II. Much of this was obtained through the retrenchment of the Belgian welfare state: reduction in the share of public employment and reduction in the 'excessively generous' system of welfare payments, by cutting family allowances and unemployment insurance benefits, and increasing the retirement age (IMF, 2012, p. 118).

3.2.5. Austerity and the assistance programmes to peripheral countries

Indeed, most of the adjustment programmes designed by the assisted countries with the 'Troika' (the IMF, the ECB and the European Commission) had been informed by and contained these theoretical premises: fiscal

---

28 See Herndon *et al.* (2014).

consolidation was not only needed, but it was a 'good' thing as it could bring those countries back to the path of economic growth and debt sustainability. The adjustment programmes of course meant a break with the fiscal stimulus panorama that had been established in Europe in 2008. Now, with the enthronement of fiscal consolidation, it could be argued (from the perspective of its defendants) that the EMU was 'getting back on track'. Fiscal consolidation (now treated as austerity) indeed meant a return to the old normality contained in the EMU's fiscal policy legal framework, since at least the inception of the Stability and Growth Pact, SGP, based on powerful economic and fiscal reasons. The changes introduced to the SGP (in 2011 and in 2013) and the signing of the so-called *Fiscal Compact* in 2012 would, in the end, fully legitimize this new policy direction.[29]

Finally, one should acknowledge that this policy reorientation was not unexpected and abnormal, when considering the presence and role of the IMF as a 'member' of the 'Troika'. The reasons have already been detailed here, and amongst those reasons rising government debt levels was one of the most important: these adjustment programmes were a first response to the surge in the European sovereign debt crisis. Hence, one can say that the main purpose of the programmes was to bail out countries most affected by the crisis and that commitments to fiscal consolidation (and other reforms) were considered natural consequences of the assistance provided. *Conditionality*, coupled with macroeconomic surveillance, is indeed one of the basic historical features of the 'rules-based system' established in 1944, when the IMF Agreement was enacted. One of the statutory objectives of the IMF is to provide financial assistance to partners suffering from macroeconomic imbalances, particularly with respect to their balance-to-payments. Assisted countries must then enter into a Memorandum of Understanding (MoU) with the IMF, establishing obligations for the assisted country regarding either fiscal or monetary policies, and eventually economic policy as a whole. Fiscal consolidation measures are usually included in the package. The MoU is thus the basic instrument to contain the conditionality principle and works as a benchmark for macroeconomic surveillance.[30]

---

29 I will come back to this issue further on in Part II.
30 It should also be noted that over time, conditionality and surveillance have evolved, partly due to the changing scope of the policy objectives and policy instruments used in the assistance programmes. In fact, "policy objectives encompassed external variables (balance of payments or the exchange rate) as well as domestic variables (output, employment, prices). Policy instruments included monetary, fiscal, and incomes policies, as well as external debt management and structural policies that directly addressed resource allocation and thus aimed at efficiency and supply enhancement." Over the years, two major changes: "one was the need to focus on an array of policy instruments beyond the strictly macroeconomic sphere, and the other was allowance for a time framework and scale of assistance commensurate with the broader policy package and aims" (information collected from the IMF's website: www.imf.org/external/pubs/ft/pam/pam46/pam4604.htm).

The main assistance programmes applied to GIPSI countries after 2010[31,32] were:

a) Greece: First Programme, Greek Loan Facility (2010)[33]; Second Programme (2012); Third Programme (2015), under the European Stability Mechanism (ESM) framework. Conclusion of the Programme(s): August 2018.

b) Ireland: The Economic Adjustment Programme for Ireland (2010). Conclusion: December 2013.

c) Portugal: The Economic Adjustment Programme for Portugal (2011). Conclusion: June 2014.

d) Spain: Bank Recapitalization Programme (2012).

3.2.6. The multiple dimensions of austerity: from fiscal adjustment to structural reforms

In the most fragile of these countries – Greece and Portugal – austerity was not only a process of fiscal consolidation. I agree with the definition given by Blyth (2013), previously quoted here, according to which austerity was mostly a process of internal devaluation (through prices and wages), to a large extent made to replace (nominal) exchange rate depreciation, no longer possible within the monetary union.

As noted by Cabral (2013), 'austerity' is indeed a polysemic concept that can involve three different dimensions. Firstly, it can mean a (simple) process of fiscal consolidation or fiscal adjustment. The idea – previously described – of 'expansionist austerity' is indeed related to the concept of fiscal consolidation, as proposed by the leading academics of the Bocconi School. Austerity – as it was applied to countries under financial assistance (and others) – was then conceived as a way to solve a public finance crisis (a sovereign debt crisis), aiming to improve the budget balance, notably by reducing the structural primary deficit. Note that, according to this same doctrine, fiscal adjustment could be successful under certain conditions (e.g. when it relies on expenditure cuts instead of tax rises), thus fostering economic growth. Austerity is hence a means to achieve economic growth (in the short run), by improving the fiscal outlook of the country and by improving the respective conditions to obtain funding in the financial markets. Curiously, though, some of these adjustment programmes failed to comply with

---

31 Detailed information can be found in the European Commission official website, available at: https://ec.europa.eu/info/business-economy-euro/economic-and-fiscal-policy-coordination/eu-financial-assistance_en.

32 Besides GIPSI, financial assistance was given to three other countries: Cyprus, Latvia and Romania.

33 See European Commission (2010).

the prescription enshrined in the 'expansionist doctrine', as much of the fiscal consolidation was made not only through expenditure reduction but also (and mostly) through tax increases.[34]

The second dimension of austerity is that which involves a process of internal devaluation aiming to replace nominal exchange rate depreciation, no longer possible within the monetary union. With austerity, domestic prices would become lower than external prices (e.g. through wage reduction), and this would allow for competitiveness gains in the economy (e.g. increase in exports, decrease in imports) that would help to restore its external balance. This would imply not only a reorientation of the economy from the non-tradable to the tradable sector, which is a long-term process of economic profile change (see *infra*), but also (and mostly) an immediate action to reduce the pressure towards imports. In fact, in the external field, the effect of a government policy action is more immediate and surgical when it is meant to address imports (in comparison to measures affecting exports). Most of the fiscal policy actions, either on the revenue side (e.g. direct tax increases, VAT tax rate increase for non-tradables, e.g. restaurants, hairdressers and fitness centres) or on the expenditure side, notably with respect to personal incomes in social segments with a high marginal propensity to consume (e.g. cuts in civil servant salaries and pensions) were made to reduce private demand and, with this, to reduce pressures on imports of goods and services. Additionally, the so-called 'structural reforms'[35] aiming to increase flexibility in factor markets, particularly in labour markets, by facilitating employee firing and subsequent hiring (with lower wages) would

---

34 This was, for example, the case with Portugal (at least in the first years of the implementation of the adjustment programme): see Mota (2017, pp. 139–143) for a description of the contents of the successive Fiscal Strategy Documents adopted during the assistance period (replacing the Stability Programmes required under the Stability and Growth Pact). Tax measures (involving either direct or indirect taxes) consisted either of an increase in the tax base and in the tax rates or the creation of additional taxes or surcharges on existing taxes. On the other hand, the Portuguese Public Finance Council (CFP, 2012, p. 4), highlighted that "compared to international experience, the adjustment may have relied too much on the revenue side in the first year, which is probably due to the fact that governments can react to fiscal crises faster by raising new revenues than by cutting expenditures. The emphasis on the revenue side continued into 2012, with 72.8 percent of the total adjustment explained by an increase in revenue. The following years seem much more promising as a successful adjustment strategy as, from 2012 onwards, most of the fiscal adjustment is planned to occur on the spending side." More recently, in the Report related to the (final) Fiscal Strategy Document (FSD) (2014–2018), the CFP (2014, p. ii) mentioned the need to evolve from a revenue-side type consolidation to an expenditure-side type one. For an assessment of the first years of the 'Troika' programme in Portugal, see the collective book: Ferreira (Coord.) (2013).

35 Recall that the OECD (2012) considered the crisis as an important 'catalyst for structural reforms' (e.g. reforms in labour and product markets), giving as examples the ones adopted in southern EU countries.

certainly grant the economy with additional competitiveness conditions arising from the reduction in production costs.[36,37]

However, as stressed by Stiglitz (2016, p. 232), internal devaluations may not work (as much as expected), for the following three reasons: (i) wages may not fall; (ii) the fall in wages may not lead to a fall in the price of export goods, or at least not enough of a decline; and (iii) the fall in prices may not lead to an increase in exports, or at least enough of an increase.

Each of these elements played out in the euro crisis. As for the first reason, Stiglitz (2016, p. 233) recalls the usual temptation of 'blaming the victim': with unemployment, wages were supposed to decrease and adjust to the cycle, and yet this did not occur on many occasions – the cause for that is wage rigidity, due, in turn, to the action of trade unions, to inflexible labour legislation – in short, to social rights constitutionally assigned to workers. Blaming the victim is not, however – in the author's opinion – the best and legitimate explanation. Stiglitz recalls instead his previous research into the matter – known as the 'efficiency wage theory' – focused on the well-documented fact that cutting wages undermines worker productivity (either by reducing worker incentives and morale or by affecting the ability of firms to hire good workers).

One important issue in this regard is the impact of the crisis upon social rights, eventually leading to a permanent change, a permanent *retrenchment* of European welfare states (recall, on this matter, the seminal book of Pierson, 1995). As noted by Carmona (2014, pp. 33–40), austerity involved a severe regression in different domains of welfare provision, notably: (i) The erosion of social protection systems – implementation of welfare 'reforms' that indeed meant cuts to social protection benefits such as unemployment, child support and disability benefits; (ii) cuts in spending on social services – including health and education services, disability, community and voluntary services, domestic violence shelters and drug outreach initiatives; (iii)

36 In the case of Portugal, Turrini (2011) addressed the impact of the MoU (signed in 2011, May) with respect to labour markets. One of the issues was the alleged dual nature and segmentation of the labour markets in Portugal: under-protected in the case of fixed term contracts, over-protected in the case of open-termed contracts. Additionally, the author refers to the effects of 'employment protection legislation' (EPL) in the incentives given to job-to-job mobility. As noted, therefore, the reform in the EPL system foreseen in the financial assistance programme was built on four pillars: (i) equalizing the severance payment regime of open-ended contracts with that of fixed-term contracts; (ii) aligning the level of severance payments to that of other EU countries; (iii) making the definition of fair dismissal for open-ended contracts less restrictive; (iv) financing part of the severance payments by means of a mutual fund operated by employers. Indeed, many of these measures were adopted with the changes introduced to the Portuguese Labour Code in 2012.

37 With respect to this, Belke and Gros (2017) compare the cases of wage adjustment that took place in countries like Greece and Portugal under the Troika assistance with other cases, considered as more successful: the German case after reunification and, more recently, the Latvia case.

reduction in wage bills, notably in the public sector – including the reduction of the public sector workforce and the cutting and freezing of civil servants' wages; (iv) implementation of regressive taxation measures – notably with the increase in sales taxes or Value-Added Tax (VAT); (v) limitation of food subsidies.

The most important question, though, is to know whether austerity can be seen as a radical break with the previous European tradition regarding social policies (the so-called 'European social model') or if it meant just the intensification of existing policy trends – the process of the disintegration of welfare states that had started at the end of the 1970s (see O'Cinneide, 2014, p. 186). Indeed, for this same author, the European social policy and social model have become an increasingly faded dream (*Idem*, p. 200), a simple rhetorical feature entirely disconnected from reality (*Idem*, p. 170). What is more, the reality is the increasing subservience of social policies to the imperatives of economic integration and macroeconomic stability that the crisis has only exacerbated (*Idem*, p. 186). In particular, "the rhetorical commitment of European States to the concept of a 'social Europe' is not backed up by any firm legal standards at either the national or the pan-European level" (O'Cinneide, 2014, p. 193).[38]

As for the second and third reasons (above)mentioned by Stiglitz (2016, pp. 234–237), he advocates that the Troika has been consistently disappointed: the growth in exports has been smaller than expected, but the decrease in GDP has been much larger than they expected – even larger than can be accounted for by the disappointing performance of exports. In his opinion, two crucial mistakes explain the underestimation of the decline in GDP. Firstly, the Troika paid insufficient attention to what would happen to the large and important non-traded goods sector, which includes everything from restaurants and hairdressers to doctors and teachers, and typically amounts to something like two-thirds of GDP. Secondly, the effects upon the banking system were miscalculated – as the banks weakened as a result of defaults and bankruptcies, money could easily move out of banks in the weak countries to those in the strong countries within the EZ. This in turn would lead to further decreases in lending and further decreases in GDP.

The ultimate, and perhaps the most important, dimension of 'austerity' is that in which austerity encapsulates an idea of the structural adjustment of the economy. This structural adjustment can be either internal (by permanently reducing the size of the public sector and decreasing the so-called 'crowding out' effect upon private consumption and investment) or external (by transforming a dependent economy, previously based on non-tradables,

---

38 Also see, regarding the impact of the crisis on social rights, Hemerijck (2013), Anderson (2015) and Caselli *et al.* (2016).

to an economy mostly relying on the production of tradables).[39] Interestingly, austerity, in this latter sense, is a way to change (in structural terms) the profile of the economy, benefitting from fiscal policy instruments that are usually conceived as macroeconomic stabilizers, in the short term. As explained by Cabral (2013), the powerful arsenal of fiscal policy measures adopted during the Troika intervention, whether on the tax side or on the expenditure side (*supra*) was used within a double (neoclassical) assumption of mobility: on the one hand, territorial mobility, meaning excess unemployed workers, should move to other regions (in the EU or abroad); on the other hand, functional mobility, that is, professional reconversion from typical non-tradable (e.g. waiters, hairdressers, construction workers) to tradable areas. As for the former case (territorial mobility), the response can be swift, and mobility effectively took place, notably in the Portuguese case.[40] In the latter case (functional mobility), on the contrary, a long-term process of worker education and professional (re)training is required, mostly in the reshaping of economic sectors, starting with the reorientation of private investment. The effectiveness of the desired structural adjustment is hence dependent (still today) on both the ability and the speed of the reconfiguration process, which in fragile economies – as are the Greek and the Portuguese cases – have not yet been assured.[41]

39 I use the term 'dependent economy' on purpose, taking into consideration the so-called 'dependent economy model' as initially proposed by Meade (1951) and later developed by Salter (1959), Swan (1960), Corden (1960) and Dornbusch (1974, 1980). Although not as popular as the Mundell-Fleming framework (*infra*), the dependent economy model is appropriate to describe how a small economy (as are some of the countries assisted by the Troika – e.g. Greece and Portugal) can deal with internal and external macroeconomic dilemmas. Notably, it can describe the relationships between the production of two types of goods – tradables and non-tradables – and in which way (resulting from well-stated constructions within trade theory – e.g. the *Law of One Price*, the *Purchasing Power Theory* and the *Balassa-Samuelson effect*) prices of non-tradables can affect prices of tradables and therefore the competitiveness stance of the economy. For a description of the 'dependent economy' framework, see Metaxas and Weber (2013); for a detailed explanation of the *Law of One Price*, the *Purchasing Power Theory* and the *Balassa-Samuelson effect*, see Krugman *et al.* (2015), pp. 445–482.

40 In Portugal, for example, emigration increased significantly during this period (2010–2013), with a peak in 2013 of 110,000–120,000 departures from the country, affecting both lower-skilled and highly qualified workers. See the 2015 official report on emigration, available at: www.portaldascomunidades.mne.pt/images/GADG/Destaques/Relatorio_Emigracao_Portuguesa_2015.pdf.

41 See Centeno and Coelho (2018) for a broader (and more optimistic) picture of the Portuguese recovery and structural changes. Fatás (2016) analyses the issue of timeliness for implementing structural reforms. As noted, the experience of successful reformers shows that reforms are triggered by a sense of crisis. However, at the same time, "structural reforms in crisis times can be counterproductive because of the potential negative effects on demand. In particular, in the case where monetary policy is constrained by the zero-lower bound, structural reforms can lead to lower growth" (*Idem*, p. 38).

3.3. From the non-bailout clause to quantitative easing: the monetary policy during the crisis

3.3.1. The non-bailout clause in the TFEU

The fundamental principle set down in the Treaty on the Functioning of the European Union (TFEU) with respect to the existence of a backstop – either on the monetary policy side or the fiscal side – is the *non-bailout clause* (see Table 3.2). However, some safeguards (e.g. exemptions) were gradually provided during the crisis, entailing a more flexible interpretation and applicability of the principle.

When considering next the evolution of the ECB's intervention in the aftermath of the crisis, I will discuss in which way non-conventional monetary policy instruments clash with the bailout prohibition clause (Article 123 TFEU). At the same time I will introduce links to the non-bailout clause on the fiscal policy side (Article 125 TFEU), to be developed further on.

3.3.2. Central banks' intervention to rescue the banking sector: the 'lender-of-last-resort' function

The intervention immediately adopted by central banks was associated with the so-called 'lender-of-last-resort' function (LOLR), that is, the provision of liquidity to an individual financial institution or to the market as a whole in

Table 3.2 The EU legal base of the non-bailout clause

The non-bailout clause on the monetary policy side	The non-bailout clause on the fiscal policy side
Article 123/1 TFUE: "Overdraft facilities or any other type of credit facility with the European Central Bank or with the central banks of the Member States (hereinafter referred to as 'national central banks') in favour of Union institutions, bodies, offices or agencies, central governments, regional, local or other public authorities, other bodies governed by public law, or public undertakings of Member States shall be prohibited, as shall the purchase directly from them by the European Central Bank or national central banks of debt instruments."	Article 125/1 TFUE: "The Union shall not be liable for or assume the commitments of central governments, regional, local or other public authorities, other bodies governed by public law, or public undertakings of any Member State, without prejudice to mutual financial guarantees for the joint execution of a specific project. A Member State shall not be liable for or assume the commitments of central governments, regional, local or other public authorities, other bodies governed by public law, or public undertakings of another Member State, without prejudice to mutual financial guarantees for the joint execution of a specific project."

reaction to an abnormal increase in demand for liquidity that cannot be met from an alternative source.[42] In these situations, the LOLR is often referred to as 'emergency liquidity assistance' (ELA) (Freixas *et al.*, 1999; Domanski *et al.*, 2014).[43]

According to Domanski *et al.* (2013, p. 6–16), immediately after the crisis, central banks carried out three types of supporting measures. Firstly, they provided credit to individual troubled and systematically critical institutions. This occurred mostly between September 2007 and August 2008, before Lehman Brothers' default: in this case the support was basically aimed at ensuring an orderly resolution of liquidity difficulties perceived as systematically important. It was the case with the ELA, a form of support given to single financial institutions or groups of similar institutions that illustrates this type of individual idiosyncratic support. Secondly, between August 2007 and early 2009, central banks extended credit to address a malfunctioning of interbank markets. In this case, they expanded provision of liquidity in response to three types of liquidity shortcomings experienced by the whole banking system. (i) the range of counterparties and eligible collateral was broadened to cope with insufficient access to reserves within the banking system as a whole; (ii) central banks carried out exceptional long-term open market operations in order to cope with the squeeze (since autumn 2007) of term funding in interbank markets; (iii) the central banks established swap lines to address shortages of foreign currency reserves. Thirdly, central banks provided funding to increase liquidity in specific financial markets, either by alleviating constraints in private funding markets (e.g. the Term Securities Facility, the Primary Dealer Credit Facility in the case of the Fed, and the Special Liquidity Scheme in the case of the Bank of England), or by ensuring liquidity provision to 'shadow banks'.

This emergency assistance was henceforth given by most central banks in the U.S. and in Europe, including in the euro area. In a first stage – while liquidity support was assumed by the ECB, asset restructuring and resolution in the EMU was handled mostly by national central banks (e.g. asset relief programmes) (Claessens *et al.*, 2011, p. 7). In most cases, these measures took the form of true state aid measures, which were divided into four different categories (Lannoo, 2015a, pp. 147–148): (i) capital support to strengthen the capital base of financial institutions – in recapitalization programmes, governments inject funds in exchange for direct equity, preferred shares or subordinated debt; (ii) asset relief *proprio sensu* – e.g. the creation of a 'bad bank', in which assets are protected or guaranteed by the state in separate legal entities, which can help the 'good' banks to strengthen their balance sheet, re-gain access to liquidity and reduce leverage; (iii) guarantees

---

42 King *et al.* (2017) define market liquidity as the ability to buy or to sell a security without significantly affecting its price.

43 Further details on the notion of LOLR are provided by King *et al.* (2017, p. 5).

given by governments to bank deposits and/or other bank liabilities; (iv) other types of liquidity support (emergency liquidity support) – notably direct loans from governments to banks.

As also noted by Lannoo (2015a, p. 151), during the period of 2008–2009 (the financial crisis stage) and 2010–2012 (the sovereign debt crisis stage), massive state aid was provided to banks: the total amount added up to €5.4 trillion, 39.7% of the EU's GDP. It consisted mostly of general and ad hoc support for financial institutions, including debt guarantees, short-term liquidity support, equity (recapitalization) and debt (subordinated debt) financing, and support for bad bank schemes. Of this amount, €1.9 trillion (14.3% of the EU GDP) was effectively used by banks.[44]

However, when confronting the ECB's action with the Fed's and the BoE's intervention, interesting differences regarding the LOLR function and the related "Buyer-of-Last-Resource" (BOLR) function immediately arise. Firstly, there is a significant difference in funding conditions and market structures. Continental Europe countries rely more on bank-based rather than market-based financial systems than Anglo-Saxon countries such as the U.S. (Oganesyan, 2013, p. 28). As a consequence, the support given by the ECB in the EMU was directed mostly to the banking sector, while in the U.S., the Fed acted more as market-maker for their securities, notably within its BOLR function (Oganesyan, 2014, p. 28).

Secondly, and more importantly, one should be aware that in the European case the evolution from a 'simple' LOLR to BOLR was mostly justified (unlike that which happened, for example, with the Fed and even with the BoE) through the mutation of the financial crisis into a sovereign debt crisis. For this very reason, the BOLR function in the U.S. was mostly related to shadow banking and processes of securitization, whereas in the EMU the

---

44 A mention should be made to the so-called Bagehot's rules. In Bagehot's own words (Bagehot, 1873, pp. 187–188): "In time of panic it (the Bank of England) must advance freely and vigorously to the public out of the reserve." Bagehot claimed that the LOLR function should involve high interest rates and good collateral, meaning that only illiquid, but solvent institutions, should be supported. Both conditions were challenged as time went by. Firstly, as for the condition of high penalty rates – made to reduce moral hazard – in many circumstances they were not needed (Domanski, 2014, p. 5). Secondly, as for the constraint of good collateral and that insolvent entities should not be supported, the recent financial crisis has definitively questioned this requirement. In fact, if in normal times it is not difficult to distinguish liquidity from solvency problems (where the LOLR aims to support a viable bank providing breathing space to restore its normal functioning), in times of financial stress illiquid and solvency issues become intertwined (Dobler et al., 2016, p. 18). In particular, the assessment of solvency becomes more problematic, for three main reasons (Ibidem, p. 19): (i) in crisis times, the mark-to-market value of financial assets can become extremely volatile, making the assessment of solvency difficult; (ii) The valuation of non-tradable assets (e.g. loans) and collateral may lie beyond the central bank's expertise and can be impaired by macroeconomic shocks; (iii) The assessment made by supervisors can be biased, notably due to reputational risk.

BOLR included – as its most significant element – the purchase of government bonds in the secondary markets. In fact, the ECB was focused mostly on the breakdown of the transmission mechanism of monetary policy that in turn was intimately linked to the sovereign-banking debt 'doom looping'. It did so, on the one hand, by easing credit to banks and, on the other hand, by purchasing sovereign bonds.[45]

Finally, some critics have pointed out the late ECB intervention through Quantitative Easing (or, more generally, in using non-conventional monetary policy tools): while the Fed started expanding its balance sheet early (in due time) by purchasing assets with minimum risk as Treasury bonds and Government Sponsored Enterprises (GSE) bonds, the ECB delayed that action until at least 2012 (with the OMT announcement). In addition, as noted by Oganesyan (2013, pp. 28–29), the Fed's activities were more extensive and timely, because the Fed was able to receive support from the Treasury through the Troubled Asset Relief Programme (TARP). In short, the ECB lacked a fiscal backstop, unlike that which happened in the U.S.

I will next detail precisely how EBC's monetary policy evolved in the course of the crisis.

3.3.3. The ECB's non-conventional monetary policy; credit easing versus quantitative easing

The distinction between conventional and non-conventional monetary policy was drawn by Smaghi (2009), according to whom "monetary policy mainly acts by setting a target for the overnight interest rate in the interbank money market and adjusting the supply of central bank money to that target through open market operations."[46] This is achieved mostly by steering the level of key interest rates, through which "the central bank effectively manages the liquidity conditions in money markets and pursues its primary

---

45 This aspect was indeed most significant in the EMU. Note, in particular, that the transmission mechanism of monetary policy is first and foremost related to the functioning of money markets. A smooth transmission mechanism depends critically on the behaviour of banks and on their willingness to entertain smooth exchanges of liquidity in the interbank market. Dysfunctional money markets can weaken the capacity of monetary policy to influence the outlook for price stability through interest rate adjustments alone (ECB, 2011, pp. 62–63). Therefore, in order to keep this mechanism fully operational and to ensure the maintenance of price stability over the medium term, a central bank may need to introduce non-standard policy measures, i.e. liquidity interventions aimed at facilitating the transmission of the interest rate policy and enhancing the flows of credit to the broad economy (ECB, *Idem*, p. 63).

46 In fact, the menu of policy instruments within conventional monetary policy includes 'open-market operations' (e.g. the ECB's main refinancing operations, longer-term refinancing operations, fine-tuning operations and structural operations), but also 'standing facilities' (e.g. the ECB's lending and deposit facilities) (ECB, 2011, p. 95).

objective of maintaining price stability over the medium term."[47] Additionally, and to minimise

> the risk exposure of the central bank's balance sheet, all liquidity-providing operations normally take place in the form of reverse transactions against a menu of eligible collateral. In other words, in *normal times* the central bank is neither involved in direct lending to the private sector or the government, nor in outright purchases of government bonds, corporate debt or other types of debt instrument.
>
> (Smaghi, 2009, emphasis in original)

There are, however, abnormal situations in which conventional instruments are no longer sufficient to ensure a proper functioning of the transmission mechanism of monetary policy. Two main reasons are highlighted. Firstly, the economic shock is so powerful that the nominal interest rate needs to be brought down to zero. Secondly, non-conventional measures may be warranted even when the policy interest rate is above zero if the monetary policy transmission process is significantly impaired (Smaghi, 2009).

In turn, Borio and Zabai (2016) propose a taxonomy of non-conventional monetary policy operations that include: *i) balance sheet operations* (quantitative easing measures); *ii) forward guidance*, which, while not a novelty, nonetheless took on greater significance in the context of the 'zero lower bound' constraint; at this point, if central banks wished (as they did) to ease financial conditions further, they had to steer inflation expectations more actively (which is done through guidance, either quantitative or qualitative guidance); (iii) *negative policy rates*. An ultimate, almost eccentric alternative to non-conventional monetary policy operations is the so-called *helicopter money* – a direct injection of money into the economy aiming to stimulate aggregate demand and boost economic growth (Bernanke, 2003). As also noted by Borio and Zabai (2016), this direct injection of money would increase the nominal purchasing power of economic agents in the form of a permanent addition to their money balances. This is equivalent to an increase in government deficit that is financed by an equivalent and permanent increase in non-interest-bearing central bank liabilities. This is a permanent operation, rather than a reversible one: thus, the central banks commit to never withdrawing the increase to the reserves.

One can thus say that the ECB's initial intervention relied mostly on credit easing (CE), to the banking sector, whereas in the subsequent stages – when

---

47 In a similar vein, Fawley and Neely (2013, p. 53) explain that central banks ordinarily conduct "monetary policy by buying and selling short-term debt securities. These purchases and sales of assets change both short-term interest rates and the monetary base."

the sovereign debt crisis emerged – that intervention evolved to quantitative easing (QE).[48,49]

It should be emphasized that *credit easing* – at least as it was applied in the initial ECB interventions – comprises policies aiming at reducing specific interest rates and/or restoring market function, while *quantitative easing* refers to any policy that unusually increases the magnitude of central bank liabilities – currency and bank reserves – particularly at the zero lower bound (Fawley and Neely, 2013, p. 55).

A more usual definition establishes this the other way round, that QE basically consists of large-scale purchases of existing assets or extensions of new credit by the central bank (Ball *et al.*, 2016, p. 31). These assets can be long-term government bonds, or private bonds, equities and real estate investment trusts. Central banks pay for QE by issuing highly liquid liabilities: through the interest rates it pays on these liabilities, the central bank effectively sets the economy-wide level of the short-term risk-free interest rate (*Idem*, p. 32). QE encourages investors to buy other assets, raising the prices of those assets and reducing risk premiums (*Idem*, p. 51). Finally, the same authors identify the main purposes of QE as: (i) expanding the central bank's balance sheet; (ii) reducing funding costs and increasing credit availability to certain sectors of the economy (Ball *et al.*, 2016, p. 31).

48 Praet (2016b, 2017b) identifies three main phases important in characterizing the evolution of the ECB intervention: The first phase was the phase of the liquidity crisis triggered by the Lehman Brothers collapse. The second phase was the sovereign debt crisis (2011–2012) and its extension through the 'bank-sovereign' nexus. The third phase was coincident with the recognition of the malfunctioning of bank-based transmission and growing signs of a credit crunch (in part due to the process of bank deleveraging itself): by the end of 2013, the annual growth rate of loans to the private sector contracted by more than 2%. By mid-2014, it also became clear that economic recovery was slowing its pace and inflation rates were decreasing. The ECB, therefore, faced a pressing need to reinforce the degree of policy accommodation in view of persistently low inflation. Mendonça (2017) in turn distinguishes three different phases: Phase 1 (September 2008–June 2014) – conventional monetary policy, notably through direct liquidity injection into the market; Phase 2 (June 2014–March 2016) – unconventional monetary policy; Phase 3 (March 2016–present) – unconventional monetary policy, marked by a liquidity trap.

49 Several other European central banks were pushed to provide additional monetary stimuli that also included (as an alternative or complement to QE) the introduction of a negative interest rate policy. This was the case with the Danmarks Nationalbank (DN), the Severiges Riksbank (SB), the Swiss National Bank and even the ECB (Bech and Malkhozov, 2016). Ball *et al.* (2016), in turn, analyses the way in which negative interest rates transmit to the economy. This is done mostly through these basic channels. Firstly, transmission to bonds and money markets – reductions of policy rates into negative territory have generally been associated with reductions along the rest of the yield curve. Secondly, transmission to bank interest rates, which is, however, a sluggish process, due to the resistance of banks to pass those rates along to their retail depositors – indeed, as noted in turn by Borio and Zabai (2016), the transmission of negative interest rates to bank rates (e.g. retail deposits) has proved to be problematic and non-linear. Finally, transmission to exchange rates.

As such, the main ECB's programmes (some of them juxtaposing in time) were: (i) 2007–2008, Fine Tuning Operations/Swap Lines (liquidity provision to the banking sector, preventing disruption in the interbank market); (ii) 2008–present,[50] Main Refinancing Operations (MRO) and Long-Term Refinancing Operations (LTRO) (avoiding disruption in the interbank market); (iii) 2008–2009, Enhanced Credit Support and ELA (activated by the national central banks); (iv) 2009–2010 and 2011–2012, Covered Bond Purchase Programme (CBPP) (facilitating lending to the economy; reinforcing funding conditions); (v) 2010–2012, Securities Market Programme (SMP) (to restore the transmission mechanism of the monetary policy); (vi) 2012 (announcement), Outright Monetary Transactions (OMT) (to restore the transmission mechanism of the monetary policy; to cease 'doom looping' between sovereign and banking sector debt; to cease financial fragmentation in the EMU, notably within sovereign debt markets; to save the euro)[51,52,53]; (vii) 2014–present, the expanded Asset Purchase Programme (APP).[54,55]

---

50 New programmes within these conventional-type instruments were implemented further on (after the sovereign debt crisis outbreak). In December 2011, the ECB announced three-year LTRO liquidity injections for that same year (LTRO 1) and a subsequent one in February 2012 (LTRO 2), aiming at enhancing bank lending and liquidity in the Eurozone money markets (Acharya *et al.*, 2016). Furthermore, in 2014, the first series of a new instrument – Targeted Longer-Term Refinancing Operations (TLTRO–I) – was launched with a maturity of up to four years at attractive conditions. A second series was launched in 2016 (TLTRO–II). The main purpose of these latter instruments was/is to ease private sector credit conditions and stimulate bank funding to households and firms. See the information on the ECB website, available at: www.ecb.europa.eu/mopo/implement/omo/tltro/html/index.en.html.

51 Recall that the announcement of the OMT was coincident with the famous speech of Mario Draghi (the ECB President) in July 2012, in which he proclaimed: "Within our mandate, the ECB is ready to do whatever it takes to preserve the euro. And believe me it will be enough."

52 As noted by Acharya *et al.* (2016, p. 12), the OMT programme differed from other previous programmes in which the ECB acted as BOLR – the case with the SMP – for the following reasons: (i) the OMT was subject to strict conditionality; (ii) the ECB improved transparency, by publishing OMT holdings, the duration, the issuer and the market value; (iii) the duration of the different purchased assets; (iv) the ECB did not establish itself as a senior claimant under the OMT programme; (v) the possibility that unlimited amounts of sovereign bonds could be purchased under the programme in order to attain its objectives.

53 Acharya *et al.* (2016) analysed the effectiveness of the OMT, comparing it with previous interventions, notably the LTRO 1 and LTRO 2 launched some months previously. The simple announcement of the OMT had a more profound and positive effect (despite not having been activated), by either helping to significantly reduce sovereign yields and sovereign credit default swap spreads in peripheral countries (e.g. Italy and Spain) or by reducing the domestic bank-sovereign loop (Acharya *et al.*, 2016, p. 41). Regarding the effects of OMT on pricing of sovereign debt, either directly or indirectly, see Afonso *et al.* (2018).

54 The APP, in turn, included four programmes: (i) the corporate sector purchase programme (CSPP); (ii) the public sector purchase programme (PSPP); (iii) the asset-backed securities purchase programme (ABSPP); (iv) the third covered bond purchase programme (CBPP3).

55 See also Claeys and Leandro (2016).

The adoption of QE measures (notably under the APP) occurs when the conventional monetary policy tool of lowering short-term interest rates is constrained by the *zero lower bound*, i.e. the reluctance to (further) cut the nominal interest rate (Demertzis and Wolff, 2016, p. 2). When the economy is facing a recession, central banks may wish to use a more aggressive monetary policy to stimulate the economy, even when interest rates are already so low that eventually the real interest rate decreases to levels below zero. But monetary policy room for manoeuvre largely depends on inflation rates. The real interest rate can be negative only when the inflation rate is positive because nominal interest rates in principle cannot go below zero (Gagnon, 2011, p. 25). [56],[57]

It should be noted, however, that this evolution leading to lower interest rates, even if exacerbated by the crisis, started before. There is indeed a *(long-term) cycle of ultra-low interest rates* that can be attributed to structural causes related either to the behaviour of financial assets or to the overall economic and demographic conditions in European and other developed economies.

As for structural conditions regarding the profitability of financial assets, Constâncio (2016) finds a gradual decline in interest rates – departing from the 'long-term real equilibrium interest rate' (the rate that reflects an economy at full employment, with stable inflation close to the monetary target)[58] – mostly due to three types of financial factors: (i) expected inflation over the lifespan of the asset; (ii) inflation and real term premia; and (iii) expected path for the short-term real interest rate. Looking at the available data, the author shows that, as regards the first component, long-term inflation expectations have declined since the beginning of the 1980s to stabilize in the 1990s at around 2%. As for the second element, the nominal term premium (which in turn consists of inflation and real term premia), despite data limitations, a declining trend over the past decades can also be observed. An additional factor exerting downward pressure on the real term premium was the imbalance between the reduction in the supply of and the

---

56 See, for further details, Coenen *et al.* (2003), Gerlach and Lewis (2010) and Ball *et al.* (2016, pp. 7–8).

57 Eventually, though, EMU entered the 'negative rates club' (Gros, 2016a). Debtor countries, such as the U.S. and the UK, benefitted from a low interest rate environment, favouring debt servicing, investment and economic recovery, and due to this it was possible to start normalizing monetary policy. In contrast, for creditor countries or blocs – as in the case of the Euro area and Japan – since that environment of low rates was not yet effective at that time, the policy response has been a paradoxical never-ending lowering process, eventually *ad absurdum*.

58 Related to this notion is the concept of 'divine coincidence' that lies behind several analyses within neo-Keynesian models and that at some point is present in the 'dual mandate' of the Fed (price stability and promotion of employment). According to the notion of 'divine coincidence,' stabilizing inflation is the same, for policy purposes, as stabilizing output.

increased demand for safe assets at a global level, a phenomenon that has been exacerbated by the financial crisis. This preference for safe assets has thus added to the increase in the respective price and to the compression of the related yields. Finally, the last factor is related to the real short-term rate over the life of the asset: the financial crisis has also contributed to this downward pressure, but there are also long-term factors – e.g. pessimistic views about the long-term growth prospects for the advanced economies – which have played a role.

In fact, there are other, more general factors related to the overall economic and demographic context that have played a significant role in the long-term process of the reduction of interest rates. These factors are exogenous because they go beyond the handling of monetary policy by the central banks. Zettelmeyer (2017, p. 160), for example, adds some of these general and global factors: (i) low productivity growth; (ii) expected ageing – increasing savings under pension plans and the yield compression; (iii) debt overhang.

3.3.4. The effects of the APP

3.3.4.1. The effectiveness of the APP

By mid-2014, it became clear that the economic recovery was slowing its pace and inflation rates were decreasing. The euro area economy was indeed facing disinflationary pressures that risked spiralling into outright deflation (Praet, 2018b). The ECB, therefore, faced a pressing need to reinforce the level of policy accommodation in view of persistently low inflation. The focus of providing monetary accommodation had to shift from an approach based on adjusting the interest rate corridor of the ECB's monetary policy framework – which steers the very short end of the yield curve – to one that more directly affects the whole constellation of interest rates across the yield curve (*Idem*).[59]

Despite this complex and problematic environment, the ECB acclaimed the success of such a policy mix. Praet (2017c) concludes that the monetary

---

59 Recall that the operational framework of the ECB (as of other central banks) includes two main type of operations: (i) *open market operations* (e.g. main refinancing operations) that play an important role in steering interest rates, signalling the monetary policy stance and managing the liquidity conditions for the euro area banking sector (ECB, 2011, p. 96); (ii) *standing facilities* that include, on the one hand, deposit facilities and, on the other hand, marginal lending facilities. The interest rate paid in the former is usually lower than that paid in money markets, whereas the rate claimed in the latter is higher than that of those same markets. Therefore, the difference – over a certain period of time – between these two rates is the so-called 'corridor' of the standing facilities. In particular, they provide a ceiling and a floor for the overnight market interest rate, measured by the euro overnight index average (EONIA) (ECB, 2011, p. 100).

policy adopted "has contributed to a major easing of euro area financing conditions and, through this channel, to a more robust and sustained economic recovery." There was, in particular, a positive effect of monetary policy on wholesale funding conditions. Furthermore, the data presented shows that the dispersion of lending rates has declined in vulnerable economies, thereby reducing asymmetries in the overall policy transmission across the euro area. The decline of bank lending rates has, in turn, had a twofold expansionary effect (Praet, 2016c): Firstly, it frees up purchasing power that was previously locked up in high loan servicing costs; Secondly, on the liability side, Praet (2017b) highlights the reduction in the average of the cost of funding from banks – very low short-term rates have encouraged banks to rebalance their liability structures away from more expensive debt securities and towards deposits, providing funding cost relief. What is more, deflationary risks seemed to have vanished (Praet, 2017b).[60]

In this regard, Dunne *et al.* (2015), Andrade *et al.* (2016), Claeys and Leandro (2016), Demertzis and Wolff (2016) and Gambetti and Musso (2017) have investigated the effectiveness of the APP, which was certainly the supreme expression of the ECB's QE policy. They aimed to identify whether and in which way the APP had a positive impact on output, employment, inflation expectations and exchange rates.[61] It should be recalled that QE attempts to cope with a situation in which monetary policy is constrained, namely due to the zero lower bound. It can be said that, in general terms, this is achieved through three main channels (Coenen *et al.*, 2003, p. 2): (i) lowering long-term interest rates to improve investment conditions and discourage savings (interest rate channel); (ii) purchasing relatively long-term assets, thereby driving investors into riskier investments (portfolio rebalancing channel); (iii) weakening the exchange rate (exchange rate channel).

Dunne *et al.* (2015) describe the three transmission channels of asset purchases to the macro economy (ultimately influencing inflation levels). The first channel is the *portfolio balancing channel*, the positive effects of which are either due to a 'wealth effect' (e.g. the APP bolsters the demand for assets, which increases their price, thus raising asset holder wealth) or for 'borrowing cost reduction'. The second is the *bank lending channel*, related to the idea of the QE (in particular the APP) as a source for money creation that can occur mostly indirectly: the non-bank investor sells government bonds to the central bank, and the cash it receives is deposited at its commercial bank; if this cash is not used to invest in an alternative asset, the deposits

60 Alcidi *et al.* (2016) considered that at this stage (2016) the risk of deflation did not exist any longer (considering overall economic conditions – the GDP deflator – instead of consumer price index normally used to measure the evolution of inflation), and for this reason, monetary policy should be normalized.

61 See details in Demertzis and Wolff (2016, pp. 6–8), Gambetti and Musso (2017) and Couré (2017).

held by the commercial bank expand; the bank may choose to employ these new deposits by expanding its credit supply to the real economy. In contrast, however, the opposite effect can occur: the reduction in long-term interest rates can negatively affect the bank's lending capacity. Indeed, lower interest rates can lower banks' net interest margins and, if they are capital constrained, reduce their ability to lend to the real economy (Dunne *et al.*, 2015, pp. 68–69). Finally, the third channel is the *signalling effect channel*, according to which the simple announcement of the APP is understood by the market as the intention of the central banker to meet its inflation objective and signals that it expects to maintain interest rates at a low level for a sustained period.

Constâncio (2016) and Praet (2017a, 2017b, 2017c) explain that the monetary policy toolkit, including not only the asset purchase programmes but also additional measures such as the negative interest rate on deposit facility (excess reserves) and forward guidance, proved to be effective in the light of these channels.

Praet (2017a, 2018b) highlights the strong complementarities between all the policy instruments adopted over the crisis period: for example, the downward pressure induced by the APP on term premia is reinforced by the negative interest rate policy and the rate forward guidance. As also noted by Constâncio (2016), the portfolio rebalancing effect is empowered by negative deposit facility rates, as banks with high amounts of excess liquidity holdings have a strong incentive to reduce these holdings and to put their reserves to work. Conversely, the APP empowers forward guidance on policy rates, as the credibility of indications about the setting of the policy rates are enhanced by the APP today. In fact, asset purchases tend to provide a strong signal that policy rates will remain low for an extended period of time. In short, asset purchases strengthen the signalling effect of rate forward guidance, while the latter reinforces the impact of purchases by adding to the reduction in the duration risk that is associated with these purchases.[62]

Despite the advantages and the alleged success of the programme, the risks involved are not ignored. Three main risks are usually indicated: (i) risks for financial stability; (ii) risk for bank profitability; (iii) risks associated with the redistributive effects of QE.

As for the first risk, it should be recalled what was mentioned in the Introduction regarding the relationship between an environment of low interest

---

62 More recently, Afonso and Jalles (2019) investigated the impact of QE on sovereign yield spreads, considering not only the announcement of the OMT program but also of the subsequent programmes including the APP. An important conclusion is that the ECB's intervention did contribute to contain sovereign yield spreads, implying indirectly expansionary monetary developments and direct monetary impact stemming from the effect of the MRO rate tenders in decreasing yield spreads. The decision to discontinue the program can moreover involve additional risks for more risky and vulnerable countries.

rates and (the risks for) financial stability. Significant literature was presented then. The monetary policy toolkit – involving large asset purchases, reference rates close to or below zero, long maturity lending to banks and forward guidance – may, if prolonged for longer than necessary, have pervasive effects on financial stability, by causing, for example, excessive risk taking and 'search for yield' behaviour.

The second risk is related to bank performance. If it is true that accommodative monetary policy has been able to reduce bank funding costs, to allow for higher asset valuations and to ensure a more robust recovery (Praet, 2016b, 2016c), also true appears to be the effects of this policy on bank profits: when interest rates are close to zero or even negative, banks become reluctant to pass this to their depositors (by charging them), because this might lead to a run on those deposits. There is a physical limit for this 'apparent never-ending' lowering process: the limit resides in the opportunity cost of holding cash. Then, when this limit is passed, losses coming from low interest rates will outweigh gains for banking sector profitability and, then, the monetary policy faces a dilemma (Couré, 2017). As a way out of the dilemma, Idem (2017) anticipates two plausible effects: (i) an incentive given for the development of financial disintermediation, and consequently; (ii) the shift toward a more market-based financial structure (lees reliant on banks) – the case with the promotion of the Capital Markets Union – that would eventually help the economy to better cope with the long-lasting low interest rate environment.

Finally, as for the third risk, it is argued that QE might increase inequality between the wealthy and the poor, and even between different regions when they have different financial structures; furthermore, as older people tend to have larger savings and might sell them in order to maintain consumption in the future, while younger households usually buy these assets in the future in order to save for retirement, QE might also entail intergenerational redistributive effects (Claeys and Leandro, 2016, p. 11).

3.3.4.2. The APP and the transmission mechanism of the monetary policy

One usual argument – already mentioned here before – is that QE was aimed to restore the *transmission mechanism of the monetary policy* that the financial crisis had cut down.[63] In particular, the first moment of this mechanism, the so-called 'pass-through of monetary policy' (from reference short-term money market interest rates to retail interest rates, notably long-term rates) was apparently impaired by the crisis. In Gambacorta *et al.* (2014)'s opinion, the standard long-term relationship tying together policy and lending rates

---

63 See ECB (2011).

broke down during the crisis. Notwithstanding this, the long-term structural change was due to a strong re-pricing of risk (a change in banks' pricing of the credit risk of their non-financial borrowers) and the need to repair banks' own balance sheets, which means that monetary policy would be transmitted differently, rather than being impaired (see also Illes *et al.*, 2015).

Indeed, even in normal circumstances, the 'signal' given by monetary policy can be curbed by different kinds of factors, and so an expansionary monetary policy (involving a reduction in reference interest rates) may not translate into more credit provided to the economy (firms and households), ultimately meaning less money creation than at first sight could be expected.

McLeay *et al.* (2014) in turn take into consideration precisely the relationship between monetary policy and money creation. It should be noted that money creation is due mostly to the lending process carried out by banks within the economy: banks create deposits by making new loans, and deposits are the main form of broad money (currency being the minor part). It is a fact that the monetary policy signal is determinant in the process of money creation: the central bank, either directly through the interest rates charged to banks, or indirectly through the overall impact of monetary policy on output and inflation, ensures money growth (as long as this is consistent with its main statutory objectives, notably price stability).

There are, nonetheless, exogenous limitations to money creation, and these can be of two types (McLeay *et al.*, 2014, p. 17): (i) On the one hand, banks face limits on the amount of money they can lend.[64] (ii) On the other hand, money creation is constrained by the behaviour of money holders (households and businesses) – the latter, when receiving the newly created money, may respond to that easiness by undertaking transactions that immediately destroy the money, for example by repaying outstanding loans.

As noted by McLeay *et al.* (2014, p. 24), QE involves a shift in the focus of monetary policy to the quantity of money (in comparison with conventional forms): the central bank purchases a quantity of assets, financed by the creation of broad money and a corresponding increase in the amount of central bank reserves. QE boosts broad money without directly leading to, or requiring, an increase in lending (*Idem*, p. 25). Only indirectly may this effect take place (the increase in bank lending), as QE may reduce bank funding costs or, more generally, because it can increase credit by boosting activity. However, these are not direct QE transmission channels: instead, QE works by circumventing the banking sector, aiming to increase private sector spending directly (*Idem*, p. 25).

Rule (2015, p. 7), in turn, distinguishes between whether the intervention of the central bank is 'liability' or 'asset' driven. In the case of the

---

64 These limits, in turn, can be self-imposed (resulting from banks' own business models) or hetero-imposed (determined by the applicable regulatory framework).

ECB, early credit easing interventions – e.g. MRO, LTRO, credit enhanced facility – were mostly liability driven, because the central bank was basically facilitating the use of existing reserves. In contrast, when adopting the APP (quantitative easing), the ECB intervention was asset driven, because the purchase of assets involved, on the liability side, the creation of new reserves (corresponding to the 'new' money credited in the bank accounts of the beneficiary institutions).

Moreover, recall that the purchase of assets can be of private bonds, equities and real estate investment trusts, or of long-term government bonds. Indeed, when considering the ECB programme more deeply related to the resolution of the sovereign debt crisis – the PSPP[65] – it can be verified that QE not only has consequences for the owners of sovereign bonds/debt balance sheets (through the aforementioned APP channels), but ultimately interlinks government and central bank balance sheets. In fact, QE is in this sense a 'quasi-fiscal' type intervention that can be seen as an alternative either to debt monetization[66] or to direct purchases of sovereign debt in the primary markets, even if closer to the latter than to the former. Indeed, unlike debt monetization, asset purchases do not cancel the repayment obligation.[67]

---

65 Note that when we focus on this remarkable asset – government bonds/debt – it should be recognized that the respective financing can rely on capital markets or on banks. Banks can thus be the sovereign bond/debt holders. This is a crucial point, since – as previously mentioned – one of the most striking elements of the 'doom looping' involving sovereign and banking debts was the 'nationalization' of sovereign debt (reflected in domestic bank balance sheets), following strategies of financial repression or of risk shifting.

66 Notice that typically debt monetization involves transforming high-interest government debt into low-interest reserves, that is, converting debt into money. As noted by Rule (2015, p. 17), "if over time government spending is not financed by taxation, debt sales or borrowing from commercial banks, the central bank will lend to offset the deficit in the fiscal account. In doing so the central bank credits the reserves accounts of commercial bank with reserves in lieu of funds from government." In most cases of debt monetization, the central bank is actually merged with the Treasury, where money issuance directly funds deficits without the need to issue new debt. In this case, one can thus better perceive central bank and Treasury balance sheets in a consolidated way.

67 With the Euro crisis, it was not only the ECB that saw its balance sheet increase and thus increase its role in the implementation of monetary policy. The national central banks (NCBs) were also given new tasks and an expansion of their respective balance sheets. Indeed, as noted by Gros (2017a), during the first decade of the EMU, NCBs operated basically as local 'access terminals' for the Eurosystem's tender operations. After the crisis, their role improved significantly. Two kinds of operations acquired importance: the ELA and the PSPP. The former is contained in Article 14 of the Statute of the ESCB, but it has been used only in a systemic fashion during the crisis. The PSPP is a major part of the APP. Eighty per cent of PSPP purchases are carried out by NCBs, and they buy only marketable debt instruments issued by their central government. Furthermore, the type of bonds, including the duration or maturity, is left at their discretion (Gros, 2017a, p. 6). The author stresses that the PSPP implied the end of the single monetary policy and a step towards a more decentralized monetary policy – an outcome that, in his opinion, is not desirable. In particular,

3.3.5. ECB's monetary policy and the role of the Court
of Justice of the EU

One of the most usual criticisms pointed to in the intervention of the ECB was that if with banks it has acted promptly as an immediate rescuer, with governments the "ECB was gripped by hesitation" (De Grauwe, 2011a). A stop-and-go policy ensued in which it provided liquidity in the government bond markets at some moments and withdrew it at others (*Idem*).[68]

However, the APP programme faced some resistance since its inception. On political grounds, the main objections were that the APP could lead to inflation (putting at stake the principal mandate of the ECB),[69] that it would carry on the transmission of fiscal losses to the ECB[70] and finally, but no less important, that it would increase governmental moral hazard behaviour[71] – the same as saying that QE would favour fiscal profligacy and irresponsibility.

Many of the arguments used on legal grounds reproduced considerable political suspicion. The basic arguments against QE (in particular the purchase of sovereign bonds in secondary markets) can still be found in the 2014 jurisprudence regarding the OMT programme, a programme that was actually never implemented, but the simple announcement of which had an immediate positive impact on the financial markets. As appropriately noted by Tridimas and Xanthoulis (2016, p. 18), "the announcement proved an exemplary exercise of 'regulation by information', calming markets and reducing interest spreads, thus rendering its actual application unnecessary." Yet the simple announcement of the programme raised controversy and triggered an insightful judicial debate. In the decision,[72] the BverG considered

---

an immediate consequence is that the PSPP (and QE in general) does not increase the ECB's seigniorage revenues, as they end up being mostly distributed by the NCBs (Gros, 2016a).

68 See other arguments in Buiter and Rahbari (2012).

69 This argument is disputed by De Grauwe (2011a), for whom the LOLR does not necessarily entail inflation. When the central banks buy government bonds or other assets, this increases the money base, but this does not necessarily translate (as previously mentioned here, *supra*) into an increase in lending (or effective money creation). In fact, in times of crises, the monetary base and monetary supply can be quite disconnected, notably because banks may eventually choose to hoard the liquidity provided by the central banks instead of using it in credit provision to the private sector.

70 For De Grauwe (2011a), the LOLR may actually involve fiscal consequences (if the government fails to service their debts, the central banks face losses) but not more than those which may occur within conventional open market operations.

71 This argument is also refuted by De Grauwe (2011a). In his opinion, the risk of moral hazard is no more significant in this case than when it involves the banking sector itself – the way to deal with it is to impose rules that will constrain governments in issuing debt, very much like when in the banking sector moral hazard is tackled by imposing limits on risk-taking by banks.

72 BverG, Case No. 2 BvR 2728/13, 14.1.2014. Available at: www.bundesverfassungsgericht. de/SharedDocs/Entscheidungen/EN/2014/01/rs20140114_2bvr272813en.html.

that the OMT programme was not covered by the ECB's mandate under the Treaties, being an action driven from economic instead of monetary policy, and which also violated the non-bailout clause set in Article 123 of the TFUE.

The matter was analysed to the Court of Justice of the European Union (CJEU), under preliminary ruling,[73] and the Court decided for the compatibility of the OMT programme with the Treaties. The CJEU addressed the main arguments under dispute. Firstly, the compatibility of the OMT with Article 119 of the TFEU and Article 127(1)–(2) of the TFEU and with Articles 17 to 24 of the Protocol of the European System of Central Banks (ESCB). Differently from the BverG decision, the CJEU considered that the OMT did not violate the mandates of the ECB and of the ESCB. Notably, it still qualified as an action of monetary policy (and not of economic policy), as its main objectives were to ensure proper monetary policy transmission and the singleness of monetary policy. In particular, the CJEU considered the selective nature of measures included in the OMT programme (targeting secondary markets of euro economies in distress) not as a way to distort market functioning and risk perception (with respect to interest rate differentials), but as a natural consequence of its initial focus on the transmission of monetary policy (Craig and Markakis, 2016, p. 12).

Secondly, the CJEU addressed the argument that OMT was violating the prohibition on monetary financing contained in Article 123 of the TFEU. The Court started by recalling that this article does not preclude the possibility of bond purchasing in secondary markets – indeed, such a possibility is expressively permitted in Article 18(1) of the Statute of the ESCB and of the ECB, as long as the nature of open market operations is not disregarded (Tridimas and Xanthoulis, 2016, p. 28). The CJEU considered that the OMT included sufficient safeguards to avoid purchases in secondary markets being made to hide purchases in primary markets. With these arguments, in short, the CJEU concluded that the non-bailout clause had not been violated with the OMT programme announcement.

More recently, the CJEU was asked to decide about the validity of the PSPP subsequent to the BverG judgement, which had questioned the validity of the programme. In the CJEU judgement,[74] the Court considered that the PSPP did not exceed the ECB's mandate – the programme was confined to monetary policy, in respect to which the EU had exclusive competence, and respected the principle of proportionality. On the other hand, the CJEU found that the PSPP did not infringe the no-bailout rule, since the programme neither corresponded to a purchase of bonds in primary markets nor positively discriminated in favour of certain countries to the detriment of others.

---

73 Case C-62/14, *Gauweiler and Others v. Deutscher Bundestag*, EU:C: 2015:400. See also Opinion of Advocate General Cruz Villalón in Case C-62/14, *Gauweiler and Others v. Deutscher Bundestag*, EU:C:2015:7.

74 Case C-493/17, Heinrich Weiss and Others, of 11 December 2018.

The Court also highlighted the limited nature of the PSPP in several terms: quantitative – limits on the monthly purchase of assets; subjective – due to the distributions of purchases between national banks according to the guide to subscribing to ECB capital; objective – this required collateral, and temporal – the programme was time-limited.

3.3.6. The normalization of monetary policy?

Before concluding this subsection, I will address two remaining issues concerning the implementation of the APP programme. The first issue is related to the relative importance of the ECB after the crisis. There is a broad consensus amongst academics that the ECB played an increasing role in crisis management and, over the crisis, has become an even more crucial institution within the institutional framework of the EMU. As noted by Majone (2014, p. 54), the crisis has dramatically altered both the ECB's behaviour and the political and economic context in which it operates. With time, the main concern of the ECB ceased to be ensuring price stability and mostly became ensuring the survival of the euro. Moreover, the crisis has led to a qualitative change in the ECB's role and scope: if with respect to monetary policy, it has evolved from conventional to non-conventional measures (as we have seen in this subsection), the fact is that the ECB has expanded its functions to new areas – in particular, assuming new supervisory and even regulatory tasks within the Banking Union – that has eventually meant significant institutional changes and taking on a growing dimension. Breuss (2017, p. 201) appropriately qualifies the new ECB as a 'multi-tasking' ECB.

Moreover, the effectiveness of monetary policy, recognized not only by the ECB itself but also from academics and analysts in general, has led the ECB to increase its reputation and credibility. From an institutional point of view, it should be stressed that the ECB was the main winner of the euro crisis (see Breuss, 2017, p. 201). Ultimately, by challenging the non-bail clause of the Treaty (with its QE measures), the ECB dared to act as a quasi-fiscal institution and to be a substitute, within the limits of its possibilities, for the non-existing Treasury or fiscal backstop mechanisms. The future role of the ECB, with respect not only to monetary policy but also to the Banking Union, the European Stability Mechanism and the possible institution of risk-sharing mechanisms (e.g. stabilization funds and debt poolers or debt risk minimizers) will say much about its relative importance vis-à-vis other EMU's institutions even beyond its natural function, and if it will effectively perform as a quasi-fiscal institution.

For some authors, the increasing role of the ECB meant, after all, an increase in the dominance of monetary policy over fiscal policy (Sluis, 2014, p. 114). The asymmetry within the two branches of macroeconomic governance – monetary policy on the one side, fiscal policy on the other – that has existed since the EMU's inception has nevertheless grown during the crisis, not only due to the bold and active role the ECB decided to adopt (notably from 2012 onwards), but because this role has not been accompanied (for the time being) by an identical evolution on the fiscal policy side. As noted by Sluis (2014, p. 114), the ECB has no economic policy partner. Even if the nature and level of independence of the ECB was inspired in the German model of the Bundesbank, the fact is that, unlike what happens with the latter – which has an economic counterpart in the German government (e.g. a strong central budget and a strong Finance minister) – the same does not happen in the EMU's economic institutional framework. Indeed, the position of the ECB in the construct of the EMU is important not only because it has a strongly enshrined legal position, but also because it is the only economic player with such a position (*Idem*, p. 114). In a similar vein, Majone (2014, p. 52), considers that the ECB is not a politically independent institution operating in the context of a democratic government, like the Bundesbank in Germany. Rather, it is a 'disembedded' non-majoritarian institution that operates in a political vacuum, without a European government or, at least, a European finance minister.

The second issue is related to the future stance of monetary policy, given the decision of the ECB to discontinue QE. The idea was that policy normalization would take place gradually. Caution and calibration were needed. Indeed, in the absence of perfect knowledge about the way market participants will react to the announcement of monetary policy adjustments, and about how those reactions will feed back to the ECB's main objective – the target inflation rate – it may be optimal to adjust policy more cautiously and in smaller steps (Praet, 2018b). Since its inception, the scope of the APP – as has happened with its occasional redesign (e.g. the monthly volume of purchases) and extension – which has been made to fine-tune the programme in line with the prospects of the inflation rate vis-à-vis the inflation target. Now, the same should happen, *a fortiori*, with its (gradual) discontinuity. Asymmetric effects of monetary policy in general – and the case of unconventional policy – should not be disregarded (Ravn and Sola, 2004).

The decision to phase out the asset purchase programme by the end of 2018 was announced in Mario Draghi's press conference after the meeting of the ECB in Riga, late June 2018 and confirmed in December.[75]

---

75 In his last press conference (12 September 2019) before the end of his term in the Governing Council of the ECB, Draghi announced the reinforcement of the expansionist toolkit. Besides lowering the interest rate applied in TLTRO III operations for banks whose eligible net lending exceeds a benchmark, and to extend the maturity of these operations from two to three years, the ECB has decided to restart, in a rather extraordinary manner, net purchases under its APP at a monthly pace of €20 billion from 1 November onwards.

Yet some uncertainty remains, as continuously reaffirmed by the ECB's main leaders.[76] For this reason, the halting of the QE is not absolute, since the ECB has maintained the possibility to reinvest QE money once current bonds mature. Moreover, such a decision should not be interpreted as definitive or irrevocable, as the ECB can always restore or reshape QE measures in the event of future economic deterioration. Even if the European economy has been growing consistently above current estimates of potential growth (Draghi, 2018), the fact is that the prospects about the development of inflation remain subdued (Praet, 2018a).

76 This explains the important decision to maintain the accommodative profile of the monetary policy with two additional measures for 2019: firstly, to keep the key ECB interest rates unchanged (that is, 0% for main long-term refinancing operations; and −0.4% and 0.25%, respectively, for the marginal deposit and the marginal loan facility); secondly, to launch a new series of quarterly targeted longer-term refinancing operations (TLTRO-III), starting in September 2019 and ending in March 2021, each with a maturity of two years, in order to preserve favourable bank lending conditions and the smooth transmission of monetary policy. In this regard, see this information on the ECB website: www.ecb.europa. eu/press/pressconf/2019/html/ecb.is190307~de1fdbd0b0.en.html.

Part II

GOVERNMENTAL RISK-SHARING MECHANISMS AFTER THE CRISIS

From a fiscal union to a fiscal capacity

4

THE 'EMU'S GREAT REFORM'
AS AN IMPERATIVE

4.1. The evolution of the (mainstream) discourse about the crisis over the years: from national failures to E(M)U flaws

4.1.1. Introduction: from national failures to E(M)U failures

When in March 2017, former Eurogroup President Jeroen Dijsselbloem, in an interview with the German newspaper *Frankfurter Allgemeine Zeitung*, said that the crisis-hit European countries had wasted their money on "drinks and women," this immediately sparked controversy. Such words were rapidly repudiated by various other politicians and by some areas of public opinion, and qualified as "insulting" and "vulgar."[1] In fact, they were interpreted as an attack on southern countries based on the assumption (a prejudice) according to which they are countries of a lazy, prodigal and irresponsible nature, in radical contrast to northern countries.

Such a view underlies the understanding of the causes of the crisis: according to it, the main culprits of the sovereign debt crisis were the peripheral countries (in particular those from the South). In fact, as noted by Treichel (2012), in the views of many analysts, the European debt crisis was caused by fiscal profligacy on the part of the countries driven primarily by the expansion of the welfare state and rising public sector wages. Proponents of this view argued that if countries had balanced their budgets and avoided the temptation to create a welfare state, excessive private spending would not have occurred, and banks and investors would have been more aware of the risks involved. Even for those, like Majone (2014, p. 139), for whom the institutional and legal framework of the EMU fostered moral hazard and adverse selection, the fact is that the conduct of Greece and other (assisted) countries was labelled as a case of pre-contractual and post-contractual opportunism.

---

1 See the news about the original polemical words and subsequent reactions in the online version of the *Financial Times* (21 March 2017), available at: www.ft.com/content/249 8740e-b911-3dbf-942d-ecce511a351e.

Such an understanding is not new, though. Many consider that at the origin of this divergence mostly lies the opposition between the French and the German traditions, with the latter connoted with the rules-based economic and legal system known as *ordoliberalism*. Brunnermeier *et al.* (2016a, p. 66) indicate as elements of the German economic intellectual tradition the following: (i) a focus on the legal, moral and political foundation of a free market in agreed rules; (ii) a strong emphasis on accountability and responsibility; (iii) a concern with the potential for moral hazard of lender of last resort activities; (iv) a concern that the LOLR activity can pollute or corrupt monetary policy, because a central bank may, in this case, give priority to financial stability instead of price stability; (v) a belief that formal or binding rules can shield monetary policy from fiscal dominance; (vi) a strict approach to government debt and to debt ceilings; (vii) a belief that growth can mostly be achieved with structural reforms; (viii) a belief that present virtue – austerity – is rewarded by future benefits.

Differently, the French intellectual tradition with respect to economic policy has the following aspects (*Idem*, p. 74): (i) rules should be subject to the political process and hence can be renegotiated; (ii) crisis management requires flexible management; (iii) constraining the freedom of government to act and to borrow would be undemocratic; (iv) monetary policy needs to be used to serve more general goals than simply price stability, such as being concerned with economic growth; (v) international imbalances should be taken symmetrically, with countries in surplus doing their part; (vi) as multiple equilibria are possible, choosing an unpleasant trajectory for the present is likely to perpetuate rather than remove constraints on growth; (vii) present virtue is self-contradictory and self-defeating.

In this same book – *The Euro and the Battle of Ideas* (Brunnermeier *et al.*, 2016a) – as well as in the volume entitled *Ordoliberalism: A German Oddity?* (Beck and Kotz, eds., 2017), the prevalent underlying idea is that the euro crisis – and the responses conceived over the crisis years, the hesitation, the political contradictions, the misguiding signs – in fact reflected the vivid tension between these two contrasting views. However, this was not a novelty. Such confrontation had also been visible in the past, in other moments of the EMU's history, and when it was initially created. As noted by Landamann (2017, p. 131), the euro area was built based on the premise that the European economy would be self-stabilizing if proper incentives were given, and a proper policy framework was put into motion to ensure price stability and the efficient operation of the markets. This belief is certainly a cornerstone of the ordoliberal school of thought, which, being prevalent at that time, was/is not free from controversy.[2]

---

2 For example, when the convergence path was defined for countries wishing to adopt the new common currency, the opposition between two contrasting lines was vivid. On the one

In turn, Frankel (2017, pp. 134–136) agrees that German ordoliberals got some things right when the terms of the EMU were settled at Maastricht in 1991. They recognized that the danger of excessive national budget deficits would be exacerbated by moral hazard from the anticipated likelihood of bailouts in the event of difficulty. These concerns were primarily addressed through defining the following rules: (i) the nominal convergence rules for public finances, with a limit of 3% for public deficit with regard to the GDP and 60% for government debt to GDP; (ii) the approval of the Stability and Growth Pact (SGP) in 1997, which included these same quantitative fiscal rules for the members of the EZ and for those to enter in the future; (iii) the non-bailout clause regarding both monetary and fiscal policies.

If the evolution in the EMU, since its inception (and particularly in the period after the crisis) has reflected the tension between these two different intellectual traditions – the German and the French traditions – the fact is that France and Germany share similarities (they are more close than apart): continental legal orders, the strong role of the central government, geographical proximity, and similar economic structures. Both are indeed EMU core countries.

Therefore, I think that the crisis has exacerbated another more significant division within Europe that resides elsewhere, in a southern parallel. Note that this North-South opposition corresponds first to a long-lasting civilizational and cultural schism that has given rise to two different traditions or mentalities in Europe: the southern Catholic tradition versus the northern Protestant one. This basic civilizational split was primarily described in Max Weber's magnum opus *Die protestantische Ethik und der Geist des Kapitalismus*, dated 1905 and first published in English in 1930 (Weber, 1930). Kantian-type asceticism and parsimony have fostered the capitalist spirit of saving and investment that together with innovation and organization were to make northern European countries (from the seventeenth century onwards) a paradigm of economic success. In turn, Catholic countries, not embedded in the same philosophical and religious landscape, threw away the advantages provided by the Maritime Discoveries and first colonization process (in the fifteenth and sixteenth centuries) and lost their path of economic progress. In fact, those countries stayed definitely apart from the (new) capitalist mood and were instead wrapped within profligacy, conservatism and economic leniency.

---

side, the 'monetarists' (featuring mostly France and Luxembourg) advocated that the adoption of the euro would foster convergence between European economies and so the former should precede the latter. On the other side, the 'economists' (represented mostly by Germany and the Netherlands) considered that before adopting the euro, candidate countries should converge with respect to the main nominal variables – entrance to the euro should be a 'coronation' of the well-succeeded process of convergence. Macroeconomic convergence should hence precede the adoption of the euro. This latter view eventually prevailed.

However, if these ancient philosophical reasons for the North-South opposition hold true, the fact is that such civilizational, economic and geographical divergence seems to have accentuated in recent years, and the sovereign debt crisis itself may have played a role. It is not just being peripheral: except for Ireland, all the affected countries are southern countries. Hence, after the crisis, the North became more northern and the South more southern. With respect to this cleavage, Guiso *et al.* (2013), when mentioning the incompatibility of national cultures (within Europe), confronts those countries obsessed with 'cheating' (Greece) with those obsessed with 'punishment' (Germany).

The outrageous acronym 'PIIGS' (Portugal, Ireland, Italy, Greece and Spain) reveals this same great civilizational contrast: an imagery of the dirt and disorder in a sty; of course, so very different from the plain and organized house of the North. The substitution, in several spheres, of this acronym by a different one, the 'GIPSI' countries (that I myself have been using in this work for abbreviation purposes) is definitely less hostile and politically more correct. However, it is not completely devoid of a certain xenophobic flavour.

In any event, one should acknowledge that mainstream discourse about the crisis and its causes evolved as time went by. As the crisis changed its nature, in a process of metamorphosis previously described, opinion about its main causes also changed. Some (paternalist) condescension with the previously accused – peripheral countries – could be glimpsed behind the recognition of other different causes, added to explain the mutation in and depth of the crisis.

In a rather anticipatory fashion, Dadush and Stancil (2010, pp. 8–15) considered that the euro crisis was mostly due to the bad behaviour of a few euro-area countries (the GIPSI), but acknowledged that blame should also be assigned to the institutional architecture of the euro. The seven reasons – 'seven capital sins' (?) – for that shared responsibility were at that time appropriately summarised (Dadush and Stancil, 2010, p. 8):

i)   *Confidence regarding growth levels in the GIPSI – nourished by the introduction of the Euro – made those countries benefit from abnormally low interest rates.*

This reason was, in turn, qualified by Stiglitz (2016) as an *internal misalignment* – through the low interest rates of the euro. This misalignment fostered easy access to credit for all euro-area countries, regardless of their individual debt profile and economic outlook, fostering in particular access to credit by peripheral economies involved in a process of economic catching up vis-à-vis core countries, furthermore benefitting, for that purpose, from easy access to structural funds.

ii) *Low interest rates fostered domestic demand, and investors and con-sumers were given an incentive to increase spending and run up debts, often owed abroad as foreign capital flowed in.*

Domestic demand in peripheral countries was henceforth fed mostly by the increase in imports – and this caused a rise in external imbalances and debt. Actually, such imbalances were also fostered by an *external misalignment* – through the exchange rates of the euro. This misalignment was due to "an exchange rate (taking account of local prices) that was too high in several countries, so that their imports systematically exceeded exports" (Stiglitz, 2016, p. 261). This would in turn give rise, in those countries, to a trade imbalance financed mostly through rising (external) debt.

Yet, since the EMU served as a camouflage for idiosyncratic country risks, foreign investors were caught by a sentiment of euro-euphoria: they could loosely lend money to all euro-area countries, because they were risk-free and the latter could very easily borrow from the former, relying on their confidence (Stiglitz, 2016). Indeed, before the crisis, it was not only the good economic moment that had fostered the optimism of financial mar-kets. Monetary and regulatory policies at the EMU level played their role as well. With respect to the latter, Véron (2011) stresses that for regulatory calculations, the risk of euro-area central government bonds was weighted at zero. In turn, as for monetary policy, it is mentioned that the ECB treated such debt with no haircut – basically as risk-free – when these bonds were offered as collateral for repos and other collateral financing trades. In view of this, the markets were at that time completely blind to sovereign risks.

iii) *The increase in demand accelerated prices, mostly in non-tradables (i.e. housing and construction) in comparison with the prices of tradable goods and services (investment was mostly channelled to less productive non-tradable sectors and away from export industries).*

Validating this idea, Treichel (2012) mentions that the abundance of capital in non-core countries indeed exacerbated weak competitiveness that had nega-tively affected those countries before the adoption of the euro. Furthermore, the loss of external competitiveness led to a shift away from manufacturing sectors towards service and non-tradables – a Dutch disease-type phenomenon.

iv) *Meanwhile, exports from core countries (such as Germany and the Neth-erlands) vis-à-vis the GIPSI countries rose sharply, increasing external imbalances between these two groups of countries.*

With respect to this, Dadush and Eidelman (2010, pp. 17–21) explain the reason why, despite the heavy costs of its reunification (during the last decade of the twentieth century), Germany was able to take advantage of the introduction of the euro and obtain substantial competitive gains (e.g. an increase in the respective external surplus). Two major factors are mentioned. Firstly, the euro was a currency relatively less valued than the Deutsch mark was expected to be (in the absence of the single currency). Secondly, the structural reforms adopted in that decade, including wage moderation and industrial restructuring, not only improved competitiveness in the export sector but also made domestic demand more sluggish, with its lowering pressure on imports.

Germany has indeed the single highest current account surplus in the world. The surplus has continued to grow since 2001 and reached 8.5% of GDP in 2016 (Felbermayr *et al.*, 2017, p. 187). Steinberg (2017) in turn identifies the main factors explaining Germany's current account surplus. Some of these factors are directly influenced by economic policy (e.g. declining public investment, conditions for private investment oriented to export sectors, structural reforms and fiscal policy), while others go beyond policy control. Amongst the latter a distinction between temporary and fundamental factors is drawn: favourable exchange rates, low commodity prices (e.g. oil prices), decreasing wage trends and global economic trends are considered as temporary in nature, whereas demographic trends (e.g. ageing), (high) returns on foreign investments, a competitive economic structure, based on diversification and specialization, and international interdependency are characterised as fundamental (structural) factors.

All these factors are linked: Germany's three domestic sectors (households, firms and the government) are savers by nature, including the government sector (unlike that which happens in many other countries). Indeed, some authors advocate that higher savings – more than low investment (public and private) – are the main cause of the surplus (Felbermayr *et al.*, 2017, p. 187).[3] In turn, these high savings are today partly related to demographic change, and to the structural reforms adopted in the 2000s (with respect to pension systems) aiming to increase private savings for retirement (instead of strict pay-as-you-go financing). As a consequence of the current surplus, Germany invests significantly abroad, especially in Europe, North America and China. German financial institutions also invest considerably abroad, including (before 2010) in Greek government bonds (Cooper, 2017, p. 184) and Greek financial institutions.

On the other hand, much of the competitive economic structure that today characterizes Germany is supported by competitive productions costs, stemming from energy and labour. Wage moderation (for some, in truth, 'wage dumping'; Felbermayr *et al.*, 2017, p. 191) is a result of wage negotiations

---

3 De Grauwe and Ji (2016a, p. 67) illustrate this idea, showing that in 2013, public investment in Germany amounted to a bare 1.6% of GDP versus 2.3% in the rest of the Eurozone.

that rely more on collective bargaining between firms and workers than on government intervention (Steinberg, 2017, p. 172). Even so, over the years, this process of wage moderation has certainly found support in policy action.

v) *The domestic boom in demand in the GIPSI countries induced rapid wage growth that outpaced productivity, increasing unit labour costs and eroding external competitiveness further.*

Treichel (2012) stresses that one of the factors contributing to this loss of competitiveness was the sharp rise in wages in non-core countries – wage increases and growth in government spending in those countries led to large increases in aggregate demand and to appreciation of the real exchange wage. Given fixed exchange rates, such divergent trends in wage inflation go hand in hand with a relative loss in competitiveness for the debtor countries. That is, unit labour costs for these countries increase in comparison to the same costs in creditor countries (Brunnermeier *et al.*, 2016a, pp. 78–79).

vi) *The single ECB monetary policy was, however, considered too loose for countries such as the GIPSI and too tight for countries like Germany, the domestic demand and wages of which grew very slowly compared to the European average. This factor also reinforced the loss of competitiveness in the GIPSI countries.*

In a divergent inflation scenario (where debtor countries face a pressure for inflation to increase, notably driven by wage inflation), there is the risk of another destabilizing effect (known as 'Walter's critique'): given a single monetary policy with capital moving freely, inflation divergence means in effect that the real interest rate is actually lower in debtor countries than in creditor countries. This lower real interest rate provides an incentive for the former to borrow and an incentive for the latter to save (Brunnermeier *et al.*, 2016a, p. 79) – thus the imbalances keep growing in an ongoing spiral.

As a final remark, note that the EMU used both the single monetary policy and the European payment system(s) as an interface and vehicle for those imbalances, instead of seeking to correct them. This was summarized in this vein by Stiglitz (2016, p. 268):

> As soon as some of the countries in the eurozone owed money to other member countries, the currency union had changed: rather than a partnership of equals striving to adopt policies that benefit each other, the ECB and eurozone authorities have become credit collection agencies for the lender nations, with Germany particularly influential.[4]

4 Further on, I will return to the role of the European payment system (TARGET 2) in exhibiting such trade imbalances and economic divergences within the EMU.

vii) *The domestic demand increase boosted tax revenues which, in turn, were used to raise government spending, with this raising public deficits and debt.*

Moreover, this abnormal consequence may also be highlighted: the euro has created a new kind of debt – apparently a domestic debt as issued in euros (and note that domestic debt can favour national control over debt issuance, management and restructuring).[5] Yet, this is in reality an external debt, simply because debtor countries have no individual control over the euro (see also Stiglitz, 2016, p. 265).

In a similar vein, De Grauwe (2011b, p. 1) explained that,

> when entering a monetary union, member countries change the nature of their sovereign debt in a fundamental way, i.e. they cease to have control over the currency in which their debt is issued. As a result, financial markets can force these countries' sovereigns into default. In this sense, member countries of a monetary union are downgraded to the status of emerging economies.

This works as the 'original sin' of monetary unions that leads these countries into an unsound equilibrium full of pain and misery (*Idem*, p. 6).[6]

In view of all this, the ultimate causes of the crisis could after all be assigned to the EMU itself, that is, to its institutional and legal framework and to the reckless policy undertaken at the EMU level since the creation of the euro. National failures were thus replaced by the euro's flaws (Stiglitz, 2016, 2017).

4.1.2. EMU failures in the tests for optimality; decentralization versus centralization of fiscal policy

4.1.2.1. Introductory remarks: a currency area as an exacerbation of a fixed exchange rate system

A currency area, and notably a currency area with the features of the EMU, is an extreme version of a fixed exchange rate system,[7] because in this case

---

5 Recall *supra* (subsection 2.2.1.1) what was mentioned about processes of debt re-nationalization.
6 See also Rossi and Dafflon (2012).
7 For a typology of exchange rate regimes, see Frankel (1999). Ishfaq (2010) arranges these regimes into three main categories, two polar-opposite categories and an in-between, intermediate one: (i) within fixed arrangements – currency unions, currency boards and a truly fixed exchange rate; (ii) within intermediate arrangements – adjustable peg, crawling peg, basket peg and target zones or bands; (iii) within floating arrangements – managed floats and free floats. Polar, radical solutions – 'pure' fixed exchange rates or 'pure' floating rates – are

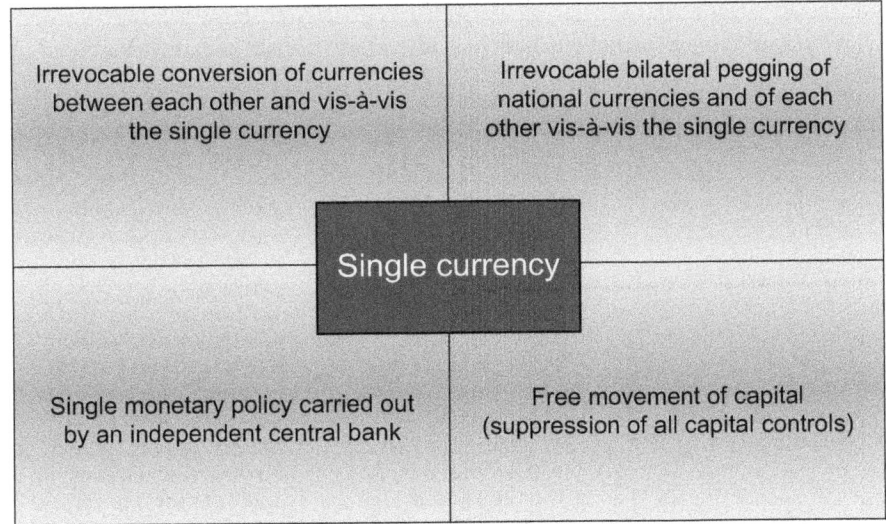

Figure 4.1 Main elements of the EMU
Source: The Author

previous national currencies were fixed both between each other and with respect to a new currency (the euro), and this fixing occurred in an irrevocable manner. This means that no subsequent realignments are allowed, unlike that which may occur in 'normal' pegged exchange rate systems. Furthermore, a currency union is a fixed exchange rate system that relies either on an implicit leading absorbent currency or on a 'democratic' currency's basket, or on a mixed version of both (Figure 4.1).[8]

The advantages and disadvantages of each of these two polarized arrangements are the obverse and the reverse of each other (see Stockman,

---

forced by the so-called 'impossible trinity' (Frankel, 1999): this principle states that a country should give up one of the following policy goals: capital mobility, fixed exchange rates or autonomous monetary policy. Intermediate exchange rate solutions are accepted because one can have a half-way regime with half-way capital mobility and/or some moderate monetary policy independence. As noted by Gagnon (2011, p. 18), "the choice is not all or nothing; it is possible to give up some monetary independence to gain some exchange rate independence, as in a managed float regime. However, the more tightly the exchange rate is controlled, the less freedom there is to set the interest rate."

8 The euro, as a store of value and unit of account, implicitly corresponds on a weighted basis to the value of the European currencies that belong to the euro area. Recall that the value of the euro was, at the date of its legal inception (31 December 1998) equivalent on a one-to-one basis to its embryo and predecessor, the ECU. The ECU in turn was a basket-type currency (and the system with it a basket peg) in which the Deutsch mark had been dominant. For further analysis of the nature and differences between these two units of account, and legal implications, see Kaufmann (1997), Patrício (1998) and Gonçalves (2010, 2019).

Table 4.1 Advantages and disadvantages of two polarized exchange rate systems

Advantages/disadvantages	Floating exchange rate	Fixed exchange rate
Economic structures	Different economic structures benefit; similar economic structures do not	Similar economic structures benefit; different economic structures do not
The role of monetary policy	Flexibility/loss of credibility	Credibility and stability (monetary anchor)/loss of flexibility and of monetary autonomy
	Monetary policy as a macroeconomic stabilizer/inflation risk	Reduction of policy shocks and policy discretion/ risk of deflation and of economic contraction
Currency value and fundamentals	Is 'market-driven' (the currency value is determined by the supply and demand of currency related to economic fundamentals); volatility due to non-fundamental noise	Is 'command-driven' (authorities act to prevent massive fluctuations and inflation); fosters speculative attacks

Source: The Author

1999). Three main types of arguments are usually mentioned when making such a contrast (Table 4.1): (i) economic structures – different economic structures should result in different exchange rate regimes; (ii) monetary policy – the benefit of flexibility and autonomy can be obtained at the cost of loss of credibility and stability (and vice versa); (iii) currency value and fundamentals – with the benefits and costs of 'market driven' systems, which are, the other way round, the costs and benefits of 'command-driven' systems.[9]

Considering Table 4.1, some additional remarks can be made. In the light of the notable 'Mundell-Fleming' model (Mundell, 1960, 1963; Fleming, 1962) and assuming free capital mobility, when a country adopts a flexible exchange rate regime vis-à-vis other countries of the world, monetary policy tends to be *the* effective stabilizer policy.[10] In contrast, the use of fis-

---

9 See in this respect Duttagupta *et al.* (2005) and Gagnon (2011).

10 In a floating exchange rate arrangement, the capacity of the monetary policy to affect real economic variables is wider, both directly, by affecting the *nominal exchange rate* (and with it the value of the domestic currency vis-à-vis foreign currencies), and indirectly, by affecting, through several channels starting with the interest rate channel (recall the transmission

cal policy for stabilization purposes (to promote output and employment or to stabilize inflation) becomes more problematic, due to the unwarranted effects on the exchange rate of the domestic currency that may eventually neutralize the initial fiscal policy movement. On the contrary, in a fixed exchange rate system, fiscal policy is effective whereas monetary policy is not. Monetary policy tends to be less effective, because the initial movement involving money supply tends to be neutralized by the pressure it can cause on the domestic currency value, a value that is fixed, which then forces the monetary authority to undo such movement (for further details, see Gagnon, 2011, pp. 13–18).

Indeed, in a fixed exchange rate system, the capacity of the central bank to create non-systematic changes in money supply is limited (see Stockman, 1999, p. 1488). Fiscal policy and other government policies can therefore play a major (substitutive) role: 'internal devaluation' (through prices and wages) is an example of how, in the context of fixed exchange rate systems, the economy can adjust to macroeconomic shocks (e.g. shocks to the balance of payments), in the absence of the possibility to directly affect the nominal exchange rate (recall austerity measures adopted in bailed-out countries, where adjustment measures involved precisely internal devaluation as a substitute for exchange rate depreciation no longer possible within the union).

In a fixed exchange rate system, a nominal anchor to the domestic currency ensures both external and internal stability (price stability). But fixed exchange rate systems – since their historical foundation with the 'gold standard' system – are not deprived of shortcomings. Under Hume's well-known *price specie flow mechanism*, the same way the system was, in principle, able to automatically ensure a country's external balance, prices and wages were supposed to do the hard rebalancing work (Baldwin and Wyplosz, 2015, p. 329) – the system could experience significant episodes of austerity, depression and deflation, and the capacity to adjust was harsh and slow (see also Mota, 2017).

Some of these observations fit – *ceteris paribus* – within the functioning of the fixed exchange rate system that lies behind the EMU. As noted before in the analysis concerning the mutation of the EMU crisis, the crisis is in large part related to the imbalances in the external positions of the members of the area, some being chronically surplus countries (the case of Germany), the others chronically deficit countries (the case with some peripheral countries) – a situation that not only is a fate but also seems to be a need in order to ensure the EMU's very survival.

For now, some summarising observations can be added. The first observation is that the EMU, as a currency union, has *a fortiori*, the same kind of

---

mechanism of the monetary policy), the overall stance of the economy and the level of domestic prices, and with this affecting the *real exchange rate*.

advantages and disadvantages of fixed exchange rate regimes summarized in Table 4.1.

Secondly, following Mundell-Fleming's didactic model, it can be said that *in the relationships of the EMU vis-à-vis the rest of the world* (and considering that with the rest of the world, the main regime is one of a – managed – floating exchange rate) a single monetary policy is effective in its macro stabilizer role for the area as a whole, both internally through the interest rates of the euro and externally through the exchange rate of this same currency. Instead, a centralized fiscal policy seems to be dispensable, as in the context of a floating exchange rate regime fiscal policy tends to be ineffective or counterproductive. Hence, a first argument for fiscal policy decentralization can be found here.

Thirdly, in the light of the same model, it can be said that, *within the area*, the usage of monetary policy is totally and irrevocably impaired, because the creation of a single currency translates into an exacerbation of the limitations usually faced by countries in a fixed exchange rate environment (notably those that decide to peg their currency to another leading one), including limitations in the use of monetary policy and foreign exchange rate intervention. But whereas in a fixed exchange rate, the usage of countries' monetary policies, although limited (as this tends to be ineffective), formally remains, in a currency union (with a single currency), the underlying decision to peg currencies involves the option to formally abdicate this.[11]

In turn, within the area, fiscal policy seems to remain effective, meaning that each of the partners with fixed exchange rates vis-à-vis the others (and with respect to the single currency) can take advantage of fiscal policy for stabilizing purposes, notably with respect to their balance-of-payments (e.g. internal devaluation). At first sight, another strong argument for fiscal policy decentralization can be found here, as the fiscal policy of each of the partners is *naturally* effective in the context of a fixed exchange rate regime.

However, and as the final observation, recall that a currency union is not *simply* a fixed exchange rate regime. A currency union is an exacerbation of the fixed exchange rate because it is a new monetary identity that should involve not only a new monetary sovereignty with macro stabilizing properties regarding the area as a whole, but also, additionally, the other ingredients of macroeconomic stabilization, that is, the centralization of fiscal policy. Indeed, a currency union tends to be a drag force containing the completion of the macro stabilizing puzzle by adding the fiscal policy piece.

---

11 Recall that according to the 'impossible trinity', the combination of fixed exchange rate with capital mobility involves abdicating monetary policy independence. 'Currency boards' are another typical example of fixed exchange rate regimes with loss of monetary autonomy (e.g. Argentina during 1991–2002, by pegging the peso to the dollar).

4.1.2.2. EMU failures in the tests for optimality

Much of the understanding of the EMU's creation and development, as well as all the historical hazards of the monetary integration process, including the recent crisis, is made possible under the widely recognized approach of the 'Optimum Currency Areas' (OCA). The theoretical foundations of OCA were launched decades ago, in the seminal articles from Mundell (1961), McKinnon (1963) and Kenen (1969), to which were added other contributions such as those of Ingram (1962), Mintz (1970) and Corden (1972).[12]

A review of economic literature on OCA unveils an analytical path that addresses specific customary subjects. The most important topic is referred to as the *conditions for the optimum in a monetary union*. Notwithstanding, Baldwin and Wyplosz (2015, p. 361) consider that the OCA "is a misnomer," for two basic reasons. Firstly, the theory does not really deal with optimality, as it simply balances costs and benefits. Secondly, it does not provide a definitive answer to the fundamental question that is: "Which countries should share the same currency?" In any case, one can say that the most important feature of this theoretical construction, as summarized by Emerson *et al.* (1990, p. 45), "is that the adoption of a single currency involves a trade-off between, on the one hand, the benefits arising from monetary integration and, on the other hand, the costs incurred when the exchange rate is lost as an adjustment instrument."

In the years immediately preceding the launching of the EMU, only the Report *One Market, One Money* (Emerson *et al.*, 1990) made explicit mention of the theory of OCA, whereas in other official reports – notably in the *Padoa-Schioppa Report* (Padoa-Schioppa *et al.*, 1987) and the *Delors Report* (Delors, 1989) – the acknowledgement of the main conditions set by the theory were merely implicit. Moreover, one can say that the basic insights of the OCA were left behind in the initial decade of the EMU as the currency union worked well in those first years of existence. Interest in OCA prescriptions were reborn, though, with the euro crisis, and in recent literature, when accessing the main flaws of the E(M)U, such prescriptions are often remembered. After their analysis and confrontation, the 'natural' conclusion is that the EMU is not an OCA (see, in this regard, De Grauwe, 2014, pp. 74–75).[13]

In particular, if one sees the OCA's conditions (defined by the aforementioned proponents) as successive tests of optimality, one can see that the basic flaws of the EMU correspond to failures to the tests (see Mongelli *et al.*, 2017). Table 4.2 details the successive tests developed by its main

---

12 For a detailed literature review of the theory of OCA, see Broz (2005), Corsetti (2008), Mongelli (2008) and Baldwin and Wyplosz (2015, pp. 361–376).

13 As also noted by De Grauwe (2014), there exists, however, an equally strong conviction that for a subset of E(M)U countries (namely Germany, the Benelux countries, Austria and France) the monetary union fulfils optimality conditions.

Table 4.2 OCA tests and the EMU

OCA proponents	Identification of the condition (test)	The EMU's failures regarding the OCA tests (or low scores)
Mundell (1961), Corden (1972)	– Mobility of factors (e.g. labour) – Flexibility of prices and wages	– Insufficient and diversified labour mobility across Europe (due to cultural, language and economic restraints); different labour legislation; different degrees of qualifications and skills; different social security systems; different models and degrees of generosity with respect to social protection. – Labour markets function differently across Europe; different role for trade unions and collective negotiations; different rules regarding wage contracts and employment stability (versus flexibility); the existence or not of a minimum wage; wage rigidity of variable degrees across Europe; different rates of (un)employment; different levels of social protection in case of unemployment; the different role and dimension of non-standard types of employment.
McKinnon (1963)	– Degrees of openness or the ratio between tradables and non-tradables (small open economies can benefit more from joining a currency union)	– Many European economies fulfil the openness condition, starting with core countries. Core countries indeed form an OCA (De Grauwe, 2014). On the contrary, some (peripheral) countries rely more on non-tradables and/or on the production of tradables with less value added (and hence less competitive) (see, on the differences in trade openness amongst E(M)U countries and consequences for growth and convergence, Simões et al., 2017).
Kenen (1969)	– Product diversification – Similar economic structures	– Different degrees of product diversification between EMU countries and hence a different capacity to cope with an economic shock (e.g. demand shock due to a change in consumers' preferences); different demand patterns. – Different economic structures between EMU countries (Mongelli et al., 2017); different forms of sectorial specialization (e.g. different types of industries) (Idem); other significant differences in 'real' economic variables – e.g. labour and capital productivity; GDP per capita; qualification levels.

Ingram (1962)	– Financial integration (through capital flows aiming at cushioning negative shocks)	– Despite capital mobility, financial markets are not totally integrated within the euro area and financial fragmentation prevails (see details *infra*).
Kenen (1969)	– Fiscal integration (a fiscal transfer system would help a region more affected by an asymmetric shock to cope with that shock, requiring less nominal exchange rate adjustments). – Political integration	– The EMU lacks any kind of a fiscal transfer system (inside or outside the EU budget) meant to address macroeconomic shocks (see details *infra*).
Mintz (1970)		– The EMU, unlike other currency areas, is not an 'embedded' area, and this occurs because it is not politically sustained (McNamara, 2015).[1]

Source: The Author

[1] As a matter of fact, McNamara (2015) presents an alternative approach to the OCA theoretical framework, according to which the Eurozone's problems result from the fact that the zone is not a politically 'embedded' currency area. And 'embeddedness' is a condition for success, depending on four key elements: (i) a legitimated generator of market confidence and liquidity (a true lender of last resort); (ii) mechanisms for fiscal redistribution and economic adjustment; (iii) regulation of financial risk and uncertainty; (iv) political solidarity.

proponents over the years and includes some short observations on why and in which way the EMU fails to pass the tests (or at least does not manage to obtain high scores).

In general terms, it can be stressed that if a currency union fails to pass the tests, this means that the costs of adopting a common currency are not circumvented (Corsetti, 2008, pp. 4–5). If those same costs exceed the benefits of the currency union, the future sustainability of the union is jeopardized. It should be recalled that the benefits of a currency union are related to reduction in trading costs both directly and indirectly, e.g. by removing exchange rate risks and the cost of currency hedging (Mongelli, 2008, 7); while its costs are related both to the loss of *seigniorage* income, including the possibility of eroding public debt by printing money and creating inflation, and to the loss of the exchange rate instrument as a mechanism of economic stabilization in the case of (macro)economic shocks .

Indeed, since its theoretical inception, one can say that the OCA framework is mostly 'shock-response centred'. It is possible, in turn, to disentangle two types of approaches: (i) an 'exogenous-type approach', according to which the purpose is to identify which types of cyclical shocks, symmetric or asymmetric, might justify two or more economies joining a monetary union; (ii) an 'endogenous-type approach', in which the focus is on whether a currency area can minimize the occurrence of asymmetric shocks and make shocks more symmetric. Another related issue within this approach is to verify whether a monetary union leads to better synchronization of the business cycles in its member countries.

Concerning the *exogenous-type approach*, Bayoumi and Eichengreen (1992, p. 5) highlight that "the incidence of disturbances across regions is a critical determinant of the design of the currency areas." Note, on the other hand, that the discussion at this stage is primarily associated with the advantages and disadvantages of the two main exchange rate regimes – fixed and flexible exchange rate regimes. Thus, as noted previously, a fixed exchange rate regime (and, *a fortiori*, a single currency area) is preferable whenever nations have similar economic structures and experience similar exogenous shocks (see Stockman, 1999, p. 1488). The magnitude of shocks also matters: the larger the size of the shocks, the more difficult it may be to sustain a fixed exchange rate system (Bayoumi and Eichengreen, 1992) and ultimately a currency union. This is particularly true in the case of supply shocks, which may require more painful adjustment (*Idem*) and hence require the use of monetary policy tools and policy autonomy that a fixed exchange does not allow.

As for the *endogenous-type approach*, the question is whether a currency area minimizes the occurrence of asymmetric shocks and makes shocks become more symmetric. Therefore, under this 'shock-response' perspective, conditions of optimality for the currency union result from the nature of the shocks involved (e.g. common or idiosyncratic) and the nature and effectiveness of the response given (symmetric or asymmetric) (Kouparitsas, 1999).

De Grauwe (2014, pp. 23–24) and Mongelli *et al.* (2017, pp. 49–53) mention two contrasting visions on this matter. According to the *optimist view* – found in the aforementioned *One Market, One Money Report* (Emerson *et al.*, 1990), differential shocks in demand will occur less frequently in a monetary union. The report does not ignore the risks in creating a European monetary union, acknowledging, for example, that in Europe labour mobility was weak. Balancing costs with benefits, the report considers that the "benefit-cost balance (is) more favourable in the case of the Community" (*Idem*, p. 28). The arguments for this are, on the one hand, that the monetary union will foster price stability, notably amongst small and open countries; and, on the other hand, because the currency union would reduce the incidence of economic shocks and therefore the need for exchange rate changes, particularly for those economies with diversified industrial structure and with more intra-industry trade than narrow specializations in particular commodities.

De Grauwe (2014) notes that according to the optimist view, the monetary union tends to make shocks more symmetric. This is so precisely because trade between European nations is mostly intra-industry and relies on economies of scale and imperfect competition (product differentiation). Hence, amongst themselves, countries buy and sell the same categories of products, thereby ensuring that demand shocks hit them in a similar way.

On the contrary, according to the pessimistic vision – mostly related to the New Economic Geography theory (NEG) (Krugman, 1991) – industrial specialization promoted by trade integration can eventually lead to asynchronous business cycles, thereby resulting in specific industry/sector shocks (Broz, 2005, p. 63). Moreover, trade integration, pushed by economies of scale and other centripetal factors, leads to regional concentration of industrial activities whereby sector-specific shocks may turn into country-specific shocks.[14] To summarize, according to this vision, monetary integration may increase the propensity of asymmetric shocks for each of the member countries (De Grauwe, 2014, p. 26).

Ultimately, the question is whether a currency union fosters the *synchronization of business cycles*.[15] Indeed, it can be accepted that "a region which

---

14 Contributors to the NEG (Krugman, 1987, 1991; Krugman and Venales, 1990; Puga and Venales, 1996) argue that by promoting trade and factor mobility, deeper integration will produce new economies of scale, activity specialization and economic agglomeration which could lead to regional disparities and ultimately to economic divergence (on this topic, see also Ascani *et al.*, 2012; Bouvet, 2003; Shankar and Shah, 2008, pp. 147–148).

15 Business cycle synchronization refers to the level of co-movement of the boom-bust economic phases of (currency areas of) member countries over time (Degiannakis *et al.*, 2014).

shows a high degree of business cycle homogeneity is an OCA" (Cuaresma and Amador, 2010a).

Before the launch of the EMU, some economists were cautious, not to say pessimistic, about the path of business cycle synchronization in Europe. Eichengreen (1991) and Bayoumi and Eichengreen (1992) distinguished between the European Community's 'core' and peripheral countries (the core was constituted by Germany, France, the Netherlands, Denmark and Belgium while the periphery included Italy, Spain, Ireland, Portugal and Greece). The main conclusion was: as in the U.S. case, in the European Community it was possible to distinguish core regions where supply and demand shocks were highly correlated and a periphery in which the correlation of shocks was less pronounced.

Despite these remarks, an optimist view prevailed. In this respect, mention should be made to the so-called *endogeneity hypothesis* of the OCA developed under the seminal contributions of Frankel and Rose (1997, 2000), Rose (1999) and Frankel (2009). According to this hypothesis, currency areas, and particularly the European Union, have the 'endogenous' property to foster trade amongst its members (taking an explanation from the 'gravity model').[16] As this trade in turn is mostly of an intra-industry type, increase in trade will naturally result in more highly correlated business cycles. In this case, then, the accomplishment of OCA's main conditions occurs in an *ex post* rather than in an *ex ante* fashion (Cuaresma and Amador, 2010a).

Other similar, contemporaneous studies can be added, such as those of Fatás (1997), Bentoglio *et al.* (2001), Haan *et al.* (2002), and Altavilla (2004), the main findings of which corroborated that trade integration steered the synchronization regarding the business cycle for the economies involved (both in Europe and in the U.S.). More recently, Montoya and De Hann (2007) have supported the hypothesis of a 'national border' effect, which fosters synchronization.[17]

The crucial question relates to the impact of the GFC on the synchronization of the business cycle in EMU countries. Literature on this matter is still scarce (see as an exception Degiannakis *et al.*, 2014; Belke *et al.*, 2016). Even so, one can say that the economic consequences of the crisis empowered the arguments against the optimistic view that had been, since the EMU's inception, mostly associated with the Rose-Frankel endogeneity hypothesis. In contrast, the 'core-periphery' fate seems to be more obvious than ever. Belke *et al.* (2016) provide evidence for such a conclusion: using a quarterly

---

16 As explained by Rose (1999, p. 7), the 'gravity model' in trade theory explains the size of international trade between countries. As a 'pure gravity one', it models the flows of international trade between a pair of countries as being proportional to their economic 'mass' (national income) and inversely proportional to the distance between them.

17 See also further studies: Gayer (2007), Cuaresma and Amador (2010a, 2010b) and Afonso and Sequeira (2010).

index for business cycle synchronization, the panel data suggest that after the last quarter of 2007, core countries experienced increased synchronization, whereas peripheral countries decreased synchronization with regards to the core, non-EMU countries and among themselves. Another significant conclusion is that even countries with the same business cycle have nevertheless, after the crisis, experienced different cyclical positions (e.g. a different amplitude of national cycles).

4.1.2.3. Decentralization versus centralization of fiscal policy; EMU atypical solution

Recall that one of the ingredients of an OCA – a condition for optimality – is the creation of a fiscal union (Kenen, 1969). For some authors, the process of economic and monetary integration would imply, necessarily, fiscal integration as a final stage.

Courchene (2008, p. 25), for example, expressed an idea of integration as a *continuum* departing from 'autarky' to arrive at a 'unified socio-economic space' and passing through the following (usual) steps: free trade agreement, customs union, common market (until this step, only negative integration operates), and then, subsequently, economic and monetary union, and social union (these steps are already marked by positive integration).

Thirion (2017), in turn, also conceived the five building blocks of the (future) fiscal union in gradual terms: (i) sharing sovereignty – fiscal rules and fiscal coordination; (ii) crisis management mechanisms; (iii) banking union – with common fiscal backstop; (iv) fiscal insurance (e.g. unemployment insurance, rainy-day funds); (v) joint debt issuance. As also noted (*Idem*), while French and Italian governments support a fiscal risk-sharing capacity in the EMU, which implies resource-sharing, the traditional German view is of further sovereignty sharing, with the centralization of fiscal rules (a stability union).

Carnot et al. (2015, p. 5) state that "the current architecture of EMU relies on decentralised fiscal policies under a rule based-framework."[18] In other words, the EMU is a fiscal union without a fiscal capacity, and for this reason it is an incomplete monetary union (De Grauwe, 2014).[19]

In fact, the current model in the EMU is atypical, and it can be considered a mix of the U.S. and German models. Enderlein et al. (2012, p. 36) describe these two models. The first – called 'market-based system' – is a system in which sub-central units are induced by capital markets to conduct

---

18 The academic definition of fiscal policy (in an open-economy): the Government policy relying on public spending and tax revenue decisions aiming to influence – short-term – economic growth (both through the internal and the external component of the GDP), employment and inflation.

19 See also, in this regard, Wyplosz and Pisani-Ferry (1990).

responsible fiscal policies and fiscal rules – if existent – are defined in a decentralized fashion.[20] This system is usually based in a no-bailout clause, defaults are possible, and there is a prohibition of debt monetisation. The second model – named 'hierarchical incentive system' – is a system in which sub-central fiscal discipline is enforced by central rules. Such system usually has a lender of last resort that can assist SCG in case of fiscal stress.[21] Enderlein *et al.* (2012, p. 36) stress that the system contained in the Maastricht Treaty was a mixed system, with elements of both systems: central rules (from the hierarchical model) are combined with some 'market-based' elements for debt default control and the prohibition of both bailout and debt monetisation.[22]

As noted, on the other hand, by Eichengreen (1997, p. 64), "historically, most federal unions established common currencies before adopting extensive systems of fiscal federalism." In particular, some features of the U.S. Fiscal Federalism model – used as a paramount example for the EMU framework – can illustrate the idea that a monetary union can subsist without a complete fiscal union.

Indeed, at first sight, there are parallels in the sequencing of monetary and political integration in the U.S. and Europe (Schelkle, 2017, p. 94). Apparently, a monetary union (with a single currency) preceded a fiscal union and ended by fostering a political union. It should be recalled that the U.S. political federalism is of a 'bottom up' nature: decentralized states gave rise – with forward and backward movements over more than three centuries – to a centralized union. Currency was not necessarily, in the first moments of U.S. history, a synonym for political integration. Indeed, the currency prolonged the divisions of the civil war into peacetime (Schelkle, 2017, p. 95). Boom-bust cycles only stopped once fiat money, tight financial regulation and stabilizing interfaces and public finance had been created, mainly in the aftermath of the Great Depression (*Idem*, p. 95).

The history of the U.S. federal government and the relationship with the states was marked by five main stages (Henning and Kessler, 2012): (i) Alexander Hamilton's reforms under the U.S. Constitution of 1789 (e.g. the Hamilton Plan of 1791); (ii) state defaults during the 1840s; (iii) a series of defaults at the state and local government levels after the Civil War; (iv) the Great Depression of the 1930s; (v) scattered defaults during 1970–2010.

During the nineteenth century, the amount of debt issued by the states was low. However, as explained by Henning and Kessler (2012), the economic expansion in the West gave rise to infrastructure demands (e.g. canals and turnpikes), which could be financed only by borrowing. In 1842, prices of bonds fell significantly, and the federal government was cut off from

20 This is typically the U.S. fiscal federal model.
21 This is closer to the so-called German fiscal federal model.
22 See also Malleghem (2014).

European financiers. The 'no-bailout clause' emerged at that time. However, it is neither a clause in the U.S. Constitution nor a provision of federal law. Instead, it is the counterpart of the high degree of fiscal sovereignty (or at least autonomy) given to states and local governments. In short, the type of fiscal union that historically emerged then is – as seen before – a system where tax autonomy goes hand in hand with no bailout provisions (at least direct bailouts).

The tradition for no-bailout provisions is strong in U.S. history and remained this way throughout the entire twentieth century: isolated cases of local bankruptcies happened, and the common solution was to make each of the respective governments adopt private rescue plans (including in the case of New York City in 1975). The same has happened with state governments: with few exceptions (e.g. the District of Columbia in the 1990s), no bailout provisions have been adopted by the federal government.

On the other hand, the U.S. has meanwhile evolved (since the Great Depression and notably with the New Deal) from an incomplete to a complete fiscal union (which ultimately replaced the need for direct bailouts) that, among others, has involved the following aspects: (i) the institution of a (national) social security system, financed by payroll taxes aiming to support new social benefits, including unemployment insurance; (ii) the increasing integration of the U.S. banking system, with the creation of the Federal Deposit Insurance Corporation – FDIC (1935) that at the same time included the provision of an ultimate governmental fiscal backstop.[23]

Fiscal integration was, under the New Deal, coupled with the deepening of monetary integration. The Fed that had been created in 1913 did not immediately imply the creation of a national banking system. Rather, the new entity was conceived as a user-owned facility held by commercial banks, which joined the system (Ugolini, 2018, p. 16). Only with the Banking Acts of 1933–1935 was the Fed transformed into a federal agency, thereby definitely centralizing the undertaking of monetary policy in the newly created Federal Reserve Open Market Committee (FOMC).

As observed by Schelkle (2017, p. 121), the Great Depression therefore softened political resistance against financial and macroeconomic stabilization by the centre. The author explains that as in the case of E(M)U integration, U.S. monetary integration fell under the spell of *Monet's curse* – under

---

23 In fact, as noted by Wolff (2012, pp. 5–6), if national deposit insurance implied some fiscal burden sharing (at the federal level), then the banking union should imply the notion of budgetary union, or at least the idea of a fiscal backstop. The author mentions that despite the autonomy of FDIC, the U.S. Treasury stands behind providing credibility in times of crisis. If a similar solution were to be adopted in the EU, then "one could view a euro-area budget as the backbone for such a common fiscal backstop for a new European resolution authority and fund. Such a fiscal backstop ultimately means that the federal level has the ability to borrow on the market" (*Idem*, p. 6), restoring confidence in crisis situations.

which the union was to be forged in crisis (*Idem*, p. 122). Indeed, evolution has been marked by trial and error, ups and downs, where centripetal and centrifugal forces struggled – and where, in the end, an effective political union was settled.

In any event, despite the progress towards centralization both with respect to fiscal and monetary policies, the U.S. can be still characterized as a currency union with significant decentralizing elements, with respect to these two policies – meaning that stabilization efforts can, at least in part, be delivered to the states.

Bearing the evolution of the U.S. fiscal union in mind, the question is whether a fiscal union (that is, the centralization of fiscal policy) is really a condition – *sine qua non* – for the existence and survival of a currency union. There are indeed contrasting arguments in this regard – see Table 4.3.

Now, let me detail these contrasting arguments.

I – In favour of decentralization of the fiscal policy is the idea that a single monetary union is enough to do the job of macroeconomic stabilization within the area.

Two main arguments stemming from the basic Mundell-Fleming model are used. The first argument is that, since the main regime in the EMU's relationships with the rest of world is that of a (managed) floating exchange

Table 4.3 Arguments pro decentralization and pro centralization of fiscal policy

Arguments pro decentralization of fiscal policy	Arguments pro centralization of fiscal policy
I – A single monetary union is enough to do the job of macroeconomic stabilization within the area	I – A single monetary policy is not well suited to cope with asymmetric shocks within the monetary union
II – The coordination of fiscal policies under a common rule-based framework is sufficient to ensure the smooth functioning of the monetary union	II – Disciplinarian devices should be combined with insurance devices
III – The current set of fiscal rules allows for the build-up of macroeconomic stabilizers	III – Fiscal policy coordination (contained mostly in the SGP framework) has proved to be unsatisfactory and can be counterproductive: it can be pro-cyclical
IV – In the light of the Fiscal Federalism theoretical framework, Sub-Central Governments (SCGs) can pursuit stabilization goals	IV – There is no theoretical rationale in favour of decentralized government with respect to stabilization function: it must be kept at the central level
V – Direct and visible anti-cyclical funds within federal-type organizations are rare	V – With centralized fiscal policies, visible and invisible mechanisms to absorb shocks interact naturally with each other

Source: The Author

rate, a single monetary policy is effective in its macro stabilizer role for the area as a whole, both internally through the interest rates for the euro and externally through the exchange rate for this same currency.

The second argument, taken from the Optimum Currency Areas theory coincides with the optimistic view about the European integration which has prevailed, according to which the monetary union would foster trade integration, making the member countries' business cycle more synchronized (recall the *One Money, One Market Report*; Emerson *et al.*, 1990). For this reason, shocks would become more symmetric, and thus a single monetary policy would suffice to ensure the stabilizing role for the whole euro area.

Finally, a broader argument is related to the self-sufficiency of the monetary policy. The Washington consensus achieved the hegemony of monetary policy in the stabilization field: indeed, monetary policy is *the* stabilizer policy. Ultimately, with inflation stabilization (the main macroeconomic goal), one can achieve output stabilization – the so-called 'divine coincidence' (see on this issue Fatás and Mihov, 2012).

Differently, in favour of centralization of fiscal policy, a single monetary policy is not well suited to cope with asymmetric shocks within the monetary union. Monetary policy, while being the main instrument in addressing area-wide shocks, is, however, an incomplete answer to a very severe shock, in particular when the lower zero bound is reached and the scope of quantitative easing is limited (Wolff, 2012, p. 5). In a similar vein, Bénassy-Quéré *et al.* (2016) stress that fiscal policy should act as a supplement to monetary policy, notably, when the monetary policy is constrained at the zero lower bound. In this case, fiscal policy has to be activated to increase demand and inflation.[24,25]

Moreover, monetary policy, by definition, does not address deep recessions that are purely regional (Wolff, 2012, p. 5), the occurrences of which

24 Bénassy-Quéré *et al.* (2016) summarize the main arguments. Firstly, monetary and fiscal policies interact – when fiscal policies are loosened, and inflation expands, this may trigger a monetary policy tightening (which commonly affects all member states). Secondly, fiscal policy may supplement monetary policy – notably, when the monetary policy is constrained at the zero lower bound, fiscal policy has to be activated to increase demand and inflation. Thirdly, national fiscal policies have direct cross-border effects – in normal times, these positive spillovers are limited, but in times of crisis and notably at the zero lower bound, a fiscal stimulus in one country has positive externalities vis-à-vis its neighbours.

25 In this regard, Corsetti *et al.* (2016) explain that accommodative monetary policy alone is not sufficient to meet a large adverse disturbance such as the global financial crisis (notably when the zero lower bound was attained). Instead, an accommodative monetary and fiscal policy *together* may be needed to ensure macroeconomic stabilization. The authors then assume and test two kinds of stylized fiscal interventions: (i) temporary increases in government spending, keeping the present value of primary budget surpluses constant; (ii) measures resulting in decreasing the present value of primary budget surpluses. In both cases, it is essential that monetary policy accommodates the fiscal stimulus by keeping policy rates at the lower bound.

have become clearer, in particular following the onset of the financial crisis (unlike the initial optimistic belief) where the EMU country business cycles have proven to be more asymmetric (Corsetti *et al.*, 2016).[26]

II – In favour of decentralization of fiscal policy, it is stressed that the coordination of fiscal policies under a common rule-based framework is sufficient to ensure the smooth functioning of the monetary union.[27]

The idea of coordination in a monetary union crucially depends on two interlinked aspects: firstly, on the type of shocks that affect the union (demand versus supply shocks; symmetric versus asymmetric) and secondly on the type of policy interaction. A conventional wisdom is that symmetric shocks (notably supply-side shocks) provide a stronger rationale for policy coordination in the union. Beestma *et al.* (2001) challenged this view by stressing that coordination, notably fiscal policy coordination, is more desirable when it is hardest to achieve, that is, when shocks are strongly asymmetric.

In turn, it should be noted that policy interaction involves two dimensions: on the one side, coordination between monetary and fiscal policies; on the other side, coordination amongst the fiscal policies themselves.

With respect to the first dimension – *coordination between monetary and fiscal policy* – mention should be made of the seminal contributions of Mélitz (1997), Wyplosz (1999) and Buti *et al.* (2001). In Mélitz's (1997) paper, the author finds evidence (for panel data from 19 OECD countries regarding the 1960–1995 period) that monetary and fiscal policies tend to move in opposite directions. The two policies are indeed 'strategic substitutes': looser fiscal policy promotes tighter monetary policy, and a stricter monetary policy triggers an expansionary fiscal policy. The same evidence for strategic substitutability was found by Wyplosz (1999): the conclusion is that the central bank raises interest rates when the deficit increases.[28]

As for the *coordination between fiscal policies*, the latter is justified with the externalities that the fiscal policy of one country can cause on others belonging to the same monetary union. In fact, these externalities can be positive or negative: positive, because an increase in the internal demand will favour the import of goods and services from the partners of the area;[29]

---

26 See also Ackrill (2004).

27 See, introducing the topic, Lavigne and Villieu (1996) and Healy (1999).

28 In turn, Buti *et al.* (2001) conceive a model of interaction between fiscal and monetary policies, bearing in mind the fiscal restraint of the SGP and its 'close-to-balance rule' concerning structural deficit. Therefore, although fiscal authorities have a preferred output target, it is assumed that the constraints imposed by the Pact lead to policy activism being considered as too costly. In turn, monetary policy aims at maintaining price stability, with it also being assumed that the central bank faces a cost in changing the interest rate. See also in this regard von Hagen and Mundschenk (2002).

29 In this regard, Belke and Osowski (2016) stress that a fiscal policy impulse in one economy can affect other economies via multiple channels: (i) the *demand channel* (or *trade channel*) – as fiscal policy actions influence domestic demand, this should also affect

negative, due to the pressure for an interest rate increase (Muet, 1996).[30] In this regard, Eichengreen (1996) argues that "fiscal policy coordination is needed to discourage free riding and induce governments to internalize the negative externalities otherwise imposed on the EMU partners." Those negative spillovers can express both through the interest rate (an 'internal' crowding out effect) and the exchange rate (an 'external' crowding out effect) of the euro (Loureiro, 2008), ultimately affecting the competitiveness of the currency area member countries.

The deficit bias of governments (Alesina and Tabellini, 1990; Alesina and Bayoumi, 1996) – due to the common pool problem and the strategic behaviour of politicians (e.g. maximization gains in the political market) – give rise to special concern in a monetary union. Indeed, unsustainable fiscal policy may generate excessive macroeconomic volatility, which will complicate the goal of the central bank in maintaining stability in the EMU.

In this neoclassical theoretical framework (summarized by the well-known statement 'rules rather than discretion'), tying the governments' hands is eventually meant to ensure credibility and the time-consistency of fiscal policies. Moreover, it is meant to avoid fiscal policy shocks. In fact, under this framework, the view that prevails is that fiscal policy not only is not acknowledged as an instrument of shock response, but it becomes, by itself, a source of macroeconomic shocks – e.g. inflation and trade imbalances (Perotti, 2002, 2007; Mountford and Uhlig, 2008).

The main instrument of fiscal policy coordination is the *Stability and Growth Pact* (SGP). The SGP was conceived, from the very beginning (1997), to limit specific fiscal policy biases, and notably excessive deficits, volatile fiscal policy and procyclicality (Fatás and Mihov, 2002).

Apparently, 'soft' coordination mechanisms would not be sufficient, as they would not entirely be able to prevent free-riding effects and opportunistic behaviour. Indeed, since its inception, a discussion involving the heterodox nature of the SGP framework has been on the table. In the words of Begg and Schelkle (2004, p. 1047), fiscal policy coordination under EMU

(domestic) demand for foreign goods and services and thereby (net) exports of trading partners; (ii) the *competitiveness channel* (or *terms of trade channel*) – due to distortionary taxation, fiscal policies can influence relative prices and therefore terms of trade; (iii) the *financial market channel* – through interest rates.

30 Hence, as shown by the Mundell-Fleming model, unlike that which happens in a flexible exchange rate system, in a fixed exchange rate regime, the transmission of fiscal policy effects tends to be negative, as the increase in the international interest rates crowds out investment. This effect cannot in turn be countervailed by exchange rate depreciation, since this instrument is no longer available (Lavigne and Villieu, 1996). The possibility of accumulating public debts adds other sources of negative spillovers through the common real interest rate and the credibility of monetary policy. In contrast, a moderate deficit and moderate debt tend to entail a crowding in effect over private investment, notably by reducing tax pressure related to a lower debt service (Boulhol, 2002). See also on this issue, Healey (1999).

"currently relies on a mix of hard rules, backed by sanctions, and 'soft law' arrangements to achieve them." Therefore, the two central regulations (1466/97 and 1467/97) that were at the heart of the SGP combined soft and hard methods of coordination: (i) soft coordination is based on the surveillance procedure, mostly within the preventive arm of the SGP; (ii) hard coordination relies on the excessive deficit procedure under the corrective arm, with provisions for escalating sanctions, culminating with a fine (Begg and Schelkle, 2004, p. 1047).[31]

Although significant procedural changes have taken place over the years with respect to these two arms of the SGP (notably with the 2005 and 2011 reforms, the latter being related to the so-called 'Six Pack'), the combination of these two elements remain.

The SGP, at its inception, carried out the prevalence of fiscal discipline over stabilization. Indeed, the SGP meant the embodiment of the so-called 'stability paradigm' (Heipertz and Verdun, 2010, p. 91). The operationally related idea of 'fiscal consolidation' was made to stem the expansionary stance of fiscal policy inherited from the 'golden age' of Keynesianism and welfare-state expansion. The basic argument was that expansionist policies had led to inflation and increasing interest rates, which, in turn, had reduced investment and contributed to weakening growth and underemployment (Heipertz and Verdun, 2010, p. 94). Progressively, this theoretical idea prevailed as a dogma: fiscal discipline was no longer an ideology, and instead it became a non-disputable statement.[32]

Opposing to these arguments, *it is argued, in favour of centralization of fiscal policy, that disciplinarian devices should necessarily be combined with insurance devices.*

Schelkle (2005) drew attention to the fact that since the EMU's foundation, the respective system of fiscal policy coordination (contained in the SGP) has been seen as a disciplinarian device aimed at addressing a classical principal-agent problem, according to which government incentives in

---

31 The legal basis for the preventive arm of the SGP results from: Articles 121 and 136 of the TFUE; Council Regulation (EC) 1466/97, of 7 July 1997, as amended by Council Regulation (EC) 1055/2005, of 27 June of 2005, and Regulation (EU) 1175/2011, of the European Parliament and the Council of 16 November 2011, and specified by the Code of Conduct of the SGP (*Specification on the Implementation of the SGP and Guidelines on the Format and Content of Stability and Convergence Programmes*). The legal basis for the corrective arm of the SGP is contained in: Article 126 of the TFUE; Council Regulation (EC) 1467/97, of 7 July 1997, as amended by Council Regulation (EC) 1056/2005, of 27 June 2005, and Council Regulation (EU) 1177/2011, of 8 November 2011, and further specified in the same Code of Conduct. Additionally, Council Regulation (EU) 1173/2011, of 16 November 2011, added a system of effective and graduated enforcement mechanisms to the Pact (European Commission, 2018).

32 See also Fabbrini (2014b).

the political-partisan market (e.g. to be re-elected) can affect credibility and time-consistency in their fiscal policy implementation throughout the cycle.

An alternative approach – the insurance view – recognizes that government faces difficulties in assuring macroeconomic stabilization and posits that policy coordination should help it to stabilize better. Untying its hands does not do away with all discipline. Therefore, collective insurance requires discipline, but as a means and not as the objective of fiscal policy coordination (Schelkle, 2005, p. 389).

III – In favour of decentralization of fiscal policy, it is advocated that the current set of fiscal rules allows for the build-up of macroeconomic stabilizers.

As soon noted by Begg and Schelkle (2004), there might be a problem of consistency between the SGP's main goals – avoiding fiscal laxity, ensuring fiscal sustainability, and promoting stabilization.

The SGP's Reform in 2005 without affecting the *status quo* (the disciplinarian view still prevailed), allowed a first concession to the idea of flexibility, in particular with respect to this latter aspect (promoting stabilization): the Pact should be more sensitive to the stages of the cycle in order to allow fiscal policy to produce stabilization effects, not only through the action of fiscal multipliers but also eventually through the endogenous discretionary fiscal policy. [33]

As such, the current set of fiscal rules – coming from the 2005 revision of the SGP and reinforced with the 2011 reform and the adoption of the so-called 'Fiscal Compact'[34] in 2012 – meant, above all, the evolution from first-generation to second-generation fiscal rules. This evolution can be verified not only in the EU but also in several other countries and has been accentuated after the crisis (Schaechter *et al.*, 2012). As stressed by Eyraud *et al.* (2018) and Debrun and Jonung (2019), prior to the great financial crisis, the first generation of fiscal rules tried to combine simplicity and flexibility, with little emphasis on enforceability. In contrast, second-generation rules reflect efforts to enhance both flexibility and enforceability, at the expense of simplicity.

Indeed, this increasing (macroeconomic) flexibility and enforceability at the cost of simplicity is mostly due to the new design of several numerical rules, now relying on a structural basis rather than on a nominal basis.[35]

---

33 Fatás and Mihov (2008) indeed conceive fiscal policy as the combination of these three elements: (i) automatic stabilizers – the reaction of fiscal policy to the business cycles which is a result of the tax code and spending rules that link budgetary components to changes in GDP; (ii) endogenous discretionary fiscal policy – that includes changes in fiscal policy taken in response to changing economic conditions; (iii) exogenous discretionary fiscal policy – changes in fiscal policy that are not related to economic conditions

34 In fact, the Treaty on the Stability, Coordination and Governance of the Economic and Monetary Union (TSCG).

35 The increasing complexity is due to the fact that these structural rules are not observable (in real time) and because their calculation involves complex (and controversial)

This new conception is firstly the idea that fiscal discipline imposed on state members not only does not jeopardize but rather can favour macroeconomic stabilization.[36] Fiscal discipline is the pre-condition for gaining room for manoeuvre that can be used in downturns to accommodate a momentary deterioration of the business cycle. In particular, the existence of safety margins allows for automatic stabilizers to work properly in those negative phases of the cycle. In this respect, two possible definitions for automatic stabilizers can be given: (i) a passive definition whereby these stabilizers react to the cycle (by increasing deficit during downturns and reducing deficit during good economic periods); (ii) an active definition, whereby stabilizers are made to actively stabilize the economy, due to their contra-cyclical effects (see on this issue Fatás and Mihov, 2012).

Table 4.4 describes the three main SGP and TSCG fiscal rules, highlighting the way they internalize, in one way or another, the effects of the cycle in the assessment of compliance with each of the rules.

The opposite argument, in favour of centralization of fiscal policy, is that policy coordination (contained mostly in the SGP framework) has proved to be unsatisfactory and can be counterproductive. In this regard, Bénassy-Quéré *et al.* (2016) highlight that such coordination has proven to be unsatisfactory since the inception of the EMU, mostly due to the so-called *pro-cyclicality of fiscal policy* in the euro area:[37] on average from 1995 to 2008, both the fiscal impulse and the discretionary parts of fiscal policy were expansionary in upturns and contractionary in downturns (*Idem*, p. 5).[38]

Moreover, Alcidi and Thirion (2016) note that the SGP had been designed with the idea that *ex ante* fiscal rules would not only be able to reduce negative externalities, but also allow the build-up of sufficient fiscal buffers in order to ensure *ex post* macroeconomic stabilization in negative moments of

---

methodologies – e.g. the determination of cyclically adjusted balance (to be covered later). Moreover, in the case of the EU surveillance procedures, both under the preventive and corrective arms, the sequence and stages of these procedures (involving different European and national institutions) have also become increasingly complex over the years.

36 In a seminal article, Alesina and Bayoumi (1996), looking at the U.S. experience, showed that balanced budget rules (applicable to U.S. states) are effective in enforcing fiscal discipline, and they have no costs in terms of increased output variability. Two contrasting explanations can be given. The first is associated with the limited role of states in ensuring macroeconomic stabilization: as such, reducing its impact more – with stringent fiscal rules – has no significant effect on product variability. The second is that a fiscal restriction not only impedes 'good' anti-cyclical policies but also limits politically motivated and biased policies, which may after all have a destabilizing effect.

37 Recall in this regard the precocious remarks made by Wyplosz and Pisani-Ferry (1990).

38 Note that this conclusion partially contradicts evidence presented by von Hagen and Wyplosz (2008), for whom fiscal policy had become more counter-cyclical after 1992 (in the Maastricht era). However, as also noted, the fact that the SGP limited counter-cyclical policy in downswings made these authors conclude that the SGP produced asymmetric effects: fiscal policy became counter-cyclical in good times and acyclical in downturns. Instead, prior to 1992, fiscal policy was pro-cyclical in bad times and acyclical otherwise.

Table 4.4 The three main SGP and TSCG fiscal rules

The fiscal rule	Description	Flexibility elements: the effects of the business cycle in the assessment of the rule
Balance budget rule:[1] the structural balance	Within the preventive arm of the Pact, each EMU country is given its own 'medium-term objective' (MTO), which is defined in structural terms as the cyclically adjusted general government balance (CAB) net of one-off and other temporary measures.[2]	Country-specific lower bounds for the MTOs: (i) the safety net margin with respect to the 3% of GDP deficit limit; (ii) sustainability or rapid progress towards sustainability that considers the fiscal effort needed to stabilize the debt ratio at 60% of the GDP[3] and the ageing cost; (iii) compliance with the minimum MTO for euro area and exchange rate mechanism (ERM2) countries, of −1% of GDP.[4] The path towards the accomplishment of the MTO is also set in a structural basis: the Commission defined the value of 0.5% of GDP as a benchmark for the annual improvement in the structural budget balance. However, it also acknowledged that this annual effort could be modulated over the economic cycle.[5]
The debt rule:[6] reaching the benchmark of 60% of GDP	For countries that do not comply with the limit of 60% of GDP, they should make an effort in order to ensure a satisfactory pace of reduction until the reference value is reached.[7]	The debt reduction benchmark is judged in three configurations (European Commission, 2018): (i) the forward-looking version; (ii) the backward-looking version; (iii) the correction of the cycle. As such, this latter methodology corrects the debt level for the cyclical component of the deficit (ensuring higher debt adjustment in good times of the cycle) and corrects the GDP level for the output gap for the past three years.

(Continued)

117

Table 4.4 (Continued)

The fiscal rule	Description	Flexibility elements: the effects of the business cycle in the assessment of the rule
The expenditure benchmark[8]	For countries that have attained the MTO, annual expenditure growth should not exceed a reference medium-term rate of potential GDP growth, unless the excess is matched by discretionary revenue measures, thus allowing the member state to remain at the MTO. For member states that have not attained the MTO, annual expenditure growth should not exceed a specific lower rate, which is set below the reference medium-term rate of potential GDP growth, unless the excess is matched by discretionary revenue measures.	For the purpose of this benchmark, only the primary expenditure net of discretionary and temporary (non-recurrent) measures is considered, which means that the relevant expenditure aggregate excludes interest spending, expenditure on EU programmes fully matched by EU funds and cyclical elements of unemployment benefit expenditure (European Commission, 2018, pp. 48–49).

Source: The Author

[1] Schaechter *et al.* (2012) detail that budget balance rules provide clear operational guidance and can help ensure debt sustainability. In turn, these rules can be divided into: overall balance, structural or cyclically adjusted balance, and balance over the cycle. While the former does not consider economic stabilization features, the latter two explicitly account for economic shocks. However, estimating the adjustment typically through the output gaps makes the rule more difficult to communicate and monitor.
[2] On this issue, see Larch and Turrini (2009), Mourre *et al.* (2013), Mourre *et al.* (2014) and European Commission (2018a, 2019).
[3] Recall that this is also the reference value coming from the TFUE, firstly as a convergence indicator, and assumed by the SGP.
[4] For signatories of the TSCG, the minimum MTO is −0.5% for countries with a public debt above the reference value of 60% of GDP.
[5] Communication, *Making the Best Use of the Flexibility within the Existing Rules of the SGP*, COM (2015), 12 final, of 13 January 2015.
[6] As explained by Schaechter *et al.* (2012), the most important advantages of a 'debt rule' are that this rule is the most effective, and it is easy to communicate. However, it faces a few drawbacks, notably because debt levels take time to be impacted by budgetary measures and because such levels can be affected by developments outside government control (e.g. changes in interest rates and exchange rates), as well as the 'below-the-line' financing operations (e.g. financial sector support measures for the calling of guarantees).
[7] According to Article 4 of the TSCG, contracting parties with a higher debt ratio shall reduce this at an average rate of one twentieth per year as a benchmark.
[8] Schaechter *et al.* (2012) explain that expenditures rules set limits on total, primary or current spending, and they can be set in absolute terms or growth rates. Such rules are not directly linked to debt sustainability since they do not constrain the revenue side. Nevertheless, they can constrain spending during temporary absorption booms, when windfall revenue receipts are temporarily high and headline deficit limits are easy to comply with. However, they are easy to communicate and monitor (*Idem*, p. 9).

the cycle – the 3% deficit as an accommodative floor. However, fiscal rules have not worked effectively to create room for manoeuvre for countercyclical policy at the national level so that it could act as a response to asymmetric shocks. On the contrary, the pro-cyclicality of fiscal policy, notably with respect to the discretionary component, has become clearer since 2011 onwards. Fiscal rules have hence proven to be asymmetric (notably in times of crisis), as they tended to create a deflationary bias in the euro area, becoming more demanding in times of recession (De Grauwe, 2013).

IV – In favour of decentralization of fiscal policy, it is argued that in the light of the Fiscal Federalism theoretical framework, SCGs can pursue stabilization goals.

Again, the example of the U.S. federal model is presented as an illustration. As noted before, the U.S. can be still characterized as a currency union with significant decentralizing elements, with respect to these two policies – meaning that stabilization efforts can, at least in part, be delivered to lower levels of government (i.e. the states).

As for stabilizing fiscal policy, elements of decentralization remain, for example with respect to the payment of unemployment benefits – which are a significant ingredient of the automatic stabilizing policy. In fact, the U.S. unemployment insurance (UI) system is a 'federal-state' system (Lenaerts *et al.*, 2017), because each state finances the scheme through payroll taxes paid by employers. Besides this normal programme, the federal government also provides for Emergency Unemployment Compensation (EUC) and the permanent Extended Benefits (EB) programme, which extends the duration of benefits in the event of economic downturn (Lenaerts *et al.*, 2017). EUC and similar federal programmes are launched in a discretionary way and are fully financed by the federal government.[39]

On the contrary, now in favour of the centralization of fiscal policy, it is stated that there is no rationale in favour of decentralized government with respect to the stabilization function: it must be kept at the central level.

Indeed, the basic argument for the centralization of fiscal policy is that it can enhance the extent of insurance against macroeconomic shocks, notably due to (Poghosyan *et al.*, 2015):

i)   A centralized fiscal system allows for better risk-sharing – macroeconomic stabilization with respect to common shocks fosters simultaneously risk-sharing against regional or idiosyncratic shocks.

---

39 However, in this regard, Alcidi and Thirion (2017) explain that the semi-decentralized nature of the UI scheme limits the scope for true inter-state risk sharing, precisely because it leaves most of the funding prerogatives to the states. This hybrid nature, indeed, restricts the scope for inter-state solidarity, rather allowing for inter-generational risk sharing with future generations within a given state. In contrast, the EUC is better suited to address state-specific shocks, but it has historically accounted for a modest amount of total UI outlays (*Idem*, 2017).

ii) Centralization of fiscal policies is marked by economies of scale – an important illustration is the ability of the central government to borrow under better conditions (Spahn, 1997; von Hagen and Wyplosz, 2008).

iii) Fiscal stabilization has features of a public good (see also Majocchi, 1999, p. 85) – the impact of stabilization measures is likely to leak out to other states through interest trade spillovers; consequently, a 'free-riding' problem emerges, making decentralized fiscal policies excessively passive.

iv) In a decentralized fiscal setting, Ricardian equivalence assumptions hold, which may lead households to save in periods of expansion in anticipation that higher deficits will have to be borne by higher taxes in the future (high effect on fiscal multipliers); in contrast, in a fiscal centralized setting, Ricardian effects are weaker, as households in states running deficits may expect that the financing of those deficits will be shared with households of other states (small effect on fiscal multipliers) (see Sala-i-Martin and Sachs, 1991).

V – In favour of decentralization of fiscal policy, it is advocated that direct and visible anti-cyclical funds within federal-type organizations are rare.

Poghosyan *et al.* (2015) show that net fiscal transfers (including transfers to state budgets, gross transfers to individuals and federal taxes) have significant impact on both risk sharing and redistribution.

Less evidence on the stabilizer effects seems to exist with respect to regional redistribution (associated with the system of intergovernmental transfers, to be analysed further on). SCGs' tax revenues tend to fluctuate cyclically, i.e. the tax-to-GDP ratio tends to grow during an economic upswing and to decline during a downswing (Blöchliger and Petzold, 2009, p. 16).[40] Intergovernmental transfers – aiming at coping with vertical and horizontal fiscal gaps – could be designed in order to correct, at least partially, this pro-cyclical effect.[41] However, in practice, this does not happen in most Fiscal Federalism experiences (*Idem*). Firstly, because most of these

---

40 To a certain extent, this view is challenged by von Hagen and Wyplosz (2008), who advocate that even though redistributive transfers were not designed explicitly for that purpose, they can be considered 'insurance' mechanisms against asymmetric cyclical shocks. This happens because regions in a more favourable cyclical position than the federation on average pay transfers to regions in a less favourable position. This has the consequence of dampening the relative boom in the former and the relative recession in the latter.

41 In this regard, von Hagen and Hepp (2001) developed a methodology aiming to assess the stabilizing properties of intergovernmental transfers. For that purpose, five indicators were used: (i) correlation between year-to-year fluctuations in taxes and grants; (ii) ratio of the normalized variances of pre-transfer and post-transfer SCG revenue fluctuations; (iii) fluctuations of sub-central tax revenue with respect to GDP; (iv) fluctuations of transfer revenue with respect to GDP; (v) fluctuations of transfer revenues with respect to SCG tax revenue (see also Blöchliger and Petzold, 2009, pp. 16–17).

transfers are based on tax revenue-sharing mechanisms, which means that ultimately the impact of the business cycle is borne entirely by the recipient government. Secondly, the equalizing formulas, based on fiscal capacity, are not fit and proper to respond to asymmetric shocks: if recipient SCGs have weaker cycles than the national average, the difference between the average and an individual SCG's fiscal capacity tends to become destabilizing (Blöchliger and Petzold, 2009, pp. 17–18). In turn, for those transfers relying on the expenditure needs indicator (and particularly matching transfers), grant allocation depends on the percentage of sub-central expenditure. The more the SCG spends, the more transfers it gets: if spending varies positively with the cycle, then matching grants tend to become pro-cyclical (*Idem*, p. 18). In short, fiscal transfers tend to magnify pro-cyclical effects that stem initially from tax assignment rules.[42]

Moreover, there are few examples in OECD countries of grants (or funds) especially designed to meet regional macroeconomic shocks. Two exceptions in this regard are Canada and Germany.

Snoddon (2004, p. 176) explains that Canada's stabilization programme dates back to 1957 – the main purpose is to protect provinces from dramatic reductions in revenues. Despite their increasing role, stabilization grants account for only between 1% and 2% of federal grants to provinces (Snoddon, 2004, p. 176). In turn, it should be noted that although this is the only explicit programme made to address macroeconomic shocks, the overall design of the intergovernmental system in Canada contributes, albeit in an invisible manner, to this objective as well. This is particularly the case with matching grants for welfare spending (e.g. health and education), which also tend to be counter-cyclical (Snoddon, 2004, p. 184).

In Germany, there is also a formula-based mechanism for fiscal equalization, the *Länderfinanzausgleich* (LFA). As explained by Hepp and von Hagen (2001, p. 5), the LFA involves three stages. Firstly, VAT revenue (cyclically sensitive by nature) is redistributed to reduce the variation in per capita VAT receipts among states; states with higher-than-average VAT revenue per capita make transfers to those with lower VAT revenue per capita. Secondly, states make transfers among each other based on a more comprehensive measure of expenditure needs and tax capacity. Finally, the federal government provides additional federal grants to further narrow differences in tax capacity.

---

42 Blöchliger and Petzold (2009) suggest some changes in the design of the equalization system in order to obtain a higher macro stabilizer effect. Firstly, transfers should be linked to the effective needs of SCGs – also, decoupling transfers from tax revenue can ensure more stable transfers of allocations to SCGs. Secondly, the percentage of matching grants should be reduced, as they favour pro-cyclical pressure. Thirdly, horizontal equalisation schemes tend to be more prone to pro-cyclical effects than vertical equalization ones. Finally, the use of lagged variables can minimize pro-cyclicality, despite their shortcomings, such as a certain rigidity in responding to current SCG needs.

On the other hand, now in favour of the centralization of fiscal policy, it can be stressed that with centralized fiscal policies, visible and invisible mechanisms to absorb shocks interact naturally with each other.

As referred to in this regard by Cabral (2017, pp. 250–251),

> some of the shock absorbers are directly conceived to address cyclical shocks – in this case, they should be qualified as 'visible' and 'direct' stabilization mechanisms – whereas others have, in contrast, stabilizing effects in an 'indirect' and 'invisible' way. The latter are in fact designed to pursue other economic goals than stabilization (and only indirectly do they provide for this macroeconomic effect).

Following the same author (*Idem*, p. 256), it should be added that the invisible action of a central budget is due either to general interregional redistributive mechanisms (e.g. grants coping with a horizontal fiscal gap) or to inter-individual redistributive instruments (e.g. personal taxes and social benefits) provided by the same budget (see MacDougall *et al.*, 1977). In fact, both personal income tax and social security benefits, as instruments of economic redistribution, also act as 'invisible' mechanisms able to correct macroeconomic imbalances: high incomes go with high tax payments, and low incomes go with high revenues from the central government (*Idem*, 13).[43]

Finally, one should add as an invisible stabilizer action the actual capacity of the central government to borrow (Bénassy-Quéré *et al.*, 2016). According to this perspective, macroeconomic stabilization as a role of the central level is not necessarily due to the existence of direct and visible risk-sharing mechanisms (or shock absorbers); rather, it occurs as a result of the normal interplay of public expenditures and revenues and the way the central government (by itself and in conjunction with low-level governments) pursues its usual tasks in the fields of goods allocation and redistribution.

As noted in the seminal contribution of Sala-i-Martin and Sachs (1991), the interregional public insurance scheme in a common monetary union setup does not have to be 'conscious': a proportional income tax even if accompanied by acyclical expenditures and transfers will automatically work as a tax/transfer system that helps to defend fixed exchange rate parities (and the overall stabilization of the area). Moreover, if the income tax

---

43 Furthermore, as mentioned by von Hagen and Wyplosz (2008), even though redistributive transfers were not designed explicitly for that purpose, they can be considered insurance mechanisms against asymmetric cyclical shocks, since regions in a more favourable cyclical position than the federation on average pay transfers to regions in a less favourable position. This has the consequence of dampening the relative boom in the former and the relative recession in the latter.

is progressive and the transfer system is countercyclical, the fraction of the shocks insured by the fiscal system will be even larger.[44]

In short, it could be said that the simple functioning of the central budget ensures, albeit in an invisible manner, macroeconomic stabilization. In this sense, macroeconomic stabilization is not a goal *per se*, but rather a natural outcome of the leading functions of the government, notably in the fields of redistribution and goods allocation (to be detailed further on).

4.1.3. E(M)U as a lopsided fiscal union

4.1.3.1. A review of Fiscal Federalism literature

The main features of Fiscal Federalism theory were defined more than 60 years ago in the seminal works of Tiebout (1956), Stigler (1957), Musgrave (1959, 1983), Oates (1965, 1968), and Olson (1969).[45] As noted by Cabral (2016, pp. 1282–1283), in the early 1990s, the subject regained interest, and since then, important studies were undertaken under the auspices of international organizations such as the IMF, OECD and the World Bank. A majority of the studies were initially disseminated as non-edited papers and eventually published as collective books (e.g. the books edited by Ter-Minassian (1997), Boadway and Shah (2007, 2009) and Shah (2007a, 2008). With the OECD label, mention should be made of Jourmard and Konsgrud (2003), Bergvall *et al.* (2006), Blöchliger and King (2006), Blöchliger *et al.* (2007), Blöchliger and Petzold (2009), Charbit (2010) and Stossberg *et al.* (2016).

In addition, Fiscal Federalism theory evolved as it was influenced by a new philosophical vision of government in its relationships with society and the economy. Indeed, whereas the traditional normative approach was based on the assumption of a benevolent government, subsequent Fiscal Federalism studies were mostly impacted by Public Choice, assuming that unlike normative approach governments, politicians and officials act as self-interested players (Ahmad and Brosio, 2006b, p. 1). This new approach, qualified by Oates (2005) as the second generation of Fiscal Federalism theory, can also be referred to as the Political Economy approach, the main contributions of which were collected in the notable volume edited by Ahmad and Brosio (2006a). This approach is characterized by the influence of political processes and the behaviour of politician in decentralization experiences along with the existence of informational problems, notably with respect to information asymmetry (Oates, *Idem*, p. 356). As will be shown next, the Political

---

44 See also, in this regard, Bargain *et al.* (2012).
45 The important volume edited by Oates (1998) brought together some of the 'classics' on the study or understanding of Fiscal Federalism, notably: Buchanan (1950), Tiebout (1956), Stigler (1957), Buchanan (1965), Gramlich (1977), Fisher (1982) and Musgrave (1983).

Economy approach has added new topics to Fiscal Federalism theory and simultaneously compelled current normative studies to broaden their scope of analysis.

An important window opened by the Political Economy of Fiscal Federalism is the acknowledgement that the separation of functions and hierarchy that typically mark intergovernmental relations under normative criteria do not prevent other sorts of arrangements, driven by political economy arguments. An important argument – that dates back to Tiebout's 'voting with one's feet' model (Tiebout, 1956) – is *competition*: citizens and consumers move their residence to those jurisdictions that provide them with the quantity and quality of services that they look for at the lowest cost, especially in terms of taxation (Ahmad and Brosio, 2006b, p. 7). In turn, competition ensures the matching of the provision of services with local preferences, minimizing inefficiencies (*Idem*, p. 7).

Departing from this model, Salmon (2006) develops the concept of *horizontal competition* (e.g. between identical layers of government) – governments can compete with each other on the basis of 'mobility-facilitating' or 'arbitrage-facilitating' information (thus addressing problems of information asymmetry). Horizontal competition can in turn favour social experimentation (the so-called 'laboratory federalism') and also 'yardstick competition' between governments (to be re-elected) – in fact, voters are asked to make comparative assessments of the incumbent's performance.[46]

On the other hand, *vertical competition* takes place between central government and sub-central governments as a mechanism for the efficient assignment of functions among levels of governments (Ahmad and Brosio, 2006b, p. 8). In his seminal book, Breton (1996, p. 190) stresses that competition will force governments to specialize in the supply of goods and services in which each is more efficient and will thus help to determine the degree of equilibrium of expenditure and revenue concentration. Ultimately, in the words of Breton (2006, p. 93), vertical competition promotes a "Wicksellian connection,"[47] a link between the quantity of a particular good and service supplied by centres of power and the tax price citizens pay for that good or service (*Idem*, p. 93).

Moreover, Breton's model implicitly accepts private, Coasean-type solutions, that is, the use of contractual arrangements between these layers of government in order to ensure a more efficient provision of public and club goods. *Contractual federalism* is hence another line of thought forged by the Political Economy of Fiscal Federalism. In this regard, Spahn (2006, p. 187) notes that contractual arrangements can be developed to address

---

46 For a detailed description of Fiscal Federalism theory, and how it evolved throughout time, see Cabral (2018).

47 Recall the benefit taxation principle due to Knut Wicksell.

inter-jurisdictional spillovers or externalities. Moreover, contracts can be tailored to meet particular circumstances and to address special needs. For this reason, contractual federalism is close to 'laboratory federalism' or social experimentation. Finally, contractual forms can improve the quality of services delivery in the public sector, and this happens because they create supplier-user relationships (Spahn, 2006, p. 192).

Congleton (2006) also proposes an approach based on bargaining between SCG and the centre. An important outcome of such contractual solutions is asymmetric arrangements with respect to the internal organization of territories. Indeed, according to Congleton's (2006) view, current organization can include *asymmetric fiscal federalism*, that is, the formation of many levels and combinations of fiscal authority (notably to cope with externalities or spillovers, or simply due to policy reasons). Ultimately, asymmetry can lead to 'menu federalism', where member states choose which services they will have produced centrally in much the same way that consumers select services from larger firms in the marketplace – this voluntary nature of each 'subscription' allows non-uniform service levels to be provided while reducing the political risk associated with discriminatory central governments (Congleton, 2006, p. 139).

Finally, the *FOCJ (functional, overlapping and competing jurisdictions) model* developed by Eichenberger and Frey (2006) should be highlighted. In this model, constituent units thus have four characteristics (Ahmad and Brosio, 2006b, pp. 11–12): (i) They are functional, or mono-functional, because they are responsible for a single policy and their size is determined according to the spatial impact of the policy for which they are responsible. (ii) They overlap, meaning that several functional jurisdictions operate in the same territory (functional specialization). (iii) They 'naturally' involve competition in the public sector. (iv) A constitutional provision is needed that sanctions the rights of citizens to create new jurisdictions.

In a nutshell, it can be said that the Political Economy of Fiscal Federalism adds new ways of conceiving territorial organization and relationships between layers of governments, highlighting their variability and complexity, which are marked by (i) horizontal and/or vertical competition, (ii) contractual arrangements, (iii) internal asymmetry and (iv) functional specialization.

4.1.3.2. Normative criteria for functions and revenues assignment: the two steps of Fiscal Federalism theory

At this stage, it should be mentioned that fiscal federalism captures several forms of fiscal decentralization, whatever the type of political or administrative structure existing in a country or groups of countries: unitary state (regional or not), federation, confederation or even supranational-type

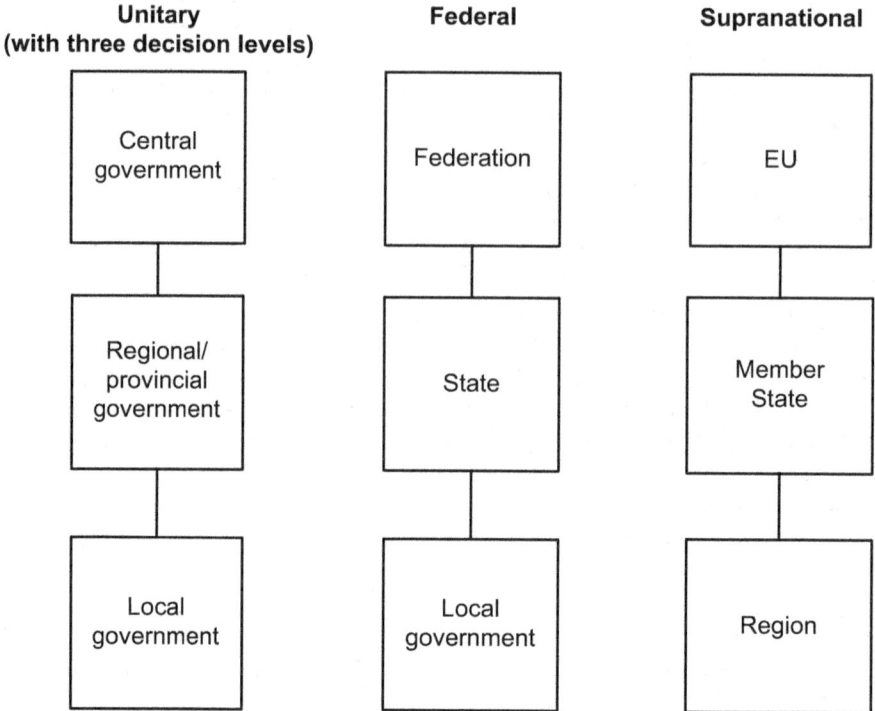

Figure 4.2 Different types of state political-administrative organization
Source: The Author

organizations as is the case with the EU (see Figure 4.2).[48] The basic conditions for Fiscal Federalism's normative prescriptions to be applied are hence the existence of different decision layers or governments with the capacity to interfere, to a certain extent, in the determination of the level of that circumscription's revenues and expenditures.

In any event, one should not ignore the fact that each experience of fiscal decentralization (in worldwide terms) is unique (due to significant cultural, historical, economic and social differences), and for this reason the attempt to use normative criteria as a global recipe must not ignore its own caveats.

Finally, it should be noted that decentralization is not a panacea able to solve all the problems a country may face, notably either with respect to government performance and fiscal discipline, or with respect to economic growth, regional convergence and inequality and poverty reduction. Decentralization can be amply justified on strong economic arguments (e.g.

48 For a complete overview of federal arrangements, see Watts (2008).

preference matching, or the reasoning behind the principle of subsidiarity) but it can also be – and usually is – explained by a specific historic political momentum (e.g. a war tends to foster centralization, whereas peace and times of prosperity may favour decentralization) or by mere circumstantial political-partisan reasons. For all these reasons, decentralization is always a learning-by-doing and a dynamic process, a path that allows for forward and backward movements, and even for some trial and error.

4.1.3.2.1. FUNCTIONS ASSIGNMENT

As explained by Cabral (2016), the conventional normative approach, in a departure from the generalized idea of "finance follows function" (Boadway and Shah, 2007, p. xxvii), proceeds to establish the normative criteria for the following – functions assignment, tax assignment, intergovernmental transfers (e.g. general objectives, types of transfers, microeconomic effects, equalization criteria), and local borrowing (see Shah, 1991). While the first item corresponds to the expenditure side, the remaining three items correspond to the revenue side (three main sources of sub-central financing).

The first step of fiscal federalism hence coincides with *functions assignment*. In this regard, considering his own seminal taxonomy of government functions, Musgrave (1959) claimed that the "heart of Fiscal Federalism" should remain with the allocation branch, while the objectives of income redistribution and macroeconomic stabilization should be mostly assigned to the central government.

Contemporary studies conducted notably by Oates (1965) and Olson (1969) managed to identify within the allocation branch the general criteria for the function assignment. The brief explanation given by Oates (2005, p. 351) is quite elucidative: The First Generation Theory (FGT) "thus envisioned a setting in which governments at different levels provided efficient levels of outputs of public goods for those goods whose spatial patterns of benefits were encompassed by the geographical scope of their jurisdictions. Such an outcome was called a 'perfect mapping' (or 'fiscal equivalence')." As noted again by Cabral (2016), the *geographical scope of the benefit* was, thus, the principal criteria used to identify whether the collective (or merit) good was a local, regional, or a national one and to determine accordingly, the level of government to which the allocation function should be assigned.

However, some other economic effects, notably the existence of spatial externalities or spillovers and the verification of economies of scale (Shah, 1991, pp. 3–4), should be considered since they could potentially lead towards a *rationale* for upgrading the decision level, i.e., a *rationale* for centralization.

Two typical mechanisms have been conceived both on theoretical and practical grounds as alternatives to a 'pure' recentralization solution. Firstly, there are *merging solutions*, as happens in the case of local government associations, including 'functional' or 'specific-functions' as opposed to 'all-purpose' associations. Secondly, there are vertical or horizontal *contractual solutions* between governments, through which the provision of the goods is ensured by one of the governments and the others, also benefiting from this provision, contract to pay for its use (see Joumard and Konsgrud, 2003).

More recently, it has been argued that expenditure decentralization not only can entail the incapacity to exploit economies of scale and to internalize spillover effects, but it also can involve both negative and positive conflicts in functions assignment. Indeed, when functions, roles and tasks are not clearly delimited, concurrent governments can either refuse to ensure the provision of the goods, sending the responsibility to the other decision layer, or they can both assume responsibilities with respect to provision of the goods and wish to do the same. In the former case (negative conflicts of competences) the outcome will be an under-provision of the goods or services. In the latter (positive conflicts of competences) the result will be one of overlapping functions, involving cost redundancies, waste and duplication of efforts (see on this issue Joumard and Konsgrud, 2003; IMF, 2009).

In the study of federalism, an academic distinction is made between dual and cooperative federalism (Shah, 2007b, pp. 5–6). Under *dual federalism* (which in turn can be in the form of 'layer-cake' or 'coordinate-authority'), the responsibilities of the different governments are separate and distinct. Under *cooperative federalism* (which in turn can be in the form of 'interdependent spheres', 'marble cake' and 'independent spheres'), the responsibilities of various orders are interlinked.

In either case, though, one can say that with exception to areas that are the exclusive competence of the central government (e.g. national defence), in all other areas, in one way or another, concurrent authorities or powers exist. This is so because the central level always reserves some kind of intervention for itself, at least to set the basic or minimum standards – the (Constitutional) core of the public policy – or the basic regulatory and/or supervisory prescriptions, which by their nature involve the whole nation. This does not prevent remaining legislative and regulatory powers being able to be assigned to intermediate and even low-level governments, but always respecting the previously defined core rules. Therefore, with respect to concurrent functional areas, two types of solutions can take place: (i) the case where all layers of government have both legislative (and/or regulatory) and administrative powers; (ii) the case where the higher levels (central government and possibly state or regional governments) possess legislative competence, whereas low-level governments are endowed only with executive/administrative powers.[49]

---

49 In this regard, it should be noted that functions assignment typically involves three main kinds of responsibilities (IMF, 2009, pp. 16–17): (i) the (legislative) *formulation* of the

It should be noted that the aforementioned problems – of negative and positive conflicts of competences – occur more often in the former situation, that is, when all layers of government have both legislative and administrative powers, including financing and supervisory powers.

These problems, involving concurrent functions assignment, can be solved only by a clear legal definition of 'who does what'. The clarification of responsibilities is hence a crucial aspect to prevent under-provision or overlapping functions, particularly when it comes to such concurrent areas (i.e., health care, education, social welfare).

4.1.3.2.2. REVENUES ASSIGNMENT

The second step of Fiscal Federalism was identified as *revenues assignment*. It includes three orders of financing: (a) tax assignment; (b) intergovernmental transfers; (c) borrowing (debt).

a) Tax assignment Starting with the first order of SCG financing – tax assignment – both Musgrave (1983) and Shah (1991) provide some normative criteria in this regard. Whereas Musgrave (1983) mostly relates to the role taxes play (according to his own taxonomy of fiscal functions), Shah (1991, p. 13) uses both equity (consistency of revenue means with expenditure needs) and efficiency (minimizing resource cost) criteria.

Notwithstanding this, some common principles can be envisaged: (i) progressive redistributive taxes should be centralized (coinciding with the allocation of the redistributive function primarily to the central government); (ii) taxes suited for economic stabilization should be centralized (*idem*); (iii) tax bases distributed unequally between jurisdictions should be centralized; (iv) taxes on mobile factors should be centralized (in order to avoid beggar-my-neighbour policies, trade leakages and perverse tax competition); (v) resident-based taxes such as taxes on sales or excises are better suited for intermediate governments (e.g. regions or states); (vi) taxes on natural resources should be allocated to either the central or intermediate level or both the central and intermediate level; (vii) taxes on immobile factors are best suited for the local level; (viii) benefit taxes and user charges should be used by all levels, according to the 'Wicksellian' benefit principle of taxation.[50]

---

spending programme, including the definition of policy goals and standards; (ii) the *financing* of the programme; (iii) the (administrative and executive) *implementation* of the programme. Additionally, I would include a fourth type of responsibility: (iv) the *control, auditing and assessment* of programme implementation.

50 Based on the tax base as an efficiency condition (benefit versus ability to pay), Oates (2004, p. 18) considers that "efficiency requires not only that decentralized jurisdictions refrain

Tax assignment (the attribution of tax revenues to different layers of government) must not, in turn, be confounded with the idea of *tax autonomy*. As noted by Blöchliger and Rabesona (2009), tax autonomy or taxing power captures various aspects of the freedom sub-central governments (SCGs) have over their own taxes.[51] It encompasses features such as SCGs' right to introduce or abolish tax, to set tax rates, to define the tax base or to grant tax allowances or reliefs to individuals or firms. Moreover, tax decentralization can involve not only tax powers over tax base and/or rates, but also the concurrent exploitation of tax bases by different levels of governments: most notably in the case of 'piggy-backing' or when different levels of the government apply their own rates to the same tax base.[52]

Note that the share of revenue assignment is not necessarily related to higher or less tax autonomy (notably over tax revenues they receive); indeed, countries with the highest share of tax revenues may not be the ones with more tax powers, and vice versa. In any case, SCGs had, in the documented year of 2011, some base or rate-setting autonomy over three quarters of the tax revenues they received (Stossberg *et al.*, 2016, p. 11).

Note, in turn, that the argument in favour of functions assignment is stronger than with tax assignment, and this is partly due to efficiency or equity costs related to tax decentralization, including tax autonomy, which are not found on the expenditure side (Boadway *et al.*, 1994). The *efficiency* of the internal market is affected by distortions in the allocation of mobile factors, and this is mostly due to tax externalities (Boadway and Shah, 2009, pp. 87–88).

In fact, decentralized tax policies distort the free flow of products and/ or factors of productions between states or regions – generating either positive tax externalities, such as (perverse) tax competition and beggar-my-neighbour policies, or negative tax externalities, as is the case with tax exporting. In this latter case, the marginal cost of public funds (MCPF) will be perceived as higher than it really is. This gives the low-level government an incentive to set taxes on mobile tax bases that are too low from an efficiency point of view (Hayashi and Boadway, 2000).

Different capacities in raising tax revenues also entail *equity* problems. In particular, when both the central and the intermediate (or low-level) governments levy broad-based taxes (as is the case with personal income taxes), increases in state/region tax rates tend to reduce the size of the tax base (competing amongst them for redistribution above the optimal level), thereby affecting the capacity of the central government to conduct a

---

from non-benefit taxation of mobile economic units, but that these actively engage in benefit taxation where the public sector provides services to these units."

51 See also Blöchliger and Nettley (2011).

52 See also Pola (1999).

national, uniform distributional tax policy – which can be seen as a negative externality (Boadway and Shah, 2009, p. 90).

Tax assignment is the first source of sub-central financing. To a large extent, tax assignment is not 'expenditure needs based', as the respective assignment criteria are mostly related to the type of tax (each tax profile is suited to finance a specific government layer) and to the kind of externalities each of these taxes may or may not produce, and whether such externalities should be prevented.

B) Intergovernmental transfers   On the contrary, *intergovernmental transfers* (i.e. *grants*) – the second order of SCG financing – are mostly expenditure needs based, as their first goal (a passive objective) is to overcome vertical fiscal imbalance (Boadway, 2007, p. 55; Shah, 2007b, 2007c). In fact, intergovernmental transfers aim at providing SCGs with additional financial resources, thus filling the gap between own tax revenues and expenditure needs (Blöchliger and Rabesona, 2009, p. 11).

Additionally, intergovernmental transfers also fulfil (active objectives of) equalization of fiscal disparities (Boadway, 2007, p. 55), the internalization of expenditure or tax externalities (*supra*) and possibly the pursuit of policy goals the central government does not wish to abdicate – e.g. to cope with territorial spillovers or externalities related to the provision of goods and services by one circumscription, to set national minimum standards for services provision and to ensure national cohesion.

In turn, it should be noted that intergovernmental transfers should not be confused with tax sharing, even though mixed arrangements can be found in several countries (some intergovernmental transfers depart from and rely on a tax sharing framework). As mentioned by Blöchliger and King (2006, p. 17), tax sharing is an arrangement in which a certain amount is allocated to each level of government out of the total revenue (generated from a single tax or a pool of taxes), whereby: (i) the share is predefined and cannot be changed in the course of the fiscal year (the assignment is therefore automatic); (ii) the revenue to SCGs is not earmarked; (iii) the revenue allocated to a single sub-central government either corresponds to the revenue it has collected or is distributed across jurisdictions on a *per capita* basis. Therefore, in a tax-sharing environment, SCGs face the overall impact of the business cycle and the risk of revenue fluctuations: in good times the share of the revenue tends to increase, whereas in bad periods a natural decrease in the shared amount is expected.

The two main categories of intergovernmental transfers are general-purpose (non-earmarked) transfers and specific-purpose (earmarked) transfers. The former are provided as general budget support, with no conditions attached – for this reason they are also described as non-conditional grants. Sometimes, these transfers are also described as 'block grants' when they are used to provide broad support in a general area of subnational expenditure (e.g. education) while allowing recipients some discretion in allocating the funds amongst specific uses (Shah, 2007c, p. 25). These grants are, for these reasons, more suitable for correcting vertical fiscal imbalance and promoting horizontal equalization. On the other hand, such grants, while producing an income effect – leading in turn to the so-called 'flypaper effect' (Courant *et al.*, 1979) – do not affect 'consumption goods' relative prices (thus not carrying out a substitution effect) (Shah, 1991, p. 24).

Earmarked (conditional) transfers are intended to provide incentives for governments to undertake specific programmes or activities (Shah, 2007c, p. 25). These grants are hence more suited to promoting certain policy goals considered as having priority by the central government. As such, they entail both income and substitution effects.

Conditional transfers may also incorporate matching provisions ('matching grants') requiring grant recipients to finance a specified percentage of expenditures using their own resources (Shah, *Idem*, p. 26). The main advantage is that they increase accountability and scrutiny in the usage of the funds, but they can represent a greater burden for a recipient jurisdiction with limited fiscal capacity (*Idem*, p. 26).[53]

One of the most challenging and complex aspects in the design of an intergovernmental transfer system is related to so-called *horizontal fiscal equalization*. However, horizontal regional/state equalization is not the same and does not imply interpersonal income inequality reduction. In general, Fiscal Federalism theory (since the seminal contribution of Musgrave, 1959) assumes that the central government is best suited to ensuring individual redistribution – redistribution is a national goal that should not be distorted by subnational intrusion notably driven by increasing powers on the tax side. In any case, local and regional governments have experienced increasing powers with respect to both tax (including distributional taxes) and expenditure sides. In particular, local and regional governments have in general, over the years, assumed more responsibility in areas that are typically related to distributional effects, such as health care, education, social assistance, housing, etc.

As noted previously, tax decentralization involves equity drawbacks that intergovernmental transfers are supposed to partially offset. In particular, SCGs with higher autonomous taxes may need higher equalizations grants – this is so because of an externality resulting from unequal tax bases or due to an *ex ante* desire for equal services provision (Charbit, 2010, p. 4). Indeed, when the intergovernmental transfer system relies on the fiscal capacity criteria (*infra*), the degree of tax autonomy by the low-level

---

53 On alternative taxonomies of intergovernmental transfers, see Bergvall *et al.* (2006) and Boadway (2007).

governments can ultimately affect the net fiscal benefit of the respective constituents. Equalization transfers benefit those jurisdictions where tax capacity remains below the average. This implies that if a recipient government raises one of its taxes, this will lower the respective tax base, which will be made up for (at least partially) by the equalization entitlements (Hayashi and Boadway, 2000).

In this regard, Buchanan (1950) considered the *fiscal residuum* (net fiscal benefit, NFB) as the basic driving force for horizontal equalization. To define this fiscal residuum, which can be negative or positive (implying respectively positive and negative transfers), one should not consider the tax treatment alone. The balance between the contributions made and the value of public services returned to the individual should be the relevant figure (Buchanan, 1950, p. 352).[54,55]

Indeed, most equalization transfer systems in OECD countries rely on the referred notion of NFB, defined as imputed benefits from public spending minus tax burden (Shah, 2006, 2012). On these grounds, the two main equalization criteria are *fiscal capacity* and *expenditure needs*.

The former can be measured either by using macroeconomic indicators (e.g. state gross domestic product, state personal income, etc.) or through a representative tax system (measuring the fiscal capacity of a state by the revenue that could be raised if the government employed all the standard sources at the average intensity of use nationwide) (Shah, 2006).

In turn, *expenditure needs* can result from: (i) *ad hoc* determination (simple measures of expenditure needs and their respective weight are arbitrarily determined);[56] or (ii) the representative expenditure system (similar to the tax representative system for the expenditure side, using direct imputation methods or a standardized cost approach) (see Shah, 2012, for more details).

c) Borrowing (debt); coping with soft budget constraints   The last, should I say residual, source of sub-central financing is *state or local borrowing*. The topic was not given the same attention under the first initial normative approaches but has regained importance in the last two decades under the influence of the Political Economy approach (Cabral, 2016). Decentralization

---

54 However, if such grants are made to cope with state/regional equity problems, there is no clear evidence that they can also ensure 'interpersonal income equalization' (that the poorest individuals of all regions will become less poor). Sepulveda and Martinez-Vasques (2010) and Stossberg *et al.* (2016) investigated the role of fiscal decentralization regarding increase in income inequality.

55 The 'other-way-around' question is whether the current tax-transfer system (social insurance plus social assistance minus taxes paid) aiming to ensure inequality reduction at the individual level will also cause inequality reduction at the regional level (see Betson and Haveman, 1984).

56 Used in many general-purpose transfers: population size, population density, age, gender, unemployment, mortality, rural costs, elderly living alone, etc.

was previously criticized due to the fact that it could either prevent fiscal discipline (Tanzi, 1996) or result in bad governance, corruption and rent seeking (Prud'Homme, 1995). Both criticisms are affiliated with Public Choice's Leviathan model and were a starting point for economic studies that related: (i) on the one hand, decentralization to the common pool problem and pork barrel politics; (ii) on the other hand, sub-central borrowing with soft budget constraints and bailout.

In this latter vein, Wildasin (1997), Eichengreen (1997) and Rodden (2006) identify the main factors that can explain the softening of budget constraints and a weak commitment from the central government in not bailing out sub-central governments in the event of debt default or bankruptcy. Rodden (2006) develops a 'bailout game' based on Alexander Hamilton's paradox,[57] in which this American statesman of the late eighteenth century lays side by side the promises and the perils of federalism.

The first factor determinant of the weak commitment for SCG bailout is economic in nature and is mostly related to the size of negative externalities driven from an SCG bankruptcy (the costs imposed on the centre) – e.g. reputational costs, economic, military and political sanctions, future access to funding, sovereign risk premia increase and investor reluctance. The higher the externalities, the higher the likelihood of a bailout. The size and dimension of such externalities are, in turn, also related to the size of jurisdictions: bailouts are less likely when jurisdictions are small, whereas large jurisdictions benefit from the so called 'too-big-to-fail effect,' and for this reason the likelihood of a bailout is higher.

The second factor is political and partisan in nature, because the bailout is more likely when SCGs have strong political representation in the central chamber(s) or if the same political party supports both the central government and the SCG requiring the bailout.

Finally, there is also a strict financial factor. As noted by Rodden (2006, p. 75), "perceptions of the center's commitment not to intervene in subnational financial crises are shaped in large part by the intergovernmental fiscal system of taxes, revenue shares and transfers." When SCGs rely heavily on grants, loans and revenue-sharing mechanisms as opposed to own taxes and fees, the central government's *ex ante* commitment to a policy of no bailouts lacks credibility (*Idem*, p. 75). In such a case, the provision of collective goods, the centre becomes responsible for the provision of purely local goods or responsible for the provision of goods that are perceived as national entitlements, such as health care and education, even when current expenditure is in the hands of SCGs. Moreover, due to the so-called 'common pool' problem (which in fact is a case of fiscal illusion), there is a break in the link between the revenue side and the expenditure side (that does not happen under a strict local taxation model), ultimately creating

---

57 Hamilton (1778).

an appearance that local expenditures are funded by non-residents (*Idem*, p. 77). Consequently, concludes Rodden (2006, p. 78), "when the central government is responsible for providing a large and growing share of local budgets, in the event of a local financial crisis, the eyes of voters and creditors will quickly turn to the central rather to than to the local government for a resolution."[58]

Indeed, as noted by the IMF (2009, p. 8), the effectiveness of fiscal decentralization can be hindered by two main causes. Firstly, local policymakers fail to internalize the full cost of local spending when they are financed through grants or revenue sharing that are funded by taxpayers of other jurisdictions (the *common pool* problem). Secondly, local politicians may expect the central government to bail them out in the case of need, thus undermining their incentives to behave in a responsible manner (*soft budget constraints*).

If it is a fact that a heavy reliance on intergovernmental transfers, as a way of coping with the vertical fiscal gap, can foster a weak commitment from the centre to bailout a SCG, also true is that the enhancement of tax autonomy and tax decentralization does not in itself ensure either the strengthening of the commitment for non-bailout, or even a hardening of the budget constraints. On the contrary, in certain cases, fiscal discipline imposed by the centre is easier when the centre maintains some control over SCG financing sources – hard budget constraints imposed at the central level are the counterpart for the heavy reliance of SCGs on transfers coming from the centre. In fact, as noted by Pisauro (2001, p. 15), "a bailout is precisely a backdoor to the common pool of tax resources. If it is not possible to keep that backdoor locked, the central government by allowing some access through the front door (financing part of local expenditures through grants) can better control the deployment of the pool and avoid the more disruptive access through the back door." The IMF (2009, p. 10) also recognizes that the more decentralized spending and taxing decisions are, the more difficult it is for the central government to ensure compliance with fiscal targets for the general government as a whole.

In any case, a high degree of SCG expenditure autonomy associated with variable degrees of tax autonomy and/or reliance of intergovernmental transfers has, since the late 1990s, been constructed as the main source of fiscal concern and eventually identified as one of the main perils concerning the functioning of governmental structures. Based on the Political Economy approach, an important strand of literature was then produced. Under the auspices of the IMF, the World Bank and the OECD, the need to harden budget constraints, notably through the imposition of fiscal rules, became 'fashionable'.[59] It should be noted, in turn, that in the EMU this new pub-

---

58 See also, in this regard, Governatori and Yim (2012).
59 A rules-based approach is indeed an alternative approach to other ways to address the problem of soft budget constraints, such as: (i) market-based approach (market discipline);

lic finance framework based on fiscal rules coincided with the launching, within the second stage of the EMU, of the SGP (in 1997) that enforced quantitative rules for member states' deficits and debt (see Philip, 2002; Begg and Schelkle, 2004; Tanzi, 2005).[60]

Fiscal rules were then defined as a permanent constraint on fiscal policy, expressed in terms of a summary indicator of fiscal performance, such as the government budget deficit, borrowing, debt or a major component thereof (Kopits and Symansky, 1998).[61, 62] Their basic purpose, as noted by Kopits (2001), is to confer credibility on the conduct of macroeconomic policies by removing discretionary intervention. In particular, as also noted, the usefulness of a well-designed set of fiscal rules, preventing deficit bias, consists of establishing a depoliticized framework for fiscal policy – in a similar vein, an inflation targeting (rule) goes for monetary policy (Kopits, 2001).

In fact, the fiscal rules approach corresponds to a new philosophical perception regarding government action (the Leviathan uncrowns the Benevolent government) and involves, to a certain extent, the replacement of a democratic-based legitimacy by a new independent technocratic landscape aiming to limit government action. The need for such limitation is based on the alleged opportunistic management of the political decision process necessarily causing fiscal profligacy.

Fiscal rules are meant to be applied both at the central (national) and subcentral levels. At the national level, Kopits (2001) considers that the basic purpose is to reduce public debt and to keep it at a prudent level. As for the respective institutional design, fiscal rules should be: (i) simple (the indicator even if fixed for the medium term should be ability to control on a budgetary basis; (ii) flexible (e.g. a cyclically adjusted balance rule allows for some anti-cyclical flexibility – budget deficits in downturns and surpluses in good times); (iii) growth-oriented (tolerance vis-à-vis investment expenditure or growth-oriented expenditure).

In turn, at the sub-central level (state, regional or local), the basic argument is to prevent moral hazard that might arise among SCGs if they incurred fiscal imbalances with repercussions on the borrowing costs at the central level (Kopits, 2001).

As noted by the IMF (2009), fiscal rules can be procedural or numerical in nature. Procedural rules aim to enhance transparency, accountability and fiscal management. Numerical rules, in turn, refer to quantitative targets,

---

(ii) cooperative approach; and (iii) administrative controls approach (Ter-Minassian and Craig, 1997).

60 I will come back to this issue later on.

61 Ter-Minassian (2006), in turn, distinguishes between procedural and quantitative fiscal rules, the latter aiming to set quantitative limits or ceilings to the main budgetary variables – e.g. budget deficit, debt, expenditure or revenue.

62 For a broad picture of fiscal rules, see Martins (2014).

hence intending to impose permanent constraints on fiscal policy. Such rules can help to reduce expenditure bias and to avoid time-inconsistency problems (IMF, 2009). Nevertheless, fiscal rules can involve policy inflexibility and foster, for this very reason, creative accounting practices in order to circumvent their applicability.

Hence, the design of fiscal rules for SCGs should be marked by simplicity and flexibility, and above all should be able to prevent pro-cyclicality, that is, the hardening of the quantitative limits in bad times and the softening on good days. Ultimately, fiscal rules should ensure the carrying out of fiscal policy in line with the business cycle, implying either the creation of implicit fiscal reserves (e.g. by obtaining fiscal surpluses) or of explicit reserves (e.g. 'rainy-day funds') in moments of expansion aiming to create fiscal space for moments of economic downturn.[63]

On the other hand, *ex ante* borrowing regulation should be complemented by *ex post* insolvency mechanisms: these two elements combined should indeed constitute the overall 'hard-budget constraint framework'. As noted by Liu and Waibel (2008, p. 222) a well-designed insolvency mechanism helps enforce the commitment device and hard budget constraints at the local level. At the same time, insolvency procedures help subnational governments to maintain essential services while restructuring their debts. This latter aspect is indeed crucial. Unlike that which happens in the case of a private company bankruptcy, where the insolvency mechanism is an asset liquidation type, in the case of insolvent (subnational) governments, the mechanism is generally of a reorganization type (Liu and Waibel, 2008, p. 226). In fact, in this case, debt restructuring lies at the heart of any insolvency framework (*Idem*, p. 229).[64]

4.1.3.3. Initial attempts to transpose the Fiscal Federalism framework to European integration

The first attempts to transpose the basic principles of Fiscal Federalism to the European Community (EC) date back to the 1970s.

This ambition was first found in the *Marjolin Report* (Marjolin *et al.*, 1975). This report was very much conditioned by the effects of the preceding oil crises and focused on how to solve their damaging economic effects,

---

63 See, in this regard, Ter-Minassian and Craig (1997), Joumard and Konsgrud (2003), Sutherland *et al.* (2005), Ahmad *et al.* (2006), Ter-Minassian (2006), Vigneault (2007), Liu and Waibel (2008), IMF (2009), and Governatori and Yim (2012).

64 Later on, I will analyse the fact that in the E(M)U there does not exist any kind of *ex post* insolvency mechanism adequately established to ensure a 'smooth bankruptcy' of member states, enabling them to ensure provision of services while restructuring their debts. I will furthermore detail the differences between private and government debts as they can justify different resolution/restructuring mechanisms, and *ex ante* insurance approaches as well.

notably an increased in unemployment, inflation taking off and external imbalances affecting several European countries.

Interestingly enough, the report suggests, on the one hand, the creation of an Exchange Rate Stabilization Fund (aiming to prevent exchange rate over-fluctuation pushed by massive capital in or outflows) and, on the other hand, the institution of a Joint Loan Authority.

Anticipating the future creation of a 'European unit of account', the report identified the main steps towards an economic and monetary union. The conditions for such a union were assumed to be the following (Marjolin et al., 1975, p. 27): (i) large parts of the population having a feeling of belonging to the union; (ii) the existence of a decision-making centre in which the three classic powers – legislative, executive and judiciary – are represented; (iii) The centralization of monetary policy in a single central bank; (iv) free movement of goods, services, workers and capital; (v) Central authorities with relatively important budgets (by then, 13% in the case of Germany, 16%–18% in the case of Canada); (vi) centralized tax and social security systems, (vii) a very high degree of openness of economies involved; (viii) the ownership of capital on enterprise is widely distributed throughout the Union's territory.

Bearing this in mind, Marjolin et al. (1975) suggested that at the end of the process the Community's budget should be able to fulfil the three conventional 'Musgravian' functions, i.e. the allocation function, the stabilization policy and the redistributive policy. Moreover, in order to achieve these goals, "it should seem particularly helpful to complete the Community's taxation powers forthwith by a borrowing power" (p. 33).

Finally, as an ultimate mechanism of redressing fiscal imbalances, the report suggests the institution of a 'Community Unemployment Benefit Fund' (Marjolin et al., 1975, pp. 34–35) anticipating in a rather innovative way the debate, currently going on, about the institution of an unemployment benefit scheme managed at the E(M)U central level (to be detailed in what follows).

Immediately after this, a group of experts – led by Sir Donald MacDougall – was appointed to study the role of public finance in European integration. The study gave rise to the so-called *MacDougall Report* (MacDougall et al., 1977). In hindsight, one can now acknowledge how *avant-garde* the report was in the anticipation of specific drawbacks along with the measures and steps that should be taken in order to enhance Fiscal Federalism in Europe.[65] One of the most important alerts made then was that a fiscal federation was a pre-condition that would facilitate the creation of a monetary union (MacDougall et al., 1977, p. 21). The report indeed, departing from the so-called *status quo*, envisaged three alternatives for future evolution: (i) pre-federal

---

65 See also in this regard Denton (1977).

integration; (ii) federation with a small public sector at the Community level; (iii) federation with a large public sector at the Community level.

The difference between these two last, 'federalist' options was that in the former (small public sector), the supply of social and welfare services would essentially remain at the national level (with equalizing transfers between them), while in the latter (large public sector), major social and welfare functions (e.g. social security) would be assigned to the higher level. Correspondingly, in the small public sector version, a central expenditure amounting to 5%–7% would suffice (respectively, for the case without and with defence expenditure at the central level), whereas the large public sector version would bring public expenditure to levels between 20% and 25% (as in existing federations, e.g. the U.S.). Additionally, in this latter solution, there would be a predominance of federal over state taxes, and intergovernmental transfers (grants) would play both an equalizing and stabilizing role.

A few years later, the *Padoa-Schioppa Report* (Padoa-Schioppa *et al.*, 1987), also relying in 'Musgravian' fiscal functions, managed to identify the major developments (achieved and to be achieved in the near future) at the Community level as the following: (i) the resource allocation function was recognized to be dependent on the completion of the European internal market; (ii) the stabilization function was mostly related to the steps related to the implementation of the Economic and Monetary Union (further on to be detailed in the Delors Report[66] and the *One Market, One Money Report*[67]), notably the enhancement of capital mobility and the development of the European Monetary System; (iii) finally, with respect to the redistribution function, the report mostly highlights the regional dimension and the need to reform structural funds, which in turn should mainly concentrate on the following problems: backward regions, declining industrial regions, long term-unemployment, employment of young people and agricultural and rural development.

As can be seen, a political evolution took place in the period between the adoption of the Marjolin and MacDougall Reports (Marjolin *et al.*, 1975; MacDougall *et al.*, 1977) and that of the adoption of the Padoa-Schioppa (1987) Report. A shift from centralization towards decentralization meaning at the same time a shift from governmental to market-driven solutions had occurred by then. It should be recalled that the Padoa-Schioppa Report was coincident with the implementation of the Single European Act and the corresponding creation of the single market. The basic prospects of Fiscal Federalism, which after all would imply the centralization of the decision-making process notably for purposes of macroeconomic stabilization, would then be effectively abandoned.

66 Delors (1989).
67 Emerson *et al.* (1990).

What is more, the proposals regarding the creation of a fiscal union at the European level lost significance as the EMU took the first steps in its existence (that is, since 1992 onwards). Stage 1 and (especially) stage 2 involved, in general terms, a successful convergence of candidate countries with respect to the main nominal variables (inflation rates, interest rates, exchange rates and public finance variables). After the adoption of the euro (in stage 3), the enthusiasm involving its institutional architecture and future outcomes took root. In particular, the optimism contained in the aforementioned *One Market, One Money Report* seemed to have been achieved: the EMU, relying on the smooth functioning of the internal market and of the single currency, would be able to foster trade integration, business cycle synchronization and economic convergence.

4.1.3.4. General and specific limitations in the transposition of the main prescriptions of Fiscal Federalism

The resurgence of the 'issue' of Fiscal Federalism has come with the crisis and with the subsequent debate about reform of the EMU.[68] This is most likely the main political and medial agenda for the next months/years to come.

The resistance involving the deepening of the central budget is strong and seems to prevent any chance of evolving to a federal-type budget; it seems clear that the euro crisis reopened the debate about whether the EU could evolve into a 'classic' Fiscal Federalism model (Hinajeros, 2014, p. 19). So far this has been an academic debate, with no relevant connection with reality, firstly and foremost since as noted by Begg (2009, p. 9), "there is simply too big a gap between the political realities of the EU and the sort of fiscal constitution that would emerge if the models were even partly applied." Indeed, even though Fiscal Federalism is not equal to political federalism, which means that the EU is not obliged to transform itself into a federation, it still requires some kind of political support. This is the main reason why for the EU, it is so difficult to admit that the prescriptions of Fiscal Federalism, in their classic form, can ever be a reality.

The obstacles for the transposition of the theoretical prescriptions of Fiscal Federalism to the E(M)U were identified by Cabral (2016). I wish now to develop these obstacles. For this purpose, I will maintain the distinction made then (Cabral, 2016) between 'general' and 'specific' limitations, the former referring to political and institutional obstacles related to the nature and design not only of the EMU but of the EU itself, and the latter concerning the difficulties on the transposition of economic (normative) criteria

---

68 Further on, I will analyse the most significant 'roadmaps' for E(M)U reform, starting with the so-called *Four Presidents' Report* (Van Rompuy *et al.*, 2012).

traced by Fiscal Federalism theory with respect both to functions and revenue (tax) assignment.

4.1.3.4.1. GENERAL LIMITATIONS: E(M)U AMBIGUITIES

a) E(M)U ontological ambiguities The crisis has highlighted the flaws of the euro but also the flaws, or at least the ambiguities, of the European Union itself. Throughout the integration process much has been discussed about the legal nature of the EU (as had been before about the EC). In many of the analyses it is acknowledged that the EU is a 'novel hybrid' (McNamara, 2015, p. 39), swinging between a federation and an intergovernmental organization, pulled either by centrifugal or by centripetal forces.[69]

Moreover, it can be said that the EU is the product of a combination of intergovernmental, domestic, (neo)functionalist and 'expertocratic' approaches (see Heipertz and Verdun, 2010).[70] Such combination has, in turn, favoured a process of integration pulled by Monet's curse ("Europe will be forged by crisis") (Schelkle, 2017, pp. 41–42) and by a bipolar response to the crises that alternates catastrophism with a simplistic voluntarism, an over-optimistic attitude, for which those crises will be, at the end of the day, solved with 'more Europe' (Majone, 2014, p. 69). Reigning in this domain is the so-called 'bicycle theory' of European integration, according to which integration must be kept moving forward, especially in a crisis, for the bicycle (the EMU) not to fall (Majone, *Idem*, p. 59).

---

69 For a broad picture of the tension between centrifugal and centripetal forces throughout the integration process, and in particular since the recent crisis, see Cunha (2009, 2013, 2019). See also Burgess (2000), for an analysis of the federal features in the building process of Europe until the EU. See, on this same issue, Fossum and Jachtenfuchs (eds.) (2018).

70 *Liberal intergovernmentalism*, mostly due to the analysis of Andrew Moravcsik in the 1990s, "argues that national preferences are shaped by the economic interests of powerful domestic groups in a situation of international interdependence; substantive agreements reflect the constellation of national preferences and bargaining power; and the design of international institutions is a function of the kind and size of co-operation problems they are supposed to manage" (Schimmelfennig, 2015, p. 178). *Neofunctionalism* expects integration to occur when domestic actors can no longer solve a particular policy problem at the domestic level, and they then have to turn to the European level (Heipertz and Verdun, 2010, p. 9). As noted in turn by Schimmelfennig (2014), "what unites the different versions of neofunctionalism is the idea of a dynamic and progressive integration process that transcends its intergovernmental origins as a result of endogenous interdependencies, spillovers, and path-dependencies." Finally, construction of the EU and in particular the EMU has been also shaped by an *expertocratic approach*. This approach stresses the importance of a paradigm (as we will see, the 'stability paradigm') as a way to conduct economic policy. The actor experts try to shape functionalist logic to comply with their paradigm – an example is that the need for 'structural reforms' is relabelled as a functional consequence of monetary integration (Heipertz and Verdun, 2010, p. 105).

The EMU is a 'club of clubs' (Majone, 2014, p. 321) driven by national preferences (a different preference constellation)[71] that has in one way or another forged, over the years, a sense of 'common interest'. By attaining this level of the integration process, reversal seems no longer possible – an idea of *fait accompli* as mentioned by Majone (2014, p. 58). The euro crisis has once again exhibited the features of this theory. Despite the moments of enormous political stress experienced in this period (of which the tension with the Greek government in 2015 was shown to be the worst) in the end, on balance, "the common interest of preserving the Euro and the Eurozone was paramount to the different preferences of highly solvent and highly indebted member states. And the costs of preserving and fixing the Eurozone were preferable to the risks of shrinking or even dissolving it. This common interest changed the structure of intergovernmental bargaining and bargaining power" (Schimmelfennig, 2014, p. 12). Indeed, as noted by the same author (*Idem*, p. 12), returning to the *status quo ante* was no longer an option.

> First, the euro contains considerable 'sunk costs' for states, firms, and citizens resulting from introducing a new currency and adapting to a new monetary regime. Second, monetary union strengthened transnational capital movement and interlocking among financial services in the Eurozone. Monetary union thus created additional, endogenous interdependence, which increases the incentives to preserve the Eurozone. Third, the institutional hurdles are high: there's no orderly exit procedure for the Eurozone unless a country leaves the EU altogether. Finally, and most importantly, all members of the Eurozone were highly uncertain and risk-sensitive about a breakup of the Eurozone.

The bargaining scenario thus evolved throughout the crisis – extreme, antagonistic positions were to be resolved in a cooperative manner with a 'bailing-out outcome conditioned to commitment': firstly, the political agreement on financial assistance to Greece (the first bailout programmes); secondly, threats of a forced 'Grexit' and refusal of solidarity (e.g. permanent and/or unconditional transfers); thirdly, agreement on extended bailout mechanisms (e.g. the European Stability Mechanism and the 'lender-of-last-resort

---

71 Bento (2013) highlights that the creation of the EMU was based on different preferences regarding inflation. On one side, there was the group of countries that were totally inflation averse (the Netherlands, some Eastern countries and first and foremost Germany, still guided by the historical remembrance of the hyperinflation period in the aftermath of the First World War). On the other side, a group of countries (France and mostly southern countries) emerged showing inflation tolerance. These different social preferences correspond to two irreconcilable monetary regimes: on the one hand, an inflationary regime leading to a weak currency ('the weak euro'); on the other hand, a monetary regime price-stability oriented and conducive to a strong currency ('the strong euro') (Bento, 2013, p. 33).

function' of the ECB), as long as assisted countries were committed with a principle of fiscal discipline (under new stringent rules of the SGP and the 'Fiscal Compact'). Ultimately, even highly indebted countries resigned to honour their 'constrained' commitments and to reform their public finances and economy in order to be a legitimate part of the monetary union (Bongardt and Torres, 2017, p. 25). In the end, the sense of 'reforms' ownership seems to have prevailed (Bongardt and Torres, *Idem*, p. 24).[72]

Another interesting element of the process under this logic of collective action is that governing a commons in the EMU case[73] has made problems resolution a by-product of private incentives (and not necessarily a product of 'well-designed' responses at the governmental level), and with risk sharing emerging only by accident or default (Schelkle, 2017, pp. 40–41). In fact, the most effective risk-sharing solutions did/do not need to be directly designed as such. Instead they are a product of 'natural' forces led by self-interest and even (in some cases) by hegemonic power (from EMU's leading countries). The most significant example is the case of the EMU's payment system (TARGET 2), which was not designed to be a risk-sharing mechanism but which during the crisis ended up by accidently absorbing the risk of a 'sudden stop' of capital flows and the flight of deposits (*Idem*, p. 41).[74]

Note, in turn, that throughout the crisis, "governments have learned to contain the constraining dissensus by isolating crisis management from politicization" (Schimmelfennig, 2014, p. 15). This has been carried out, according to the same author, through three types of escapes: euro-compatible coalition formation, avoidance of referendums, and supranational delegation (*Idem*, p. 17).

It should be highlighted, on the other hand, that this last type of escape – supranational delegation – is strictly connected to the EU's ontological ambiguity. In fact, such ambiguity runs through several domains of the political decision-making process, and notably with respect to two main aspects: firstly, the division of political power amongst the main institutions of the EU and the way this power is exerted; secondly, and as a consequence, the kind of law these institutions enact.

With respect to the former aspect (the way power is exerted), recall that the EU political system is atypical. The EU is indeed a barely drawn and traced outline of conventional democratic regimes in contemporaneous developed countries. The European Parliament (EP) does not represent (a non-existent) European people in the same sense in which a national parliament represents an historically defined *demos*, and thus cannot represent a generalized European interest which should be much more than the sum of

---

72 See also, on the institutional impact of the crisis, De Streel (2014) and Soares (2016).
73 An expression used by Schelkle (2017), and imported from the seminal book of Elinor Ostrom (1990) to explain how the EMU (a common good) can be maintained.
74 I will come back to this issue further on.

national interests (Majone, 2014, pp. 55–56). Furthermore, legislative procedures are complex and bicephalous as they usually involve two branches of the legislative authority – the EP and the Council of the European Communities – and where the proponent institution and also the executive body of the EU – the European Commission – unlike national governments is not sustained by democratic legitimacy.

Another relevant feature is the creation, out of the political spectrum, of independent institutions, whose mandates and design make them quasi-European institutions receiving important competences through a process of delegation of powers, and yet totally spared from mechanisms of political checks and balances that exist at the national level. The case of the ECB is that referred to the most. As noted by Majone (2014, p. 173), unlike the U.S. Federal Reserve, which is placed within a political structure where the Congress, the President and the Treasury supply all the necessary political counterweights, the ECB is free to operate in a 'political vacuum', without a European government to balance its powers.

The other relevant example is the European Stability Mechanism (ESM), the institutive Treaty signed in 2012 (see Article 3, referring the main objectives of the ESM). Note that due to its institutive act (not an EU legal act, but rather an Intergovernmental Treaty) and the design of the ESM, one can say this is an intergovernmental institutional that functions parallel to the E(M)U institutional framework (Dimopoulos, 2014, p. 44). For these reasons, Bardutzky and Fahey (2014, pp. 346–347) consider the ESM Treaty (besides the TSCG) as an example of 'legal postnationalism', which in turn can be identified by the proliferation of new forms of law and politics, interactions between legal orders and the creation of political disordering.

In particular, the decision-making powers of the ESM are awarded to new intergovernmental bodies (the Board of Governors and the Board of Directors), while decision-making is dependent on the capital contributions of the signatories, thus distinguishing itself from the governance rules that exist under EU Treaties (*Idem*, p. 44).

And yet euro-area countries[75] felt the need to merge this 'special agreement' in the EU institutional framework starting with the precocious amendment, in 2011,[76] of Article 136 of the TFEU, by adding a new paragraph[77] that conveyed a basis for the EU to legally legitimize this new mechanism.

---

75 Note, on the other hand, that the ESM Treaty was also signed by non-EMU countries, for example, the UK.

76 European Council Decision 2011/199/EU, of 25 March 2011.

77 The new paragraph 3 states the following: "The Member States whose currency is the euro may establish a stability mechanism to be activated if indispensable to safeguard the stability of the euro area as a whole. The granting of any required financial assistance under the mechanism will be made subject to strict conditionality."

Moreover, the ESM has borrowed the EU institutions – notably the Commission – for certain tasks, notably for carrying out, implementing and monitoring the decisions adopted by the ESM Boards (Dimopoulos, 2014, p. 44).

The last case of supranational delegation has occurred in informal bodies that on the basis of functional and 'expertocratic' justifications (e.g. to manage better the crisis) have gained influence and power. Moreover, although lacking direct democratic legitimacy, these bodies rely on a new form of technocratic and pragmatic legitimacy. At the same time, as being subject to the oversight of other legitimate institutions, they also benefit from a 'mediated legitimacy' (Lindseth, 2014, p. 383). This is so, first and foremost, with the Eurogroup. This is a non-formal intergovernmental institution that has, over the years, gained decisional powers within the multilateral SGP surveillance procedure, in particular in the so-called 'European semester' that was eventually acknowledged by the EU law (e.g. the changes introduced to the SGP by the 'Six Pack' and the 'Two Pack').

The E(M)U has indeed been a trial balloon for testing new sources of legal production, out of the conventional legislative and regulatory mode and marked by the predominance of a 'modern administrative governance' that combines delegation of competences with fragmentation and functional diffusion of regulatory power (Lindseth, 2014, p. 382).

In a nutshell, the EU can be viewed as (i) a novel hybrid – an association of sovereign states, somewhere in between a sovereign country and an intergovernmental organization, (ii) that imperfectly replicates a democratic regime, (iii) that has undertaken supranational delegation not only in conventional EU institutions but in new atypical ones (formal and informal EU institutions or bodies out of the conventional spectrum) and (iv) that has forged an exotic legal system over the years juxtaposing with EU law new sources of non-EU law which are adopted or framed by the EU legal system, eventually merging with it.

b) General limitations in the transposition of Fiscal Federalism's prescriptions for the E(M)U scenario. The main general obstacles are hence those listed as follows.

Firstly, the E(M)U is neither a politically embedded entity (recall McNamara, 2015) nor even culturally embedded. In a globalized world, elements of sovereignty remain, and they translate into a sense of fellowship. Note that on the bases of the theory of Fiscal Federalism, this sense of fellowship is a pre-condition for its prescriptions to be sustained. Indeed, even for highly decentralized countries where nationalist feelings are strong, there is always a *residuum* of partnership, i.e. the feeling of belonging to the same country – in short, an identity. This *residuum*, even if smaller, allows for mechanisms of solidarity that usually overcome the particular interests of each of the sub-central governments and overcome accounting details. Hence, mechanisms of risk sharing and equalization instruments are accepted even if at the expense of moral hazard. The E(M)U, not being a sovereign country, lacks a sense of cohesion, a common identity (Verdun, 2010), which, for example, explains taxpayer resistance, in normal times, to finance mechanisms of risk sharing at the cost of moral hazard.

In an interesting analysis, Trein (2017) points out that despite similarities with federations, the E(M)U exhibits more contrasting elements. An important feature of federation occurs in times of stress or economic crisis: these occasions result in the opportunistic behaviour of the member states of the federation that seek to defend their interests against other member states and the federal government; to circumvent this, the central government puts policy responses to the crisis into motion which entail a temporary centralization of discretion at the federal level; in the end, this centralization of discretion and stabilizing institutions avoids opportunistic interests of member states and tendencies to overturn solidarity turned into systemic conflicts in the federation. In contrast, the same author (Trein, 2017) notes that the E(M)U did not provide institutional mechanisms to cope with member state opportunism, and it lacked the policy capacity to counteract asymmetric effects of the euro crisis. As a consequence, the E(M)U experienced 'strong desolidarization', which resulted in a political crisis regarding European integration.

For these reasons, risk-sharing mechanisms are forged only by accident, notably when facing the abyss and the fear of major losses is acknowledged. In fact, the E(M)U is moved by crisis and by a natural, self-interest instinct for survival – member countries which act as risk averse are those which value the losses of an uncontrolled disintegration caused by insufficient 'solidarity' more when it is needed.

The second general obstacle, the fact that the EU is not an all-purpose organization (Cabral, 2016) should also be noted, because it has mostly been assigned powers related to economic policies (either as exclusive, or concurrent powers with member states). Since the Maastricht Treaty (1992), there has been a considerable rise in the EU's political scope – most notably instituting the idea of European citizenship and including new powers in political areas (internal affairs and justice). Yet, despite that, the EU is not a universal supranational organization. Consequently, when it comes to identifying, on a normative basis, which collective goods should be allocated to the highest decision level (the EU level), the normative criteria fails to be applied simply because the EU has not been assigned any 'constitutional' powers regarding those issues (see for instance, the case of defence).

Thirdly, as noted before by Cabral (2016), in the EMU, the central level has the power to issue money but has no political sovereignty – a currency without a state (Cunha, 2000), whereas the member countries (the sub-central level) although sovereigns are deprived of money-issuing power – and this is also atypical in the light of Fiscal Federalism theory – creating difficulties notably when it comes to assigning stabilization functions.

Finally, it should be noted that the Fiscal Federalism theory works in a matching geographical scenario both for fiscal and monetary policies (the upper borders of both monetary and fiscal policies coincide and their scopes correspond to the overall national territory – the highest decision level). On the contrary, the European integration process has created a disjointed territory where monetary policy is mostly restricted to the Eurozone (managed by the ECB and the Eurosystem); while tax collection and expenditure commitments, whenever referred to the central level, correspond to a territory with a larger dimension, i.e. the EU territory. In fact, the European Community Budget refers to all EU countries, thus implying that resources and expenditures are owed from and assigned to the 28 EU member states. Notwithstanding this, even though revenues and expenditures are related to the EU overall budget, for macroeconomic stabilization purposes this budget is unsuitable, primarily due to its reduced dimension and also because it does not provide for specific fiscal policy devices to cope with macroeconomic imbalances. In fact, the EU budget was not made to accommodate any kind of fiscal policy.

Moreover, the only mechanisms with direct stabilization purposes have, in turn, a more limited territorial scope, corresponding not to the EU, but to the Eurozone, and in a more restricted manner. An example of this is precisely the ESM, the new European institution created to provide for financial assistance to needed countries. This entails that, unlike that which is expected to happen in the light of Fiscal Federalism's ideas, stabilization is not a role of the central (EU) budget but of an 'outsider' mechanism which has particular rules for financing, limited territorial scope and incomplete effectiveness.

c) EMU and the Political Economy of Fiscal Federalism: influence and limitations   This atypical nature of the E(M)U could be an argument for finding here the proper landscape for new Fiscal Federalism arrangements, firstly studied by the aforementioned second generation of Fiscal Federalism theory. As noted then, the Political Economy of Fiscal Federalism added new ways of conceiving territorial organization and relationships amongst layers of governments under the general idea of 'laboratory or menu federalism', the main expressions of which are: (i) horizontal and/or vertical competition, (ii) contractual arrangements, (iii) internal asymmetry and (iv) functional specialization.

However, most of these expressions fail to accomplish their outcomes in the E(M)U panorama. As such, as for *(horizontal) competition*, Breton (1996, pp. 275–276) explained that

> within the confines of Europe, there is no hegemonic power to monitor horizontal competition and to enforce the rules of competition;

in addition, the central bodies of the community are poorly equipped for these tasks. Unmonitored and the rules not enforced, competition is unstable. To prevent the occurrence of instability, competition is minimized through excessive harmonization of a substantial fraction of social, economic, and other policies. Harmonization is not complete, but if one compare the degree of harmonization with that in Canada, the United States, and other federations, one is impressed by the extent to which it is greater in Europe than in the federations.

However, as added in this regard by Majone (2014, p. 270), the fact is that excessive harmonization was not sufficient to ensure the stability of the EU. On the contrary, it was the cause of the present instability: monetary union is, after all, an extreme form of total harmonization. In contrast, all other approaches that could foster competition without implying more harmonization, although promising, failed to be seen as a real alternative. The author (Majone, 2014, pp. 270–271) refers the 'open method of coordination' (OMC) as an example: this method forged in the Lisbon European Council in 2000 implied non-binding objectives and guidelines, commonly agreed indicators, benchmarking and persuasion, aiming at inducing changes in social policies. Despite its promising features, it failed to meet the expectations for delivering further changes in those same policies through increasing competition between member states.

As for *contract federalism*, Spahn (2006, p. 189), when comparing the EU with the German federation, consider that the former exhibits more flexibility than the latter. This happens because the EU respects the principle of equivalence and the corporatist spirit of the *acquis* has in the EU case been supplemented by the *géométrie variable* or multispeed approach with contractual opting-in and opting-out provisions that add flexibility.

Once again, Majone (2014) challenges this view, stressing that legal centralism put private order into question, with the *acquis communautaire* becoming indisputably linked to the creation of the EMU, and competition was minimized through excessive harmonization. 'More Europe' has indeed suppressed initial elements of flexibility, and possible contractual schemes were replaced by more rigid, uniform and 'one-size-fits-all' decisions.

As for *asymmetric federalism*, Congleton (2006, p. 148) considers that in the EU, significant asymmetries exist within major policy areas where menu-like choices are possible. Moreover, some non-EU country (e.g. Norway) members of the European Economic Area were granted significant autonomy regarding fisheries, agriculture, indirect taxation, etc. Finally, there are exceptions in several areas from certain countries – starting with the opting-out clause regarding the single currency itself. Yet, the author acknowledges the EU has implemented a 'generality rule', according to which principles and law should be uniformly applicable to all members (Congleton, 2006, p. 148), a trend that has been reinforced over the years.

The basis for *functional integration* (Majone, 2014, p. 113) is the theory of clubs (Buchanan, 1965).[78] Indeed, as noted by Majone (2014, p. 318), this theory provides a good conceptual foundation for the functional (rather than territorial) approach to international governance. Recall in this regard the functional specialization principle underlying the 'FOCJ' model. This possibility has not yet been entirely explored within the E(M)U scenario. Majone (2014, p. 322) considers that in the context of a union with 28 (27!) members at different stages of economic development, preferences, geopolitical concerns and diverse policy priorities, the model for a future integration could rely precisely on a flexible model of functional integration, henceforth overcoming the traditional national state model.

4.1.3.4.2. SPECIFIC LIMITATIONS IN THE TRANSPOSITION TO THE EU OF FISCAL FEDERALISM PRESCRIPTIONS

Previously, I have referred to the general limitations that can be anticipated when Fiscal Federalism ideas are applied to the EU. These general limitations result from the *sui generis* institutional nature of the EU and translate its peculiar philosophic *leitmotiv* – a federal dream without a federal sentiment. Now, departing from the main topics of Fiscal Federalism, I shall attempt to identify how Fiscal Federalism prescriptions could be transposed to the EU, with attention being given to specific drawbacks.[79]

Nevertheless, certain features emphasized by the normative Fiscal Federalism theory have already been mastered by the EU, even if in a haphazard manner. With regards to the *macroeconomic stabilization function* (and related to monetary policy), the idea that responsibility should remain with the central government has already been accomplished in the EU as monetary policy is carried out by the ECB. However, my previous remark that the territory of the centralized monetary union is not the EU but a smaller area within the EU, i.e. the EMU, should be borne in mind.

Furthermore, within the framework of function assignment and in particular the *allocation function*, it can be established that the completion of the internal market is in line with Fiscal Federalism prescriptions. In fact, the creation of a level playing field in terms of competition, for the whole territory, is a way to prevent predatory competition or beggar-my-neighbour policies that might occur in the absence of common rules. It is also true that,

---

78 Public goods which are excludable but only partially rivalrous lie at the centre of this theory. The first disputed issue is the optimal size (dimension) and population of the club: optimality is given by the condition that, in equilibrium, the cost of admitting an additional member must equal the average cost of providing a public good (Casella and Frey, 1992, p. 642). Clubs with a higher number of members than the optimum suffer from congestion; clubs with fewer members than the optimum suffer from desertification. Both cases are sub-optimal.

79 See again, on this issue, Cabral (2016).

within the same internal market, the EU has evolved to centralize powers in areas characterized by externalities or economies of scale – for instance, the case of specific policies, such as R&D, transport and communications, and regulatory policies. The EU has also made progress in other areas and increased its powers with the assistance of the aforementioned normative insight of 'fiscal equivalence', which establishes that whenever the scope of the benefit corresponds to the central level, the provision of the goods should be centralized (this is the case, for example, with foreign aid and external affairs). Another observation is that the principle of subsidiarity – collective good should be provided by the low level(s) of government as they are closer to the population, unless it can be proven that the highest level can provide it more efficiently and effectively – also supports the aforementioned Fiscal Federalism prescription that, unless proven otherwise, the core of decentralization relies upon the allocation branch. Both social policies, like education and health, and cultural policies are examples of areas where there is a strong *rationale* for decentralization to member states (or to their respective regional or local governments) on the grounds of subsidiarity and fiscal equivalence.

Finally, concerning the *distribution function*, the EU already has financial instruments that exhibit interregional redistributive impact, albeit in a restrictive manner. That is the case, as we will see, for the Cohesion and Structural Funds.

However, the gaps between prescriptions of normative Fiscal Federalism and the EU reality are larger than the accomplishments. I will now identify those main gaps.

a) Functions assignment The most important divergence highlighted by economic literature is in relation to the stabilization branch. Unlike that which happens in most OECD countries (unitary or federal countries), the EU budget is not capable of ensuring the macroeconomic stabilization function since it is too small in comparison with national budgets. Begg (2012) explains that in most mature economies, the federal or central government performs this crucial role, partly through the action of automatic stabilizers which arise through the interaction of public expenditure and taxation – tending to offset any fall in demand – and partly through discretionary changes in public expenditures or tax rates. The EU budget does not fulfil this function because:

i)   The *EU budget is too small* as a proportion of the EU GDP, and so it is simply incapable of stabilizing the EU economy as a whole (Begg, 2012).

This characteristic of the EU budget, since its inception, has not seen much change from the initial (related to the EU's GDP) to the current dimension. Hence, as pointed out by De Grauwe (2014, p. 8), the EU's budget amounts to only 1% of EU GDP while national budgets typically absorb 40%–50% of GDP. Moreover, as stressed by Begg (2009, p. 11), in typical federal systems, the highest level of government is responsible for a sizeable proportion of public expenditure and taxation (the same happens *a fortiori* with unitary countries). Thus, in the U.S., it is in excess of 20% of GNI and the proportions in other major federations are of similar magnitude. Depending upon its significant magnitude, a central budget can usually provide for automatic transfers, thereby reducing the social costs of a monetary union (De Grauwe, 2014, p. 207).

ii) The *pattern of taxes and of expenditure of the EU budget is not sensitive to cyclical fluctuations* (Begg, 2012).

Note that the simple existence of a central budget – a system of collecting taxes and assigning expenditures – allows for stabilization mechanisms to operate whenever regional shocks occur. Uniquely enough, in a Fiscal Federalism system, stabilization can occur not necessarily in a direct and 'visible' manner through specific stabilization mechanisms (e.g. insurance instruments to share risks, cyclical grants to local or regional governments, a cyclical convergence facility), but also through inter-individual redistributive instruments (e.g. personal taxes and social benefits) provided by the central budget (recall that according to Musgrave's taxonomy, inter-individual redistribution is mostly a responsibility of the central government). Accordingly, as mentioned previously, the stabilization branch goes hand in hand with the redistribution branch.

As referred to in the *MacDougall Report* (MacDougall *et al.*, 1977, p. 36), clearly the personal income tax is a predominant instrument of progressive redistribution, and the main expenditure programmes and social security benefit schemes also have substantial redistributive effects. Due to these 'invisible' mechanisms, high incomes go with high tax payments, and low incomes go with high receipts of centrally provided services and transfer payments (*Idem*, p. 13). The stabilization effects related to this redistributive system are, thus, of two types: firstly, allowing for the correction of deficits in the balance of payments on current account of the poorer regions, through corresponding surpluses in the richer regions; and secondly, by cushioning short-term and cyclical fluctuations (a substantial part or a short-term loss of primary income in a region due to a fall in its external sales which may be automatically offset through lower payments of taxes and insurance contributions to the centre and higher receipts of unemployment and other benefits – *Idem*, p. 12).

In the case of the EU budget, the centre is deprived of important fiscal policy instruments, both on the tax and expenditure side, so it cannot properly manage the stabilization function. Moreover, on the tax revenue side (and as we will see further on) the existing EU own resources system was not designed to pursue any king of stabilizing role. In turn, with reference to the expenditure side, and due to the principle of subsidiarity (which in the EU legal framework is extended to its ultimate consequences), the EU is also deprived of a substantial part of social policy instruments (namely social security benefits that can work as automatic stabilizers) that could effectively contribute towards stabilization in the case of macroeconomic shocks. That is again true in the case of unemployment benefits, which exist as decentralized benefits in EU member states but on normative grounds should firstly act as a central device of macroeconomic stabilization. The principle of subsidiarity has in fact given strong support to decentralization in the EU, sometimes even in a heterodox and counterproductive way (Cabral, 2016).

iii) The Treaty requirement (Article 310 TFUE) to *balance the annual budget* means that the EU is not able to borrow (or run a surplus) as means of managing demand (Begg, 2012).

This strict balance rule is in turn related to the specific nature of the EU budgetary system wherein the annual budget is integrated in a 'Multiannual Financial Framework' (MFF).[80] Framing the annual budget in a medium-term document of expenditure planning and defining a top-down approach helps in achieving fiscal discipline and micro budgeting efficiency (allocation of resources to prior objectives during the programming period). Nonetheless, this also tends to curtail the capability of the annual budget to face short-term economic shocks. In fact, the rigid nature of expenditure headings set in the MFF hampers the EU's budget capability to respond to those shocks and obstruct any counter-cyclical policy (Tondl, 2000, p. 236), thereby, once again, jeopardizing the capability of the EU's budget of ensuring macroeconomic stabilization. Although this problem is not new, the changes in the EU Treaty, introduced by the Lisbon Treaty in 2009, have not changed the *status quo*.

b) Tax assignment   It can also be shown that most Fiscal Federalism prescriptions fail to apply. Departing from the aforementioned assignment rules developed by Musgrave (1983), it is obvious that the EU does not fulfil the criteria, or at least not with respect to all types of taxes. It is true that for indirect taxation, the current setup closely resembles a federal system (Cabral, 2016). In fact, unlike that which happens with direct taxation (personal income taxes), there is legal harmonization in the EU

---

80 The current package is MFF 2014–2020, which is mostly related to the implementation of the Lisbon Strategy and the achievement of the so-called 'Europe 2020' objectives. I will come back to this further on.

concerning Value-Added Tax (VAT), which is the main indirect tax collected in the member countries (tax harmonization is a good condition to sustain 'piggy-backing' amongst different levels of government), and a part of the VAT revenue is effectively assigned to the EU budget (corresponding to a uniform rate of 0.3% levied on the harmonized VAT base of each member state). Another relevant aspect is that the VAT harmonization and the respective 'piggy-backing' mechanism are also in accordance with normative Fiscal Federalism, in the sense that centralization in these kinds of general consumption taxes is a way to prevent distortions that can affect the functioning of the common market and induce beggar-my-neighbour policies (Cabral, 2016).

However, as noted by Cabral (2016) with VAT harmonization, the EU's resemblance to a federal tax system ends. Unlike that which happens with indirect taxation, personal income tax, with redistributive purposes, is not assigned to the central level and hence remains payable to the intermediate level (the member states). On the other hand, within the EU's own resource system, it can be affirmed that the GNI tax revenue (through which each member state transfers a standard percentage of its GNI to the EU) does not have the profile to become a central personal income tax.[81] Furthermore, the creation of tax-sharing or 'piggy-backing' mechanisms, which allows for the central government to share the same tax base with national governments and, based on that, to define some sort of progressive tax arrangement related to this kind of tax in the EU, does not seem plausible in the short to the medium term.

Lastly, in general terms, it can be said that despite the 2014 reform of the EU's own resources system, the criticisms made by Begg (2009, pp. 36–40) and Dullien and Schwarzer (2009, p. 163) remain pertinent: national contributions have a limited connection to fiscal federalism theories, not taking properly into account member states' wealth, and also face several distortions, as was always the case with the UK rebate.

c) Intergovernmental transfers (grants) The gaps between theoretical proposals and the reality of the E(M)U are also significant. As previously stated, grants serve two main purposes: to correct vertical fiscal imbalances that occur whenever there is a mismatch between revenue means and expenditure needs (translating into a shortfall suffered by the lower level of government); and to correct horizontal fiscal gaps, i.e. to promote internal cohesion and equalization.

Strangely enough, since the process of decentralization in the EU is a 'reverse-type' process fed by the subsidiarity principle, the resulting vertical fiscal imbalance suffered by the member states is a *natural state*, to the

---

81 I will come back to this point further on, when analysing the EU's own resource system.

extent that it cannot be corrected. Hence, the creation of general-purpose grants aiming to redress vertical fiscal imbalances is out of the question (Cabral, 2016).

On the contrary, the topic of (horizontal) fiscal equalization is not ignored and has gained importance with the euro crisis. The equalization objective is twofold – it has a short-term perspective where it serves as a fiscal instrument to ensure, at any moment, the correction of horizontal imbalances between regions or municipalities of the same country; and a long-term perspective, the theoretical origins of which are long-term growth theories and trade theories, where equalization is related to convergence purposes (referred to earlier). In fact, the EU's main interregional redistributive instruments – the Structural and Cohesion Fund – appear quite frequently in relation to convergence issues (see Bouvet, 2004; Martin, 2005; Shankar and Shah, 2009).A general conclusion that can be arrived at through these empirical studies is that while the Structural and Cohesion Funds initiated the process of convergence between countries, they were not so effective at ensuring convergence within the countries (see Martin, 2005, p. 86).

On the other hand, it should be highlighted that the existing Funds are not conceived of as typical equalization instruments, which can correct horizontal imbalances and cope with differential net fiscal benefits across states. This is the case primarily for the following reasons. Firstly, even though some of these Funds (this is the case with the Cohesion and European Regional Development Funds) have had low income states or regions as previous beneficiaries, they do not include in most cases redistributive formulas, typical of equalization transfers, based on fiscal capacity (e.g. macro indicators or the representative tax system) or expenditures needs (e.g. *ad hoc* criteria or the representative expenditure system). Secondly, these Funds are specific purpose grants (e.g. projects in specific areas, such as the environment, R&D, to support small and medium-sized enterprises, etc.), and not general non-conditional grants with a typical equalizing role. Thirdly, most of these grants are also matching grants which involve financial effort from both the donor's side and recipient's side, an effort that the latter is sometimes not in a position to make (Cabral, 2016).

Finally, it should be stressed that the current design of intergovernmental transfers in the EU is made to counteract typical problems that occur in these kinds of transfers, properly highlighted by the second generation of Fiscal Federalism theory, notably moral hazard issues, the common pool problem and pork barrel politics. However, this involves a trade-off: the loss of an unconditional equalization mechanism, solely based on fiscal capacity, that would "assure to poor, small and peripheral member states economic, welfare and public services standards not too far below those of the main body of the Community" (MacDougall *et al.*, 1977, p. 64).

4.2. Catalogue of proposals for the 'Great EMU's Reform': roadmaps or crossroads?

Table 4.5 contains the catalogue for the main roadmaps for EMU reform. I have differentiated the proposals by considering their main provenience: on the one side, institutional proposals, that is, proposals made directly by European institutions; on the other side, proposals as a by-product of academia and 'think-tanks'.[82]

The so-called *Four Presidents' Report* (Van Rompuy *et al.*, 2012) enclosing the seminal roadmap 'towards a genuine Economic and Monetary Union' set out the process for EMU reform, and that it should be based on three main stages:

Table 4.5 The catalogue for the main roadmaps for EMU reform

Institutional	Academia/think-tanks
i) *Four Presidents' Report* (Van Rompuy *et al.*, 2012, "Towards a Genuine Economic and Monetary Union")	i) *Report of the 'Tommaso Padoa-Schioppa Group'* (Enderlein *et al.*, 2012, "Completing the Euro – A Road Map towards Fiscal Union in Europe").
ii) *Five Presidents' Report* (Juncker *et al.*, 2015, "Completing Europe's Economic and Monetary Union")	ii) *Report under the auspices of the Jacques Delors Institute* (Enderlein *et al.*, 2016, "Repair and Prepare – Growth and the Euro after Brexit").
iii) *Dombrovskis and Moscovici Reflection Paper* (European Commission, 2017a, "Reflection Paper on the Deepening of the Economic and Monetary Union").	iii) *CEPR Reports* (Baldwin and Giavazzi (eds), 2016, How to Fix Europe's monetary union – Views of Leading Economists and Bénassy-Quéré and Giavazzi (eds.), 2017, Europe's Political Spring – Fixing the Eurozone and Beyond)
iv) President Juncker, *Roadmap for a More United, Stronger and More Democratic Union* (Juncker *et al.*, 2017)[1]	iv) *CEPS Task Force Report* (Hübner *et al.*, 2017, Regroup and Reform – Ideas for a More Responsive and Effective European Union)
	v) *French-German independent economists' proposals* (Bénassy-Quéré *et al.*, 2018, "Reconciling Risk Sharing with Market Discipline: A Constructive Approach to Euro Area Reform")

Source: The Author

[1] Information available at: https://ec.europa.eu/commission/sites/beta-political/files/roadmap-soteu-factsheet_en.pdf.

82 See also in this regard (with a detailed description of these and several other proposals for EMU reform) Cabral *et al.* (2017).

i) Stage 1 (End 2012–2013): aiming at ensuring the consolidation of public finances and breaking the link between sovereign and banking debts,
which would imply the following elements: a stronger framework for
fiscal governance; the launching of the Banking Union (BU); the setting up of the operational framework for direct bank recapitalization
through the ESM.

ii) Stage 2 (2013–2014): aiming at completing the integrated financial
framework and promoting sound structural policies.

iii) Stage 3 (post 2014): intending to improve EMU resilience through the
creation of a shock-absorption function at the central level.

Later on, in 2015, the *Five Presidents Report* (Juncker *et al.*, 2015) updated
the path to EMU reform. The report is even more ambitious in the sense
that it broadens the scope of reform to four main fronts (*Idem*, pp. 4–5):
firstly, towards a genuine *Economic Union* that ensures each economy
has the proper economic features to prosper within the monetary union;
secondly, towards a *Financial Union* that increases risk sharing with the
private sector (by completing both the BU and the CMU); thirdly, towards a
Fiscal Union that delivers both fiscal sustainability and fiscal stabilization;
fourthly, towards a *Political Union* that brings genuine democratic accountability, legitimacy and institutional strengthening to the EMU level.

The roadmap in this work has been laid out.

i) Stage 1 (July 2015–30 June 2017) is described as the stage 'deepening
by doing', that is, using the current legal framework to proceed with
immediate steps on these several areas, notably: *Economic Union*, a new
boost to convergence, jobs and growth (e.g. strengthening the Macroeconomic Imbalance Procedure and stronger coordination of economic
policies); *Financial Union*, the completion of the BU and by launching
the CMU; *Fiscal Union* – a new advisory European Fiscal Board; and
Political Union – revamping the European semester and strengthening
the control of the European Parliament over this Semester.

ii) Stage 2 (2017–2025) is called the stage of 'completing the EMU',
where changes in the EMU's economic and institutional architecture
are required and to ensure convergence towards commonly agreed
benchmarks.

iii) Stage 3 (from 2025 onwards) will be a genuine EMU with the conditions to be completed.

As regards the Five Presidents Report, the Vice-President of the Commission, Valdis Dombrovskis, and the Commissioner, Pierre Moscovici, released
the *Reflection Paper on the Deepening of the Economic and Monetary Union*
(European Commission, 2017a). The three key areas of action are then identified: firstly, competing a genuine Financial Union (including the completion

of the BU and of the CMU); secondly, achieving a more integrated Economic and Fiscal Union, notably through the implementation at the E(M)U level of a macroeconomic stabilization function;[83] thirdly, anchoring democratic accountability and strengthening euro-area institutions. Indeed, the commissioners propose a sequence of steps for each of these areas of progress, so that by 2025 a deepened EMU is formed.

Finally, after his State of the Union Speech in September 2017, President Juncker set up his "Roadmap for a More United, Stronger and More Democratic Union." This proposal covered the period of 2017–2019, whereby several initiatives regarding the EU and in particular the EMU were to be taken, notably in the following areas (see also Gros, 2017c): transformation of the ESM into a European Monetary Fund (EMF); creation of a dedicated euro area budget line within the EU budget; and creation of a European Minister of the Economy and Finance.

As for non-institutional reports, produced in an academic or 'think-tank' context, the so-called 'Tommaso Padoa-Schiopa Group' (Enderlein et al., 2012) started these off, proposing "Completing the Euro: A Road Map towards Fiscal Union in Europe." The authors (Enderlein et al., 2012, p. 5) envisaged achieving a sui generis form of fiscal federalism, "which derives from the functional deficiencies of the current common currency framework while respecting to the largest extent the budgetary autonomy of euro area member countries."

The report proposes (Enderlein et al., 2012, pp. 6–7) policy actions in the following four areas. In the first place, action is needed for the completion of the Single Market in order to allow the real exchange rate channel to work more effectively. Secondly, action is required for the implementation of a cyclical stabilization insurance fund to counter some of the effects of the 'one-size-fits-none' policy. In the third place, a rebalancing of the fiscal rights and fiscal duties in the EMU is advocated, under the core principle 'sovereignty ends when solvency ends'. However, at the same time, the euro area should ensure sovereign access to financing even in times of economic and fiscal stress. For this purpose, the creation of a European Debt Agency (EDA) is suggested that should allow the possibility of flexible financing to

---

83 In the *Reflection Paper*, three possible options for this stabilization function are assumed. (i) A *European Investment Protection Scheme* would protect investment in the event of a downturn by supporting well-identified priorities and already planned projects or activities at a national level, such as infrastructure or skills development; in the case of an economic downturn the protection scheme would ensure that projects be continued, and consequently firms and citizens could overcome the crisis more quickly and robustly. (ii) A *European Unemployment Reinsurance Scheme* would act as a reinsurance fund for national unemployment schemes; this scheme would provide more breathing space for national public finances and help to emerge from the crisis faster and stronger. (iii) A *rainy day fund* could accumulate funds on a regular basis; disbursements from the fund would be triggered on a discretionary basis to cushion a large shock (European Commission, 2017a, p. 26).

countries in exchange for a stepwise transfer of sovereignty.[84] Finally, the fourth area of intervention is the BU, required to solve the paradoxical setup of financial market integration and banking supervision, notably through the creation of a euro-area banking supervision authority.

Later on, in the aftermath of the euro crisis and after the Brexit decision, a group of these same researchers (to whom were joined others), now under the auspices of the Jacques Delors Institut, published the Report "Repair and Prepare – Growth and the Euro after Brexit" (Enderlein *et al.*, 2016). In this report (*Idem*, pp. 19 ff.), a 'three-pronged action plan' was suggested based on the following building blocks:

a) *A first aid kit for the EMU*, aiming at protecting the euro against a possible new crisis in the short to the medium term (e.g. transforming the ESM into an ESM+, with a €200 billion rapid-response facility; within the BU, introducing a mechanism able to create some risk sharing among national deposit insurance schemes and creating a fiscal backstop to the Single Resolution Fund).

b) *Reforms and investment for growth* (e.g. suitable structural reforms, for example in product and labour markets; a comprehensive public and private investment initiative).

c) *Risk sharing and sovereignty sharing* through the implementation of a full-fledged euro-area budget and better counter-cyclical stabilizers.

A similar contribution came from a group of CEPR researchers, whose research was divided into two stages. In stage 1, the purpose was to set an 'agreement on the crisis narrative' (e.g. the causes of the EZ crisis) (Baldwin *et al.*, 2015). Then, stage 2 meant to gather a consensus on 'how to fix Europe's monetary union' and 'rebooting Europe' (see the e-book of Baldwin and Giavazzi (eds.) (2016).[85] A similar CEPR e-book, from Bénassy-Quéré and Giavazzi (eds.) (2017) was eventually published in 2017.[86]

With a broader scope, through considering the effects of both the euro and the refugee crisis and therefore envisaging the entire EU, the CEPS Task Force in 2017 published the report "Regroup and Reform – Ideas for a More Responsive and Effective European Union" (Hübner, 2017), where recommendations are made with respect to two main areas: (i) euro-area

---

84 I will come back to this proposal later on.
85 See also Baldwin and Giavazzi (eds.) (2015a). See, for example, Eichengreen and Wyplosz (2016, pp. 36–43), who clarify the main conditions for the survival of the euro.
86 Several proposals were presented in both e-books, such as: (i) stabilization funds, either new ones (Bénassy-Quéré, 2016) or extending the profile of the ESM (De Grauwe and Ji, 2016b); (ii) stability bonds and the supervision of national debt policies (Tabellini, 2016) or an asset management company for the EZ (Beck, 2017); (iii) the completion of the BU under the reinsurance approach, e.g. a European Deposit Insurance System (EDIS) (Gros, 2016b, 2017b).

management – enhancing compliance of fiscal rules through an incentive-based enforcement mechanism, completing the BU through the creation of an insurance deposit scheme, creating the euro-area Finance Minister and a fiscal capacity;[87] and (ii) the social dimension of European economic policy – by multiplying investment (e.g. under the European Fund for Strategic Investments), improving social stabilizers (e.g. under the European Pillar of Social Rights) and recalibrating EU trade policy.

In a more recent contribution, a group of independent French-German economists (Bénassy-Quéré et al., 2018, p. 4), related to the CEPR, proposed a 'blueprint for reform' along three main axes: (a) *reform of the financial sector architecture* (private risk-sharing); (b) *reform of the fiscal architecture* (increasing national ownership of fiscal rules); c) *reform of the institutional architecture* (separating the role of the surveillance watchdog and political decision-maker by either creating an independent watchdog within the European Commission or moving this role outside the Commission).

As a final comment on all these proposals,[88] it can be said that despite their different provenience and theoretical background, they share some common features. Firstly, they all acknowledge the existence of flaws ('the original sin') in the construction of the EMU, and these flaws explain not only the development of macroeconomic imbalances since the adoption of the single currency, but also the difficulty in dealing with the effects of the crisis. As mentioned by Enderlein et al. (2012, p. 25), the euro area was confronted with two types of economic heterogeneities: on the one hand, *structural divergences* reflecting different historical models and patterns of economic specialization, leading to differences in terms of wealth (e.g. GDP per capita); on the other hand, *cyclical divergences* that point to the relative position of the business cycle of a country in comparison to the business cycle position of the rest of the euro area.

Secondly, in all these proposals there is a consensus that tackling these cyclical divergences may require the combination of private along with

---

87 With respect to this issue, Hübner et al. (2017, p. 26) advocate the creation of a euro-area budget as a complementary part of the EU budget, financed through a newly introduced own resource, raised with euro-area member states and earmarked for the exclusive use of the euro-area fiscal capacity. Such assigned revenue would not be included in the ceilings of the multi-annual financial framework, and this budget would complement, not replace, the EU budget. The authors (*Ibidem*, p. 26) then propose that the implementation of this fiscal capacity should be achieved through three main steps. Firstly, the fiscal capacity should rely on the aforementioned incentive-based enforcement mechanism to achieve progress in convergence and sustainable structural reforms. Secondly, the incentive-based enforcement mechanism should be complemented by a mechanism absorbing asymmetric shocks such as a rainy-day fund reinsuring national unemployment benefit schemes or a genuine European Unemployment Benefit Scheme (see more details further on). Finally, the fiscal capacity could be expanded to a mechanism absorbing asymmetric shocks.

88 See also, as a contribution for the discussion about the future of Europe, the collective book: Quadros and Sidjanski (eds.) (2017).

governmental risk-sharing mechanisms. All the proposals accentuate the need to complete both the BU and the CMU.

As such, it can be said that blueprints for reforms usually involve holistic and cross-pillar approaches, and at the same time an idea of gradualism, accepting a medium-term work-in-progress until the full conclusion of a complete EMU. In fact, in all these proposals, the outcome implies moving European integration forwards and not backwards, and ultimately moving it to a scenario of Fiscal Federalism even if a *sui generis* Fiscal Federalism.

Enshrined in the acceptance of a fiscal capacity in the EMU, it is also commonly accepted that mechanisms for orderly sovereign debt restructuring should be implemented and eventually managed at the central level, although the level and nature of some kind of debt pooling at the EMU level is still controversial.

In fact, despite the common features, divergences remain with respect to the nature and design of risk-sharing mechanisms, particularly regarding the design of the so-called fiscal capacity.

5

RISK-SHARING MECHANISMS AS A PANACEA FOR SAVING THE EURO

A fiscal capacity for the EMU

5.1. Basic conceptual elements of the notion of 'risk sharing'; a first justification for governmental risk-sharing mechanisms

5.1.1. Consumption smoothing versus international risk sharing; private versus governmental risk-sharing instruments

The general notion of 'risk sharing' (*lato sensu*) incorporates two interlinked notions: firstly, the concept of consumption smoothing, and secondly, the notion of international (or spatial) risk sharing.[1] Both are a feature or a consequence of the functioning of insurance devices (*infra*), either of a private (market) or governmental nature (in this latter case, as we will see further on, coming from the invisible stabilizing role of fiscal policy or from the visible action of similar devices).

> *Consumption smoothing*, according to Alcidi and Thirion (2016, p. 9), posits a consumption choice of different dates, it is an intertemporal concept according to which individuals (or countries) can maintain a steady level of consumption over time in face of the temporary shocks that may result in fluctuations in income, which in turn translate into fluctuations in consumption.

In a strict intertemporal and individual manner, consumption smoothing would be ensured – in perfect markets without credit rationing – through

---

1 Note that this conceptual division is not new and can be found in seminal contributions from von Hagen (1992, 1998, 2007). According to this author, risk-sharing mechanisms can indeed be analysed according to two basic approaches – regional stabilization and consumption smoothing approaches. Asdrubali *et al.* (1996), in turn, also identify the main channels of risk sharing which include: (i) international capital markets (private risk sharing of assets or income smoothing) related to portfolio diversification; (ii) credit markets and consumption smoothing (inter-temporal risk sharing); (iii) government redistribution (fiscal risk sharing).

savings and borrowings: consumers would save in good times and be able to borrow in bad times.

In turn, *international (or spatial) risk-sharing mechanisms* is

> a concept that relates to the idea of risk diversification and is linked to the existence of different 'states of nature', some good and others bad, that could materialise and the fact that people want to protect themselves against the risk that bad states adversely affect their well-being. In broad terms, (market) risk sharing requires access to international capital markets and occurs either through having a diversified portfolio of international assets or an explicit insurance policy, hence it is based on ex-ante arrangements that kick in automatically to smooth domestic income in the event of a shock.
>
> (Alcidi and Thirion, 2016, p. 9)[2]

Private risk-sharing mechanisms work through two main channels (Cimadomo *et al.*, 2018, p. 86). (i) The *savings channel* (also known as the credit channel) operates via cross-border saving/borrowing, i.e. the public sector, households and firms can borrow internationally (or inter-jurisdictionally) to sustain consumption or investment levels in the event of adverse shocks. (ii) The *capital market channel* operates through internationally (or inter-jurisdictionally) diversified private investment portfolios.[3] Additionally (*Idem*, p. 86), a third 'public' channel relies on cross-regional fiscal transfers, where transfers are used to smooth the impact of shocks at the state or regional level.

In this regard, it should be noted that in the seminal paper by Asdrubali *et al.* (1996), who analysed data for the U.S. from 1963 to 1990, the most important findings were that most shocks to the gross state product were absorbed by capital markets (39%), while federal government smoothing applied to only 13% and credit market smoothing to 23% (with 6% remaining for non-smoothed shocks). In turn, Hoffmann and Sørensen (2012) claim that from the three existing risk-sharing channels – the fiscal insurance, the credit market and the capital market channels – the most effective is the latter.

As noted by Cimadomo *et al.* (2018, pp. 90–91), at the start of the EMU, the belief was that the creation of a single currency would by itself enhance income and consumption smoothing. The EMU would reduce trading and information gathering costs, leading to a higher cross-country ownership of financial assets. Moreover, the removal of the currency risk would foster

---

2 For a broad picture of the subject, relating it to financial globalization, see Kose *et al.* (2008).
3 For an explanation of which way equity and bond markets work as a private insurance mechanism in case of asymmetric shocks, see De Grauwe (2014, pp. 18–19).

foreign direct investment and greater integration of bond markets, therefore creating more liquid markets for lending and borrowing.

However, as noted by the same authors, empirical results from the literature on the pre-EMU and EMU periods are mixed (Cimadomo *et al.*, 2018, p. 91). Sørensen and Yosha (1998) analysed risk-sharing patterns among EU member states (together with OECD countries) between 1966 and 1990; they concluded that 50% of the shock is smoothed (below the 75% for the U.S.), and find that this is achieved through corporate savings and budget deficits, not through capital markets.[4] In turn, for a panel of 25 European countries, Afonso and Furceri (2008b) found that only 43% of shocks to GDP were smoothed in the pre-EMU phase (mostly through private and government savings) and that this share decreased to 37% after the introduction of the euro. In a non-distinct vein, Furceri and Zdzienicka (2013) found that factor income flows did not contribute to smooth income across countries in the EMU: in fact, although the amounts increased, they became less counter-cyclical. Moreover, in their opinion, the bulk of risk sharing has come mainly through the credit channel, through borrowing and savings. However, it is unclear whether the higher degree of integration in the interbank market meant a positive effect in terms of shock absorption (see also Alcidi and Thirion, 2016). As noted by Alcidi and Thirion (2016), one crucial feature of the credit channel is that it tends to be ineffective during crises. Overall, this feature suggests that large shocks can strongly impair consumption smoothing by constraining the private and public sectors' capacity to borrow.

More recently, Alcidi (2017), Alcidi and Thirion (2017) and Alcidi *et al.* (2017a) investigated the capacity to smooth the impact of asymmetric shocks in the U.S. and the EMU and examined the various mechanisms of shock absorption. The main findings taken from Alcidi (2017a) are as follows. (i) Capital markets in the U.S. perform far better than in the euro area in terms of supplying risk-sharing. (ii) The results for the euro area are mostly driven by dynamics in peripheral countries, where the unsmoothed part of the risks is higher than in core countries. (iii) The persistence of shocks is also an issue in the EMU relative to the U.S., for two reasons – firstly, because total savings and borrowing in the EMU (including households, corporate and government savings) play a more significant role than in the U.S., where instead capital markets provide the largest part of risk-sharing; and secondly, since shock absorption through savings and borrowing does not usually respond well to permanent/persistent shocks, the persistence of the euro area debt crisis may explain why, after 2010, the unsmoothed part of the shocks increased much more in the EMU than in the U.S.

Governmental risk sharing action can be justified on the grounds of both consumption smoothing and international (regional) risk-sharing purposes.

---

4 See also Balli and Sørensen (2007).

Fatás (1998) explains that the government – through fiscal policy – can help consumers to smooth consumption, notably when, due to market imperfections, they are unable to use financial markets to borrow against their future income (credit rationing). In turn, it can be said that government risk sharing is a substitute for capital markets when the latter suffer from market frictions and incompleteness (von Hagen, 1998). Regional governments can self-insure their regions against temporary shocks by borrowing and lending in the national or international credit market. A depressed region could borrow and spend the proceeds on domestic output, whereas the prospering region would invest its higher tax revenues in national and international assets. In the long run, a region's borrowing and lending would be zero on average (von Hagen, 1998, p. 7).[5]

5.1.2. Refining the notion of (governmental) risk sharing: types of shocks; stabilization lato sensu versus insurance

In fact, as seen previously when detailing the insights from Fiscal Federalism, it is possible to split the redistribution and the stabilization functions. As noted by von Hagen (1992), the central budget plays a key role in redistribution among territories within a federation. Starting with a certain structure of revenues and expenditures, redistribution translates into an equalization function, since the existence of progressive taxes and uniformly distributed regional transfers means that those regions with a lower level of income will receive transfers from the rest (Bajo-Rubio and Díaz-Roldán, 2003, p. 74).

Additionally, the central budget may also play a stabilizing role, through direct transfers and progressive taxes – in the case where all regions experienced a recession, tax revenues would decrease, and transfers would increase (*Idem*, p. 74) – aiming at accommodating the functioning either of automatic stabilizers or discretionary measures.[6]

In a common Fiscal Federalism framework, the stabilization function – at the central level – would operate as a response to common shocks hitting the regions (states) of the economy. In this regard, the idea according to which in the case of common shocks monetary policy would be sufficient to resolve them should be recalled. In contrast, in the case where one region suffers

---

5 Assuming the justification for governmental risk sharing both on the grounds of consumption smoothing and spatial risk sharing, the question is ultimately about the impact of regional shocks on other regions' tax liabilities. The issue has been discussed by Bayoumi and Masson (1998), where the distinction between Ricardian versus non-Ricardian consumers appears to be crucial. This reasoning can, in turn, be associated with other types of reflexion, such as that of Persson and Tabellini (1996) and von Hagen (1998, 2007).

6 As an interesting point of departure – for the current *status quo* (where a 'true' central budget at the EU level does not exist) – Dolls *et al.* (2010) propose an exercise to assess the role of macro automatic stabilizers in Europe and in the U.S, in the event of an economic crisis (e.g. income and unemployment shocks).

a shock not affecting the others (asymmetric shock),[7] a unique monetary policy is no longer an adequate or sufficient response (recall previous arguments pro centralization of fiscal policies). Therefore, in the case of asymmetric shocks, fiscal policy would be the best candidate for macroeconomic stabilization, through net transfers by the central government to the affected region. The stabilization function would ultimately involve a (central) budget deficit to be financed through debt issuance and made to accommodate the functioning either of automatic stabilizers (e.g. unemployment benefits) or discretionary measures (e.g. investment expenditure).

Additionally, it has been stressed by some economists that what distinguishes fiscal policy in the case of common versus asymmetric shocks is that while in the former case we are in the presence of a typical stabilization function, in the latter a stabilization function would give rise to an insurance function (see, for example, Eichengreen, 1998).

In turn, to be considered as a *typical insurance mechanism*, the device has to fulfil the main purposes and features of the insurance framework. Those purposes and features are the following:

a) The first is to precisely be an insurance instrument *qua tale*, that is, a *direct* and *visible mechanism* aiming at ensuring risk coverage and management. Moreover, it should be automatic in the sense that the insurance is activated whenever the relevant trigger (related to the occurrence of risk) effectively materializes.

b) The main driver for the demand for insurance is that people (or institutions) be considered as *risk averse*, which means that its utility function is concave (Klein, 2014). Therefore, if someone is risk averse, they are willing to pay something for insurance to keep what they have rather than take a chance of having a loss – what they are willing to pay for this security or reduction in uncertainty (i.e. objective risk) is called a 'risk premium' (Klein, 2014). Note that the demand for insurance is also affected by the information and the perception people have of the risks they face – sometimes these risks are underestimated, and in other cases they are overestimated (*Idem*).

c) Furthermore, the demand for insurance is influenced by *income and wealth* (where people with higher income tend to buy more insurance). Moreover, as people compare the relative costs and benefits of different risk transfer options, and if they have other alternatives to insurance, they would most likely choose a low-cost option. As noted by Klein (2014), there are different *non-insurance alternatives for risk transfer*, such as defaults on debt

---

7 Bajo-Rubio and Díaz-Roldán (2003, p. 75) explain that asymmetric shocks can be of two types: specific, which affect just one region or country (i.e. asymmetric both in origin and impact); and common to several regions or countries but having a different impact on them (i.e. symmetric in origin but asymmetric in impact).

obligations, charity and government financial assistance. If, for example, it is found less costly to enter bankruptcy than to buy an insurance device, then the risk transfer would not be carried out through the latter.

d) Uncertainty together with the law of large numbers explain why risks can be faced through mechanisms designed to diversify or spread the risk across a wider base of exposures and/or over time (Klein, 2014). This is done through *risk diversification* and *risk pooling*. Given this, assuming that pool members are risk averse, pool members will be willing to pay a risk premium to cover the administrative and transaction costs of the pool to benefit from that risk reduction (*Idem*). In particular, when paying a risk premium (insurers pay for insurance above the actuarially fair price), all people will buy (full) insurance even if this is not fairly priced for all individuals – this is the notion of 'pooling equilibrium' (Gruber, 2013, p. 332).

e) The idea of *equity* in the insurance market is not straightforward. For some it should be based on the ability to pay – those with greater resources should pay higher premiums. Some rely strictly on a principle of benefit – payment would be made according to the benefits obtained (Klein, 2014). According to this latter version – that is, a pure and strict insurance version – equity is achieved when beneficiaries pay premiums commensurate with their relative risk, i.e. the high-risk insured pay higher premiums than the low risk-insured (Klein, 2014).

f) This second version of the idea of equity can in turn be related to the need to cope with market failures in the insurance market, the first of which is *adverse selection*.[8] In order to prevent the implosion of the market (due to the presence of 'lemons'; Akerlof, 1970), the premium can be differentiated according to the risk profile and exposure, including more severe conditions after the occurrence of a risk. This is indeed the so-called *experience rating*, where the insurer charges a price for insurance that is a function of realized outcomes (Gruber, 2013, p. 333). Experience rating is in fact an *ex post* equivalent of actuarial adjustment: while actuarial adjustment charges a price as a function of expected experience, experience rating charges a price based on actual or realized experience (Gruber, 2013, p. 333). Additionally, other instruments can be applied: for example, waiting periods after the coverage purchase (Klein, 2014).

g) The other typical market failure is *moral hazard* – the exposure to the risk including less effort to avoid losses.[9] Insurers address moral hazard by imposing deductibles, policy limits and co-insurance provisions that

---

8 For a detailed notion of adverse selection and a review of the most significant literature on the topic, see Araújo (2005, pp. 304–309; 2007, pp. 286–287).

9 For a detailed notion of moral hazard and a review of the most significant literature on the topic, see Araújo (2005, pp. 309–311; 2007, pp. 287–290).

force the insured to bear some portion of the respective loss (Klein, 2014). Alternatively, insurers may increase safety incentives by offering discounts for loss prevention measures and by declining to sell insurance to those that refuse to commit to safety (Klein, 2014). The latter tend to be complementary to the former: they are complementary obligations vis-à-vis principal insurance provisions. Finally, another way to avoid moral hazard is through risk selectivity: only large or severe risks, not small ones, are covered by the insurance scheme.

h) As a final remark, it should be noted that both mechanisms to cope with adverse selection and moral hazard are also intended to ensure the so-called long-term budget neutrality of the insurance 'fund', that is, an insurance fund should not be a mechanism of redistribution (or solidarity) between its members. Risk pooling is indeed not the same thing as redistribution.

The attempt to use these features in the case of governmental insurance devices to cope with regional shocks is not new. Italianer and Vanheukelen (1992), Goodhart and Smith (1993), the Commission of the European Communities (1993) and Hammond and von Hagen (1995) addressed this issue, by identifying several conceptual properties of the schemes, notably the following: (i) the scheme must operate with simplicity and be automatic; (ii) it must avoid moral hazard; (iii) it must avoid wide coverage and guarantee budget neutrality so that regions not hit by the shock should contribute relatively more, and only the regions affected should receive transfers; (iv) the whole amount collected should always be distributed, avoiding deficits and surpluses regarding the mechanism; (v) the scheme should insure the regions, not individuals; vi) it should offer insurance only against serious economic difficulties (see also in this regard Pacheco, 2000; Bajo-Rubio and Díaz-Roldán, 2003).

However, the fact is that in the context of a public risk-sharing scheme, the purity of insurance features give way to heterodoxy. This is so first and foremost because it is not always easy to disentangle redistributive (or even allocation purposes) from stabilization ones, as it is not easy to sustain whether a stabilization device is typically an insurance scheme, because some of the features may simply not be present.

5.1.3. First generation of proposals for the creation of insurance devices at the European level

5.1.3.1. Analysis of the level of insurance in pre-existing fiscal federal experiences

Prior to proposals on the implementation of insurance devices for the European Community/E(M)U, and mostly during the 1990s, a considerable number of economists investigated the degree of insurance (shock absorption or shock smoothing) found in the central budget – considering the typical interplay of taxes and transfers/benefits – and carried out that research for several countries, in particular the U.S., Canada and the UK (see Table 5.1).[10]

Table 5.1 The level of insurance in pre-existing fiscal federal experiences: investigations and main findings

Identification of the study and main conclusion	*Technical issues*
Sala-i-Martin and Sachs (1991) regress federal government's tax revenues and transfers on final disposable income for nine U.S. regions – an overall cushioning effect of around 40%[1].	i) Trigger: a regional income shock. ii) Nature of shock: temporary. iii) Stabilization instruments: the combination of the tax system (34% of income smoothing) and the transfer system (6%). iv) Stabilizer impact: the impact of stabilizers (tax system and transfers) on the final disposable per capita income; the predominant role of the progressive tax system, which also means that the stabilization process is automatic rather than discretionary. v) Methodology: regression analysis (period covered: 1970–1988).
Von Hagen (1992, 1998) – see additionally, Hammond and von Hagen (1995) and Kletzer and von Hagen (2000). In the former study, von Hagen (1992) estimated, for the 50 states and the District of Columbia in the U.S., an insurance effect of 10%.	i) Trigger: state gross products. ii) Nature of shock: temporary. iii) Stabilization instruments: the combination of the tax system and the transfer system, but excluding social security benefits. iv) Stabilizer impact: upon income. v) Methodology: regression analysis (period covered: 1981–1986).
Italianer and Pisani-Ferry (1992) and Pisani-Ferry *et al.* (1993) developed a neo-Keynesian macro-model relying on a set of hypotheses for the behaviour of an economy. Such hypotheses included the degree of integration for the goods and labour markets, as well as for the capital markets. With respect to	i) Trigger: GDP shocks. ii) Nature of shock: asymmetric and common shocks. iii) Stabilization instruments: the combination of the tax system (7.3% in the U.S.), social security contributions (8.7% in the U.S.) and the transfer system (1.1% in the U.S).

10 For more details in this regard, see also von Hagen (1998) and Bajo-Rubio and Díaz-Roldán (2003).

Identification of the study and main conclusion	*Technical issues*
the fiscal block, the model considered several parameters for both tax and transfers, as well as considered the respective elasticity (e.g. income tax elasticity to revenue; revenue elasticity of transfers related to revenue). The authors then simulated the stabilization impact of transfers, taxes and social security contributions for the U.S. and some European countries (Germany and France). For the U.S., the overall stabilization effects was 17%, lower than that for France (37.4%) and Germany (33%–42%).	iv) Stabilizer impact: upon income. v) Methodology: simulation exercise.
Goodhart and Smith (1993) found an insurance effect of 11% for the U.S. (the cases of Canada and UK were also analysed with an insurance effects of 12%–17% in the former case and 21% in the latter).	i) Trigger: state gross products. ii) Nature of shock: temporary. iii) Stabilization instruments: the combination of the tax system and the transfer system, excluding the unemployment benefit (because it is not managed at the central level). iv) Stabilizer impact: upon income (but also consumption smoothing was tested). v) Methodology: regression analysis (period covered: U.S., 1981–1986; Canada 1965–1988; and the UK, 1983–1987); simulation exercise.
Asdrubali *et al.* (1996) have empirically tested for the U.S. case that from the shocks to gross state product, a significant part (39%) was absorbed by capital markets, credit markets smoothed 23%, while federal government smoothing was only at 13% (with 6% remaining of non-smoothed shocks).	i) Trigger: shock to gross state product. ii) Nature of shock: temporary (also tested persistent shocks). iii) Stabilization instruments: the combination of the tax system (4.3% of income smoothing); the transfer system (not including unemployment benefits, 6.3%); unemployment benefits (1.9%) and interregional grants (2.5%). iv) Stabilizer impact: upon income (but also tested consumption smoothing). v) Methodology: regression analysis (period covered: 1963–1990).

(Continue)

Table 5.1 (Continued)

Identification of the study and main conclusion	Technical issues
Bayoumi and Masson (1995, 1998) disentangle redistribution and insurance functions, and obtain for 48 U.S. states a degree of insurance of 30% (for Canada, a lower value of 17%).	i) Trigger: income shock. ii) Nature of shock: temporary. iii) Stabilization instruments: the combination of the tax system (34% of income smoothing) and the transfer system (6%). iv) Stabilizer impact: the impact of stabilizers (tax system and transfers) on the final disposable per capita income. v) Methodology: regression analysis (period covered: for the U.S., 1969–1986; for Canada, 1965–1988).
Fatás (1998), assuming a stabilization effect of 30% (in line with Sala-i-Martin, 1991; Bayoumi and Masson, 1995), isolated the insurance effect (defined as the reduction, in percentage, of volatility, measured by the standard deviation, of state permanent income). He considered that the estimate for insurance is much lower than the result from the static analysis that focused on stabilization of disposable income and ignored the implications of the intertemporal budget constraint of the federal budget. Indeed, the amount of insurance was around one third of the estimates of the static analysis.	i) Trigger: income shock. ii) Nature of shock: temporary. iii) Stabilization instruments: the combination of the tax system and the transfer system. iv) Stabilizer impact: (reduction of) volatility of state permanent income. v) Methodology: regression analysis (period covered: 1960–1990).

Source: The Author

[1] The results of this study were challenged (notably by von Hagen, 1992) for not having well separated the redistribution function from the insurance function: for this reason the stabilization impact was much larger than on subsequent investigations, where that separation was made. Von Hagen's (1992) investigation allows the intercepts of his panel regression to account for the U.S. business cycle.

5.1.3.2. Seminal proposals for the creation of insurance devices at the European level: main conceptual elements

It should be noted that the first contributions to the discussion (during the last quarter of the twentieth century) were very much in line with the *MacDougall Report*, therefore assuming a fully federal model in which actual spending and revenues were shifted to the euro-area level (Pisani-Ferry *et al.*, 2013, p. 4) and which could, for that reason, have other economic goals than stabilization. Only recently, in the after-crisis literature, has the emphasis been put more on those typical visible insurance mechanisms, because unlike previous literature, it acknowledges the incomplete nature of the European fiscal union (Cabral, 2017).

Indeed, starting in the 1990s and until the great financial crisis, a sequence of proposals for the creation of insurance devices at the European level emerged. When analysing these proposals, it can be seen that in the majority of them, one can find the usual conceptual elements, both with respect to the macro-environment justifying the mechanism to be activated and the features and properties of the instrument conceived to respond to this.

5.1.3.2.1. THE FIRST CONCEPTUAL ELEMENT IS THE TYPE OF SHOCK

In most of the seminal proposals, there is a 'ring facing' of asymmetric and temporary shocks: the idea of a typical insurance device is to address these kinds of shocks.[11]

The other aspect – the magnitude or severity of the shocks – was at that time less discussed. Even so, the Commission of the European Communities (1993) pleaded that this would be only when serious economic difficulties were at stake. In recent years, this issue has been significant. Carnot et al. (2015), when proposing (four types of) insurance schemes for the euro area, disentangle schemes aiming at insuring states, irrespective of the size of the shocks, and those that should mainly address large shocks. The advantages of this latter solution are drawn up. Firstly, income stabilization would be perceived less like a 'euro tax' and more like a true 'euro insurance'. Secondly, the SGP makes that distinction, and so a similar flavour would be captured in the income stabilization scheme in focusing on gross movements in the output gap – the SGP and the income stabilization scheme would form a coherent pair. Thirdly, large national cyclical busts are more costly than small slumps – this is so because the ability to deal with the former is limited in the case of a single monetary union and where a common exchange rate is made to frame the euro area as a whole. Therefore, concentrating the scheme's action on paying out large amounts to avoid big slumps has strong merits.

---

11 Carnot et al. (2015) recently discussed the creation of different types of schemes within the euro area, one of which should be able to respond not only to asymmetric but also to common shocks. Although this kind of scheme has the advantage of ensuring a higher degree of income smoothing (by saving across Europe as a whole in good times), increased stabilization power against favourable shocks could be made only by increasing total borrowing at moments of distress. Eventually, this might jeopardize fiscal discipline. As such, stronger requirements would be needed in order to preserve the credibility of the overall framework (Carnot et al., 2015). See also Kalemli-Ozcan (2004).

Wolff (2012) in turn stresses that only for large recessions would support be needed, and this should take the form of temporary but real transfers. For smaller deviations from potential output, a well-established national balance budget rule is sufficient. In short, creating a euro-area budget to address small shocks does not appear warranted.

Finally, Gros (2014) claims that the institution of a shock absorber within the Eurozone should take into account 'economics of insurance' – not only to prevent moral hazard behaviour but also to ensure that the mechanism is effective when *effectively* needed. In his opinion, the Eurozone does not need a system that offsets all shocks by some small fraction, but a system protecting against shocks that could be potentially catastrophic. For this reason, a system of fiscal insurance with a fixed deductible would therefore be preferable to a fiscal shock absorber that offsets a certain percentage of all fiscal shocks.[12]

5.1.3.2.2. THE SECOND CONCEPTUAL ELEMENT IS THE NATURE OF THE INSURANCE MECHANISM

As we have seen previously, although the distinction between stabilization and insurance (*qua tale*) is not always easy to draw, and assuming that stabilization devices may in turn imply (or not) some degree of redistribution, the fact is that seminal proposals in the 1990s were already focused on creating typical and visible insurance devices.

A first proposal to be noted was presented by Italianer and Vanheukelen (1992).[13] The authors proposed two versions of automatic stabilization mechanism. On the one hand, a 'full stabilization mechanism' would be activated for all asymmetric shocks irrespective of their size. On the other hand, a 'limited stabilization mechanism' would be activated automatically or on a discretionary basis for shocks attaining a certain magnitude.

The trigger for the scheme would be the variation of the unemployment rate (a percentage difference, lower in the former scheme and higher in the latter, of the country's rate with respect to the average European rate). Then, whenever activated, the scheme would ensure direct transfers to member countries, but not through the payment of individual unemployment benefits.[14]

---

12 Furceri and Zdzienicka (2013) present a supranational fiscal stabilization mechanism to insure countries against income shocks. The results suggest that this mechanism, although funded by a relatively small contribution, would be able to provide full insurance against very severe, persistent and non-anticipated shocks.

13 See also, for a detailed characterization, Pacheco (2000).

14 Monthly transfers under the full stabilization scheme (see notation in Pacheco, 2000) would be:

$$T_i(t) = 0, \qquad \text{if } dU_i - dU_{iEC}(t) \le 0 \qquad \text{or} \qquad dU_i(t) \le 0$$

And would be of:

Secondly, Mélitz and Vori (1993) proposed an insurance fund for income per capita or for the unemployment rate, but with no redistributive purposes, even that of income stabilization (see Pacheco, 2000). In contrast to Italianer and Vanheukelen (1992), the trigger would be deviations of the national unemployment level from the national average level. The authors argued that any system trying to compensate for deviations from the Community average would indeed imply income redistribution (see more details in Pacheco, 2000).[15]

At the same time, but in a different vein, Majocchi and Rey (1993) developed the idea of a 'conjunctural convergence facility' (previously described in the *MacDougall Report*; MacDougall *et al.*, 1977). In order to cope with asymmetric shocks, the authors proposed a contingency fund, financed on an *ad hoc* basis by member states (Strauss, 2016). Moreover, the mechanism would be activated in a discretionary form – the assistance would consist of grants and loans of up to 1% of GDP of the recipient member state, so limited to a maximum nominal amount; to avoid time-lag problems associated with discretionary action, a first tranche equal to 25% would be released (Strauss, 2016).

Finally, Hammond and von Hagen (1995) propose an insurance mechanism that would insure countries against deviations, both transitory and specific, from a common trend related to their economies' long-term equilibrium path (see again Pacheco, 2000). The authors proposed three approaches for the scheme: (i) the 'innovation approach' where transfers are related to annual deviations, not correlated and conditionally unexpected, of EU countries' income per capita from a common stochastic trend; (ii) the 'deviation approach' that ties payments to the asymmetric deviations that a given economy exhibits with respect to a common trend; (iii) the 'naïve approach', where the purpose is to stabilize the rate of growth of real per capita GDP around the annual average growth rate (for a synthesis, *Idem*).

$$T_i = \alpha . (dU_i(t) - dU_{iEC}(t)) . GDP_t, \qquad \text{if }, 0 < dU_i(t) - dU_{iEC}(t) \leq 2$$

$$T_i(t) = \alpha . 2 . GDP_i, \qquad \text{if } dU_i(t) - dU_{iEC}(t) > 2$$

Where $T_i(t)$ is monthly transfer, equal to one given percentage α of 1/12 of the country's i GDP in the previous year. Given this, fixing that percentage α at 1%, the maximum monthly payment to a member state would be equal to 2% of 1/12 of its annual GDP (Pacheco, 2000).

In turn, under the 'limited stabilization scheme', transfers would be activated only if there was a significant divergence in the unemployment rates, surpassing a given minimum level (for example, fixed at 0.3 p.p.) (for more details, see also Pacheco, 2000).

15 The scheme would rely on this relationship (Pacheco, 2000 for notation): where is the value to insure (income per capita or unemployment rate); is the national reference value and is the averaged sum of the deviations in the Union. In the case of income per capita, negative values for the expression would imply payments from the other member states. In the case of the unemployment rate, positive values would trigger those same payments (*Idem*, 2000).

5.1.3.2.3. THE THIRD CONCEPTUAL ELEMENT RELIES PRECISELY ON THE IDENTIFICATION OF THE TRIGGER AND ON THE AUTOMATICITY OF THE SCHEME

In the proposals for the creation of insurance mechanisms, the trigger usually alternates between the unemployment rate (deviations from a certain benchmark) and the output gap. More recently, Wolff (2012) highlighted other technical possibilities, such as credit growth, current accounts and interest rates.

Another relevant issue in this regard – and the 'debate' between Italianer and Vanheukelen (1992) on the one hand and Mélitz and Vori (1993) on the other illustrates this – is to identify what the benchmark or reference value will be: a national or a Community average. In either case, a 'proper' insurance mechanism relies on automaticity, that is, the mechanism is activated as soon as the trigger is switched on.

In turn, it should be noted that the trigger makes not only the mechanism automatic, but also its stabilizer reaction: the response should be given mostly through the action of automatic stabilizers (e.g. unemployment benefits or income-type transfers) instead of discretionary spending. As explained by Wolff (2012), automatic stabilizers can be agreed on *ex ante* and therefore have the advantage of being easily enforceable in the event of a shock. Moreover, as the scheme is activated in the event of cyclical fluctuations, an expenditure automatic response will better correspond to the size of the shock and at the same time provide a sizeable (and matched) response to that same shock. Finally, it should be stated that a system relying on automatic stabilizers can more easily be associated to instruments aiming to prevent or correct moral hazard. As we will see, a reaction through automatic stabilizers is better suited to be interlinked with the SGP framework and with the rules of fiscal discipline. These rules could be *naturally* used as means to prevent moral hazard in the context of a future bailout or insurance device.[16]

5.1.3.2.4. THE FOURTH CONCEPTUAL ELEMENT RELATES TO THE INSTRUMENTS AIMING AT PREVENTING AND CORRECTING MORAL HAZARD (AND POSSIBLE ADVERSE SELECTION)

As noted indeed in the seminal contribution of Persson and Tabellini (1992), in a system of federal transfers to the lower government levels, "a likely trade-off between risk sharing and moral hazard emerges."

With respect to this, it is possible to disentangle two possible solutions (that can be combined): (i) a *'typical' insurance solution*, which can imply,

---

16 In contrast, as also noted by Wolff (2012), discretionary spending has the advantage of requiring a strong decision-making centre that would be able to take quick decisions in favour of countries in need. As such, discretionary spending is desirable to address specific shocks in a targeted way.

in turn, *ex ante* devices – e.g. the requirement of a deductible (recall Gros, 2014) – or *ex post* devices – e.g. penalties, an experience rating system, raising of the premium; (ii) a *'non-typical' insurance solution*, but mimicking the former, by linking the insurance scheme to a fiscal discipline requirement.

One can indeed state that fiscal discipline can play a similar role – preventing and correcting moral hazard – in a governmental-type insurance scheme that *ex ante* and *ex post* insurance devices play in a common 'private' insurance scheme. Considering the EMU fiscal framework, the link settled between the insurance scheme and the fiscal discipline requirement can be, on the other hand, of two different natures (Cabral, 2017):

- A *functional-type link*, where fiscal discipline (enclosed in the SGP rules) is simply a condition of risk protection.[17] Note that this might imply either fiscal discipline enhancement as an *ex ante* condition to be eligible for funding, or an *ex post* penalty for countries that circumvent SGP rules – e.g. overstating potential GDP in order to reduce their payment to the Fund (von Hagen and Wyplosz, 2008, p. 17) – then withdrawing the protection.

- A *structural-type link* where insurance instruments are encapsulated in the SGP framework and work as an extension of the latter, therefore ensuring medium-term (or cyclically adjusted) management of the insurance scheme itself. An example of this is the *automatic transfer scheme* proposed by Wolff (2012) and Pisani-Ferry *et al.* (2013), a system of financial support based on the business cycle and using potential output as a benchmark. The idea would be to complement the SGP, which is centred on the budget balance net of business cycle effects, with a system of financial support based on the business cycle. Countries whose output is significantly below the potential output would be allowed to run deficits and would be supported by common resources (Wolff, 2012). In the scheme, absolute (not relative) deviations of output from potential output would trigger transfers to the countries hit by the shock. Moreover, since the business cycles are correlated in the euro area, the instrument would need to borrow during recessions and would balance out only over the business cycle (e.g. extracting payments from countries with output above potential in good times) (Pisani-Ferry *et al.*, 2013, p. 5).

In a similar vein, Cabral (2017) suggests a more radical version of the system, where the funding of the scheme would also go through the rules of the

---

17 As mentioned by Schelkle (2005), the idea would be to complement the disciplinarian view present in the SGP with an insurance device, while controlling moral hazard.

SGP. Indeed, in this case, the (structural) budget balance rule would be used as a pendulum for the system, both in good and bad times. In good times, countries with budget surpluses would have to contribute to the Fund that would hence work as a buffer to support those same countries whenever facing a downturn. On the other hand, in bad times, countries would also be allowed to run deficits (cyclically motivated deficits) but only under the condition of having accomplished SGP and Fiscal Compact rules, e.g. the compliance with the medium term objective (MTO). In fact, past and current structural balance should be a condition not only to run deficits but also to benefit from financial support in the event of an adverse shock.[18]

Another option would be to link the insurance mechanism to the SGP framework through the expenditure benchmark. It should be recalled that to verify the compliance of the benchmark, either when the MTO is attained or not, the primary expenditure net of discretionary and temporary (non-recurrent) measures is considered, which means that the relevant expenditure aggregate excludes interest spending, expenditure on EU programmes fully matched by EU funds and cyclical elements of unemployment benefit expenditure (European Commission, 2018a, pp. 48–49). In this case, expenditures with the funding of the scheme could be, in good times, excluded from the aggregate as the cyclical elements of the unemployment benefit are excluded in bad times (other insurance/cyclical transfers to be created may also be excluded).

5.2. From a full-fledged fiscal union to a fiscal capacity in the EMU

5.2.1. The design of the fiscal capacity

5.2.1.1. Justification for creating a fiscal capacity

An important line of thought is that one should not expect too much from the European fiscal union. Instead, as a preferable route, the unfinished integration of European capital markets should be completed (Hoffman and Sørensen, 2012). Relying on Asdrubali et al. (1996), the same authors found (for the U.S.) an overall capacity for shock absorption of 75%–80% that results from the combined action of three channels: 40% capital income flows, 10%–15% from fiscal transfers and 25% from credit markets (Hoffman and Sørensen, 2012).

The authors then recognize that in the case of a downturn, risk sharing attained through a fiscal mechanism or through credit markets is limited

---

18 Moreover, note that this structural type-link should furthermore require technical arrangements in order to adapt the new financial scheme to the SGP framework, notably vis-à-vis the calculation of the GDP potential and output gaps.

by the borrowing capacity of private and sovereign debtors. Private credit markets can dry up, making risk sharing impossible when it is most needed (*Idem*). In a similar vein, Alcidi and Thirion (2016) note that one crucial feature of the credit channel is that it tends to be ineffective during crises. Overall, this feature suggests that large shocks can strongly impair consumption smoothing by constraining the private and public sector's capacity to borrow.

In contrast, risk sharing through capital markets is the result of diversification of ownership, which works quite seamlessly once disaster strikes (Hoffman and Sørensen, 2012). Financial globalisation over the last decade has surely changed the nature of risk, as portfolios have become more diversified (*Idem*, p. 12), and this has ensured risk sharing and consumption smoothing across many countries of the world.[19]

The U.S. case is usually mentioned as being paramount. The (well) functioning of the capital markets – in particular, equity and bond markets, but also FDI – explains to a large extent why the response to the crisis was much more effective in the U.S. than in Europe. It should be recalled that according to Hoffman and Sørensen (2012), 40% of the capacity of shock absorption is due to capital income flows. This predominance of capital markets affects both non-financial and financial companies, starting with the banking sector itself. In the U.S., not only is there a banking union, but there is also a 'private' banking union, that is, a truly integrated banking market (Gros and Belke, 2015). In contrast, in Europe, the banking market – as an important expression of the capital markets – is not in itself completely integrated (Cabral, 2017).[20,21]

19 Recall, in this regard, Agénor *et al.* (2001) and Kose *et al.* (2006).

20 Recall in this regard the main features of financial integration and the nature of capital flows in Europe – Lane (2006, 2013) and ECB (2016).

21 Lane and Milesi-Ferretti (2017) discuss changes in the patterns of international financial integration after the great financial crisis. The first change is the reduction in cross-border banking activity and, in turn, the significant increase in FDI (foreign direct investment) positions. This increase is mostly explained by FDI positions vis-à-vis the financial centres, which include the special role assumed by special purpose vehicles. Another justificatory factor is the increased tendency of multinational companies to move their domicile to a financial centre. Indeed, this is the other changing pattern after the crisis: in geographical terms, a disproportionate role has been played by financial centres (e.g. Ireland, Luxembourg, Switzerland and the Cayman Islands) in total holdings. Another change is related to foreign holdings of portfolios of debt securities. These include a shift from international bank-intermediated debt liabilities to international portfolio debt liabilities, due to an increase in the issuance of portfolio debt instruments by emerging economies and higher foreign participation in their securities markets. Additionally, a reduction of foreign holdings of domestic debt securities for euro-area countries more severely hit by the crisis is denoted (Lane and Milesi-Ferretti, 2017, p. 16). Finally, the last changing pattern points to the role in financial integration played by emerging countries, and in particular by China, notably in the case of foreign exchange reserves and FDI.

Against this line of thought there is the position of those who claim the need for a fiscal capacity in the EMU. Buti and Carnot (2018) address the three main criticisms of its opponents, with the following arguments. Firstly, against the criticism according to which sizeable asymmetric shocks are infrequent in the monetary union, the authors recall that business cycle fluctuations have remained significant since the inception of the euro. Moreover, simple decompositions of the cycle suggest that such fluctuations comprise both a common component and asymmetric developments. In fact, national business cycles are imperfectly correlated, and when they are, their amplitudes may differ.

Secondly, Buti and Carnot (2018) respond to the (aforementioned) criticism that the completion of private risk sharing mechanisms (e.g. the BU and the CMU) should be sufficient to ensure shock absorption in the EMU. The question here is whether financial integration should be seen as a substitute for a fiscal capacity or should function as complements. In this regard, as noted (Buti and Carnot, 2018) the evidence suggests that financial and fiscal unions may substitute shock absorbers in normal times but need each other in bad times. Indeed, private mechanisms may behave pro-cyclically when left entirely on their own (Furceri and Zdzienicka, 2013 and Alcidi and Thirion, 2016). This pro-cyclicality may partially be explained by the inadequate structure of financial flows that, as seen earlier, may rely more on debt than on equity. As such, in Buti and Carnot's (2018) opinion, either the CMU or the BU should be completed with forms of public risk sharing, including – in this latter case – the institution of a fiscal backstop for the deposit scheme. In fact, as also explained (Buti and Carnot, 2018), these forms of public risk sharing are "crucial in order to make the system robust by strengthening financial stability, reducing pro-cyclicality, and maximising its capacity to smooth asymmetric shocks via private sector risk sharing."

In this regard, Alcidi and Thirion (2016) go even further, recalling Farhi and Werning (2012). For these latter authors, even under the assumption of complete financial markets, the level of risk sharing achieved through private markets is not Pareto efficient. The main reason for this is that private agents do not purchase efficient amounts of private insurance because they do not internalize the positive externalities from the macroeconomic stabilization effects of their portfolio choices.

The final criticism addressed by Buti and Carnot (2018) is that a fiscal capacity at the EMU level is unnecessary, as national fiscal stabilizers within the SGP suffice to smooth the remaining shocks. The authors point out that on several occasions, member states failed to have enough fiscal space to accommodate the effects of a downturn. In particular, states with high levels of debt are in a fragile position: when faced with an economic slowdown that shortens tax revenues, they quickly fall under the suspicion of the markets; they indeed risk a self-fulfilling spiral of higher deficits and interest costs. As such, as concluded (Buti and Carnot, 2018), "in those circumstances, an element of risk sharing can tip both policies and expectations towards a better equilibrium and prevent the materialization of self-destructing austerity or a full-blown meltdown."[22,23]

5.2.1.2. Financing issues of the fiscal capacity

5.2.1.2.1. TAX ASSIGNMENT: THE EU 'OWN RESOURCES SYSTEM' AND FUTURE PROSPECTS

a) Tax assignment in the EU　When considering the creation of a new fiscal capacity, the first question concerns how the mechanism will be financed – that is, through the existing setup of tax revenues, or by different ones to be created.

I will start by analysing how the EU system of own resources can evolve in the near future, including the possible creation of new taxes and the redesign of the existing ones, notably to accommodate the creation of the new fiscal capacity. However, it should be noted that much of the discussion regarding the future system of own resources stands on its own, regardless its association with the financing of a future new fiscal capacity.

As we have seen before, the transposition of Fiscal Federalism tax assignment principles for the EU (as the central or higher-level government) faces the limitations of being in the presence of a *sui generis* central government, that corresponds to a sectorial, non-all-purpose institution that lacks the typical Musgravian functions, notably the (inter-individual) redistribution and the stabilization functions. Given this, the redistributive (and by nature stabilizing) taxes (e.g. personal income tax) are not assigned – as in a typical fiscal federal framework – to the central level, but instead to intermediate levels, the member states. As such, the first prescription, coming from Musgrave's lesson – redistributive (and stabilizing taxes) should be assigned to the central level – fails to apply in the EU budgetary system.

22　When preparing the proposal for the introduction of a European stabilization function in the EMU (see *infra*), the European Commission (2018b, p. 16) justified its creation with several drivers. (i) *External drivers*: national business cycles remain strong and only partially synchronized; private cross-sector risk sharing through financial markets could be improved, but may need a minimum of fiscal risk-sharing to work at critical times; monetary policy is at risk of being over-burned. (ii) *Internal drivers*: the legacy of high public debt will take time to wind down; fiscal buffers need to be built in good times, but even the national sovereigns may be constrained in providing stabilization; fiscal adjustment undertaken under pressure tends to be overly reliant on cuts in public investment.

23　Strásky and Claveres (2019) investigated the stabilization effects of a fiscal capacity in the EMU, considering the stance of the monetary policy. One of the main conclusions is that the fiscal capacity improves macroeconomic stabilization when the monetary policy is constrained.

On the other hand, the second of Musgrave's prescriptions for tax assignment to the central government – that is, taxes on mobile factors should be centralized, although resident-based taxes such as taxes on sales or excises should preferably be assigned to intermediate governments – has been accepted since the creation of the first Economic Communities, and especially when the respective budgetary system was forged in the late 1970s.[24]

In fact, since the very beginning of the European construction, there was a clear perception that the assignment of mobile factors to the central level would be necessary to ensure the deepening of the internal market: a principle of tax centralization was indeed necessary to avoid the negative outcomes of horizontal tax competition, coming from tax externalities such as (perverse) tax competition and beggar-my-neighbour policies. In short, one can say that – at least until the 1980s when the GNP resource was created – the fundamental dictum underlying the European 'own resources system' was that it should serve the purposes of ensuring the mobility of free goods within the customs union and ultimately the construction of a true single market.

As for the final function, macro stabilization – usually assigned, also in line with Musgrave (1959), to the central government – it should be recalled that the current 'own resources system' that exists in the EU was not conceived to produce any kind of stabilization effect. As noted before, this is so not only due to the small size of the EU budget but also due to the fact that their own resources – agricultural levies, customs duties, Value-Added Tax (VAT) and GNP-based own resource – are not cyclically sensitive, at least as much as national taxes (e.g. personal income and corporate taxes and social security contributions) tend to be (Cabral, 2017). As noted by the same author (*Idem*), unlike national taxes that pursue overall and indistinctive goals (e.g. inter-individual redistribution through tax progressivity), tax resources assigned to the EU's budget are 'one-purpose', which means that they are conceived to be targeted at sectorial areas (e.g. the Common Agricultural Policy and Regional Policies), also being capped by the expenditure levels settled by the Multiannual Financial Framework.

b) The evolution of the EU Own Resources System   Let me first explain the main stages in the evolution of the European budgetary system.[25]

---

24 Since the seminal book of Strasser (1975), several other contributions to the study of the EC/EU's budgetary system (and its own resource system) have been made, such as: Franco *et al.* (1994), Swann (1995), Archer and Butler (1996), Begg and Grimwade (1998), Neal and Barbezat (1998), Nugent (1999), Tondl (2000), Ardy (2004), Porto (2006, 2012, 2017), Matthijs (2010), Catarino (2012), Tavares (2012), Cipriani (2014), Schratzenstaller (2014), Pardal (2015) and Ferrer *et al.* (2016).

25 See in this regard Franco *et al.* (1994) and Tavares (2012).

After an initial attempt – within the European Coal and Steel Commission – to introduce an own resource – a tax on coal and steel production – the fact is that within the European Economic Community (EEC), the *first stage* (between 1957 and the beginning of the 1970s) was very close to a budgetary system of conventional international organizations, that is, a budget mostly financed by contributions from the member states, as such.

The *second stage* (between 1970 and 1977) set the foundations for a system of own finances, with the approval of Council Decision 70/243/ECSC, of 21 April 1970, that institutes, from 1971 onwards, a system of own resources, therefore ensuring the financial autonomy of the EEC. This Decision instituted the so-called 'traditional own resources' (TOR) that includes customs duties, agricultural duties, and sugar and isoglucose levies. In addition, the VAT-based own resource was introduced in 1979,

> originally as a residual financing source with a uniform call rate from a harmonized tax base which is limited to 50 percent of a national Gross National Income (GNI) (capping). At its introduction, the (maximum) call rate was fixed at 1 percent.
>
> (Schratzenstaller, 2014, p. 333)

Note that this latter limitation – of the tax base as a function of the GNI – results on the other hand from the institution (in 1988) of the GNI resource (*infra*) and was aimed at reducing the alleged regressive effect of the VAT-based resource for relatively low-income member states (Cipriani, 2014, p. 3).

The *third stage* (between 1977 and 1987) saw the consolidation of the system of financial autonomy, which was in turn contemporaneous with the creation of the single market after the signature of the Single European Act (1986). During this period, the VAT call rate started to increase (1985), but after the creation of the GNI resource (in 1988), the call rate has been progressively declining. In the MFF 2007–2013, it was set at 0.3%.

Finally, the *fourth stage*, from 1987 onwards, optimistically described by Franco *et al.* (1994) and Tavares (2012) as a "model for the progress of federal finances," was marked by important changes. Firstly, with respect to the revenue side, there was the stabilization of the own resource system following the creation, in 1988, of the Gross National Product (GNP) resource (later on, in 2000, replaced by the Gross National Income, GNI resource). As noted by Schratzenstaller (2014, p. 334), as a residual financing source it serves to balance the budget subject to the own resources ceiling; as a consequence, the call rates are updated each year. Secondly, with respect to the expenditure side, there was the implementation of the multiannual financial framework (MFF) within the budgetary procedure, with the approval of the Delors I financial package for the period 1988–1992. This package would be followed by the Delors II package (1993–1999), Agenda 2000

(2000–2006), financial perspectives for 2007–2013 and for 2013–2020, and now the latest package, 2020–2027, is already under negotiation. Currently, the main sections of the MFF are: (i) Economic, Social and Territorial Cohesion; (ii) Sustainable Growth and Natural Resources; (iii) Competitiveness for Growth and Jobs.

Regarding the EU own resources system, a first observation is that although the EU has legally independent revenue, this revenue is derived from national governments' tax revenues and is highly controlled by those governments (Ardy, 2004, p. 86). Thus the typical revenue sources of federal governments, such as income tax, corporation tax, sales taxes and social security contributions, are not available to the EU (*Idem*, p. 86).

On the other hand, as noted by Cipriani (2014, p. 9),

> while legal texts define all EU financing sources as 'own resources' only TOR revenue (13% of own resources in the period 2007–2013) can be considered to be a 'true' financing source, since the EU is the legitimate institutional recipient of duties levied on a specific and identifiable taxable operation. Also, as there is often no coincidence between the place of collection and the final consumption of goods, this revenue could not be attributed to a specific member state.

By contrast, as also noted by the same author (*Idem*, p. 9),

> the assessment basis of the VAT and GNI-based resources (87% of 'own resources' in the period 2007–2013) derive from a member states' calculation, mostly based on statistical data. These resources are not 'collected' but put at the disposal of the EU budget as financial transfers from the cashbox of overall national taxation. In particular, the VAT-based resource is not levied directly on national taxable persons (and therefore on consumers), but on member states' 'notional' harmonized VAT basis.

Another relevant feature is the profound evolution in the pattern of revenue over the years. TOR received directly by the EU lost importance due to the fall of custom revenues in the course of trade liberalization (within the GATT[26] and the WTO[27]) and EU enlargement: whereas in 1980 they accounted for almost 50% of total revenues, they have been about 15% since 2005 (Schratzenstaller, 2014, p. 335). Thus, the financing of the EU budget rests increasingly on direct contributions from member states' national budgets, which means that there was a reversion to a conventional

---

26 General Agreement on Tariffs and Trade.
27 World Trade Organization.

scheme of intergovernmental organization financing in sharp contrast with a tax assignment scheme typical of a fiscal federal model.

Moreover, the concept of 'own resources' should have meant a shift of sovereignty from member states to the EU institutions, allowing the EU to exert direct power of taxation over EU citizens (Cipriani, 2014, p. 7). Ultimately, a tax directly borne by EU citizens should not even appear in the budget of the member states. However, this is not the case: as we have seen, most countries describe their own contribution as a transfer (an expenditure) to the EU budget.

Another contrasting feature to a typical tax assignment scheme is that EU financing depends strictly on the EU expenditure ceilings according to a principle of 'budgetary discipline' (Cipriani, 2014, p. 7). This means that not only is the overall EU revenue limited (since 1988) by an 'own resources' ceiling (for the MFF 2014–2020, payments shall not exceed 1.23% of the EU GNI), but also the EU budget is subject to a principle of equilibrium, meaning that in each year revenue is determined in relation to expenditure – an expenditure that, in turn, is also very limited in this financial setup (*Idem*, pp. 7–8).

Additionally, the financing system of the EU has over the years moved away from a fiscal federal typical scheme, exhibiting instead some tautological features. Indeed, the current funding system, essentially fed by GNI-based national contributions (including VAT itself[28]), and being treated as national expenditures vis-à-vis the EU budget, tempts member states to calculate their 'net returns'. As mentioned by Le Cacheux (2007, p. 5), "it is therefore tempting to regard this contribution as a fee for membership in the EU 'club' and to compare it to an evaluation of (private) benefits derived from being a member." Given this, an 'accounting logic' predominates almost exclusively guided by the notions of 'net national contributions' and 'fair returns' (*Idem*, p. 5). In fact, as added by Cipriani (2014, pp. 12–13),

> EU expenditures represent the financial 'return' of national contributions paid to the EU. This explains that a large part of the expenditures (agricultural market-related expenditure and direct payments to farmers, fisheries and cohesion, representing some 70% of the 2014–2020 MFF) is directly or de facto pre-allocated on a country basis as a part of the MFF deal.

This very logic of 'net contributions' and 'fair returns' was at the origin of the so-called 'UK rebate' (set in 1984 at the European Council of Fontainebleau): it aimed at reducing the UK's contributions with the argument that

---

28 In fact, due "to the 'capping mechanism', the VAT-based resource has since 1988 become the *de facto* GNP/GNI-based resource for the countries concerned" (Cipriani, 2014, pp. 9–10).

they were too high relative to the respective wealth and the benefits obtained from the EU budget. The same argument would be used later on in favour of other countries that have also benefitted from their own rebate – e.g. Germany, the Netherlands, Austria and Sweden.

Finally, one should be aware that the combination of this 'fair returns' logic with a principle (set in 1966) of unanimity in budgetary decisions has been, over the years, "a major source of trouble in collective decision-making" (Le Cacheux, 2007, p. 9). In fact, minimizing the overall size of the budget in order to minimize 'net national contributions' is inevitably the most tempting strategy for 'net contributors', whereas 'net beneficiaries' will try to obtain the largest share of individual transfers – after all, the system tends to encourage petty bargaining and 'pork-barrel politics' (*Idem*, p. 9).

Despite all these abnormal outcomes, the fact is that, in the EU, non-typical own resources (member states' contributions) were those that have increased over the years. Firstly, it was the share of VAT-based own resources, reaching a peak of 70% in 1986 and then declining since then to 12% in 2011; then it was the GNI-resource that has risen steadily since its creation to reach 74% in 2011 (Schratzenstaller, 2014, p. 335).

The two main reasons for this move from VAT towards GNI-based own resources were, firstly, to widen the financial scope of the EU budget, and secondly, to ease the financial burden of the weaker member states. Indeed, while contributions on the basis of VAT have a regressive effect, the contributions linked to GNI better reflect a country's economic capacity (Schratzenstaller, 2014, p. 335). On the other hand, VAT along with other indirect taxes is referred as being a least sensitive source of revenue in cyclical terms, as consumption is relatively smooth over the business cycle (Dullien and Schwarzer, 2009, p. 163).[29,30]

Related to this, an important question would be to verify whether some of the EU's own resources could be used to provide for certain stabilization effects. According to Cabral (2017), amongst the two possible candidates, VAT and GNI own resources, the latter seems to be preferable,[31] firstly because it has evolved to become the main financing source of the EU's budget. But for that, some changes in the design of the GNI based-resource would be required (Cabral, 2017). Notably, the following technical

29 For example, in the measurement of the output gap and of the cyclically adjusted balance budget, it is assumed that indirect taxes have a unitary elasticity with respect to output gap, unlike that with social contributions and direct taxation. On this issue, see Mourre *et al.* (2014).

30 In a different vein, von Hagen and Wyplosz (2008, pp. 14–15) stress that VAT is closer to demand shocks than income and payroll taxes and that the former reacts faster to cyclical movements in the economy than the latter.

31 Further on, I will mention some other proposals stressing for modification of the VAT own resource, also improving the respective stabilizing role (for example, Cipriani, 2014).

features should be discussed. Firstly, there is the substitution/completion of the GNI as an assignment base for/by another tax assignment base that would more accurately translate cyclical movements or variations in the output gap (this would at the same time entail a stronger link with the SPG framework and the methodology used to compute the structural balance). Secondly, the assignment rate would become an individual, country-based and also a constant, non-changeable, flat rate (not dependent on VAT collection or expenditure needs) that would permit tax-sharing mechanisms to operate properly and that would allow the (positive or negative) cyclical movements to be translated each year into a (higher or lower) contribution by each country – countries more affected by negative shocks would contribute less (Cabral, 2017).

For the time being, the atypical nature of this own resource when compared to the assignment of tax revenues coming from income taxes in a normal 'state-layer' interplay comes not only from the fact that this is not borne directly by taxpayers (instead by member countries) but also because the features of the GNI resource are not typically redistributive ones.

In more general terms, it can be said that the difficulty to create a 'true' tax on income, with redistributive features and the capacity to be cyclically sensitive, in the EU, has led EU institutions to accept a different path: narrowing the scope and dimension of the public risk-sharing mechanism – the so-called 'fiscal capacity' for the E(M)U – means admitting specific earmarked taxes, not necessarily with a redistributive and/or a macro stabilizer profile, but that can be accepted as financing sources of that stabilizer device. In such a case, the mechanism would be a stabilizer due to the stabilizing properties of the expenditure side and not necessarily due to the financing side. The only exception – considering the proposals further on analysed here – is the case with the European Unemployment Benefit Scheme (EUBS), in its genuine version (see *infra*), to be financed entirely through employers' and employees' contributions – which are by nature important macro stabilizer (type of) taxes.

c) Proposals (in 2011 and 2018) for new Own Resources: respective advantages and shortcomings The idea of diversifying away own resources in the EU and at the same time transforming the existing system into a 'true own resource system' is not new. In 1998, the Commission discussed new potential own resources, notably a CO_2 or energy tax, modified VAT, excises on tobacco, alcohol and mineral oil, corporate tax, tax on transport and telecommunication services, income tax, interest income tax, and a tax on the ECB gains for seigniorage (Schratzenstaller, 2014, p. 348). In 2004, the possibilities were limited to three options – energy tax, revised VAT and corporate tax. In 2011, in the proposals for the reform of the own resources system, a financial transaction tax and financial activity tax, revenues from auctioning under the greenhouse gas Emissions Trading System, a charge related to air transport, an EU VAT, an EU energy tax and an EU corporate tax were discussed (Schratzenstaller, 2014, p. 348).

Amongst these proposals, the Commission in 2011 considered as preferable a new VAT own resource and a resource based on a financial transaction tax (FTT) in considering reducing the contribution of member states to the EU budget (Cipriani, 2014, p. 36).[32]

With respect to the *new VAT own resource*, two options were discussed: a parallel system to that operating in member states and a revenue transfer mechanism. The former was discarded, as it would in practice create a double VAT system (Cipriani, 2014, p. 37). As for the second option, the VAT-based resource would hence derive from the application of a single EU rate (maximum 2%) on the net value of supplies of goods and services, intra-EU acquisitions of goods and the importation of goods that are subject to the standard VAT rate in every member state – the tax base would in fact correspond to the smallest common denominator of national VAT systems (Cipriani, 2014, p. 38). The VAT resource would have required the Commission to calculate a single EU-wide average proportion of VAT receipts from common standard-rated transactions in every member state and each member state to apply this proportion to its total VAT receipts (*Idem*, p. 38).[33]

The proposal for a new VAT resource is attractive for several reasons. VAT is a general tax with a broad and relative price-inelastic basis; as a pillar of the EU single market, VAT is regulated by EU law, and it is part of the *acquis communautaire* (Cipriani, 2016). Moreover, VAT is ultimately borne by final consumers: it is charged as a percentage of prices, which means that the actual tax burden is visible to taxpayers (*Idem*). Moreover, as noted by Ferrer *et al.* (2016, p. 87), the yield from VAT taxation is directly related to economic activity, though less subject to cyclical fluctuations than many other taxes, which gives this instrument relatively good automatic-stabilizer properties without causing unduly large imbalances in the case of economic downturns.

Despite these positive properties making it a good candidate to adjust and remain as an own resource, VAT is nevertheless prone to certain drawbacks. In particular, it is vulnerable to fraud, with estimates across countries ranging from 2% to 20% (Ferrer *et al.*, 2016, p. 88). Moreover, although there is some correlation between the VAT rate and yield, the relationship is not

---

32 Later on, the European Commission released the Communication "On an Action Plan on VAT – Towards a Single EU VAT Area – Time to Decide," COM (2016) 148 final.

33 Cipriani (2014, pp. 38–39) addressed several criticisms concerning the proposal, arguing that since the new VAT would be levied on member states and not on citizens, it would not seek to provide a solution for the opacity of the EU financing system. Moreover, due to the absence of an explicit link to the taxpayer, this resource would have continued to be perceived as national expenditure.

linear, even if the notion that it is regressive among member states is contradicted by the high VAT yield in the Nordic countries (*Idem*, p. 88).

More recently, the European Commission (2018c) renewed the discussion about the system of own resources of the EU. In the proposal presented to the Council,[34] the main weakness of the current VAT own resource system was said to be its complexity in the calculation of the tax base, due to the several statistical compensations needed to harmonize 28 VAT bases of the member states. For this reason, the European Commission (2018c) proposed the reform of the system, with the main objective of simplifying calculations while enhancing the connection with the single market and maintaining fairness across member states.[35]

The other alternative option that resurged (in the aftermath of the crisis) and was considered plausible by the European Commission in 2011 was the *financial transaction tax* (FTT). Indeed, as noted by Cipriani (2014), by that time, the FTT was proposed as an EU-regulated 'Robin Hood' tax to make the financial sector contribute to the cost of the crisis. Indeed, the 'S' triangle of financial innovation – identified as one of the major sources of the crisis – included shadow banking, securitization and short-selling as its vertices. In particular, the link between securitization to swap instruments in the mortgage-backed securities market was denounced in the aftermath of the crisis. It is not by chance, therefore, that international examples of FTT (as they have evolved over the crisis) include not only taxation of spot share trading[36] but also other types of transactions such as derivatives.

Darvas and von Wiezsäcker (2010) start by identifying the main reasons that should justify a FTT: firstly, to collect revenues for public expenditures; secondly, to discourage activities that are deemed to have negative side effects not properly taken into account by market participants.

The authors consider that from a purely revenue-raising perspective, the case for a financial transaction tax is not particularly strong. The reason is that a large number of financial transactions should be regarded as 'intermediate production', not final consumption (Darvas and von Wiezsäcker, 2010). Then, they discuss the main arguments usually referred to in support

---

34 Proposal of a Council Decision on the system of Own Resources of the European Union, COM (2018) 325 final.

35 The steps for the calculation of the VAT own resource base would be as follows: (i) Take the VAT receipts collected by each member state; receipts from standard-rated supplies would be then determined by applying a 45% common union share to these receipts. (ii) Then calculate the standard-rated taxable base (SRTB), i.e. the value of goods and services on which the member state levied the VAT receipts (SRTB = SR receipts/standard rate). (iii) Apply a uniform call rate, i.e. the same for all EU member states to the SRTB. The new own resource would be simple and transparent, reducing administrative costs and calculated using only fiscal data (European Commission, 2018c).

36 As noted by Darvas and von Wiezsäcker (2010), the most well-known example is the UK's stamp duty: it is a 0.5% tax on the value of spot transactions in shares of UK companies.

of the taxation of the financial sector (especially financial products and instruments) – the fact that this is an under-taxed sector; the fact that this taxation could work as an 'insurance fee' for the systemic risk created by the financial sector.

As regards the idea of discouraging activities with negative side effects and hence 'internalising negative externalities', the FTT would then have behaved as a typical Pigouvian tax. An FTT would then back up the insufficiency of regulation and would properly address financial market imperfections and fragility. In particular, it would be able to address one of the roots of the crisis, that is, the heavy reliance on short-term arrangements (i.e. short-term financing for its funding needs, e.g. the interbank market, commercial paper) and, more broadly, on excessive systemically relevant leverage (*Idem*).[37]

A similar argument is related to transaction costs and volatility. As noted again by Darvas and von Wiezsäcker (2010), advocates of financial transaction taxes suggest that by making short-horizon trading more costly compared to long-horizon trading, both short-term volatility (i.e. 'noise') and long-term volatility (i.e. persistent deviation from a 'fundamental equilibrium') would lessen. However, as also noted, there is also the opposite argument that financial transaction taxes, by reducing liquidity, risk increasing the volatility of markets (*Idem*). Evidence on this matter is not clear.

As noted in turn by Ferrer *at al.* (2016), considerations of vertical fairness among member states may also arise, notably because the weight of the financial sector differs in each economy. If, on the one hand, the performance of the FTT with regard to vertical equity is not to be achieved through progressive taxation, it seems logical, on the other hand, that richer economic actors would be more likely to bear the application of the FTT (*Idem*). However, this assumption is not without its shortcomings: (i) the passing of the tax burden from financial providers to financial product consumers; (ii) the tax treatment of activities that are by no means speculative; (iii) the effectiveness of the measure as a way to prevent future bubbles and financial crises.

Considering the pros and cons of the institution of an FTT, notably at the EU level, Darvas and von Wiezsäcker (2010) consider that the preferable option, from an efficiency point of view, would be a small but non-zero tax, that is, a sufficiently small tax so that the respective welfare benefits exceed the welfare costs.

---

37 In this regard, Beck and Huizinga (2011, p. 68) consider that FTT is not the right instrument to reduce risk-taking and fragility in the financial sector, as all transactions are taxed at the same rate, independently of their risk profile. The alternative could be a 'financial activities tax' (FAT) to be applied to the combined profits and wage bill of financial institutions and thus would be a broad tax on income generated in the financial sector (*Idem*, p. 69).

In the European Commission's (2018c) staff working document, it is acknowledged that such a proposal, with the implementation of all the regulatory reforms after the crisis, has in the meanwhile become outdated. Moreover, the European Commission (2018c) recalls that the legal difficulty in adopting such a proposal after the 2011 proposal was due to the imposition of the unanimity principle, which was not overcome at that time.[38] Even so, the European Commission (2018c) has not discarded an FTT as a viable candidate to expand the system of own resources, considering that it fulfils many criteria to be regulated and assigned at the EU (central) level – in particular its mobile tax base and cross-border nature.

Interestingly, greater importance and detail are given now to the implementation of a *common consolidated corporate tax base own resource* (European Commission, 2018c). As mentioned by Le Cacheux (2007, p. 21),

> one major argument in favour of making (part of) the corporate income a European tax is that differences in current national corporate tax systems, both in the definition of the tax base and in rates, are a major source of distortions in location decisions of firms within the internal market and/or of profit-shifting within the EU multinational corporations.

The corporate tax has become an instrument of tax competition that has clearly resulted in a 'race to the bottom' in statutory rates as well as in marginal and average effective rates on corporate profits, bringing EU national tax rates below those observed in the rest of OECD countries (*Idem*).[39] Indeed, the idea is not new; however it has faced the limitations arising from the unanimity principle, as well as the general difficulty of reinforcing tax harmonization at the EU level.

The fact is that harmonization of the tax base is considered a precondition for transforming this tax into a candidate as an EU own resource. At the same time, such harmonization is viewed as a condition for the enhancement of the single market. From a single market perspective, national tax laws conflict with the non-discrimination principle and the free movement of services and capital (Wasserfallen, 2013). Despite these advantages coming from tax integration, the fact is that tax structures remain highly diversified in the EU, leading to asymmetric effects coming from tax competition dynamics in the single market (recall the idea

---

38 On the legal issues and difficulties involving the creation of the FTT on this occasion, see Fabbrini (2014c).

39 Bénassy-Quéré *et al.* (2014) explain that tax competition can take place both though tax rates and tax bases. Either way, this induces distortions in the single market and a 'race to the bottom' mostly involving mobile taxes, which may lead to the under-provision of public goods or to a shift of the tax burden from mobile to immobile taxes.

of 'predatory competition'). This kind of asymmetric effects is felt more intensively in the case of corporate taxation – countries that benefit from tax competition dynamics, which are typically low-tax countries, have no interest in supporting tax harmonization, being in principle more resistant to the pooling of tax authority (Wasserfallen, 2013, p. 8).

One of the proposals in this regard was that made in 2018, in the *Manifesto for the Democratization of Europe*, the main signatory to which was the French economist Thomas Piketty (amongst other economists and politicians), and where a reform of the EU budget was proposed. The proposal contained the creation of four new European taxes: a tax on corporate profits, a progressive tax on top wealth, a progressive tax on high incomes and a tax on carbon emissions. With the exception of the latter (see further on for more details), all the other three taxes imply a redefinition of direct taxation principles at the EU level, assigning to European institutions the new role of 'standard-bearer' of the progressive taxation principle, and with it, for the first time in EU budget history, redistributive functions (recall the Musgravian criteria: the central level features redistributive functions, therefore it should be assigned with progressive taxation revenues).

In particular, with respect to the tax on corporate profits, the Manifesto starts by highlighting that, at the moment, the national rate of tax on corporate profits is on average 22% in the EU (whereas it was 45% at the beginning of the 1980s). For this reason, the signatories wish to levy a common tax on corporate profits at an additional European rate of 15% and to raise the global minimum rate to 37% (the sum of the European rate and the national rate).[40,41]

At the institutional level, one should start with highlighting attempts to harmonize direct taxation, in particular the corporate tax base, are recurrent, the most complete of which was proposed in 2016. At that time, the European Commission published four proposals for corporate tax directives to be applied in the EU member countries: (i) the Common Corporate Tax Base (CCTB) directive; (ii) the Common Consolidated Corporate Tax Base (CCCTB) directive; (iii) a proposed amendment to the Anti-Tax Avoidance Directive already in force; (iv) a directive on Double Taxation Dispute Resolution Mechanisms in the EU (see Merks *et al.*, 2016). With respect to the former two – now of more

---

40 More information on this and other proposals contained in the Manifesto is available at: http://tdem.eu/en/a-budget-for-europe/.

41 As for the other two direct taxes, based on a progressive taxation principle, the Manifesto pleads for the institution of true 'fortune taxes': on the one hand, a progressive tax on wealth, with a marginal rate of 1% on net individual estates valued at above €1 million and 2% on those above €5 million; on the other hand, a progressive tax on high incomes, with marginal European additional rates of 10% on annual individual incomes above €100,000 (€200,000 for a couple) and of 20% on those above €200,000 (€400,000 for a couple). The revenues estimated would be around 1% of the EU GDP. More details are available at: http://tdem.eu/en/a-budget-for-europe/.

interest for our purposes – the idea was that the CCTB directive would enter into force in January 2019, and the CCCTB in January 2021. The process has nevertheless failed to take place, once again due to political resistance.

In the CCTB directive, the intention was to set common rules to calculate and determine the taxable profits in EU member states; the tax base for multinational companies would consist of all revenues unless expressly exempted (Merks *et al.*, 2016). Additionally, other common rules could be seen in the following areas (*Idem*): (i) participation exemption regime, in order to prevent double taxation of foreign direct investment; (ii) super deduction for R&D costs, in order to support innovation in the economy; (iii) loss compensation, allowing losses to be carried forwards but not backwards; (iv) Allowance for Growth and Investment (AGI) – that is, a rule against 'debt bias' – in order to neutralize the current framework that discourages equity financing (this rule would in turn be associated with interest limitation rules).

This AGI rule is important. It should be seen as instrumental of the single market, in particular of the CMU (see further on) as it seeks to replace the debt bias in the financing of EU companies by other ways of financing now relying on the capital markets (e.g. equity and bonds). As we have seen before, it is believed that the reinforcement of capital market instruments instead of debt instruments is a way not only to strengthen (capitalize) more non-financial and financial companies, but also to ensure more effective private risk sharing in cases of economic distress. Indeed, as seen previously, credit markets tend to be more reactive and pro-cyclical in the event of a downturn (sudden stops often occur), therefore amplifying the effects of the crisis. Instead, the reliance of the finance structure of a company more on 'capital' (equity) and not so much on leverage makes it more resilient in those bad moments.

Despite the abovementioned difficulties in the field of corporate tax harmonization, the fact is that in the recent proposal by the (European Commission, 2018c) on the reform of the own resource system, the CCCTB regained importance. According to the proposal, the own resource based on this tax base would be calculated by applying the call rate on the value of taxable profits of those companies for which the CCCTB is compulsory, as apportioned to each member state.[42]

An area that also regained importance in the 2018 proposal was *eco-taxation*.[43] In the last couple of years, the EU has definitely assigned the

---

42 The formula would be (European Commission, 2018c): CCCTB *Own resource = call rate * apportioned tax base (mandatory part)*.

43 The issue is not new, either. Recall past proposals aiming at complementing a broad-based consumption tax through a specific tax instrument (e.g. excises duties on alcohol, tobacco and fuels), also with the argument that the different excises would generate distortions in the single market. Moreover, there is here an additional, twofold (maybe contradictory) argument of being a direct and immediate way of collecting revenue and of increasing the

'Environmental Agenda' as a policy priority and the idea of 'Sustainable Europe' as a crucial guiding principle. It is not surprising, then, that within the reform of the EU's financing system, eco-taxation has assumed a prominent place. Within this kind of taxation, two options are on the table (European Commission, 2018c).

On the one hand, the creation of an "Own Resource based on the auctioning revenue from the EU Emissions Trade System" is proposed. The Own Resources contribution would apply only to the allowances distributed to all member states on the basis of 2005–2007 emissions (excluding the allowances auctioned for aviation).[44] The estimated revenue would vary between €1.2 billion and €3.0 billion, depending on the carbon price and auction volumes (European Commission, 2018c). On the other hand, the European Commission (2018c) suggests the institution of an "Own Resource contribution based on Plastic Packaging Waste". This own resource would be proportional to the quantity of Plastic Packaging Waste that is not recycled. The contribution of member states to this Own Resource would be calculated by applying a call rate to this quantity.[45]

Last but not least, the European Commission (2018c) also drew attention to the creation of a *Digital Services Tax* that had been proposed a few months previously.[46] In this proposal, the Commission started by recognizing that current tax rules, based on the physical presence of activities, are no longer adequate to pursue the development of the digital economy.[47] Ancient principles of taxation, such as that according to which profits should be taxed where the value is created, are inadequate for the digital economy, where physical presence of the company is no longer required.

The intention in this proposal was hence to ensure a fair and harmonized system of digital services taxation, and to ensure a level playing field for businesses operating in the EU. For this purpose, the proposal aimed at harmonizing the concept of 'digital service', considered as that where the participation of a user in a digital activity constitutes an essential input for the business carrying out that activity and which enables that business to

---

relative price of goods whose consumption is intended to be discouraged (Le Cacheux, 2007, p. 20).

44 The formula would be (European Commission, 2018c): *Emission Trading System-based Own resource = call rate * allowances * auction clearing price.*

45 The formula would be (European Commission, 2018c): *Plastic Based Own resource = call rate * kg of non-recycled plastic packaging waste.*

46 Proposal for a Council Directive on the common system of a digital services tax on revenues resulting from the provision of certain digital services, COM (2018) 148 final of 21 March 2018.

47 Quoted from the Proposal for a Council Directive proposal, COM (2018) 148 final of 21 March 2018.

obtain revenues therefrom.[48] Moreover, the proposal defines the notion of 'taxable person', an entity whose worldwide revenues are pre-set quantitative thresholds and clarifies the concept of 'place of taxation', according to which the tax is due in the member state(s) where the users are located.

Ultimately, if approved, the Digital Service Tax can also be presented as a good candidate for a future own resource. Moreover, this tax would help to prevent the fragmentation of the single market and to be one of the pillars for the creation of the (recently launched) 'Digital Single Market'.[49]

d) Concluding remarks My concluding remarks on this issue involve two aspects, a formal and a substantive one. As for the formal dimension, bearing in mind these prospects for the future evolution of the EU Own Resources system, the fact is that for the time being, the assignment of tax resources to the central level – which is of a 'reverse-type or "bottom-up driven" nature' – faces the usual limitations and political resistance. It should be stressed that the insufficiency in resources assigned to the EU budget reflects, on the other hand, the limitation of the decisional capacity of the EU regarding tax policy. A major element of sovereignty – tax sovereignty – strictly belongs to the member states,[50] which means that any transferral of tax resources and powers to the central EU level (when implying tax harmonization) must obtain full consensus from the intermediate levels.

In a recent Communication, "Towards a More Efficient and Democratic Decision Making in EU Tax Policy,"[51] the Commission confronted the European Parliament, the European Council and the Council with the alleged causes and costs of non-action in EU tax policy. Not surprisingly, the major cause pointed out for the insufficient progress in the tax field is (once again) the rule of unanimity.

As for the substantive dimension, one can now detail the alleged costs of non-action in EU tax policy. Not only because this inaction jeopardizes the reinforcement of the EU budget (considering that the proposed new taxes would primarily be assigning resources to the EU budget), but also because that inaction jeopardizes the achievement of objectives of the Treaty,

---

48 The ways in which user participation can contribute to the value of a business are of very different kinds. Hence, digital businesses can derive data about user activities through digital interfaces or through the active and sustained engagement of users in multi-sided digital interfaces.

49 See the information available at: https://ec.europa.eu/digital-single-market/en.

50 Unlike that which happens to the other element, monetary sovereignty delegated to the central level (for EMU countries).

51 COM (2019) 8 final.

notably the completion of the single market. Note that the completion of the single market, notably in the production factors side (including firstly and foremost capital) seems to be essential for the reinforcement of private risk-sharing mechanisms. Curiously, insufficient action in the domain of tax policy (which implies, of course, a governmental action) is implying a cost from the point of view of the smooth functioning of the goods, services and factors markets, thus making the Union lack complete and adequate market mechanisms to address economic shocks. Considering that tax policy is one of the most important policies from the point of view of the functioning of the markets (together with regulatory policies), due to the incentives it can give and the internalization of market failures, this insufficient governmental action is indeed depriving market forces from acting properly in the large European single market.

Notwithstanding this, the recognition that tax policy is critical to the sound functioning of the internal market explains the renewed importance given in the recent Proposal of a Council Decision on the system of own resources (recall in this regard European Commission, 2018c) to market-improvement resources, in particular the revision and simplification of the VAT resource and the new CCCTB own resource. In this latter case (coupled with the Digital Service Tax), we are dealing with highly mobile factors or incomes, the base of which is prone to erosion and evasion, and for this reason, affecting the level playing field in the EU internal market.

On the other hand, it should be noted that the VAT resource and the new CCCTB own resource are 'own resources' not because they are typically EU taxes (as the TOR were), but rather because they are driven from national taxes (indirect and direct taxes) that have to be previously harmonized – notably regarding the respective base – in order to accommodate the sharing of the tax base by different layers of government, a mechanism that effectively resembles tax base 'piggy-backing'. Nonetheless, as we have seen in the case of the VAT resource, the fact is that a misjudgement of the nature of the resource occurs: VAT is usually described by member states as a public expenditure, an amount to be transferred to the EU budget.

Assuming, in the near future, the evolution of the VAT resource to a 'true' EU own resource and the effective institution of the CCCTB own resource, a number of difficulties immediately arise: on the one hand, legal problems related to the level of harmonization, and on the other hand, the determination of the tax rate defined at both the national and the central level (the call rate), because the juxtaposition of these different rates can cause problems of vertical tax competition and on equity grounds.

Fundamentally, national governments (the intermediate level) are at the heart of the EU fiscal federal setup. It is therefore a very decentralized setup. As such, deprived of functions typically given to the centre – e.g. redistributive functions – it is also natural that typical redistributive taxes remain allocated to the intermediate governments. Considering the recent proposals, one can verify that the evolution of the GNI resource – that which most resembles a redistributive (or at least not regressive) tax at the EU level – is far from confirming that redistributive nature. In fact, the GNI resource is not even a true tax (or a true own resource), as it is not borne by taxpayers, and the respective call rates are very much dependent on EU budget expenditure requirements, more than tax capacity, in the context of the respective budget balance principle and the restrictive MFF.

Curiously, the GNI resembles a 'grant', a reverse-type of grant (as reverse in the EU fiscal federal setup). Indeed, unlike 'normal' grants that go from the central government to the low levels of government, based on the tax capacity and/or expenditure needs of the recipient, in the case of the GNI resource, the process goes the other way round: the intermediate governments provide the centre with a 'grant' apparently based on the fiscal capacity of the donors (the intermediate governments) yet depending on the expenditure needs of the recipient (the central government), which in turn depends either on the needs or the (economic) capacity of the donors themselves. This is, after all, the redundant logic of 'fair return'.

5.2.1.2.2. THE CURRENT SYSTEM OF GRANTS AND PERSPECTIVES

The choice amongst different types of grants is not irrelevant, either. As previously seen, intergovernmental transfers can ensure the correction of both vertical and horizontal fiscal gaps. Note that fiscal equalization (convergence between regions and/or member states) is not ignored in the EU. However, it should be highlighted that the existing convergence-oriented Funds are not conceived of as typical equalization instruments, aiming at correcting horizontal imbalances and coping with differential net fiscal benefits across states (Cabral, 2016). As noted before, this happens primarily for the following reasons. Firstly, even though some of these Funds (the case of the Cohesion and European Regional Development Funds) have had low-income states or regions as previous beneficiaries, they do not include redistributive formulas, typical of equalization transfers, based on fiscal capacity (e.g. macro indicators or the representative tax system) or expenditure needs (e.g. *ad hoc* criteria or the representative expenditure system).[52] Secondly, these Funds are earmarked and conditional grants (e.g. projects in specific areas, such as the environment, R&D, to support small and medium-sized enterprises, etc.), and not general grants, with the principal purpose of interregional redistribution. Thirdly, most of these grants are also

---

52 On the impact of European Funds on the convergence process between EU countries and within EU countries see, over the years, Ardy *et al.* (2003), Bouvet (2004), Martin (2005), Checherita *et al.* (2009), Shankar and Shah (2008, 2009), Gros *et al.* (2018), Alcidi *et al.* (2018), and Gros (2018a).

matching grants which involve financial effort from both the donor's and recipient's sides, an effort that the latter is sometimes not in a condition to make (Cabral, 2016).

Moreover, it is commonly accepted that the existing set of structural funds (materialized through the EU budget and in particular through its MFF) was not conceived to promote any sort of macroeconomic stabilization. One first justification relies precisely in their insufficient nature as instruments of (regional) redistribution – as they do not rely on any idea of fiscal capacity or of fiscal residuum, they do have not the proper conditions to work, if needed, as an indirect stabilization mechanism. The case with the previously mentioned German equalization grants is illustrative. In the former case, the *Länderfinanzausgleich* (LFA) is meant to redistribute VAT revenue to reduce the variation in per capita VAT receipts among states. States with higher-than-average VAT revenue per capita make transfers to those with lower VAT revenue per capita (Hepp and von Hagen, 2010), thereby ensuring a stabilizer response to weak states in the event of an economic downturn.

As we will see, due to the difficulty in putting into motion this 'top-down' approach relaying in the conjunction of general redistributive with stabilizer goals – which is closer to a typical fiscal federal perspective – a new path seems to have been chosen: to use a 'bottom-up' approach, that is, the idea of seizing the existing EU budget framework – based on earmarked and matching grants for expenditure headings – and to use it for a new goal of macroeconomic stabilization. In other words, typical funds used for resource allocation and regional convergence purposes now take on a novel dimension, that is, they are used to embed a new fiscal capacity for the E(M)U.

The last related aspect is to define whether the fiscal capacity will operate through the EU budget or outside of it and, related to this, what its personal scope will be: EMU countries (including ERM II countries), or instead all the EU countries.

5.2.1.2.3. INSIDE OR OUTSIDE THE EU BUDGET; PERSONAL SCOPE OF THE SCHEME

The EU budget has a life of its own. The ongoing discussion on the future 'own resources' system can be entirely separated from the discussion on the flaws of the EMU, including the lack of a fiscal union and/or fiscal capacity (as a risk-sharing instrument). The EU budget financing options are much more centred on taxes with specific notable purposes, also related to the general policies of the EU – notably, the new 'Environmental Agenda' and the completion of a 'Sustainable Europe' – that go beyond the malfunctioning of the monetary union. Ultimately, according to this reasoning, the EU can survive without a functional monetary union, and this conclusion is obvious as some of the EU countries simply do not belong to the EMU.

In the Communication entitled "New Budgetary Instruments for a Stable Euro Area within the Union Framework,"[53] the Commission acknowledged that the EU public finances already include a vast array of tools that act together with the main headings of the MFF. Therefore, besides the three headings of the MFF – (i) Economic, Social and Territorial Cohesion; (ii) Sustainable Growth and Natural Resources; (iii) Competitiveness for Growth and Jobs – the European Commission (2017b) identifies financial assistance and short-term liquidity support as macro-financial instruments also linked to the EU budget (in particular, the BoP facility and the Macro-Financial Assistance).[54]

The BoP mechanism was adopted in 1988;[55] therefore it preceded the institution of the single currency. It remained in force until 1999 with the entry of the euro; later on it was reactivated in view of the enlargement and of the risks of new member states needing assistance. Therefore, it was revived and amended in 2002 (Council Regulation (EC) No. 332/2002)[56] for non-euro member states (Ferrer et al., 2016, p. 147). In turn, the so-called Macro-Financial Assistance (MFA) (established in 1990 and which is currently also regulated by the same Regulation No. 332/2002) – was specifically designed to support partner non-EU member countries experiencing financial crises (Ferrer et al., 2016, p. 147).

Later on, with the financial crisis, the EU introduced the European Financial Stability Mechanism (EFSM) (Council Regulation (EC) No. 407/2010),[57] offering macroeconomic support for euro-area member states experiencing severe financial difficulties, however with a limited capacity (Ferrer and Alcidi, 2018). Indeed, the EFSM was considered insufficient to address the effects of the crisis, notably in the case of EMU countries. For this reason, a temporary mechanism was created outside the EU budget – the European Financial Stability Facility (EFSF) – that provided assistance to Ireland, Greece and Portugal under the respective (first) assistance programmes (Ferrer et al., 2016, p. 148).

Unlike the EFSF (that has been set up outside the EU budget), the three former instruments – BoP facility, the MFA and the EFSM – have in common

---

53 COM (2017) 822 final, of 6.12.2017.

54 Although with a minor role (inside the EU budget), the *EU Solidarity Fund* providing limited financial aid to member states affected by a major natural disaster, and the *European Adjustment Globalization Fund*, offering one-off-assistance to workers in the context of unexpected dismissals associated with developments in global trade and economic disruption, should be added (Ferrer and Alcidi, 2018).

55 Regulation (EEC) No 1969/88 of 24 of June establishing a single facility providing medium-term financial assistance for Member States' balances of payments.

56 Council Regulation (EC) No. 332/2002 of 18 of February establishing a facility providing medium-term financial assistance for Member States' balances of payments.

57 Council Regulation (EU) No. 407/2010 of 11 May 2010, establishing a European financial stabilization mechanism.

the fact that it is the EU budget that guarantees the support given. For this purpose, the Commission is authorized to borrow on the capital markets or from financial institutions in order to finance the loans (Ferrer *et al.*, 2016, p. 148). In particular, since the creation of the EFSM for Ireland and Portugal, the EU has become a frequent benchmark issuer: since 2011, around €54 billion has been raised through 15 issues of bonds (*Idem*, p. 148).

Outside the EU budget, one can find other public finance tools. On the one hand, instruments aimed at supporting projects that contribute to economic growth and that are financed through additional funding sources rather than the EU budget.[58] This is the case with the 'European Fund for Strategic Investment' under the Juncker Plan (detailed further on), the resources of which are mobilized mostly through the European Investment Bank (EIB) Group. On the other hand, there is the European Stability Mechanism, which is – as detailed further on – an independent institution created to provide assistance to member states in a crisis event.

Given this – when considering the institution of a fiscal capacity at the E(M)U level – the question is whether the fiscal capacity should be set using the mix of taxes and expenditures of the EU budget (the existing ones or others to be created) or a new instrument (a small "budget" or fund with earmarked taxes/contributions to finance specific types of expenditures), outside the EU budget. Moreover, as we will see in the next subsection, the question is whether this new fund or (if it should be the case) the EU budget will have or increase its borrowing capacity - a capacity on behalf on the E(M)U itself (and not of each of its Member States) – eventually backed by the existing own resources or the new tax resources to be created (*supra*, e.g. eco-taxation, digital taxes, corporate tax based own resources, financial transaction taxes).

An issue commonly discussed when analysing the creation of new taxes for financing new risk sharing instruments concerns compliance with EU budgetary rules (even if this were to be a specific instrument only for EMU countries). The problems are different when considering the two plausible solutions.[59]

The first solution would be *the creation of a dedicated fund outside the EU budget*. Here, the main legal issue is the possible disrespect of budgetary principles (contained in Article 310 of the TFEU and in Regulation No. 966/2012 on the financial rules applicable to the general budget of the Union,[60] and complemented by the Council Decision of 7 June 2007 on the

---

58 As it was at the beginning of the integration process, the European Development Fund (EDF), created in 1957 by the member states and not by the European Economic Community (EEC) institutions.

59 For an analysis of this issue, in particular for the case of the European Unemployment Benefit Scheme (*infra*), see Repasi (2017).

60 Regulation (EU, Euratom) No. 966/2012, of the European Parliament and the Council of 25 October 2012.

system of the European Communities' own resources[61]). In particular, the question is whether the principles of unity and universality of the EU budget (articles 310(1) TFEU and 7 and 20 of Regulation No. 966/2012) could be affected, as they imply that all items of revenue and expenditure of the Union shall be included in estimates to be drawn up each financial year and shall be shown in the budget. Given this, any kind of separate or subsidiary budget seems to be forbidden. In Repasi's (2017) opinion, the creation of a fund of this sort outside the EU budget should be accepted provided that the European Parliament and the Council as budgetary authorities exercise a control over the fund as foreseen by EU budget law in Articles 310 *et seq.* TFEU (Repasi, 2017, p. 53).

The other option is *to channel the amounts* due to these risk-sharing mechanisms *directly through the EU budget*. The most important question, with regard to the aforementioned principles of unity and universality, relates to the possibility of establishing an earmarked contribution for a specific purpose (e.g. funding the macro stabilizing instrument). The question arises because as a consequence of those principles, Article 6 of the Own Resources Decision states that "revenue . . . shall be used without distinction to finance all expenditure entered in the general budget of the European Union." However, as noted by Repasi (2017, p. 52), one should distinguish between the establishment of expenditure directly linked to a certain own resource, which is prohibited, and the establishment of a new budget line financed by revenue originating from certain financial contributions (a possibility to be admitted, according to Article 21 of Regulation No. 966/2012).

A related question is to know whether the fiscal capacity will include *only EMU countries* or *all EU countries*. In the most relevant proposals – to be detailed further on – the scope of the device is, in principle, restricted to the EMU countries. After all, once again, we are dealing with an EMU problem to be resolved within the borders of the EMU. An interesting exception is found in Beblavý *et al.* (2015, p. 17), concerning the introduction of the European Unemployment Benefit Scheme (see *infra*). In their study, they include all EU member countries, and this is mostly because if the purpose of the scheme is to ensure countries against asymmetric shocks, then a larger pool of countries is better than a smaller one.

To be in favour of this latter solution is indeed an optimistic/evolutionist view, according to which the ultimate goal of the integration process is that the EMU will include all EU member states and so, ultimately, the EMU budget will be *the* EU budget. This evolutionist idea faces, however, real-world difficulties. The EU budget pursues 'traditional' objectives of its own (e.g. convergence policies, technological improvement, environmental goals, competition and the single market), which do not necessarily have to

---

61 Council Decision 2007/436/EC, Euratom, of 7 June 2007.

intend to be a specific response to the EMU's needs – as a currency union – for macroeconomic adjustment and fiscal policy integration. Moreover, as we have seen before, the design of the EU budget – both on the expenditure and revenue sides – is not prepared to accommodate the responses that the EMU actually needs.[62]

5.2.1.3. Discussing the borrowing capacity of the scheme; from debt restructuring to debt mutualization and debt securitization

5.2.1.3.1. INTRODUCTORY REMARKS

In the aftermath of the crisis, several topics regarding sovereign debt issuance and management have been considered either in the context of policy proposals (e.g. roadmaps for reform) or on academic and scientific grounds. The main questions in this regard, to be developed in the next subsections, are:

a) Should sovereign debt be subject to a process of debt restructuring, and if in the affirmative case, which model for debt restructuring should be adopted at the E(M)U level? Two approaches can be identified, market-based versus statutory approaches.
b) Which alternative mechanisms should be considered for a 'debt centralization' at the E(M)U level? Two contrasting models for debt issuance can be envisaged, 'debt mutualization' and 'debt securitization' models.

The former question is important, because – as we will see – several proposals involving the design or the enhancement of insurance/assistance mechanisms to countries in situation of distress (e.g. under the ESM) usually imply the institution of ordered mechanisms of debt restructuring.

As for the latter question, it should be noted that the discussion involving debt mutualization can be specifically linked to the creation of a fiscal capacity (the issue is then how to finance the scheme and whether borrowing can be accepted as a source of financing) or it can stand on its own. This is not irrelevant both from a financial and legal point of view. In the former case, the fiscal capacity can eventually imply the creation of a new European debt agency (the embryo for a European Treasury) where the borrowing capacity is legally assigned to E(M)U itself. In the latter case, it is still countries' borrowing capacity that is at stake and debt mutualisation, although allowing for risk-sharing in terms of debt service and cost

---

62 See also, on this issue, Iara (2015).

does not prevent that debt issued is still backed by national taxes and accounted as a national debt. Indeed, initial proposals for the creation of Eurobonds and other similar instruments (see further on in this chapter) were not necessarily attached to financing any kind of central fiscal capacity, or alike. The point was simply to create a possibility of risk debt pooling involving EMU countries, notably to allow countries to better cope with national debt crisis.

5.2.1.3.2. MODELS FOR DEBT RESTRUCTURING: MARKET-BASED VERSUS STATUTORY APPROACHES

Bénassy-Quéré (2015, pp. 78–79) highlighted the 'trilemma' faced during the Eurozone crisis management. Since the Treaty excludes both debt monetization and a bailout to member states, the reluctance of Europeans to proceed with debt restructuring led to one of the 'impossible trinities' widespread in the economic literature. As such, in this case, the impossible trinity (in fact, an internal contraction of the crisis management) relied on the coexistence of these three vertices: (i) no monetization; (ii) no bailout clause; (iii) no debt restructuring.

In part because of this, when the sovereign debt crisis emerged, several economists and political leaders advocated that the 'no-debt restructuring' dictum should fall. Indeed, debt restructuring was needed as a way to overcome the trilemma in the crisis management (assuming that the two first vertices were not about to be changed).

Let me start by remembering the Greek events and the debt relief decision obtained by Greece prior to the Second Adjustment Programme. Before this Programme was formalized, in March 2012, the Eurogroup decided – relying on the Private Sector Involvement (PSI) – to promote Greece's debt restructuring, in order to prevent a selective default. In the words of Xafa (2014), "the 2012 Greek debt exchange and subsequent buyback was . . . the largest debt restructuring in the history of sovereign defaults, and the first within the Eurozone." Indeed, out of a total of €205.6 billion in bonds eligible for the exchange offer, approximately €197 billion (that is, 95.7%) were exchanged involving a haircut at between 53.5% and 77.1% (Cabo, 2017, p. 180).[63]

Despite the PSI, the effective voluntary nature of this debt restructuring was not ensured and the so-called free-rider problem remained. To prevent this effect, several measures were conceived: (i) threatening potential holdouts (see *infra*) with no payment; (ii) collective action clauses (CACs; see *infra*) allowing a qualified majority of creditors to change the payment terms of the bonds against the opposition of a group of holdouts; (iii) legal devices

---

63 For more details on the specificity of this haircut, see Zettelmeyer *et al.* (2013).

or financial enhancements putting tendering bondholders at an advantage in future sovereign debt crises (Zettelmeyer *et al.*, 2013).

Even so, the holdout problem was not entirely overcome. In fact, while the aforementioned CACs ensured that the entire Greek-law bonds were exchanged, some holders of foreign-law bonds decided to hold out for full payment (€6 billion out of €28 billion in foreign law bonds) (Xafa, 2014). To avoid an Argentine-style litigation (see *infra*), holdout creditors were paid in full (Xafa, 2014).

Moreover, despite the success of the debt exchange programme, high yields on the new bonds signalled the market's view that a second default in Greece was still considered as a strong hypothesis (Zettelmeyer *et al.*, 2013). The political situation, with the ascent of the left-wing party, Syriza, as a predominant player in the Greek political spectrum, became more complex.

For these reasons, the IMF began to demand further debt relief for Greece as a condition for further IMF disbursements. Given that Greece's largest creditor at this point was the EU –through both the EFSF and the "Greek Loan Facility" (GLF) that had financed the first bailout programme – meaningful debt relief could come only from the official sector (Zettelmeyer *et al.*, 2013). As a result, an agreement with the Troika was settled, ensuring the extension of the maturity of the GLF and EFSF and the controversial proposal of EFSF funding for a partial buyback of Greece's newly issued bonds, which were still trading at a large discount (*Idem*).[64]

The final result of the debt-restructuring programme in Greece was a major shift in the Greek debt structure. As noted again by Zettelmeyer *et al.* (2013), in less than a year, the structure of Greek government debt was turned upside down, with privately held debt (bonds and T-bills) now accounting for only about 20% of the total. Most strikingly, there was a near elimination of privately held sovereign bonds.[65]

Clearly, one can see that the notion of debt restructuring is not straightforward. As noted by Cabo (2017, p. 179),

---

64 Eaton and Fernandez (1995) explain that a buyback is a mechanism of debt restructuring (at the initiative of debtors) that consists of buying back its debt in the secondary markets. They can take various forms depending on the way they are financed. In its purest form, the debtor government buys back the debt with its own foreign exchange. In other cases, foreign donors provide the resources. In 'swap' arrangements, the debtor government has exchanged domestic currency for debt at some specified price. The swap arrangement can be described as a pure buyback combined with a subsidy to direct foreign investment, with the amount of the subsidy depending upon both the price of the debt and the exchange rate.

65 Zettelmeyer *et al.* (2013) also analysed the combined effect of the debt exchange and buyback on Greece's creditors. They concluded that participating investors lost about 65% of the value of their claims on average as a result of both restructuring operations, with wide differences between holders of short maturities, who lost up to 74%, and of longer maturities, who lost far less (Zettelmeyer *et al.*, 2013).

lato sensu, sovereign debt may comprise a set of tools used for government debt management, such as exchange offers, buybacks and early redemptions, currency and interest rates swaps and other financial operations, made with the general objective of lowering the costs of servicing the public debt and fine tune debt maturities, allowing for more even distribution over the years and avoiding excessive concentration of repayments.

In turn, *stricto sensu* debt restructuring involves an element of debt relief for borrowers combined with losses for lenders (Cabo, 2017, p. 179). In particular, this can occur whenever maturities of the old debt are lengthened, interest rates are lowered, a debt *moratoria* is agreed or unilaterally imposed, or there is a reduction of the face value of the bonds/bills (*Idem*, p. 179).[66]

In principle, debt restructuring is the typical solution or outcome for a sovereign debt crisis. Recall that unlike that which happens in the case of a private company bankruptcy, where the insolvency mechanism is an asset liquidation type, in the case of insolvent (subnational) governments, the mechanism is generally of a reorganization type (Liu and Waibel, 2008, p. 226). In fact, in this case, debt restructuring lies at the heart of any insolvency framework (*Idem*, p. 229).[67]

Although debt restructuring can be seen as a *natural* response for public debt, the fact is that, as noted by Bolton and Jeanne (2008), the structure of sovereign debt is usually designed to make debt restructuring more difficult. In fact, since the debt crises in the 1980s that affected several emerging economies, the so-called 'willingness-to-pay problem' has been highlighted.[68]

---

66 Historically, there are several examples of debt restructuring and in particular of debt relief, even on a multilateral basis. In this latter case, as mentioned by Reinhart and Trebesch (2016), the Baker and Brady Plans proposed by the U.S. Secretaries of the Treasury (respectively, James Baker and Nicholas Brady) involved more than 100 countries and were supported by the IMF. The Baker plan of the mid-1980s aimed at encouraging voluntary capital inflows and structural reforms in countries in crisis. It also involved large amounts of preferential lending from commercial banks and multilateral institutions. Due to the limited success of the Baker initiative, a more ambitious plan – the Brady Plan – was announced in 1989. This plan also aimed at promoting growth, capital flows and reforms, but it involved deeper haircuts on the face value than its predecessor. In fact, as noted by the same authors (Reinhart and Trebesch, 2016), while the former implied debt flow relief via rescheduling and delayed repayments, the latter implied debt stock relief and reducing the nominal value of the outstanding debt.

67 Moreover, it can be said that a well-organized process of debt restructuring, including of debt relief, can have positive impacts on economic grounds (e.g. economic growth). On this matter, see Forni *et al.* (2016) and Reinhart and Trebesch (2016).

68 Indeed, due to its own nature, sovereign debt faces limited mechanisms for enforcement: a private agent or corporation is in principle subject to a jurisdiction and legal authority; sovereign nations are not (Aguiar and Amador, 2013). As such, if a sovereign debtor fails to make a contracted payment, creditors have limited legal recourse, relying only on overseas legal instruments and reputational considerations (*Idem*, 2013).

Moreover, all the attempts to frame, on a multilateral basis, debt restructuring processes, *per se* or enclosed in a package of financial assistance (as were/are the programmes provided by the IMF) have faced, in one manner or another, political resistance and have been only moderately successful. This was the case with the proposal for the institution of 'Sovereign Debt Restructuring Mechanisms' (SDRM), made under the auspices of the IMF in the mid-1990s This proposal can, furthermore, be described as a nuanced version of the market-based approach to debt restructuring with features of the statutory approach.

The market-based approach relies mostly on the so-called 'Collective Action Clauses' (CACs). As explained by Guzman and Stiglitz (2014), at the origin of these clauses (in the mid-1990s) was the intention of the International Capital Market Association (ICMA), supported by the IMF, to change the language of debt contracts (see also Díaz-Cassou and Erce, 2011). The new terms were to include a formula for aggregation of CACs and a clarification of the *pari passu* clause. While the former allows bondholders across different series of bonds to vote collectively in response to a restructuring proposal, and the decisions of a super-majority would be binding on all bondholders across all series, the latter clarifies that the issuer has no obligation to effect equal or rateable payment(s) at any time.

Despite the good intentions behind this approach, Guzman and Stiglitz (2014) consider that it is not sufficient to address the current problems that the restructuring process faces, notably the blockage veto from vulture funds,[69] the prevention of unjust enrichment and the existence of distortive credit default swaps. In a similar vein, Berensmann (2011, p. 197) indicated the main problems with the CACs approach, including the holdout problem, where a minority of creditors can block a debt restructuring process that could be advantageous to the majority of the creditors. On this latter aspect, the Greek case (together with the aforementioned Argentine episode) is also illustrative. As we have seen, supermajorities within the CACs can easily be blocked by specialized investors, who by buying a large share of a specific bond at very low prices can further engage in (aggressive) litigation strategies in order to obtain full payment.

Alternative models to the market-based approach have been advocated. The proposal made by Guzman and Stiglitz (2014) for the implementation of a (multinational) legal framework for sovereign debt restructuring is an illustration of what can be described as a statutory approach. Here, we are no longer uniquely facing a contractual/voluntary framework for debt restructuring. We are assuming the codification of principles, the settlement

---

69 Guzman and Stiglitz (2014), recalling the Argentine case in the 1990s, stress that the disruption of the restructuring process was due to the judicial action taken by 'vulture funds' that had bought defaulted assets (debt) and then demanded full payment, blocking the super-majority pro-restructuring assumed in the CAC.

of multilateral legal rules and possibly the institution of *super partes* multilateral courts (or arbitration courts) assigned with the task of adjudicating a restructuring decision involving the sovereign debtor and (all of) its creditors.

The evolution from a typical market-based approach to a statutory approach depends mostly on the nature of the creditors and on the type of relationship that exists between them (assuming the *status quo* relationship on non-seniority[70]), including spillovers or contagion effects. Indeed, the point of departure for the implementation of an ordered (and eventually centralized) plan for debt restructuring is the recognition that restructuring is a 'lesser evil', when the alternative is a disorderly default that can lead not only to severe reputational consequences for the defaulter,[71] but also severe contagion effects (first and foremost to the lenders themselves). The restructuring plan that was presented to Greece reflects the risks that other EMU countries (including the respective financial and banking sector) faced in the event Greece failed to meet all its obligations vis-à-vis its lenders at the time.

Debt restructuring is also related to the nature of creditors: in principle, the more disseminated debt holding is (through a plurality of bondholders), the more securitized (e.g. bonds instead of loan contracts), and the more it is held by private instead of 'official' creditors, the more difficult it is to agree and succeed in a debt restructuring process.[72]

It is not by chance that several proposals – within the reform of the EMU's fiscal governance – made in recent years include measures for orderly debt restructuring. They take into account the fact that future restructuring will be asked of countries (already) in fiscal distress, as some peripheral countries

---

70 In the next subsection, I will address this issue.

71 Recall the consequences for default and the reasons why sovereigns seldom default on their debts (Part I). One should also recall (and consider historical examples to the effect) that default countries can suffer sanctions, either explicit sanctions (and super-sanctions) – e.g. trade retaliation, fiscal house arrest and military reaction – or implicit sanctions, e.g. increasing borrowing costs that can ultimately prevent indebted countries from having access to financing markets. Reputational consequences – which in turn are related to signalling costs – should also explain the difficulty a default country may face in maintaining access to the market (see on this issue, the seminal contribution from Bulow and Rogoff, 1988; see also Eaton and Fernandez, 1995; Paoli *et al.*, 2011; Hatchondo *et al.*, 2011; Fuentes and Saravia, 2011; Mitchener and Weidenmier, 2011; Aguiar and Amador, 2013).

72 Eaton and Fernandez (1995) highlight that in the presence of multiple creditors, the problem is not just that of coordination amongst them, but also the so-called heterogeneity problem. Lenders may have different attributes: there are differences between large and small lenders and between sound and unsound lenders. Small lenders have greater incentives to free ride and so will refinance at a higher rate than large lenders. Moreover, their superior ability to free ride means that small lenders do better in a Nash equilibrium than their share of exposure would imply. A consequence is that in a negotiation between large and small lenders about refinancing the debt, the latter might successfully demand more than their share of exposure would indicate.

are. As noted before, most of these countries – such as Greece and Portugal – have as their main creditors, official creditors (that is, the 'Troika' members) and not, as until the crisis, private creditors. As such, assuming as a possible future financial bailouts through the existing mechanisms (in particular the ESM), it is expected to assume debt restructuring as an element of the package for that same assistance (Dolls *et al.*, 2015b; Bénassy-Quéré *et al.*, 2018).

The most radical and fully centralized debt restructuring proposal – historically explained by the Greek debt crisis episode (followed by other EMU peripheral countries, e.g. Portugal) – was presented by a group of economists led by Pâris and Wyplosz (2014): the proposal was coined the *PADRE plan*. The proponents started by recognizing that some of the peripheral countries had, until then, accumulated unsustainable public debts. In their opinion, unsustainability did not mean bankruptcy; rather, those countries faced a debt burden that would stunt economic growth, preventing the use of fiscal policy to deal with cyclical swings and making them too vulnerable to market sentiment (Pâris and Wyplosz, 2014).

This plan can be described as the ultimate version of the statutory approach, because it includes not only the centralized design of legal rules for debt restructuring (around which creditors should agree), but also a centralized management of the restructured debt. The plan therefore involved an (unique) agency that would acquire a share of existing public debts at face value and swap them into zero-interest perpetuities (that is, an agency for 'problematic sovereign assets management'). Moreover, since the agency had to pay interest on the debt that was bought but would not receive interest on perpetuities, the agency was supposed to face losses, with these losses being assumed forever. In the authors' opinion (Pâris and Wyplosz, 2014), the best entity to be assigned such a task would be the ECB.

5.2.1.3.3. MODELS FOR DEBT ISSUING: DEBT MUTUALIZATION VERSUS DEBT SECURITIZATION

Note the following from Riet (2017, pp. 39–40):

> over the past few years, the European financial institutions as well as the EU have stepped up their securities issuance either to financial assistance programmes (EFSF, ESM) and/or to carry out a specific mandate assigned to them under the EU Treaty (European Investment Bank, EIB, and EU). Given the explicit fiscal backing from all euro area countries, all Member States, or the EU budget, these European institutions tend to have a very high if not the highest credit ratings.

However, the E(M)U is far from having a euro-area fiscal authority (or a Treasury) able to issue 'risk-free' Eurobonds, based on a joint and several guarantee from all participating countries (Riet, 2017). In this author's opinion (*Idem*), the E(M)U faces the so-called *safety trilemma*,[73] for which one of these goals has to be dropped: euro-area stability, open capital market and national safe haven. For Riet (2017), assuming – as given – the objective of a stable monetary union based on free movement of capital, a euro safe haven is required, in order to prevent investors from the safe countries searching for yield across the risky countries in good times, while quickly returning to the safety of their home country (*flight-to-quality*) when financial distress materializes in those same risky countries. Given this, the options to resolve the trilemma, by replacing a national by a 'euro area safe haven', can be of two sorts: to pool (mutualize) national sovereign risk, or to make national public debt more equally safe.

Initial proposals for debt issuing at the E(M)U level involved some kind of mutualization (debt pooling), that is, some kind of mutual guarantee at the central level. Due to the political resistance faced by these debt-pooling approaches, more recent proposals dispense with this feature and rely on the simple idea of making those sovereign assets safer (Lannoo and Thomadakis, 2019, p. 31). Indeed, safety is achieved by some combination of diversification and seniority (Bénassy-Quéré *et al.*, 2018). Table 5.2 indicates the main proposals made in this regard, taking into consideration this distinguishable feature that translates into two different models for debt issuing at the central level.

Table 5.2 Proposals for debt issuing: models of debt mutualization and debt securitization

Models	Model of debt mutualization	Model of debt securitization
Description of the proposals	– De Grauwe and Mosen (2009): Eurobonds – Delpla and von Weizsäcker (2010): blue/red bonds – Bofinger *et al.* (2011): A European Redemption Fund – European Commission (2011): stability bonds – Enderlein *et al.* (2012): A European Debt Agency (EDA) – Ubide (2015): stability bonds	– Brunnermeier *et al.* (2012), Brunnermeier *et al.* (2016b) and ESRB (2018): European Safe Bonds (ESBies) – Leandro and Zettelmeyer (2019) and Zettelmeyer and Leandro (2019): E-bonds (even if not involving tranching)

Source: The Author

73 This trilemma can be, on the other hand, coupled to Schoenmaker's (2011) 'financial trilemma', according to which the three objectives of (i) financial stability, (ii) financial integration and (iii) autonomous financial policies are incompatible – one of them has to be abandoned.

a) Debt mutualisation   Inspired by the seminal proposal for the creation of *Eurobonds* (De Grauwe and Mosen, 2009), Delpla and von Weizsäcker (2010) proposed a model of debt pooling, relying on two categories of bonds: a blue and a red bond. As for the former, EU countries should pool up to 60% of GDP of their national debt under a joint and several liability as a senior sovereign debt, thereby reducing the borrowing cost of that part of debt. The latter would correspond to any additional debt beyond a country's blue bond allocation and would be issued as national and junior debt, with a procedure for orderly debt default. This would thus increase the marginal cost of public borrowing, which would help to enhance fiscal discipline (*Idem*). As a final note, the authors advocate that blue bond allocation to member states ought to be proposed by an Independent Stability Council and voted on by national parliaments in order to safeguard fiscal responsibility (*Idem*).[74,75]

In turn, Enderlein *et al.* (2012) suggest the creation of a European Debt Agency (EDA), intended to be more than a European Stability Fund providing emergency assistance against strict conditionality. Indeed, the EDA should be a flexible instrument covering all scenarios, from facilitating debt issuance in normal times, to assisting countries under short-term financial market pressures, and including the scenario where a euro-area member in default is bailed out by the EDA.

As for the design of the instrument, the authors suggest the following features. (i) The EDA would be jointly guaranteed by all euro area countries: in normal times, all of them would issue a pre-defined share of their debt (i.e. 10% of their GDP) through the EDA, thus establishing a very liquid market for EDA debt instruments. (ii) Should a country be affected by a solvency crisis, the EDA would allow that country to increase its EDA share to a level or strictly limited amount (e.g. another 10 percentage points of GDP); at this stage the only conditionality required would be the fulfilment of the SGP. (iii) For a country with difficulties in refinancing itself beyond this 20% of GDP, the conditions required would be much stricter, involving the signature of a Memorandum of Understanding, with increasing loss of fiscal sovereignty. (iv) For a country in need of financing more that 60% of debt

---

74 An important question discussed was how to handle the transition to the blue bond scheme. Delpla and von Weizsäcker (2010) argued for an approach where all the legacy government debt (i.e. issued before the beginning of the blue bond scheme) should be treated as senior to the red debt but junior to the blue debt. This legacy debt would then be gradually replaced by the senior blue debt and the junior red debt as the existing debt stock were rolled over.

75 A different scheme was proposed by the German Council of Economic Experts led by Peter Bofinger (see Bofinger *et al.*, 2011): the institution of a European Redemption Fund (ERF). The plan would convert into euro bonds the existing debt in excess of 60% of GDP. The ERF bonds would be paid off over 25 years. This is the opposite scheme to that presented by Delpla and von Weizsäcker (2010), where only debt issued by national authorities below the threshold of 60% would be backed by euro bonds (Frankel, 2012).

to GDP via the EDA, this would require formal approval from the latter to adopt its budget – ultimately, the fiscal policy would be effectively carried out by the EDA.

The stability bonds initially proposed by the European Commission (2011) – to be discussed with several possible options – assumed a specific design in the proposal made, a few years later, by Ubide (2015). The idea was to create a partially financed euro-area debt up to 25% of GDP along the full spectrum of maturities of the yield curve. Beyond this threshold, countries would have to finance their own debt, which would ensure market discipline and help to mitigate moral hazard. These bonds (rated AAA) would be issued by the EDA in close cooperation with national debt agencies and would be supported by tax revenues. The revenues could result from transferred national tax revenues (e.g. a shared of VAT) or, at a subsequent stage, result from a European tax (e.g. a carbon tax).

Stability bonds would ensure a response to country-specific shocks, and they would help countries to stabilize their economics. What is more, even for large euro-wide negative shocks, stability bonds could be issued in order to finance a euro-area stimulus package (*Idem*).

For their defendants, the creation of these types of bonds – involving debt mutualization – was clearly justified from the beginning. Matziorinis (2011) detailed the main advantages for their creation. Euro bonds would immediately resolve the euro debt crisis. More important, by reducing the interest rate at which states finance their debt, such new euro bonds would save governments considerable amounts of interest payments, thereby reducing future budget deficits and improving debt sustainability in the long run. By improving debt dynamics in the long run, it would also improve the fiscal outlook and justify lower financing rates. Last but not least, a new euro bond should lead to lower interest rates in the European financial market than those paid by Germany – investors would then wish to hold such a bond, not only for investment and precautionary purposes, but also for payment and transactions purposes (*Idem*).

However, as also noted by the same author, the creation of these types of bonds was not without disadvantages (Matziorinis, 2011). The first was that it might raise the interest rates of the most creditworthy countries, in particular those paid by Germany. Secondly, such bonds might remove the disciplining effect of capital markets on the ability of member states to issue more debt and would institutionalize moral hazard. At the extreme, a euro bond creditor could demand that Germany pay all of the debts a country like Greece or Italy had racked up (*Idem*).[76]

---

76 Smaghi and Marcussen (2019) consider that – due to these various difficulties associated with the introduction of euro bonds – the process has to be gradual throughout a period of transition. During this period of transition, one should not have 'true' euro bonds, but a

b) Debt securitization   In the first years of the EMU's existence, the belief was that a legal framework for sovereign safety had been created. Riet (2017, p. 6) defines a *safe asset* as "a marketable financial claim on public or private sector entities that investors consider to offer a convenience yield because of its special attributes in terms of moneyness, liquidity, volatility and in particular its safety."

As noted in this regard by Brunnermeier *et al.* (2012), modern financial systems rely heavily on safe assets. As such, prudent bank regulation – after the Basel Accords – requires banks to manage the risk in their assets in proportion to their capital; pension funds are another example of a large class of investors that must hold a significant share of safe assets (Brunnermeier *et al.*, 2012). The fact is that, unlike the U.S. – with its Treasury bills and bonds – Europe has not had such safe assets, and the equal treatment of all national government bonds as safe, prior to the crisis, has been shown to be counterproductive.

Indeed, the crisis has put this 'market sentiment' in question. Initial reforming steps (e.g. the Banking Union intending to break the 'doom loop' between sovereign and bank debts, the reinforcement of macroeconomic and fiscal governance, the inception of fiscal backstop facilities – the EFSF, the EFSM and ultimately the ESM), although necessary, are not yet considered sufficient to bring safety back to this problematic financial market.

Given this, the creation of a safe financial asset – a 'safe haven' – seems to be the condition to restore safety to sovereign debt markets, and with it, to restore financial safety in the remaining banking and financial markets. In the proponents' opinion (Brunnermeier *et al.*, 2012), the safe asset, combined with appropriate regulation that gives the correct weights to sovereign bonds, would be able to cope with two problems that the euro crisis has revealed: (i) the doom looping between sovereign debt and banking debt; (ii) the flight of capital to a safe haven in the case of distress. Cronin and Dunne (2018), in turn, argue that one of the principal motivations for this new asset is to reduce the potential for spillovers across sovereign bond markets owing to localized shocks, by reducing the self-fulfilling crisis dynamics within the euro-area sovereign bond markets.

Considering this background, Brunnermeier *et al.* (2012) therefore proposed the creation of a new class of synthetic bonds, labelled as *European Safe Bonds* (in short, ESBies):[77] they are *European*, because they are issued by an EDA in line with the EU Treaty (this does not require more fiscal integration than we have); they are *safe*, by being designed to minimize the risk

---

transitory instrument that they describe as a *purple bond* that at the end of this would be transformed into a typical euro bond (Smaghi and Marcussen, 2019).

77 Further on, also labelled as *Sovereign Bond-Backed Securities* (SBBSs) (ESBR, 2018).

of default; they are *bonds*, freely traded in markets and held by investors and central banks.

The idea is to use the techniques of securitization, diversification and tranching to engineer an instrument with an extra safety and liquidity premium in the market, without involving debt mutualization (Riet, 2017). For this objective, a special purpose vehicle (SPV) – that could be governed by the private or public sector – acquires a maximized portfolio of government bonds from all euro-area countries with market access in a fixed proportion (e.g. the weights could be derived from the relative GDP of the ECB's key capital). Against this portfolio as collateral, two tranches of a synthetic bond would be issued (*Idem*): (i) a relatively large tranche of senior bonds (the ESBies themselves) with a senior claim on the cash flow from this pool of government bonds; and (ii) a relatively small tranche of European Junior Bonds (EJBies) with a junior claim on these payments. Losses on the SPV's portfolio would first be borne by EJBies holders, leaving taxpayers safe. The SPV would be able to generate a 'risk-free' yield curve if ESBies were offered with a range of maturities (Riet, 2017).[78]

Further design issues have also been considered. The first relates to possible 'sub-tranching' in order to cater for different classes of investors. This provides for sub-tranching the junior bond into a first-loss 'equity' piece and a mezzanine tranche each catering to a different clientele: risk-averse investors, such as insurance companies and pension funds would be attracted by the mezzanine tranche, whereas other specialized investors – such as hedge funds – would prefer the first-loss piece (Brunnermeier *et al.*, 2016). The second special designing feature is that ESBies are also 'opened' for the creation of a market for derivatives, and in particular for credit default swaps, CDS (Brunnermeier *et al.*, 2012; Riet, 2017).

Contractual features of ESBies – or senior SBBSs – are also noteworthy. In fact, as can be perceived so far, such bonds combine elements of sovereign bonds, securitized bonds and covered bonds (ESRB, 2018): (i) They are similar to sovereign bonds, because cash flows that accrue from these SBBSs derive exclusively from the underlying sovereign bonds. (ii) They are like securitized and covered bonds, because they are issued by a dedicated entity with no previous trading or indebtedness. This entity would be protected from default – in short, be bankruptcy-remote.

An important remaining aspect related to the design of the SBBSs concerns regulatory policy. The issue is also addressed by Brunnermeier *et al.*

---

78 In a subsequent study, Brunnermeier *et al.* (2016b) propose a base case for the subordination level to be set at 30%, such that the junior tranche represents 30% and the senior one 70% of the underlying face value. Then, the authors proceed with simulations for three scenarios: a severe recession, a mild recession and economic expansion. In turn, Lane and Langfield (2019, p. 53) show that no single sovereign default can impose losses on senior tranches when they are protected by 30%-thick mezzanine and junior ones.

(2016) and more recently by the ESRB (2018). The main question relates to the treatment of sovereign exposures (and reforms to be introduced in this regard)[79] – the question was addressed by the Basel Committee in its meeting of December 2017, but no consensus was reached (ESRB, 2018). Under the current framework, SBBSs would be treated as securitized products entailing subordination of credit risk. This would mean that they would have an unfavourable treatment in comparison to the underlying sovereign bonds: for banks, holding a securitized product rather than the underlying portfolio gives rise to higher capital requirements, justified by higher agency risk; similarly, for insurance corporations (and pension funds), securitizations are subject to capital requirements, putting them at a disadvantage relative to direct holdings of member states' sovereign bonds (ESRB, 2018).

The results of the studies undertaken so far are clear: the appeal of ESBies would greatly depend on regulatory changes affecting sovereign exposures: if an enabling regulation for SBBSs were adopted, banks could hold senior SBBSs (rather than sovereign bonds directly) to mitigate the impact of those changes in the regulatory treatment of sovereign exposures on bank capital requirements.

Despite this belief in the safe nature of ESBies, no asset is absolutely safe – as evidenced by the price of CDS, which can be significant even for the U.S. government; ratings provide a very imperfect guide to safety (Gros, 2018b).

Moreover, SBBSs as a by-product of securitization and collateralization remind us of the origins of the subprime crisis. As noted by De Grauwe and Ji (2018), in the U.S., CDOs were created during the boom years, backed by different securities, e.g. mortgages. At the time people were enthusiastic, because they believed that this source of financial innovation would make financial (and banking) markets more efficient, leading to more financial stability (*Idem*). The fact is that none of this occurred: in contrast, securitization partially explains the outbreak of the crisis. History should not be neglected, and all the mistakes and problems that were revealed at that time should be properly taken into account, and these are explained further on.

The fact is that in De Grauwe and Ji's (2018) opinion, the creation of a safe asset does not eliminate national government bond markets: as a result, the potential for destabilizing flows across the borders of the monetary union remain. Furthermore, it is observable that during crises, the correlation pattern of yields changes dramatically: yields in high-risk assets become highly positively correlated reflecting the dynamics of contagion; at the same time, as investors are looking for safe havens, the yields in safe assets tend to decline sharply (De Grauwe and Ji, 2018).

---

79 Recall on this matter the evolution of regulatory policy affecting the exposure of banks to sovereign debt (see the 'Introduction').

In a similar vein, Lannoo and Thomadakis (2019) highlight the main problems (referred to by market practitioners, credit rating agencies, and Debt Management Offices) that the ESBies/ESJies proposal carries. Firstly, the impact of extreme market events: as sovereign risks become highly correlated among several countries in a situation of crisis, it cannot be ensured that the junior tranche will maintain its safe nature on such occasions. The demand for this tranche decreases, reducing the price of EJBies. This will cause a shift from EJBies to ESBies and push up the latter's prices. Given that arbitrage between these two classes of bonds is not perfect, there are no guarantees that the market value of each of them will cover the cost of buying the underlying government bonds. Ultimately the decreasing price of EJBies will undermine the issuance of ESBies. Secondly, and related to this, there is the risk that investor appetite for this junior tranche may dry up: as the junior and senior tranches need to be issued together, it becomes more difficult for investors interested in buying the junior one (Lannoo and Thomadakis, 2019).

Due to these shortcomings, the same authors show a preference for the alternative proposal – made by Leandro and Zettelmeyer (2018) – of E-bonds, that would be issued by a supranational entity (to cover the financial needs of the euro area) and backed by a portfolio of senior claims towards these same countries. The advantage of E-bonds in comparison to ESBies is that safety would in this case be related to the intermediary itself and not to the specific tranche of the bonds issued by the intermediary (Lannoo and Thomadakis, 2019). More recently, the proponents of E-bonds (Zettelmeyer and Leandro, 2019) have clarified that these bonds imply 'safety' (they are covered bonds) but not 'tranching' (so they are not a securitization instrument).[80]

c) Final remarks   Three final remarks should now be made. Firstly, one should compare the two models detailed here so far – debt mutualization and debt securitization – with the insights driven from Fiscal Federalism theory (and practice). In fact, one of the most important powers assigned to the central level consists precisely of the issuing of typical Treasury bonds (or bills), as a normal way to fund federal state needs. This is a mark of fiscal

---

80 A last, while very interesting, proposal in this regard was made recently by Acalin (2019). The interesting feature of this proposal is that it intends to combine GDP indexed bonds (see *infra*) with securitization: an EDA (which could be the ESM itself) would ensure coordination of the debt issuance in Europe. Each country would issue GDP indexed bonds up to 60% of their own GDP; above this threshold, countries would continue to issue individual traditional plain-vanilla bonds. On the assets side of the respective balance sheet, the EDA would hence buy GDP indexed bonds from euro-area countries: the sovereign risk is not priced since the expected return of such bonds would be equal to the return of plain-vanilla bonds over the maturity of the bond. On the liability side, the EDA would then issue two kinds of bonds: a European safe asset (paying a fixed interest rate) and a European junior asset (paying a variable interest rate) (Acalin, 2019, p. 79).

sovereignty. In the case of the EU, as I have previously noted, such a pre-rogative does not exist: the EU lacks a typical central Treasury (as happens in other federal setups, for example, the U.S. Treasury). What is more, the possibility to issue debt is – in a normal federal setup – generally related to tasks developed at the central level and that are not made in principle (only in exceptional cases) to finance intermediate or lower levels of government. In my opinion, the proposals for debt issuing at the E(M)U level (that is, issuing euro bonds and issuing safe assets) mean, at the same time, less and more than the natural profile for debt issuing in a federal setup that implies the institution of a 'true' Treasury (see Figure 5.1).

They *mean less*, because even proposals for debt mutualization do not imply, in principle, the creation of a 'true' Treasury. As noted before, in most of these proposals it is still countries' borrowing capacity that is at stake and debt mutualisation, although allowing for risk-sharing in terms of debt service and cost does not prevent that debt issued is still backed by national taxes and accounted as a national debt. The EDA may have greater or fewer competences, as a function of the model of debt issuing and according to the approach; but in any of these, the EDA is considered to be a typical Treasury. In fact, this entity is assigned competences for issuing certain types of bonds with specific features and/or to cope with specific shocks, which means that these bonds are not entirely coincident with typical Treasury bonds. Typical treasury bonds imply a full sense of debt pooling – debt issuing is made 'in the name and on behalf' of that sovereign state (including implicitly all its constituencies) – an idea that even in the Eurobonds model is not entirely assumed.

Moreover, only in some of the proposals for the new fiscal capacity – particularly when designed to be typical insurance schemes – it is accepted the respective borrowing capacity, allowing those schemes to fund them-selves in the market in situations of economic downturn when the mecha-nism is to be given traction. This is particularly the case with proposals for the creation of the so-called anti-cyclical funds and of the European Unem-ployment Benefit Scheme, to be detailed next.

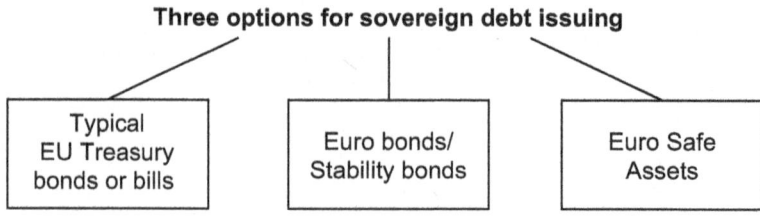

Figure 5.1 The three options for sovereign debt issuing
Source: The Author

However, at the same time, these proposals for debt pooling and debt securitization *mean more* than typical Treasury bonds. In fact, they have a specific purpose, which is to solve or prevent a debt crisis of intermediary levels of government (which are actually also sovereign governments). This is abnormal if one considers the usual fiscal federal setup: the role of the Treasury is neither made to cope with real or possible difficulties from the lower levels of government to finance themselves nor to grant their debt with a supplementary degree of trust and financial safety. In particular, in the case of the safe asset, note that this is presented to mimic the benefits of a true treasury bond (a national safe asset by nature), nevertheless using elements of financial innovation, in particular of structured finance (unlike the plain simplicity of conventional debt instruments), an endeavour that is at the same time audacious and intricate.

A second final remark is related to the fact that SBBSs mean an approximation in the treatment given to public debt to the treatment usually given to private (corporate) debt. Private and public debts are different in their management conditions. As we have seen previously, mechanisms for enforcement in sovereign or public debt tend to be weaker than in the case of private debt. Moreover, in case of default (or difficult liquidity or financial situation), the natural response is a reorganization-type solution (debt restructuring) instead of liquidation.

These specificities in debt management result in turn from differences in the respective debt structure. In fact, as noted by the IMF (2004), sovereign liability structures are not as rich as those of corporations. There are two main reasons for such a different structure.

Firstly, much of the financial structure in private companies is based on equity (stocks) or equity-like instruments, such as convertibles (e.g. bonds that can be converted into stocks on a pre-determined date at a certain exchange rate) or contingent convertibles (the conversion occurs when certain conditions are met – e.g. deterioration of capital ratios). Whenever the financial structure is based on this kind of instrument, investors share the fortunes and misfortunes suffered by the company.

Unlike private debt, in the case of sovereign debt, the financial structure does not incorporate this kind of risk-sharing mechanism that underlies a structure based on equity. Moreover, we are dealing with incomplete contracts, typically non-contingent in the sense that the contract specifies a pre-determined, non-state contingent sequence of payments in a defined currency due at defined points in time (Aguiar and Amador, 2013).

The inexistence of these equity instruments – working as risk-sharing mechanisms within the company's financial structure – can, however, be overcome in the sovereign debt financial structure. As mentioned by the IMF (2004), the benefits of risk-sharing can be mimicked through financial instruments with payment terms indexed to real variables, such as gross domestic product (GDP). Since the seminal contribution of Shiller (1993), increasing interest in this type of instrument has been noted, because they are first and foremost seen as instruments of insurance and of international risk sharing.[81]

Payoff structures of GDP-indexed bonds (that do not need to be symmetric) typically link the size of interest payments to the issuing country's rate of economic growth (Ahrend *et al.*, 2011): higher interest rates in good times and lower rates in moments of economic downturn. As also noted, GDP-indexed bonds can reduce the likelihood of debt crises by acting as an automatic stabilizer against pro-cyclical spending: when countries are hit by a negative macroeconomic shock, the lower interest payments reduce the need for fiscal adjustment (austerity) or additional external borrowing, which could become unbearable (in terms of cost) in those moments of distress (Ahrend *et al.*, 2011).

The second reason that justifies differences of structure between private and sovereign debt relates to the inexistence, in the latter, of an explicit seniority structure, which at the corporate level is naturally required by statute or through bond covenants (IMF, 2004). This is indeed the second reason why we are dealing with incomplete contracts: the repayment of the first lender cannot be made contingent on the contract with the second lender (Bolton and Jeanne, 2008).

As a result, sovereign creditors are more exposed to *debt dilution* than are their corporate counterparts: "Debt dilution occurs when new debt reduces the claim that existing creditors can hope to recover in the event of default" (IMF, 2004, p. 7).[82] As a reaction to debt dilution, investors may tend to opt (and impose) *de facto* forms of seniority, such as the replacement of long-term by short-term debt and/or by debt that is more difficult to restructure.[83] This option involves, in turn, serious dangers for the borrower counterpart, including increasing borrowing costs.

Moreover, corporations issue liabilities belonging to several classes with different priorities in the event of liquidation or bankruptcy: secured debt; ordinary unsecured debt; subordinated debt; preferred stock; common stock (IMF, 2004, p. 22). Additionally, corporations make extensive use of securitization, through structured financing (e.g. collateralized debt), as a way to meet liquidity needs and assign risks related to maturity mismatching

---

81 Pisani-Ferry *et al.* (2013) indicate as one option for the introduction of stabilization mechanisms in the EMU precisely 'debt as equity', that is, that part of debt should be issued in the form of GDP-indexed bonds.

82 As also noted in the same study, debt dilution is analogous to the dilution of equity through new equity issues: when new debt is issued, the recovery value of debt has to be shared among more creditors in the event of insolvency (IMF, 2004).

83 One reasoning for this, according to one model of corporate debt, is that the debtor's inability to commit to a debt maturity structure leads to a sub-optimally short maturity structure (Fernandez and Martin, 2015).

to other institutions (e.g. SPV) more appropriate to assume such risks. In contrast, sovereign liabilities usually fall into one single class – unsecured debt – and the secured debt is residual, where sovereign claims are collateralized by future receipts, such as oil revenue or other exportable receivables (IMF, 2004).

To cope with this peculiar structure, several proposals have been made advocating the introduction, on the one hand, of explicit mechanisms of seniority and, on the other hand, more diversified classes of secured and unsecured debt, including in-between classes.

As for the former suggestion, Chatterjee and Eyigungor (2015) explain that an explicit seniority structure on debt can mitigate the dilution problem, because existing creditors do not have to share default payments with new creditors. Explicit seniority can thus prevent *de facto* seniority as a reaction to debt dilution (e.g. the shift towards short-term debt).

The IMF (2004) suggests that an explicit seniority clause can be implemented in a number of ways, including international treaties or accords, national statutes in debtor countries, or simply on a contractual basis. Alternatively, implicit forms of seniority – e.g. implicit (negative) covenants[84] – can be introduced, in order to protect the financial interests of creditors by restricting the borrowing's financial decisions: this is the case, for example, with the imposition of quantitative fiscal rules, limiting budget deficits or placing limits on (external) debt (IMF, 2004, p. 23) and possibly expenditure ceilings.

Moreover, processes of securitization, relying on structured financing, are not out of the picture. Indeed, public debt is, in principle, also a good candidate for securitization, in particular for the creation of collateralized debt obligations (CDOs) involving tranching and the definition of different degrees of seniority (e.g. senior, mezzanine and junior tranches).

Bearing in mind these considerations, we can see the safe asset, in its various forms (because we are dealing with securitizations and/or covered bonds), implies not only the attempt to make sovereign debt more 'secured' – thereby promoting financial safety in the European debt market – meaning, above all, an approximation in the structure of sovereign debt to the structure of private corporate debt. The safe asset is indeed a way of 'privatizing' public debt.

The last remark I would like to make on this matter concerns the role of monetary policy and how it relates to the creation of safe assets. The

---

84 Note that covenants (in the corporate financing structure) can be either positive or negative, in the case of involving impositions or prohibitions to the debtor. Negative covenants – the most common – can include, for example, clauses implying limits to indebtedness or borrowing, restrictions on the distribution of dividends, negative pledge clauses, restrictions on investment, merger prohibition, etc. (see, on this issue, Oliveira, 2015).

implication is twofold: firstly, to address the question on how the SBBSs can eventually be incorporated in APP (a programme, within QE, that – as we have seen before – has been discontinued but not entirely abandoned); secondly, moreover, to explain the current signal of monetary policy (marked by very low, not to say negative, interest rates) in the light of this continuing appetite in the markets for safe assets.

The first question is related to the fact that SBBSs are not specifically covered by the Eurosystem collateral framework. However, in the sense that they can be described as 'asset-backed securities' (ABS) (e.g. because debt securities are backed by a pool of ring-fenced financial assets and issued by a special entity), then they could (under existing guidelines) be subject to ABS-specific collateral eligibility criteria (ESRB, 2018).

The second, more important, question relates to the secular decline in real interest rates (an expression of secular stagnation) related to the growing shortage of safe assets, a shortage that became acute during the GFC (Caballero and Farhi, 2014). Caballero and Farhi (2014) describe a mechanism that leads to the so-called 'safety trap'. Coping with safety traps (and with safety shortages) involves several alternatives within conventional and unconventional monetary policy: (i) helicopter money; (ii) the purchase, amongst others, of risky assets (as was the APP, and within it the PSPP); (iii) forward guidance policy, etc. Many of these alternatives have been adopted by central banks after the GFC, and by the ECB in particular.

The challenge now – in a context of economic uncertainty, fragile economic growth and apparent exhaustion of monetary policy tools – is to promote the supply of safe assets outside the frontiers of monetary policy. In most proposals, the EDA in charge of issuing safe assets (which in many of the proposals is the ESM itself) is a non-monetary policy agency. The EDA is indeed at the frontier of a fiscal (union) institution.

5.2.2. Taxonomy proposed for a fiscal capacity

5.2.2.1. Introductory remarks

In the next subsections I will analyse the four types of governmental 'risk-sharing' mechanisms that can possibly embody the idea of a fiscal capacity for the EMU. I will take into consideration the main proposals that have been made in recent years, notably since the *Four Presidents' Report*, including academic and scientific articles and the several 'roadmaps' for EMU reform (previously described).

The identification of types of financial grant instruments dates back to MacDougall *et al.* (1977), which (coupled with limited borrowing powers) could make the European Community (EC) evolve into a federal-type model of fiscal integration. Such financial grant instruments were: firstly, the implementation of an unemployment scheme at the EU level; secondly, the implementation of cyclical general purpose grants; thirdly, the establishment of a 'conjunctural convergence facility' with the objective to extend grant finance to economically weak member states in particularly difficult economic situations.

On the other hand, it should be noted that the *MacDougall Report* (MacDougall *et al.*, 1977) also suggested that apart from stabilization, the EC should deepen regional redistribution (as an alternative to a true model of inter-individual redistribution possible only in a complete federal setup). One possibility was to implement a horizontal budget equalization mechanism (of the type of the German inter-Länder equalization device – *Finanzausgleich*), with the objective of raising the per capita fiscal capacity of economically weak member states in the EC up to a minimum of 95% of the EC average.

Alternatively to this type of equalization and cyclical grant, a mimic version can be envisaged in recent proposals. The design of the instrument is to be detailed. In all cases, two possible approaches can be identified: (i) a 'top-down' approach, where a general convergence (or regional redistributive) fund would also produce a stabilizer effect – the aforementioned 'conjunctural convergence facility' of the *MacDougall Report* could lie at the origin of this approach; (ii) a 'bottom-up' approach, where sectorial grants to states or regions, that is, grants in specific sectors (e.g. investment and other expenditure related to transportation, communications, energy, environment, housing, etc.), thereby primarily ensuring a (Musgravian) function of allocation of resources, could indirectly also be used for the stabilization function. In fact, in this case, by targeting and financing expenditures with a high multiplier effect, one could ensure this double side-effect. Ultimately, therefore, it could be said that in this case, stabilization would go hand in hand with allocation of resources.

Taking this into consideration, the taxonomy proposed here includes four main types of plausible solutions for the design of a 'fiscal capacity' in the EMU. Three of these are: (i) a European unemployment insurance scheme; (ii) anti-cyclical funds; and (iii) convergence-based funds, that can in turn be subdivided into two solutions according to the two mentioned approaches, the top-down and the bottom-up approaches. Finally, (iv) I will also include in the list of these risk-sharing mechanisms the so-called 'fiscal backstops', by explaining their overall stabilizer capacity and considering their relationship with other policies. My point is that fiscal backstops – as a modality of governmental risk-sharing mechanisms – can act as 'market-makers' and ensure a better functioning of private risk-sharing mechanisms, notably by enhancing the single market (Figure 5.2)

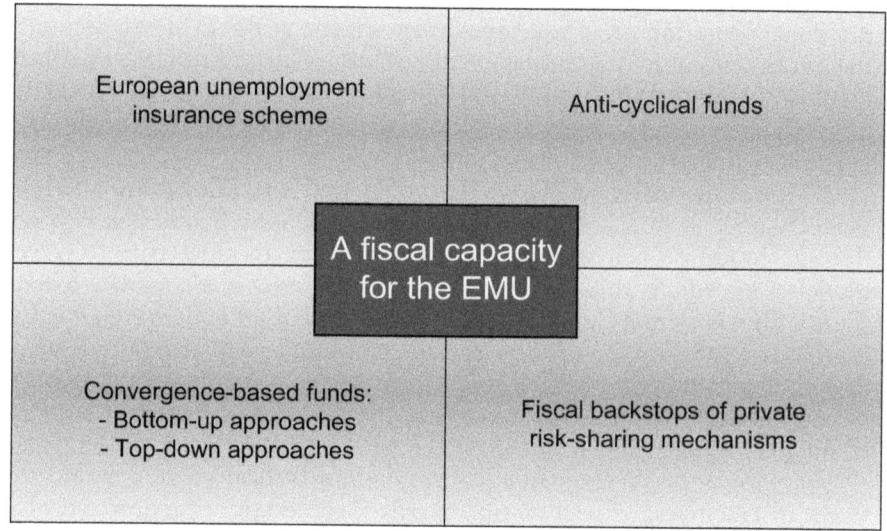

Figure 5.2 A fiscal capacity for the EMU: taxonomy proposed
Source: The Author

5.2.2.2. A European unemployment insurance scheme

The proposal for the creation of an unemployment benefit scheme in Europe dates back to the *Marjolin Report* (Marjolin, 1975).[85] At that time – an economic period marked by stagflation – concerns with high unemployment rates in Europe were at the centre of the debate. In particular, high rates of long-term or structural unemployment and their relationship with regional inequality or economic divergence between European regions and states was also a matter of political concern. Therefore, the report assumed the following main purposes of the future unemployment scheme (Marjolin, 1975): (i) to help to reduce structural and regional imbalances through transfers of income from areas with low structural unemployment to areas with high structural unemployment; (ii) to guarantee unemployed persons in the Community a common minimum level of benefits; (iii) to promote regional flexibility, making it possible to cope with changes in regional developments and in the standard of living; (iv) to help to give a visible expression to Community solidarity; (v) to allow member states considerable freedom to retain their present national schemes, with differences regarding coverage and the amount of benefits.

Due to these significant differences between national unemployment schemes, the report acknowledged that the creation of this European scheme should be gradual, in stages. In the first stage, the Community fund for

85 Also covered in the *MacDougall Report* (MacDougall *et al.*, 1977).

unemployment should be preferably financed by a Community contribution from new resources than pooling the revenue and expenditure of the national schemes. In a longer-term context, some harmonization of social security schemes should happen, at least with regard to their main features (e.g. conditions, coverage, amount and duration of benefits). Two types of schemes could be implemented: on the one hand, a proportional scheme guaranteeing unemployed persons a certain income as a percentage of their last income; on the other hand, a flat-rate amount to all beneficiaries. This instrument would be an independent institutional unit, with funds not channelled through the European budget, and the participation of social partners would be ensured in its respective management.

Despite its early inception, the fact is that in the following years the idea did not develop any further. Only in the beginning of the financial crisis, Dullien (2007) in a study that would be further developed under the auspices of the European commission (Dullien, 2012, 2013) would the proposal be reborn. Indeed, at a moment where the crisis was causing its more dramatic economic and social impacts (with the significant increase of unemployment rates in many European countries), the European Commission immediately after the *Four Presidents' Report* (Van Rompuy *et al.*, 2012) gave the issue a new political priority. At the same time, the Commission included the topic in the development of a new Social Dimension of the EMU (Strauss, 2016) that would eventually lead to the launching by President Juncker, in 2017, of the *European Pillar of Social Rights*.[86]

The model conceived for Europe is usually associated and justified with the existing federal model in the U.S. As seen previously, the U.S. unemployment insurance (UI) system is a 'federal-state' system (Lenaerts *et al.*, 2017), because each state finances the scheme through payroll taxes paid by employers.[87] Inspired by this U.S. model, the first topic related to the design of the European unemployment benefit scheme (EUBS) is if the scheme would be a *genuine* or an *equivalent* scheme. In the former, unemployment benefits are paid directly to unemployed individuals and would be funded through contributions from employers and employees (Lenaerts *et al.*, 2017). This scheme can, at least partially, replace national schemes (although it can be supplemented by national amounts and/or benefit duration periods, if higher). In the latter, financial transfers for the EUBS would occur between the state and a suprastate entity (*Idem*), usually only when triggered by a major adverse event (Gros, 2016c). This means that the equivalent scheme is also a reinsurance scheme, i.e. a scheme that does not in any way replace, but rather re-insures them (Gros, 2016c).

---

86 See information available at the EC website: https://ec.europa.eu/commission/priorities/ deeper-and-fairer-economic-and-monetary-union/european-pillar-social-rights_en.

87 For a full description of the U.S. unemployment benefits system, see also O'Leary and Barnow (2016).

The genuine model of the EUBS would in fact correspond (or at least approximate more) to the normal U.S. unemployment scheme, because here the system is financed through contributions from both employees and employers (even if with respect to the latter with some specificities related to the federal nature of the system). Instead, the equivalent scheme would very much resemble the second branch of the U.S. system, composed of the Emergency Unemployment Compensation (EUC) and the permanent Extended Benefits (EB) – a program made to extend the duration of benefits in the case of economic downturn – because they are entirely paid by the 'supra state' (in this case, the U.S. government) to the states.

In the first proposals (Dullien, 2007, 2012), only a genuine model seemed to be considered. Later on, Beblavý and Maselli (2014) and Beblavý et al. (2015) analysed the two alternative models. Further on, in the major project/study conducted by a research consortium led by the Center for European Policy Studies (CEPS),[88] and entitled *Feasibility and Added Value of a European Unemployment Benefit Scheme*, both alternative models were analysed in detail.

In this project (European Commission, 2017b, p. 22), the equivalent EUBS (in its basic form) is marked by a trigger, experience rating and claw-back mechanisms (see further on). The trigger – a condition that determines when the EUBS becomes active (i.e. when funds are paid out) – was assumed to be the short-term unemployment rate. Debt issuing captures whether the fund is allowed to issue debt to cover short-term imbalances. In the study (European Commission, 2017b, p. 22), the EUBS is triggered when a country's short-term unemployment rate in quarter t exceeds its average short-term unemployment rate in the last 40 quarters (or 10 years), plus a certain percentage (i.e. 0.1%, 1% or 2%).

As for the genuine EUBS (the basic variant), unemployment benefits are paid to all those unemployed who have worked as employees during at least 3 out of the last 12 months (eligibility) (European Commission, *Idem*, p. 23). These individuals are entitled to unemployment benefits equal to 50% of their last gross wage, capped at 150% of the national average wage (benefit level). Benefits are paid out for 9 months, from the start of the 4th month until the end of the 12th month of unemployment (*Idem*, p. 23).

With respect to the financing sources, whereas the genuine EUBS should be financed as a typical UI, that is, through contributions collected from employers and employees, the equivalent EUBS would be financed with contributions collected from the member states: each member state would contribute 0.1% of its GDP every quarter until 0.5% of EU GDP is accumulated (then, countries would cease to contribute); when the balance of the fund drops below 0.5% of EU GDP, contributions would restart (start-stop mechanism) (European Commission, *Idem*, p. 27). The study also admits – notably with respect to the equivalent EUBS – the possibility of debt-issuing as a way to address

---

88 Carried out by the main researchers Miroslav Beblavý and Karolien Lenaerts.

any short-term imbalances of the EUBS fund. The alternatives – nevertheless reducing the stabilization effect of the scheme – would be to adjust some parameters of the EUBS to reduce its costs (e.g. eligibility criteria) or to increase the contributions from the member states (*Idem*, p. 35).[89]

In any case, both solutions involve typical problems of insurance schemes. The first problem (or challenge) is *moral hazard*. Note that in the case of unemployment benefit schemes involving a federal or multi-tiered organization besides individual moral hazard, one has to deal with the so-called institutional moral hazard. The latter arises if there is a possibility for the beneficiary regions or states to influence the costs of UI borne by the federation (Vandenbroucke *et al.*, 2017). This is particularly the case when the federation is responsible for the financing and payment of the UI benefits, but where all other aspects of the management of the scheme (including eligibility criteria and activation policies) rely on the sub-central governments (SCG). Note that there is here a degree of asymmetric information, which makes it impossible for the federal government to fully disentangle the impact of pure risk factors, not controlled by the SCG, and the impact of deliberate SCG policies on the actual incidence of the risk borne by the central government (Vandenbroucke *et al.*, 2017).

Institutional moral hazard can be more perceived in the case of the equivalent EUBS than in the genuine EUBS. To address this kind of moral hazard, one can identify *ex ante*, *pari passu* and *ex post* mechanisms:

- *Ex ante* mechanisms: the introduction of a trigger, which in turn is composed of an indicator and a threshold: in every period (e.g. a month, a

---

89 Moreover, it should be noted that the implementation of the EUBS is subject to legal constraints. The question is whether the two versions of the EUBS have a legal basis in the Treaty on the Functioning of the EU (TFEU). According to the European Commission (2017b), a legal base for the equivalent EUBS can be found in Article 352(1) of the Treaty, whereas the legal base for the genuine EUBS results from the combination of Articles 175(3) and 352(1). Note also that these Articles are not subject to the 'no-bailout clause' – Article 125(1). In turn, Repasi (2017) discusses the basis for the 'financing side' of the EUBS, distinguishing whether the EUBS is implemented in or outside the EU budget. In the case of *being implemented through the EU budget*, the base would be Article 314 TFUE, together with Regulation No. 966/2012 on the financial rules applicable to the general budget of the Union. Regarding the equivalent EUBS, the main question is whether those contributions can be qualified as new 'own resources' or as 'other revenue'. As for the genuine EUBS, the fact of being financed by employees and employers (instead of member states) may raise additional difficulties for its inclusion in the EU budget. Notwithstanding, a precedent for directly raising from individuals can be found in Article 9 of Regulation (EC) No 443/2009 setting emission performance standards for new passenger cars (Repasi, 2017, p. 50). As an alternative to introducing a budget line in the general EU budget, which is financed by external assigned revenue originating from member states (equivalent EUBS) or from employers and employees (genuine EUBS), one could consider *the establishment of a Fund outside the EU budget*. The model would, for example, be the European Development Fund. The question is if the implementation of this fund would undermine or not the *principle of unity* that requires all expenditures and all revenues to be part of one EU budget (Repasi, 2017, p. 53).

semester or a year) in which the indicator exceeds the threshold, transfers are carried out to a particular country (Beblavý *et al.*, 2015). As we saw earlier, the indicator for risk sharing or insurance devices is related to the rate of change of an indicator of economic activity, rather than to its level (*Idem*). For a UI scheme, the typical indicator would hence be the change in the unemployment rate. The choice of the threshold matters: a high threshold means that only major economic shocks would trigger transfers from the EUBS, thereby limiting greater moral hazard. In a similar vein, Claveres and Strásky (2019) adopt for their model of unemployment benefits reinsurance scheme a 'double condition trigger' as a way to prevent moral hazard, that is, activation of the scheme occurs when the unemployment rate is both increasing and above the long-term average.

- *Pari passu* mechanisms: these are mostly related to the implementation of activation policies (e.g. the SCG may prevent measures to help unemployed workers re-enter labour markets from being put into motion, in order to benefit more from the unemployment grant from the central government). Therefore, a stronger harmonization of these features – imposed by the centre to low levels of government – helps to mitigate asymmetric information, and possibly also to address social dumping and a 'race to the bottom' competition with respect to social protection (Lenaerts *et al.*, 2017).

- *Ex post* mechanisms: these mechanisms that connect pay-in with payout can be of two types – 'experience rating' and 'claw-back' mechanisms. In the former, the purpose is to link the pay-in into the supranational fund to the likelihood of using it (European Commission, 2017b, p. 31). In the latter, the contribution of each country to the EUBS fund depends on the net balance of the past net contributions of that country. Note that in an equivalent EUBS, claw-back mechanisms are very much like experience rating – e.g. the pay-in of a country is increased after a certain number of years (for example, three years) of a negative balance vis-à-vis the fund that exceeds a certain percentage (of the GDP).

In turn, both the genuine and the equivalent EUBS (can) involve an individual moral hazard (that can hence be juxtaposed with the institutional moral hazard). Once again, three types of mechanisms to address individual moral hazard can now be implemented:

- *Ex ante* mechanisms: access or eligibility periods (the bigger they are, the more they can prevent moral hazard) – in actuarial terms, the existence of this eligibility period can be an alternative to the payment of a deductible or to the specification of a trigger, notably when the insurance is made to be provided upon verification of the event regardless of its dimension or severity.

- *Pari passu* mechanisms: the case where a condition to obtain and maintain unemployment benefit is that the beneficiary be actively engaged in the search for a job, or at least for a suitable job.

- *Ex post* mechanisms: through 'experience rating', where firms that expose their employers more to unemployment may have their contribution increased.

It should be noted that the preoccupation with moral hazard, first and foremost with institutional moral hazard, aims at preventing another risk (or problem) in this kind of insurance scheme: that transfers under the EUBS fund become permanent transfers, that is, a form of *permanent redistribution* between states (Gros, 2016c). The fact that the scheme is designed to be reactive to changes in employment status rather than to employment levels makes it less prone to the verification of permanent transfers (Dolls *et al.*, 2015a). Moreover, the fact that the system is targeted to short-term (rather than structural) unemployment also helps to ensure the avoidance of permanent transfers (APT).

However, as noted by the same authors (Dolls *et al.*, 2015a) it may be the case that net transfers are unevenly distributed across member states if flows into unemployment diverge permanently or if there are permanent differences in the level of short-term unemployment. Claw-back mechanisms are made precisely to mitigate this effect and therefore to ensure the neutral balance of long-term *net balance contribution* (NBC) to the fund. As noted by Beblavý *et al.* (2015), if it is right to say that NBC implies APT, the reverse is not true: NBC is a strict concept that is not implied by APT. NBC means that if a member state has a negative cumulative balance (i.e. has received more than it has paid to the fund), the scheme can adjust this situation by increasing the country's pay-in or demanding a supplementary contribution (Beblavý *et al.*, 2017, pp. 294–295).

The last (but not least important) issue related to the creation of the EUBS involves its *stabilization effects*.[90] As the EUBS is unemployment-based, it has the advantage of providing benefits that are counter-cyclical and very responsive to shocks. Moreover, they are automatic and fast, providing a quick source of income to the unemployed to support their consumption spending. Finally, it has a high multiplier effect – estimated in several studies as higher than one (European Commission, 2017b, p. 18).

At this stage, the above-mentioned distinction between spatial risk-sharing and consumption smoothing should be recalled. Indeed, as noted by Gros (2016c) and the European Commission (2017b, pp. 25–26), within the stabilization function of the EUBS, one can distinguish:

i) A *geographical (spatial) insurance role* that refers to the reallocation of resources across member states within a given period (Alcidi and Thirion, 2016) – this is 'true' risk-sharing whereby resources that are

---

90 Other additional effects of the EUBS have been highlighted. Alcidi *et al.* (2017b) in particular discuss the effect of the EUBS on labour mobility.

temporarily pooled together are distributed to those countries and regions in greater need. As this entails only distribution of the resources available at any point in time, spatial risk-sharing would not require the ability to issue debt. This kind of insurance would suffice to cover asymmetric shocks in small and medium-sized economies, but it would not be sufficient in the event of major symmetric shocks or an asymmetric shock to a significant proportion of the economy.

ii) An *intertemporal insurance role* that would involve the reallocation of resources across time (consumption smoothing) (Alcidi and Thirion, 2016). This could be achieved through debt issuing or by allowing a supranational fund to go into deficit in recession while compensating in good times (e.g. through the accumulation of reserves). This role is appropriate to deal with major asymmetric or extended downturns (European Commission, 2017b).

In turn, Dullien (2013) and Beblavý *et al.* (2015) point out another distinction regarding the stabilization effect of the EUBS. On the one hand is the so-called average country marginal stabilization effect, which is the average effect across all member countries during a recession. On the other hand is the 'true' marginal stabilization effect, that is, the effect during a recession in the most severely hit countries.

5.2.2.3. Anti-cyclical funds

Following the initial literature in this regard (the aforementioned, Goodhart and Smith, 1993; Commission of the European Communities, 1993; Hammond and von Hagen, 1995), Furceri and Zdzienicka (2013, pp. 12–13) recall that a stabilization mechanism should present certain optimal features: (i) the mechanism should be simple and automatic, also reducing strategic behaviour; (ii) contributions to the stabilization fund and transfers should not be regressive (i.e. they should not decrease as *per capita* income gets smaller); (iii) transfers should be temporary; iv) transfers should be a function of serially uncorrelated shocks (thereby reducing the risk that transfers can be manipulated by member countries, thus reducing moral hazard problems); (v) the scheme should be able to offset a large part of the shock.

Based on these premises, several proposals for the creation of an anti-cyclical device have been made since the onset of the crisis. In general terms, this concerns an automatic and visible insurance (transfer) scheme, that is, a system of financial support based on the business cycle and using deviations from potential output as an indicator or benchmark. [91]

---

91 Recall, in this regard, the *automatic transfer scheme* proposed by Wolff (2012) and Pisani-Ferry *et al.* (2013). As noted before, the idea would be to complement the SGP, which is centred on the budget balance net of business cycle effects, with a system of financial

Von Hagen and Wyplosz (2008) propose a *fiscal insurance system* aiming at insuring the tax revenues of participating governments against transitory asymmetric shocks. Such shocks may be correlated over time, but in order to guarantee the long-term neutrality of the scheme, only shocks that do not permanently affect the level of taxes can be insured. Indeed, the mechanism is able to disentangle transitory shocks from permanent ones, using for that purpose, as a shock indicator, the deviation from the potential output.

As such, assuming that tax revenues are proportional to GDP ($T_{it} = \alpha Y_{it}$), the design of the transfer scheme can be achieved by tying payments to the deviation between actual (Y) and potential GDP (Y^*),

$$t_{it} = \lambda \alpha ((Y_{it} - Y_{it}^*) - \beta(Y_t - Y_t^*))$$

where λ is the degree of insurance chosen by government, and β is the weight of country i in the euro-area potential GDP.

The authors (Von Hagen and Wyplosz, 2008) then identify a moral hazard problem, in particular in the case where the government overstates its Y^* in order to reduce its payment into the system. This problem can be addressed through two main ways: (i) *ex ante* mechanism, to delegate the computation of the potential GDP to an independent institution (e.g. the European Commission); or, alternatively, (ii) *ex post* mechanism, a penalty for cheating. This would be achieved by modifying the transfer formula in order to assure balance over time, as follows:

$$t_{it} = \lambda \alpha (Y_{it} - Y_{it}^*) - \beta(Y_t - Y_t^*) - \sum_{j=0}^{t-N} (1 + r_t)^{N+j} t_{it-N-j}$$

The new term of the equation (the latter one) is the penalty term, since in the event of cheating it reduces transfers received in period t through a part of the accumulated transfers in the past.

Enderlein *et al.* (2013) advocate the creation of a *cyclical shock insurance* scheme (CSI), aiming to reduce the difference between individual member states' business cycle positions and that of the euro area as a whole, in order to achieve higher levels of business cycle convergence. The shock indicator is the output gap, notably the difference of the gap of a euro-area member relative to the euro-area average output gap.

---

support based on the business cycle. Countries whose output is significantly below the potential output would be allowed to run deficits and would be supported by common resources (Wolff, 2012). In the scheme, absolute (not relative) deviations of output from potential output would trigger transfers to the countries hit by the shock. Moreover, since the business cycles are correlated in the euro area, this capacity would need to borrow during recessions and would balance out only over the business cycle (e.g. extracting payments from countries with output above potential output in good times) (Pisani-Ferry *et al.*, 2013, p. 5).

A country's annual transfers are calculated by the formula:

$$T_i = \alpha((Y_{EZ} - Y_{EZ}^*)/Y_{EZ}^* - (y_i - y_i^*)/y_i^*) \times y_i^*$$

The convergence variable α denotes the share of the difference between a member country and the euro-area output gap to be offset. In the baseline scenario, $\alpha = 0.5$, which results in an average reduction in the standard deviation of 40%. The basic assumptions of the estimation are: (i) CSI payments affect only actual GDP (Y) and not potential GDP (Y^*); (ii) payments are based on this year's GDP net transfers; (iii) a total fiscal multiplier of 1.2 is assumed.[92]

The authors (Enderlein et al., 2013) then address the issue of moral hazard. To deal with *ex ante* moral hazard, the introduction of a common rulebook for domestic stabilization is proposed. To deal with *ex post* moral hazard, the introduction of earmarking transfers is suggested and their advantages to both contributors and recipient sides are discussed. Earmarking can have advantages mostly in the latter case, as it implies allocating funds to expenditure increase or to tax cuts where multipliers are higher, where time lags are shorter and where this does not crowd out private spending (e.g. a decrease in social security contributions). Moreover, it is explained that the scheme should not prevent national stabilizers from operating. On the contrary, there must be an incentive (through earmarking) that funds are used in expenditures and/or taxes where national multipliers are higher.

Delbecque (2013), in turn, proposes the implementation of a *European Stabilization Fund* (ESF). This is also an insurance-type absorption mechanism to increase the resilience of member states to economic shocks. The shock indicator is the difference between real GDP growth estimates and the projected long-term real GDP growth rate. When the projected real GDP growth forecast is below the estimated long-term real GDP growth, euro-area members would benefit from a disbursement from an EMU fund (ESF). When the growth forecast is above the long-term real growth, they would make a contribution to the ESF.

The formula for the net contribution is

$$d = \alpha(Y^e - Y^*)$$

where d is the net contribution expressed as a percentage of the GDP, Y^e is the projected real GDP growth rate and Y^* is the projected long-term real GDP growth rate.[93]

The ESF would also be marked by long-term neutrality, since assets/debt would fluctuate in a narrow band around zero. In fact, the ESF would reduce

---

92　Enderlein et al. (2013) then proceed with a simulation exercise using real-time data (data set of 17,000 individual output gaps for euro-area countries, covering the period 1981–2014).

93　The simulation exercise assumes $\alpha = 0.5$, and that is the average potential real GDP growth rate observed in 1999–2013.

its debt and accumulate reserves during times of economic boom and would use its reserves or issue bonds (to borrow) in periods of recession.

The ESF is capable of dealing with moral hazard, because it works on a temporary basis (only to cushion short-term cyclical fluctuations rather than promoting economic convergence) – hence low economic growth would also reduce long-term real economic growth and thus the level of potential disbursements from the ESF. Moreover, the development of a framework that would modulate transfers from the ESF to ongoing compliance with mutually agreed commitments is accepted within the ESF.

Finally, Furceri and Zdzienicka (2013) propose the creation of a *supranational fiscal risk sharing mechanism*, a scheme that collects taxes as a share of the GNP of each member state, according to the formula

$$Stabilization\_budget_t = \Sigma_i \tau^* GNP_{it-1}$$

where τ is the gross contribution rate, and pays transfers to the countries negatively hit by shocks:

$$T_{it} = 0, \qquad\qquad\qquad\qquad \text{if } \varepsilon_{it} \geq 0$$

$$T_{it} = |\epsilon_{it}| * \frac{DNI_{it-1}}{\Sigma DNI_{it-1}} * \Sigma_i \tau * GNP_{it-1} \quad \text{if } \varepsilon_{it} < 0$$

where ϵ_{it} are the shocks for the country i at time t. The transfers are a function of three factors: (i) the size of the shock; (ii) the size of the stabilization fund; (iii) the relative size of the economy.

In the simulation exercise presented, Furceri and Zdzienicka (2013) conclude that for serially uncorrelated shocks – identified as deviations of output from potential, and deviations of growth from historical average – a small contribution from the member countries would suffice (a net contribution of around 1.3% of GNP, similar to the size of the current EU budget). This small contribution would hence be capable of providing full insurance against severe, persistent and unanticipated downturns (*Idem*).

5.2.2.4. Convergence-based funds: bottom-up versus top-down approaches

5.2.2.4.1. BOTTOM-UP APPROACHES: THE 'JUNCKER PLAN'

As noted before, in the *MacDougall Report* (MacDougall *et al.*, 1977), an alternative approach to the top-down approach (a complete budgetary union based on a 'fully federal' model) was proposed.

This approach, entitled a 'bottom-up approach', examined the specific functions of the public sector in the supply of given goods or services in areas such as agriculture, education, etc., and how the provision of these goods might imply the pursuit of broader objectives of redistribution and stabilization (MacDougall *et al.*, 1977, pp. 23, 43). What should now be highlighted is the fact that public goods provision and/or financing may instrumentally be used for some kind of macroeconomic stabilization. On this stance, recall that the EU's (budget) regional policy (e.g. Structural Funds) – an interregional redistributive instrument by nature – has a targeted nature relying on conditional and earmarked grants for the provision of certain types of public goods or private goods exhibiting high positive externalities (human capital and training, R&D, communications, transportation, environment, etc.).

Enderlein *et al.* (2012, p. 25) highlight the link between these two dimensions – the structural and the conjunctural – when explaining that, with the crisis, the euro area was confronted with two types of economic heterogeneities: on the one hand, *structural divergences* reflecting different historical models and patterns of economic specialization, and leading to differences in terms of wealth (e.g. GDP per capita); on the other hand, *cyclical divergences* that point to the relative position of the business cycle of a country in comparison to the business cycle position of the rest of the euro area.

Within this position, the regional policy that has been mostly conceived as a regional redistributive instrument aiming at promoting long-term convergence between regions in the EU (see Shankar and Shah, 2009) can also play, as mentioned in the report by Padoa-Schioppa (1987), an important role in macroeconomic stabilization by helping regions that experience short-term economic imbalances (again; Cabral, 2017). However, for that purpose, certain changes in the design or in the functioning of these conditional grants should be imposed, such as those referred to by Beblavý *et al.* (2015, p. 10) – for example, subsidizing the interest rate paid on loans taken on by the private sector from the European Investment Bank or other credit institutions, or using existing Structural Funds for regions in (short-term) economic difficulty.

Drèze and Durré (2013), in this regard, proposed the creation of a new public investment programme in the areas of social housing, renewable energy, and transportation, which should be applied to countries facing economic distress. This was the case mostly because of the high multiplier effects associated with these expenditure programmes. This proposal was interesting because it can be considered a first step in the use of funds specially conceived for public goods provision (or goods with high externalities) to 'directly' address macroeconomic shocks (Cabral, 2017).

The *Investment Plan for Europe*, launched by President Juncker in 2015 (the so-called 'Juncker Plan'), intending to promote EU investment for the following years on a massive scale in areas such as infrastructures and communications, is also justified by the acknowledgement that these three dimensions – public goods provision, interregional distribution and macroeconomic stabilization – can be interlinked (*Idem*).

The first pillar of the 'Juncker Plan' is the *European Fund for Strategic Investment* (EFSI).[94] It was created as a very large instrument outside the standard structure of the EU budget and with the potential to mobilize investments (target €315 billion) that rival the size of the cohesion policy (€351.8 billion) (Ferrer *et al.*, 2016; Rinaldi and Ferrer, 2017). This Fund provides an EU guarantee to mobilize private investment. For this objective, the Commission works together with its strategic partner, the European Investment Bank (EIB) Group.[95,96] Indeed, the EFSI is presented[97] as an initiative launched jointly by the EIB Group – the European Investment Bank and European Investment Fund – and the European Commission to help overcome the current investment gap in the EU. With EFSI support, the EIB Group aims at providing funding for economically viable projects, especially for projects with a higher risk profile than usually taken on by the Bank. It will focus on sectors of key importance for the European economy, including: (i) strategic infrastructure, including digital, transport and energy; (ii) education, research, development and innovation (RDI); (iii) renewable energy and resource efficiency; (iv) support for small and mid-sized businesses.

A crucial element of EFSI is its capacity to leverage private and public investment in Europe and the respective multiplier effect. According to Rinaldi and Ferrer (2017), the EFSI appears to be on track in leveraging private investment to reach a target multiplier of x15 for the total portfolio after three years of operations. The same authors point out that between 2015 and 2017, the higher sectorial incidence of the EFSI had been in small companies, the energy sector and RDI (Rinaldi and Ferrer, 2017).

---

94 The other two pillars are: on the one hand, the *European Investment Advisory Hub* and the *European Investment Project Portal* which provide technical assistance and greater visibility of investment opportunities; on the other hand, the improvement in the business environment by removing regulatory barriers to investment both nationally and at the EU level – notably, through the completion of the single market, the CMU, the digital single market and the Energy Union (Rinaldi and Ferrer, 2017).

95 Information is available at: https://ec.europa.eu/commission/priorities/jobs-growth-and-investment/investment-plan-europe-juncker-plan/what-investment-plan-europe_en.

96 Mertens and Thiemann (2017) explain that the Juncker Plan favoured the development of public banks and/or financial institutions, both at the European and national levels. At the European level, the EIB was equipped to leverage funds from the EU budget to mobilize private investment. At the national level, the Juncker plan favoured the appearance or growth of 'development banks', generally giving rise to the so-called 'promotional banking' (new investment programmes and financial products). This new 'hidden European investment state' is not any longer a typical Keynesian state where investment is done directly or promoted by state. Instead, this new model of investment state relies in a network based on the premise of mobilizing and leveraging funds, sharing risks, and cooperating to facilitate both public and private investment (Mertens and Thiemann, 2017).

97 See the information available at the European Investment Bank website: www.eib.org/en/efsi/what-is-efsi/index.htm.

5.2.2.4.2. TOP-DOWN APPROACHES: THE EUROPEAN INVESTMENT
STABILIZATION FUNCTION AND THE BUDGETARY INSTRU-
MENT FOR CONVERGENCE AND COMPETITIVENESS

In the last couple of years, a new route for top-down approaches has been developed in the EMU. Given the recognition that a full-fledged fiscal union seems not to be possible to be achieved in the near future, the fiscal capacity could try to mimic some of the elements of a complete fiscal union, although with a narrower scope. Interestingly, under this convergence-based approach, the idea is to link structural-convergence instruments (typically made to ensure regional redistribution) to stabilization purposes as well (recall, in this regard, the German anti-cyclical grant *Länderfinanzausgleich*).

In 2017, and considering the 2012–2027 period, the European Commission, possibly inspired by this proposal, launched the *European Investment Stabilization Function*. This Function is coupled, on the other hand, to the Structural Reform Support Programme (SRSP). The latter is an EU programme which, under the current MFF, provides technical support to member states for the preparation, design and implementation of growth-enhancing reforms. This is a tailor-made support, available to all member states upon their request; it requires no co-financing and mobilizes experts from all over Europe and beyond, from both the public and the private sectors.[98] The post-2020 SRSP will consist of three separate but complementary instruments: the Technical Support Instrument, which will build on this experience and go beyond the current SRSP, and two new instruments, the Reform Delivery Tool and the Convergence Facility.[99] More recently (June 2019), the European Commission proposed to materialize this convergence facility, a governance framework for the 'Budgetary Instrument for Convergence and Competitiveness': such an instrument aims to promote cohesion within the Union by providing euro-area member states with financial support for reforms and investment, as set out in coherent packages.[100] It should be noted that these two budgetary instruments – the European Investment Stabilization Function and the Budgetary Instrument for Convergence and Competitiveness – are meant, at first sight, to be developed on the bases of the existing MFF, therefore taking from the EU budget own resources.

On the other hand, with respect in particular to the *European Investment Stabilization Function* (EISF), the justification for the need for a fiscal capacity managed at the central level should be recalled: the recognition that austerity and in general fiscal consolidation under the SGP framework (e.g. compliance with strict fiscal rules) may leave little fiscal space for countries

---

98 Information available at: http://europa.eu/rapid/press-release_MEMO-18-3971_en.htm.
99 Information available at: http://europa.eu/rapid/press-release_MEMO-18-3971_en.htm.
100 More details are available at: https://ec.europa.eu/info/files/regulation-governance-frame work-budgetary-instrument-convergence-and-competitiveness-euro-area_en.

to be able to cope with asymmetric shocks when needed. The risk that such rules – even when flexibility is ensured – become pro-cyclical should not be ignored. Certain components of public expenditure can be sacrificed more for the sake of fiscal adjustment. Indeed, as noted by the European Commission (2018b, p. 16), fiscal adjustment undertaken under pressure tends to be overly reliant on cuts in public investment.

The EISF hence exhibits its 'Keynesian vein': on the one hand, it is typically an instrument of macroeconomic stabilization; on the other hand, it promotes that stabilization mostly through the rehabilitation of (publicly supported) investment, which is by nature a discretionary expenditure and not an automatic stabilizer.

In the aforementioned Communication of the European Commission[101] and in European Commission (2018b), the main criteria for the implementation of the EISF were outlined. (i) The instrument should be different from and complementary to the existing EU public finances toolbox, and it should complete national macro stabilizers. (ii) The EISF should be timely and effective (e.g. triggering should be activated automatically and rapidly on the basis of pre-defined parameters – the output gap; the GDP growth; an unemployment rate trigger). (iii) The EISF should be neutral over the medium term and not lead to permanent transfers between member states and therefore prevent moral hazard.[102] (iv) An important new element of the EISF is its relation with social and environmental objectives. (v) Finally, the stabilization impact is also discussed and investigated.[103]

As noted before, the Commission intends to include the EISF inside the EU budget (even if it is to be used only by euro-area and ERM II members[104]), and the tool is to comprise of two main components.[105] Firstly, a *loan component*, implying the possibility that the Commission offers (investment-related) back-to-back loans of up to €30 billion for countries facing a negative shock, but presenting sound fiscal policies previous to the shock (Claeys, 2018). Secondly, a *grant component*, consisting of a rainy-day fund with €600 million per year, financed with a share of the seigniorage profits from the Eurosystem, and to be used to provide 'an interest rate subsidy' to cover the interest rates that countries would pay on the back-to-back loans (Claeys, 2018). Interestingly, if this is so, the grant component would work

---

101 COM (2017) 822 final, of 6.12.2017.
102 See, in this regard, Buti and Carnot (2018).
103 European Commission, 2018b.
104 Arguing that the euro is the official currency of the EU, and the tools to strengthen the monetary union should not be separated from the financial architecture of the whole EU (Claeys, 2018).
105 See the main features of the proposal presented to the European Parliament, in further detail, available at: www.europarl.europa.eu/RegData/etudes/BRIE/2019/630361/EPRS_BRI(2019)630361_EN.pdf.

out as a visible insurance instrument, by bringing the European payment system to the heart of the risk-sharing system.

In turn, the *Budgetary Instrument for Convergence and Competitiveness* (BICC) is to be launched within the proposal to create a Reform Support Programme, to be included in the MFF 2021–2027 (so it will be part of the EU budget, even if its scope is to be restricted to EMU member states) – the support from the instrument will be delivered in the form of grants (i.e. direct financial contribution). The BICC is presented as "a budgetary tool dedicated to the euro area (EA). It will finance packages of structural reforms and public investments in order to strengthen the potential growth of euro area economies and the resilience of the single currency against economic shocks."[106] In sum, the BICC is typically a convergence-based instrument, with the possibility of being used as a risk-sharing mechanism, thereby presenting some degree of stabilizing effect – to be confirmed (or not) in the near future.

5.2.2.5. *Fiscal backstops of private risk-sharing mechanisms: governmental risk-sharing mechanisms as 'market-makers'*

5.2.2.5.1. INTRODUCTORY REMARKS

As we have seen, a significant part of the literature – since the seminal investigation of Asdrubali *et al.* (1996) – agrees that in a federal setup, the vast majority of risk-sharing operates through private mechanisms, and the remaining part is then ensured through governmental risk-sharing, that is, the block made of taxes/transfers to/from the central state towards the SCGs.

As mentioned earlier, in particular, private risk-sharing mechanisms work through two main channels (Cimadomo *et al.*, 2018, p. 86): (i) the *savings channel* (also known as the credit channel) that operates via cross-border saving/borrowing; (ii) the *capital market channel*, which operates through internationally diversified private investment portfolios. These channels – the former operating mostly through the banking system, the latter through the capital markets – although typically *private* risk-sharing instruments,[107]

---

106 Quotation from: www.consilium.europa.eu/en/policies/emu-deepening/bicc-faq/#
107 It should be also noted that besides these 'explicit' private risk-sharing mechanisms – as capital and banking markets – in EMU one can also find 'implicit' private risk-sharing instruments: the most noteworthy is the *TARGET 2*, the EMU's system of payment. With the alarm raised by the German researcher at Ifo Institute, Hans-Werner Sinn (Sinn, 2012), a prevalent view was that the target system is a way for current-account deficit countries to finance their deficits almost without limit. Creditor countries – as Germany – would ensure this access to credit. Schelkle (2017) challenges this view, stressing that TARGET 2 was also beneficial, during crisis times, providing insurance for other users and not only debtor countries: the diversity of users was not simply a matter of core and periphery. For some, the value of insurance consisted of maintaining trade flows and permitting gradual

can also be supported by public/governmental devices. Fiscal backstops are in this case ultimate supports to ensure a smooth functioning of the internal market in which they operate, and so they can work as effective 'market makers'. Fostering market mechanisms can be achieved through several ways: regulation (harmonization and unification of instruments), taxation and, finally, financial support. This is what happens – as we will see next – with respect to the CMU and the BU in the E(M)U. A suitable regulatory framework and fiscal backstop can be provided to make these markets more effective and efficient.

Final attention will also be given to the ESM – as it is by nature an atypical institution of financial assistance in crisis situations – it can certainly in the near future experience reinforcement of its public/governmental nature, backstopping financial and banking markets.

5.2.2.5.2. PROMOTING THE (INTERNAL) MARKET: THE CASE OF THE
      CAPITAL MARKETS UNION

As mentioned previously, financial integration in the EMU, which seems indisputable, has not yet been sufficient to ensure an effective capacity from capital markets to work as private risk-sharing mechanisms.[108] Indeed, financial integration in the EMU does not pass the triple test of effectiveness from the point of view of risk sharing, that is, the test across dimensions (ECB, 2016, pp. 81–86).

The first dimension relates to the type of cross-border financial instruments traded – debt or equity. Hence, one important element of the financial integration in the EMU (in contrast, for example, with the U.S.) is that it is biased towards debt finance, and especially towards intermediation by banks (ECB, 2016, p. 82), and this fact could have helped to magnify the impact of negative shocks on economic growth.[109] Indeed – as also noted (ECB, 2016, p. 82) – debt tends to be more prone to runs than equity. Liquid-

---

adjustment to a breakdown of credit; for others, the value of insurance was the ability to secure property rights despite the increasing fragility of the domestic banking system and the probability of collapse of the single currency (Schelkle, 2017). See also, in this regard, Rossi (2017).

108 As explained by Valiante (2016, p. 50), the forms of risk sharing through the capital markets result from the use of three main tools: foreign direct investment and equity portfolio investments; other portfolio investments (e.g. debt securities, interbank loans, etc.); and capital gains.

109 Valiante (2016) explains the funding structure both of non-financial corporations (NFC) and of households in Europe and shows this overreliance on debt (instead of capital markets). In Europe, total NFC funding intermediation (excluding cash and deposits), in the form of bank loans, corresponds to 44% of GDP, against only 18% in the U.S.; in turn, only a small part of European households' financial assets are invested in capital markets (e.g. equity and debt securities), made up mostly of cash and deposit holdings. As for NFC, the case of small and medium enterprises (SMEs) is more troublesome: bank lending is still

ity crises are often related to sudden stops in debt investment rather than to equity-type forms of finance (that exhibit features of risk sharing).[110] On the other hand, as mentioned by Allen *et al.* (2011) and the ECB (2016), cross-border capital flows tend to be more stable and create a more balanced financial integration when they are bi-directional. This is true for banking and portfolio flows, which tend to be more volatile than others. In this case, one-directional flows are in general moving from richer to poorer or less-capital-abundant countries. Gravity models (Lane, 2006) show that since the creation of the EMU, there has in fact been unbalanced large 'downhill' investments from the European core to the periphery, rather than broad-based integration in the single market fostered by a single currency (ECB, 2016).

The second dimension refers to capital instrument maturity. The EMU financing instruments are typically short-term instruments (e.g. debt instruments) and are therefore more volatile. Short-term flows have, in turn, a pro-cyclical nature, therefore increasing overall macroeconomic instability (that is, financially integrated countries that rely more on short-term debt are more exposed to crisis): easy access to credit in good times and market freeze in bad times. It should be recalled that the sovereign debt and the euro crisis were due mostly to a 'sudden stop' in capital flows, and this happened to a large extent because of a heavy reliance on short-term debt as a source of funding, notably by vulnerable and peripheral European economies.

Finally, with respect to the composition of intra-euro-area foreign bank lending, in the EMU it has relied mostly on the integration of the interbank money markets, whereas cross-border integration and retail financial services grew at a slower pace (ECB, 2016, p. 86). In this regard, Allen *et al.* (2011, p. 23) noted that if it seems clear that retail banking has remained highly fragmented in the post-EMU, it is also true that the banking sector has been the main driver of financial integration in Europe, mostly through cross-border interbank loans and deposits. This overreliance on interbank market funding may expose banks more to the market freeze and amplify

---

the most common source of external finance, with it being more difficult to find market-based finance as an alternative (Thomadakis, 2017).

110 As noted in turn by Valiante (2016, p. 127), equity markets in the EMU remain highly fragmented. There is also disagreement on the role of the euro in leading equity markets to more integration; indeed, there is some evidence that the monetary union has caused the apparent segmentation between bond and stock markets within but not outside Europe, due to flight-to-quality issues related to the incomplete nature of the monetary union with a common monetary policy. On the other hand, as for debt markets, the same author notes that these are historically the most important funding source in Europe, especially for governments and financial institutions (Valiante, 2016, p. 141). Moreover, the market for debt securities has played a key role in the financial process post-EMU.

liquidity shocks that can ultimately spill over to other financial markets (as the crisis has in fact shown).[111]

The launching of the Capital Markets Union (CMU) was hence one of the reforms adopted in the aftermath the GFC, aiming to ensure the smooth functioning of the EMU and, in particular, the smooth functioning of the so-called private or market-driven risk-sharing mechanisms.[112] Indeed, it intended to ensure the completion of the internal market with respect to capital mobility, allowing investors to share risks and consumers (of financial products) to smooth consumption. As such, the CMU was seen as a *sine qua non* condition for the creation of an OCA, in line with Mundell's (1960) basic prospects.

Furthermore, it was thought the CMU would address the so-called 'financial fragmentation' in the EMU, allowing for the proper functioning of the transmission mechanism of monetary policy. In particular, it aimed at favouring the reinforcement of cross-border capital flows, including capital flows through the banking system, also needed in order to enhance international risk sharing across the euro area. The CMU was considered thus essential to conclude an effective financial integration in the EMU.

Moreover, it was intended to change the pattern regarding sources of financing of the economy that, in the EMU, rely(ied) mostly on banking debt instead of capital markets. In the *Green Paper Building a Capital Markets Union*, launched by the Commission in 2015, several alternatives to bank lending were suggested, notably through the development of equity or bond markets (e.g. improving access to finance, including risk capital for SMEs, or the development of a more integrated European covered bond market for investment promotion). Through this diversification of financing sources, the CMU is seen as a fundamental pillar for enhancing investment and growth in the EMU.

More recently, within the framework for the completion of the CMU, a new significant goal emerged, and this goal is related to the 'new' Environmental and Sustainable Growth Agenda. In particular, the CMU can be a path to promote the so-called 'sustainable finance' (SF) goals.[113] SF indeed represents a Copernican revolution in the conception of (corporate) finance

---

111 See also Fecht *et al.* (2007).

112 For a brief characterization of the Action Plan concerning the CMU, see Valiante (2015) and Lannoo (2015a, 2015b).

113 In the Action Plan on Financing Sustainable Growth, presented by the European Commission in March 2018, sustainable finance (SF) is defined as "the process of taking due account of environmental and social considerations in investment decision-making, leading to increased investments in longer-term and sustainable activities. More specifically, environmental considerations refer to climate change mitigation and adaptation, as well as the environment more broadly and related risks (e.g. natural disasters). Social considerations may refer to issues of inequality, inclusiveness, labour relations, investment in human capital and communities."

that in turn begs for creativity, at least in the following areas: (i) the conception of new financial products (environmentally and human rights friendly); (ii) the definition of new portfolio compositions; iii) the development of new investment strategies. [114]

The inclusion of SF goals was thus a subsequent step and a novel argument for the very existence of the CMU: SF goals do indeed provide a new legitimacy and a broader scope to the CMU (Cabral, 2019).

The provisions regarding SF can be found in the *CMU Action Plan*, in the issue entitled "Investing for Long-term, Infrastructure, and Sustainable Investment" and then detailed in the aforementioned *Action Plan on Financing Sustainable Growth*. Key actions set out in the document include:[115] (i) an EU classification system – or taxonomy – of sustainable activities; (ii) EU labels for green financial products (e.g. green bonds);[116] (iii) clarification of asset managers' and institutional investors' duties regarding sustainability; (iv) strengthening the transparency of companies regarding their ESG policies; (v) a 'green supporting factor' in the EU prudential rules for banks and insurance companies.

Ultimately, the CMU can be an opportunity for the development of 'true' European financial products, products with an EU label. Lannoo (2015b) considered that Europe was lacking EU-wide, well-diversified and stable investment products. While they exist at the national level – through life insurance or pension fund products – they do not exist in the EU. A product to be included in the new regulatory framework UCITS ("Undertakings for the Collective Investment in Transferable Securities")[117] is the new the *Pan-European Pension Product* (PEPP), the main goals of which are precisely to

---

114 Under this new approach, Schoenmaker (2017) confronts the so-called 'finance as usual', where T = F (total value equal to financial value) and where only the 'shareholder value' matters, with steps towards a new approach for sustainable finance. In the first step (SF 01), associated with a 'refined shareholder value', F > S and E (where F is financial value, S is social impact and E is environmental impact). In the second step (SF 02), T = F + S + E and a shift from a simple shareholder value to a 'stakeholder value' occurs. Finally, in the last step, associated with a 'common good value', S and E > F.

115 For information on this, see: https://ec.europa.eu/info/business-economy-euro/banking-and finance/sustainable-finance_en.

116 See, in this regard, the European Commission *Study on the Potential of Green Bond Finance for Resource-Efficient Investments*. In this study, a green bond is considered to be "differentiated from a regular bond by its label, which signifies a commitment to exclusively use the funds raised to finance or re-finance 'green' projects, assets or business activities" (European Commission, 2016, p. 8).

117 This is a regulatory framework of the European Commission that creates a harmonized regime throughout Europe for the management and sale of mutual funds. UCITS funds can be registered in Europe and sold to investors worldwide using unified regulatory and investor protection requirements; UCITS fund providers who meet the standards are exempt from national regulation in individual European countries. Further information is available at: www.investopedia.com/terms/u/ucits.asp.

improve cross-border access and strengthen the single market in personal private pensions, improving coverage and take-up with appropriate security for savings[118] (see Lannoo, 2019; Rodrigues, 2019).

5.2.2.5.3. INSURING THE BANKING UNION

Much has been said and written about the Banking Union (BU).[119] The BU was assumed in the *Four Presidents' Report* (Van Rompuy *et al.*, 2012) as one of the major endeavours within the EMU reform process, being considered instrumental to the completion of the monetary union and making it more capable of addressing financial and economic shocks. Figure 5.3 summarizes the main features and background of the BU.

Figure 5.3 specifies the links with other previous and contemporaneous measures, starting with the decision to proceed – after the creation of the European Banking Authority (EBA) in 2011 – with a 'comprehensive assessment' of the systematically important banks in Europe (Xafa, 2015), which included a review of the quality of assets (of banks) and the first stress tests for the banking system. This assessment was carried out by the EBA, in association with the ECB and the national central banks.

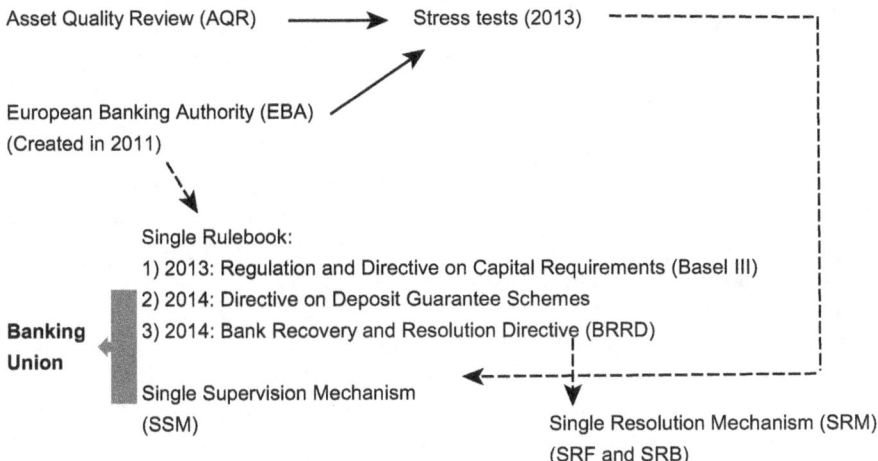

Figure 5.3 Features and background of the BU
Source: The Author

---

118 For further information, see: www.consilium.europa.eu/en/press/press-releases/2018/06/19/pensions-council-agrees-its-stance-on-pan-european-pension-product/pdf .

119 See Beck (2012), Goyal *et al.* (2013), ECB (2014), Geeroms and Karbownik (2014), Wymeersch (2014), Breuss *et al.* (2015), Gros and Belke (2015), Lannoo (2015a), Schoenmaker (2015), Véron (2015), Xafa (2015), ECB (2016), Huertas (2016), Micossi (2017), Praet (2017e), and Rodrigues and Gonçalves (2017).

These measures were indeed at the origin of the centralization – now in the ECB – of the supervisory role of the 'biggest' banks in Europe. As such, they were embryos of the single supervisory mechanism, which in fact is the first pillar of the BU.

The creation of the EBA led, in turn, to the approval of the legal package labelled as the 'Single Rulebook' of the Banking System, which incorporates some of the new regulatory environment coming from the Basel III Accord (enacted in 2010), in particular new capital requirements for banking institutions. The 2013 EU Regulation and Directive on Capital Requirements were derived precisely from this background.

The Single Rulebook moreover included two other legal elements, a Directive on (National) Deposit Guarantee/Insurance Schemes and the Bank Recovery and Resolution Directive (BRRD) (both dated from 2014) which, in turn, lie at the origin of the two other pillars of the BU: the former is the embryo for the still-expected creation of a European Deposit Insurance Scheme (EDIS); the latter was at the centre and was encapsulated in the creation of the Single Resolution Mechanism (SRM), which is the other remaining pillar of the BU, to be completed with the creation of the Single Resolution Board (SRB) and Single Resolution Fund (SRF) (see Table 5.3 for a brief characterization of the three pillars of the BU).

Having said this, I want to address two issues important for the purpose of this section. The first issue involves explaining in which way the BU can contribute to a better functioning of the E(M)U internal market and so act as a private risk-sharing mechanism. Some of the features, and the actual course of the BU, can put this intended outcome into question. The second issue relates to the need (or not) to have a fiscal backstop within the BU. This point is discussed notably with respect to the possible future creation of an EDIS – which is certainly the most controversial element regarding the completion of the BU. These two issues are related.

a) The BU as a private risk-sharing mechanism: advantages and shortcomings   As for the first issue – in which way the BU can foster the development of the internal market – let me start by highlighting the major arguments for the institution of a European BU. Firstly, the BU can be presented, from its inception, as a way to promote a 'level playing field' in the provision of banking services – within a cross-border perspective – by ensuring that providers of those services rely on similar regulatory rules and are subject to similar supervisory powers and procedures. Ultimately, the allocation to the ECB – which is a central institution – of new competences concerning banking supervision makes all large systemic European banks face similar conditions, even on competitive grounds.

Secondly, by submitting banks to similar regulatory rules (e.g. licences, capital requirements, liquidity provisions, etc.) and being subject to similar

Table 5.3 Brief characterization of the three pillars of the BU

Pillars	Legal basis	Characterization
Single Supervisory Mechanism (SSM)	Regulation (EU) No 1024/2013, of 15 October 2013.	Confers on the ECB specific tasks concerning policies relating to the prudential supervision of credit institutions, with a view to contributing to the safety and soundness of credit institutions and the stability of the financial system within the Union and each member state. Included in the object of ECB supervision are systemically important financial institutions, that is, 120 large systemic European banks; with assets valued above €30 billion. The other banks remain within the scope of supervision from national central banks.
Single Resolution Mechanism (SRM)	– Directive 2014/59 of the European Parliament and of the Council of 15 May 2014. – Regulation (EU) No 806/2014 of the European Council and of the Parliament of 15 July 2014.	Establishing a framework for the recovery and resolution of credit institutions and investment firms. Establishing uniform rules and procedures for the resolution of credit institutions and certain investment firms in the framework of an SRM and an SRF. To sum up: The EU's bank resolution rules ensure that the banks' shareholders and creditors pay their share of the respective costs based on a 'bail-in' principle. The costs of resolution would thus not be borne by taxpayers.
National Deposit Guarantee Scheme (DGS) and European Deposit Insurance Scheme (EDIS)	Directive 2014/49 of the European Parliament and of the Council of 16 April 2014.	Harmonized target level for the pre-funding of the national DGS (0.5% of covered deposits by 2024), as well as the level of deposit coverage (€100,000), the type of financing, the scope of eligible deposits, the repayment period, etc. (ECB, 2016, p. 45). EDIS (see details *infra*).

Source: The Author

conditions both of micro and macro supervision, the idea is to ensure a limitation of information asymmetry and agency problems, both between banks amongst themselves in the interbank market, and between lenders and borrowers in the retail market, thereby favouring an improvement in the quality of assets detained by banks and in particular a more effective *ex ante* control of non-performing loans.

Thirdly, the idea of breaking the 'doom looping' between sovereigns and banks – through the reinforcement of 'bail-in' mechanisms notably for bank resolution and recovery (under the SRM) – is intended not only to avoid the deterioration of the respective balance sheets of banks and sovereigns, but also to foster a more efficient functioning of the banking system, preventing taxpayers from being called on to bear the costs of bank resolutions. This could ultimately be seen as an artificial way of bailing out and maintaining non-performing banks (starting with small, non-systemic banks), thereby distorting the rules of healthy competition.

Fourthly, the idea of creating, with the BU, a 'level playing field' with regard to supervision, resolution and deposit guarantee, aiming at reversing financial fragmentation at the E(M)U level, which has prevented the functioning of risk-sharing mechanisms and the absorption of shocks through financial products and structures, and has actually amplified those same shocks. By ensuring a high level of resiliency in the whole banking system – regardless of each bank's 'nationality' – it would be possible to increase trust, eliminate or limit 'home bias' in investment decisions and definitely contribute to the geographical dissemination of investment decisions, including the decision to own a bank or a part of it – in short, international risk sharing.

Fifthly, the BU has been created to ensure a better 'transmission of the monetary policy' through its various channels, starting with the money market/interbank channel and ending with the credit channel (for non-financial corporations and households). As was noted precociously by the ECB (2013), "despite an accommodative monetary policy, bank lending conditions have remained heterogeneous in an environment of persistent debt tensions, fragile economic activity, weak capital positions and high levels of uncertainty." As such, the idea of the BU, by deterring financial fragmentation (once again through a level playing field and promoting financial robustness throughout the entire European banking sector), would also favour more homogeneous bank lending conditions to the economy, so that the effects of monetary policy on market interest rates and on the availability of credit – the so-called 'bank interest rate pass-through' – would be similar throughout the whole Euro area.

Last (but not least), it should be noted that the fragmentation of banking markets is a consequence of the non-integration of the capital markets in general terms. As mentioned in the previous subsection, euro-area members' financial systems are heavily 'bank-centred' and stock and bond markets provide a relatively modest share of financing to the private sector in most countries (Gros and Belke, 2015). If this is true, this peculiar inconsistency also appears to be true: even though the main financing channel is debt through the banking system, the banking market – as an important landscape and expression of the capital markets – is not in itself completely integrated (Cabral, 2017). Important consequences arise from this inconsistency, and the euro crisis has highlighted them: the Eurozone has once again shown itself to be a *non*-Optimum Currency Area (as integration of capital markets should be a consequence of full capital mobility, and yet it is not) that lacks appropriate responses to asymmetric shocks and that also prevents normal financing channels for households, firms and governments, ultimately impairing investment in the *real* economy (Cabral, 2017).

The BU, by promoting banking sector integration, can through this contribute towards a higher integration of capital markets. Indeed, due to important synergies between banks and the capital markets in Europe, it can be accepted that the BU supports the CMU, and vice versa (Constâncio, 2017). The BU supports the CMU, because banks are important players in the capital markets (they act as service providers, investors and issuers). Given this, Constâncio (2017) finds two types of synergies between the BU and the CMU: (i) on the one hand, a more resilient banking system supports the smooth functioning of the capital markets (resilient banks are in a better condition to act as market-makers); (ii) on the other hand, an increasingly integrated banking system should also support integration of capital markets in the EU (e.g. regulatory and supervisory convergence make cross-border operations and cross-border mergers of banks easier).

However, the reverse is also true: the CMU can support the BU. This is so because in a more integrated capital market, banks would no longer need to develop local expertise for each national market; they could exploit cross-border economies of scale by offering similar or even the same products and services in other member states (Constâncio, 2017).

To summarize, as well stated by Véron (2015), the BU was conceived to put in motion a major transformation of Europe's 'banking and financial landscape', that is, a change in the structure of the euro-area banking market and, beyond the banks, in the structure of the broader European financial system. The change would be felt particularly in the following domains. Firstly, encouraging banks with cross-border activity to engage in more integrated legal, financial and organizational structures. Secondly, accelerating cross-border mergers and acquisitions that would in turn foster the appearance of pan-European banking groups. Thirdly, diversifying the financial system in order to make it less reliant on bank intermediation.

Yet, despite this ambitious goal, the fact is that the BU, even in the light of the enhancement of the internal market, is not without its shortcomings. Firstly, because the BU is still incomplete and asymmetric: centralization of supervision and resolution rules and procedures, but with continuing decentralization in depositor insurance, responsibility for which remains at the national level, including a fiscal backstop (see *infra*, the implications of this).

Secondly, because by fostering concentration – through cross-border mergers and acquisitions – leading to the creation of pan-European banking groups, the BU may in fact be promoting a moral hazard effect – the so-called 'too-big-to-fail' problem. That is, banks increase their dimension in such a way that they become necessarily systemically important banks, and their bankruptcy can spread to the entire financial system. In particular, banking concentration can have a twofold effect: on the one hand, it contributes to increasing banks' robustness (because they become bigger), but on the other hand, it is not certain that concentration eliminates geographical risk associated with home bias and promotes effective geographical risk sharing. Instead, it may 'simply' replace national risk by regional risk (for example, the case of the acquisition and/or integration of Portuguese by Spanish big banks – this process will possibly eliminate national risk and create an Iberian one, a risk of increased magnitude).

Finally, the combination of a strict regulatory and supervisory environment with the aforementioned banking concentration, giving rise to large regional banking groups, can after all limit the access to credit by companies and households from (more) peripheral and weak countries, that is, the development of discriminatory credit policies against those countries.

b) The creation of a fiscal backstop in the context of the BU In the first place, one should remember the opinion expressed by the ECB (2016), according to which the EDIS is considered as the third pillar of the European BU and that it is required in order to complete the BU itself. In fact, the creation of the EDIS will increase consistency with regard to the SSM and the SRM by aligning liability for deposit protection and control over key factors influencing the risk of a depositor payout (ECB, 2016, p. 38). The current BU is incomplete because it is asymmetric: it implies a common framework for supervision and resolution, but not for deposit protection (*Idem*, p. 38).

Recall that member states already have, in general, national deposit guarantee schemes. Moreover, with the Directive on (National) Deposit Guarantee Schemes approved in 2014, rules in this domain have been harmonized. Within these national pre-existing schemes, an explicit or implicit fiscal backstop exists: it is required in order to promote confidence and to prevent bank runs in the event of liquidity shortage.

Yet, as noted by the ECB (2016, p. 40), the credibility of the national deposit guarantee scheme is influenced by the fiscal strength of the respective sovereign; therefore, member states with a less favourable fiscal position may be perceived as unable to provide a credible backstop to the national deposit guarantee scheme (DGSs) in the event of a systemic crisis. The rationale for an EDIS is found here:

> The financial disparity across backstops of national DGSs may create adverse incentives, contributing to market fragmentation and competitive distortion. Notably, the banks' ability and willingness to expand to other Member States and their decisions in terms of group structure (branches and subsidiaries) could be affected.
>
> (ECB, 2016, p. 41)

Given this, the main conclusion taken by the ECB (2016, p. 43) is that *only an EDIS coupled with a credible common backstop will underpin depositor confidence in the BU as a whole*, notably by offering protection in the case of large local shocks, which could otherwise overburden national DGSs.

In the Communication "Towards the Completion of the Banking Union" (of 24 November 2015), the European Commission hence advocated the institution of an EDIS. According to the proposal, this should be a gradual process marked by three stages. The first stage – described as the 'reinsurance' stage – would last at least three years, during which up to 20% of the liquidity shortfall and up to 20% of excess losses of a given national DGS are covered by the Deposit Insurance Fund (DIF), which is the Fund for the EDIS set up from the start (ECB, 2016). The second stage – named as the 'co-insurance' stage – will thus consist of a co-insurance scheme, where the DIF will cover a gradually increasing share (from 20% to 80%) of the liquidity needs and losses of participating DGSs until they are fully insured (*Idem*). In the last stage – labelled 'full insurance' – national DGSs would be fully insured by the EDIS.[120]

The remaining question is whether the EDIS should benefit or not from a fiscal backstop. In ECB (2016), although the DIF is mostly funded by accumulated resources paid by banks (a bail-in mechanism as well), in exceptional situations – when those resources are shown to be insufficient to pay out to depositors – the EDIS could find alternative sources of financing. A hypothesis, in the absence of a true fiscal backstop as exists in the U.S. under the Federal Deposit Insurance Corporation (FDIC) (Schoenmaker, 2012),[121] would be to use the ESM to play this role of quasi-fiscal backstop to the EDIS.

The creation of a fiscal backstop constitutes one of the critical points in the completion of the BU: the political impasse is mostly around this issue. Some consider that more important than creating a fiscal backstop to the BU is creating a true 'private' BU in Europe (Gros and Belke, 2015). It is

---

120 The pre-funding of EDIS is also required. The Commission proposes an ultimate target level for the DIF of 0.8% of covered deposits of all credit institutions covered by national DGSs, to be reached as of July 2024, in line with the general target of 0.8% of covered national deposits in the DGS Directive. The size of the DI would hence be approx. €45 billion (ECB, 2016, p. 51). Note, on the other hand, that the DIF can coexist with the SRF (within the SRM), which itself has a target of 1% of covered deposits. Thus, together, they would amount to 1.8% of covered deposits dedicated to resolution and insurance purposes (around €103 billion) (ECB, 2016, p. 51).

121 The ECB (2016, p. 51) recalls that, under the U.S. scheme, which accumulates the double role of deposit insurance and bank resolution, on the top of *ex ante* funds to the FDIC, there is a credible backstop for systemic cases of USD 500 billion, through the Orderly Liquidation Authority. The FDIC's Orderly Liquidation Authority aims at ensuring the rapid and orderly resolution of a systemically important financial institution, when no viable private sector alternative solution can be found and the bankruptcy could imply adverse effects on the U.S. financial sector as a whole (the 'too-big-to-fail' problem).

alleged that the European BU is not even a truly 'private' banking union, unlike that which happens in the U.S. – and this explains the way the U.S. responded quickly and more effectively to the effects of the crisis than did European countries. In fact, bank owners in the U.S. are not only 'national' owners but also 'foreign' owners (that is, owners from other American states different from those hit by negative shocks, e.g. the case in Nevada or Florida) and this helped to smooth the effects of the same shocks by distributing them over the whole territory of the U.S. That is, the U.S. BU was able to trigger an effective private sharing risk mechanism between all its members. Unlike the U.S., the predominance of domestic capital vis-à-vis the banking institutions in some Eurozone countries (e.g. Spain), explains the concentration of risks within a country and the need for government bailout of its national banks (Gros and Belke, 2015). Furthermore, market mechanisms to absorb losses in subprime or non-conforming mortgages were developed in the U.S., through insurance and securitization (*Idem*). Differently in the Eurozone, risk-sharing mechanisms provided either by institutions, backed up by the central government (as in the case of the FDIC) or by the private sector (large banks and subprime securitization) did not fully operate, which explains the response to the bailout and, in some cases, the subsequent deterioration in fiscal outlook (e.g. soaring public debt levels) (*Idem*; Cabral, 2017).

The agreement towards the institution of a fiscal backstop is also related to the design, itself, of the insurance scheme. Two main different approaches can be identified. According to the first view – a 'market-driven and national approach' for the BU – the insurance scheme would not be a maximalist EDIS, but a 'mere' reinsurance solution. Gros (2015) stresses that, indeed, the reinsurance scheme did not necessarily have to be – as in the proposal of the Commission (*supra*) – a transitory solution, but that it could well be the final and permanent solution. Under this approach, national DGSs would continue to function as before, but each would be forced to take out insurance coverage against large shocks. This idea relies on the very logic of reinsurance: national responsibility is required in order to prevent moral hazard and adverse selection, by ensuring the national DGSs have a first-loss tranche to bear (Schoenmaker and Wolff, 2015). The reinsurance scheme could be managed by the EDIS, funding for which would be made through the DIF. The funding of the DIF in turn would rely on national DGS contributions, which would have to transmit part of their fees to the DIF. As such, the scheme would consist of two tiers of deposit insurance: by the national DGSs in relationship to 'their' banks and by the European reinsurer in relationship to the national DGSs.

The second approach – a 'public-driven and European' approach for the BU (Schoenmaker, 2015; Schoenmaker and Wolff, 2015) – effectively proposes the institution of a 'true' European deposit insurance fund (in line with the aforementioned proposal from the Commission). In this view, a simple reinsurance scheme does not fully solve the problem of a fiscal backstop. In fact, for larger systemic risks, even the reinsurance is unlikely to cover the entire potentially affected deposits: even this would ultimately have to be supported by that fiscal backstop. As such, the proposal for creating a true EDIS would eventually make reinsurance dispensable, as the Fund would become capable of covering the failure of a mid-sized bank and even larger banks. The role of fiscal backstop would be played by the ESM: in fact, a credit line from the ESM would be useful – as a solution of last resort – similar to the credit line from the U.S. Treasury for the FDIC.

Finally, it should be noted that the stabilization properties of the BU actually also depend on the respective design properties. This topic was investigated by Breuss et al. (2015). The authors compared costs and benefits, for peripheral and core countries, arising from the status quo solution of national bailout, in comparison with the resolution mechanisms included in the banking union – namely through the SRM – based on the principle of 'bail-in', and with the backstop solution in the banks' recapitalization instrument within the ESM. The combination of these two instruments seemed to carry out the most significant stabilizing effect – in the case of macroeconomic shocks affecting a peripheral country – reducing GDP losses for the core countries.

In the next subsection, I will finally detail the role of the ESM – since its inception in 2012, analysing future prospects for its functioning and scope, and bearing in mind its relationship with other policies, in particular the BU. A reflexion will be made on the nature (present and future) of the ESM, which seems to offer a balance between a typical monetary institution and a quasi-fiscal one.

5.2.2.5.4. RESHAPING THE EUROPEAN STABILITY MECHANISM: A MONETARY FUND OR A (QUASI) FISCAL INSTITUTION?

The ESM – instituted with the signature of the ESM Treaty in February 2012 – is a new EMU institution, although created on the basis of an intergovernmental treaty and not under EU regulation – which has required a change in the TFEU (adding a new paragraph to Article 136),[122] a controversial modification that would lead to a judicial case in the European Court of Justice – the famous Pringle Case (previously mentioned).[123] The ECJ has also analysed the possible violation of the 'no-bailout' clauses (contained in Articles 123 and 125 of the TFEU) concluding that such violation did not occur, because the ESM was not to be assumed as a guarantor of the debts of the recipient state (see, on this issue, Lo Schiavo, 2013).[124] The ESM was

---

122 Decision of the European Council 2011/99.
123 Case C- 370/12, *Thomas Pringle v. Government of Ireland* (of 27 November 2012).
124 See also Fabbrini (2014a).

in fact created with the mission to provide financial assistance to euro-area countries experiencing or threatened by severe financing problems, and such assistance is granted only if it is proven necessary to safeguard the financial stability of the euro area as a whole and ESM members.

Since its creation, the ESM has worked in association with the European Financial Stabilization Facility (EFSF), a temporary credit-enhanced SPV with minimal capitalization created to raise funds from the capital markets on its investment grade rating and provide financial assistance to distressed member states at lower interest rates than those available to the latter (Olivares-Caminal, 2011). The EFSF – which financed the first assistance programmes to Ireland, Portugal and Greece (the Second Adjustment Programme) – will be progressively discontinued, so that it will give rise to a permanent assistance mechanism, the ESM itself (Alcidi et al., 2017c). Although both institutions were made to provide financial assistance in situations of financial distress, there are two main differences between them (Alcidi et al., 2017c, pp. 17–18). Firstly, of the €700 billion ESM-subscribed capital (in accordance with the GDP and population of each of the members), €80 billion are paid in capital shares, and €620 billion are callable shares. This ensures its AAA rating even in the absence of credit-enhanced schemes (instead, the EFSF had an over-guarantee, cash buffer and reserves). Secondly, while the EFSF has the same credit right as any other sovereign claim, the ESM enjoys a status of preferred creditor in a similar fashion to the IMF.

On the other hand, however, unlike other instruments for temporary financial assistance that already exist within the EU budget – which is the case with the European Financial Stabilization Mechanism (EFSM) and the BoP facility – the ESM is a separate financial instrument, outside the EU budget and with its own governance structure (Alcidi et al., 2017c).

The ESM, under a principle of strict conditionality (involving the signature of a Memorandum of Understanding by the member state which requires the assistance and a commitment towards fiscal and financial adjustment measures and even structural reforms), provides the following types of financial assistance: (i) loans within a macroeconomic adjustment programme; (ii) primary market purchases; (iii) secondary market purchases; (iv) precautionary credit line; (v) loans for indirect bank recapitalization; (vi) direct recapitalization of institutions.

These two latter types of assistance suggest in particular a plausible overlapping role with the BU (see the previous subsection), notably with the SRM – which is also aimed at adopting recapitalization measures involving the banking sector. Linking of these two instruments – the action of the SRM and the recapitalization instrument within the ESM – is absolutely essential.

Another issue previously addressed was the link between the ESM and the possible institution of an EDIS (the third pillar of the BU). In this regard, as noted by Sapir and Schoenmaker (2017), the ESM would serve as a (fiscal) backstop to the euro-area banking system. This would mean three things

(Sapir and Schoenmaker, 2017): firstly, the procedure for recapitalization should be simplified in order to be deployed as soon as needed; secondly, the ESM should be allowed to participate in precautionary recapitalizations; thirdly, the ESM should be able to provide a credit line to the SRF and DIF (or a new Fund combining the two, similar to the U.S. FDIC model).

In these authors' opinion, the problem of moral hazard through the use of the ESM as a fiscal backstop of the EDIS can be overcome by ensuring not only the reduction of non-performing loans but also, and above all, a suitable and tight regulatory treatment of sovereign exposure by banks, in conjunction with a new European Sovereign Debt Restructuring Mechanism (ESDRM) (Sapir and Schoenmaker, 2017). The ESM can indeed be at the centre of a new ESDRM and simultaneously be a bridge to the institution of debt pooling instruments (*supra*), where the ESM itself could eventually emerge as an EDA, that is, the central Treasury of the EMU.

When anticipating the future of the ESM, it appears that the role it plays within the EMU's governance framework will increase. Typically, it can give rise to a 'true' European Monetary Fund (Gros and Mayer, 2017; Sapir and Schoenmaker, 2017), inspired by the IMF model – a financial assistance institution with a special creditor status. Interestingly, it could also assume fiscal functions that would involve, on the one hand, a role as a fiscal backstop to private risk-sharing instruments (as the BU) and, on the other hand, the actions of a typical fiscal institution – as a debt agency and treasury. Indeed, the ESM would, in this maximalist model, emerge as a heterodox and manifold institution made to adapt to the specificities of the EMU as a lopsided fiscal union.

5.2.3. Concluding remarks

Recall the two main intersecting questions initially presented, in the Introduction. Firstly, to verify whether the governmental risk-sharing mechanism is an insurance device (*stricto sensu*) or a stabilizer instrument (*lato sensu*) but with no specific features of an insurance mechanism.[125] Secondly, the question of knowing whether the fiscal capacity acts primarily as a visible stabilization device or is instead an instrument where the stabilizing effect is only indirect and invisible – that is, a collateral effect of other policy goals, e.g. redistribution or allocation of resources.

---

125 It should also be recalled that to be considered an insurance device, the instrument must present some of these features: (i) be automatic (the trigger activates automatically the mechanism and the reaction is automatic); (ii) covering large and idiosyncratic shocks; (iii) no permanent transfers (no redistribution) and the fund should be balanced in the long-run; (iv) able to address moral hazard, either on an *ex ante* basis (e.g. contributions; deductibles; commitment with certain behaviour – fiscal discipline or sustainability) or *ex post* basis (e.g. penalties; clawback mechanisms; etc.).

When looking at the catalogue of proposals made in recent years (recalling the taxonomy presented – Figure 5.2), it can be said that only the EUBS and 'classical' anti-cyclical funds give an affirmative answer to both questions.

On the other hand, one can see that, at an institutional level (considering measures adopted or proposed by the Juncker Commission) – the model so far preferred seems to have moved aside from this typical macro stabilizer instrument with insurance features.

The model has evolved to preferably be a convergence-based 'bottom-up' model or to a new route for 'top-down' approaches, where the idea is to derive stabilization objectives from structural-convergence instruments (typically made to ensure allocation of resources and regional redistribution). In either case, the main focus is given over to the pursuit of sectorial policies, that is, the provision of certain types of public goods or private goods exhibiting high positive externalities according to the dominant political agenda expressed in each MFF – for the next MFF, considering the policy priorities already announced by the new Commission, issues such as the *digital economy* and *environmental challenges* will be at the frontline.

Moreover, we are dealing basically with earmarked grants, supporting private and public investment, which by their nature are not able to act as a typical automatic stabilizer. This is the case with the EFSI, a core pillar of the Juncker Investment Plan, and it is also the case with EISF and the recently announced BICC. In these latter cases, despite their apparent purpose to work as stabilizer devices, they are still investment and earmarked programmes, promoting stabilization mostly through the rehabilitation of (publicly supported) investment, by nature a discretionary expenditure and not an automatic stabilizer.

In turn, it can be stated that for the time being, as these instruments are meant to take hold of EU budget resources and eventually be merged in the MFF, they exhibit their conservative nature, respecting the EU budget *status quo*. The new fiscal capacity is apparently a small fund echoing other pre-existing funds or EU budget allocations, therefore with no clear autonomous or innovative goal, and where the proclaimed initial intention to serve as a governmental risk-sharing mechanism seems diluted.

In turn, it is interesting to note that the rehabilitation of fiscal policy in a context of apparent exhaustion of monetary policy is mostly achieved through the rehabilitation of *investment*. At the national level, voices have recently risen pleading for a policy shift towards fiscal stimulus – in Germany. At the European level, the former Juncker Commission seemed to lead Europe to a post-Keynesian world, where European institutions (the EU budget together with 'promotional banking', e.g. the EIB) aimed at giving rise, together with national financial and non-financial institutions, to a great network of funding and leveraging for investment promotion – either public or private investment. Investment is actually now acknowledged as the last resource to overcome the pervasive secular stagnation in Europe. In this regard, the misguiding signs and shifts in policy direction undertaken by European leaders during the peak of the financial crisis should not be forgotten.

At the same time, although assuming the rehabilitation of fiscal policy and, with it, governmental risk-sharing mechanisms, the tension is still there: how to reconcile risk-sharing with market 'discipline'. The discussion involving the completion of the BU is curious in this regard: as seen before, some argue that a fiscal backstop can actually prevent the smooth functioning and the implicit mechanisms of adjustment of the private banking market. Even if well-accepted, the fiscal backstop will mainly be an instrument made to ensure a better functioning of the internal market, notably by supporting private risk-sharing mechanisms ultimately acting as a 'market-maker'.

The abundant menu of (governmental) 'risk-sharing mechanisms' in the EMU is still a work in progress, and the final model is yet unclear. A lot has to be done to give substance and meaning to the new fiscal capacity. The evolution of the economic situation in the near future and the political action of the new EU leaders (notably under the new European Commission) will confirm whether these instruments came to stay and to save the euro.

EPILOGUE

The Coronavirus (COVID-19) pandemic crisis and its major effects

As I write these final words, the world has been hit by a major and destructive pandemic crisis caused by a new Coronavirus disease, COVID-19. Besides the losses of precious human lives and the costs and pressure put upon health care systems, the risks of a major economic disruption across several countries become ever more real with each day that passes. Ultimately, a severe depression, previously unknown in times of peace, is not out of the question; the magnitude of the economic crisis will depend mostly on the duration of the effects of the pandemic and with these the need to maintain contention measures and the emergency states already declared by various governments. The disruption is twofold, affecting both the demand and the supply side of the economy. In the long run, the production capacity of economic units across the world – starting with those in countries with weaker economic structures – will be at stake.

Anticipating such disruptive effects in the production channels and in overall conditions for production, impressive rescue packages (both in terms of their size and heterodox nature) have already been adopted by both governments and monetary authorities. For example, in the U.S., and additionally to sustain the unprecedented turbulence on Wall Street, the Fed immediately announced an almost-unlimited asset purchase of Treasury bills and mortgage-backed securities, in order to favour smooth market functioning and an effective transmission of monetary policy to broader financial conditions. In Germany, the government announced the largest support programme for businesses, including first and foremost the powerful manufacturing sector, together with employment compensation for employees. In order to finance these emergency packages, the German government allowed the lifting of the limits on debt established by constitutional law (the so-called 'debt-brake'), to finance the new funds required to support private and public sectors of the economy (including the states and local governments). The main concern underlying all these policy measures across the world is, in this way, to urgently provide liquidity to firms and families, preventing the shutdown of economic activity leading to massive unemployment and the loss of income that would increase the pain and suffering of the population even more.

COVID-19 and the 'Monet curse' again: a new opportunity for the E(M)U?

Besides the decisions to provide support at the EU level for national health care systems, notably supporting the supply of medical equipment and medication to countries in need and for research, the first significant reaction in terms of economic policy made to address the disruptive effects of the pandemic was the announcement of the ECB's €750 billion Pandemic Emergency Purchase Programme (PEPP). This is the highest monthly purchase programme ever launched by the ECB, being undertaken until the end of 2020 and including all the asset categories eligible under the existing APP.[1] In its initial moment (on 18 March 2020), the programme seemed to face similar limitations to those of APP, notably the cap that the ECB should not hold more than 33% of any one country's debt. On 26 March, this limitation was dropped, meaning that the ECB allowed for a revolutionary and legally controversial possibility of unlimited money-printing[2] to address the coronavirus outbreak.

But for some, Europe should go even further and the time for 'helicopter money' is now (in fact a debt monetization initiative where the Central Bank engages into a quasi-fiscal bailout policy). As stressed in this regard by Galí (2020),

> the central bank could credit the government's account (or governments, in the case of the ECB) for the amount of the additional transfers and for the duration of the programme. That credit would not be repayable, i.e. it would amount to a transfer from the central bank to the government . . . Note that such a transfer from the central bank to the government would be equivalent to a commensurate purchase of government debt by the central bank, followed by its immediate writing-off, thus no longer having an impact on the government's effective debt liabilities.

Besides monetary policy, COVID-19 definitely poses new challenges for fiscal policy as well at the EMU level. A first radical and novel move was already taken by the European Commission. On 20 March, President Ursula von der Leyen proposed the activation of the general escape clause of the SGP to enable full flexibility in the application of the Pact's fiscal rules during 2020. The Eurogroup, in turn, agreed with the European Commission

---

1 More details available here: https://www.ecb.europa.eu/press/pr/date/2020/html/ecb.pr200318_1~3949d6f266.en.html
2 Recall the constitutional problems raised in national courts (especially in Germany) and in the Court of the Justice of the EU regarding previous programmes, notably the OMT and the APP.

iniciative, on moving forward with the new "Corona Response Investment Initiative" which immediately mobilized around €37 billion for urgent needs, by introducing a modification to the common provision regulation of the existing structural funds. Furthermore, in the Eurogroup April meetings, there was an agreement involving three main iniciatives (equivalent to a total of €540 billion rescue package): i) a temporary instrument to support national employment protection measures – a programme named by the Commision as 'SURE'; ii) the European Investment Bank iniciative, aiming at guarenteing lending especially to SMEs; iii) the new Pandemic Crisis Support safeguard, using for that purpose the provisions of the ESM Treaty building on the framework of the existing Enhanced Conditions Credit Line (ECCL) up to 2% of each country's GDP. Two important shortcomings were, however, attached to this latter solution during the political debate: firstly, ESM credit lines typically involve some degree of conditionality (resembling the austerity countries had to face during the sovereign debt crisis in exchange for financial assistance); secondly, this would imply some kind of stigma for those that would have to apply for this specific support.

In a joint letter of 24 March, addressed by nine EU prime ministers to the European Council President, Charles Michel, a new and much more controversial proposal stepped into the political debate, namely the issuance of 'coronabonds'. Based on the model of the Eurobonds, the idea was to allow a joint issuance of debt by affected countries aiming at financing the costs related to COVID-19 and the economic recovery measures following the pandemic crisis. Significantly, a major programme of investment can be put into operation financed by this new joint instrument. For the time being, indeed, a major financial effort has already been shown to be necessary in all European countries to sustain national health care systems and also to support all the significant pieces of the respective economies. Countries would see public expenditure escalate abruptly and at the same time observe tax revenues shrinking due to the economic shutdown. The issuance of these common bonds would hence ensure – as a typical risk-sharing mechanism to address a common shock – smooth market access conditions, both in terms of interest rate costs and maturity. It would ultimately prevent new 'sudden stops' in debt and other financial markets and the increase in spreads between core and peripheral countries. In sum, it would eventually contribute to impairing the rise of a new sovereign debt crisis in the E(M)U. The main argument was that unlike that which happened in 2010, this is not a public finance crisis; this is not an idiosyncratic crisis; this is a common shock driven from an exogenous and uncontrolled factor which has hit all EMU countries in a similar fashion and where moral hazard does not take place. The political debate on this matter would be hard, counting with initial opposition from Germany, the Netherlands, Finland and Austria to this kind of mutualized financing solution.

As can be seen, despite being faced with a different kind of shock, all the measures on the table to counteract the effects of the COVID-19 crisis were still inspired by the menu of risk-sharing solutions, born after the last financial and sovereign debt crisis both on the side of monetary and fiscal policies. The new PEPP was inspired by the APP, but it went beyond this, approximating more to a typical money-printing solution. The Pandemic Crisis Support safeguard was thought to rely on ESM credit lines but could eventually go further, with the relaxation of conditionality. Other measures aiming at supporting employment – such as the SURE programme – could now be accelerated given the risk of unemployment increasing on a very large scale, ultimately justifying to move on with the creation of a true EUBS. In turn, the proposal for the issuance of coronabonds was clearly inspired in the Eurobonds model, implying a debt pooling instrument as a way to ensure risk sharing between all affected economies. Lastly, the possible creation of a new recovery instrument (linked to the European Budget under the next MFF 2021–2027) is embedded in the 'convergence-based funds' approach, here previously detailed, where the idea is to derive some kind of stabilizing goal (e.g. the response to macroeconomic shocks) from convergence earmarked grants (typically made to ensure allocation of resources and regional redistribution).

The 'Pandora's box' of the relaxation of the no-bailout clause, in the cases of both monetary and fiscal policy, is definitely about to be opened as of this writing. The coronavirus crisis pushed the EMU to an existential crossroads with two paths signposted – 'the fiscal federal path (or more Europe)' and the *status quo*. This major and unprecedented crisis (again, the 'Monet curse') forces decision makers – even the sceptical ones – to look at the 'fiscal federal path', if they acknowledge the '*status quo* path' may be even more dangerous at this critical stage, and where the risk of the disintegration of the E(M)U as a political project is not out of the question.

REFERENCES

Acalin, Julien (2019). "Turning National Growth-Indexed Bonds into European Assets: A Proposal to Strengthen the Euro Area", Jean Pisany-Ferry and Jeromin Zettelmeyer (eds.), *Risk-Sharing Plus Market Discipline: A New Paradigm for Euro Area Reform? A Debate*, A VosEU.org Book, London: CEPR Press, pp. 74–81.

Acharya, Viral V. and Steffen, Sascha (2011). "The 'Greatest' Carry Trade Ever? Understanding Eurozone Bank Risks", *Journal of Financial Economics*, 115(2), pp. 215–236.

Acharya, Viral V. *et al.* (2011). "A Pyrrhic Victory? Bank Bailouts and Sovereign Credit Risk", NYU Working Paper No. 2451/31331. Available at SSRN: https://ssrn.com/abstract=2284650

Acharya, Viral V. *et al.* (2016). "Lender of Last Resort versus Buyer of Last Resort – Evidence from European Sovereign Debt Crisis", ZEW – Centre for European Economic Research Discussion Paper No. 16–019, Swiss Finance Institute Research Paper No. 18–35.

Ackrill, Robert (2004). "Stabilization in EMU", Mark Baimbridge and Philip Whyman (eds.), *Fiscal Federalism and European Economic Integration*, London and New York: Routledge, pp. 103–118.

Afonso, António and Furceri, Davide (2008a). "Government Size, Composition, Volatility and Economic Growth", European Central Bank Working Paper Series, No 849.

Afonso, António and Furceri, Davide (2008b). "EMU Enlargement, Stabilization Costs and Insurance Mechanisms", *Journal of International Money and Finance*, 27(2), pp. 169–187.

Afonso, António and Jalles, João (2019). "Quantitative Easing and Sovereign Yield Spreads: Euro-Area Time-Varying Evidence", *Journal of International Financial Markets, Institutions & Money*, 58(2018), pp. 208–224.

Afonso, António and Sequeira, Ana (2010). "Revisiting Business Cycle Synchronization in the European Union", ISEG Working Papers, WP/22/DE/UECE. Available at: http://pascal.iseg.utl.pt/~depeco/wp/wp222010.pdf

Afonso, António *et al.* (2018). "'Whatever It Takes' to Resolve the European Sovereign Debt Crisis? Bond Pricing Regime Switches and Monetary Policy Effects", *Journal of International Money and Finance*, 86, pp. 1–30.

Agénor, Pierre-Richard (2001). "Benefits and Costs of International Financial Integration: Theory and Facts", World Bank Policy Research Working Paper No. 2699. Available at: https://papers.ssrn.com/sol3/papers.cfm?abstract_id=632768

Aguiar, Mark and Amador, Manuel (2013). "Sovereign Debt", NBER Working Paper, No. 19388. Available at: www.nber.org/papers/w19388

Ahmad, Ehtisham and Brosio, Giorgio (eds.) (2006a). *Handbook of Fiscal Federalism*, Cheltenham, UK: Edward Elgar.

Ahmad, Ehtisham and Brosio, Giorgio (2006b). "Introduction: Fiscal Federalism – A Review of Developments in the Literature and Policy", Ehtisham Ahmad and Giorgio Brosio (eds.), *Handbook of Fiscal Federalism*, Cheltenham, UK: Edward Elgar, pp. 1–29.

Ahmad, Ehtisham *et al.* (2006). "Subnational Public Financial Management: Institutions and Macroeconomic Considerations", Ehtisham Ahmad and Giorgio Brosio (eds.), *Handbook of Fiscal Federalism*, Cheltenham, UK: Edward Elgar, pp. 405–427.

Ahrend, Rudiger *et al.* (2011). "The Sharing of Macroeconomic Risk – Who Loses (and Gains) from Macroeconomic Shocks", OECD Economics Department Working Papers No. 877.

Akerlof, George (1970). "The Market of 'Lemons': Quality Uncertainty and the Market Mechanism", *Quarterly Journal of Economics*, 84, pp. 488–500.

Akin, Ozlem *et al.* (2014). "The Real Estate and Credit Bubble: Evidence from Spain", Barcelona GSE Working Paper Series, Working Paper No. 772.

Alcidi, Cinzia (2017). "Fiscal Policy Stabilization and the Financial Cycle in the Euro Area", European Commission Discussion Paper 052, July 2017.

Alcidi, Cinzia and Thirion, Gilles (2016). "Assessing the Euro Area's Shock-Absorption Capacity – Risk-Sharing, Consumption Smoothing and Fiscal Policy", CEPS Special Report, No. 146, September 2016.

Alcidi, Cinzia and Thirion, Gilles (2017). "Fiscal Risk Sharing and Resilience to Shocks: Lesson for the Euro Area from the US", CEPS Working Document No. 210/17, May 2017.

Alcidi, Cinzia *et al.* (2016). "Is There a Need for Additional Monetary Stimulus? Insights from the Original Taylor Rule", CEPS Policy Brief, No. 232, April 2016.

Alcidi, Cinzia *et al.* (2017a). "Risk-sharing and Consumption-smoothing Patterns in the US and the Euro Area: A Comprehensive Comparison", CEPS Working Document No. 2017/04, May 2017.

Alcidi, Cinzia *et al.* (2017b). "Additional Effects of a European Unemployment Benefit Scheme", Social Europe, Brussels: European Commission.

Alcidi, Cinzia *et al.* (2017c). "The Instruments Providing Macro-Financial Support to EU Member States", CEPS Research Report, No. 2017/06, March 2017.

Alcidi, Cinzia *et al.* (2018). "Income Convergence in the EU: Within-country Regional Patterns", CEPS Commentary. Available at: www.ceps.eu/ceps-publications/income-convergence-eu-within-country-regional-patterns/

Alesina, Alberto and Ardagna, Silvia (1998). "Tales of Fiscal Adjustment", *Economic Policy*, 13(27), pp. 489–585.

Alesina, Alberto and Ardagna, Silvia (2009). "Large Changes in Fiscal Policy: Taxes versus Spending", NBER Working Paper 15438. Available at: www.nber.org/papers/w15438.pdf

Alesina, Alberto and Ardagna, Silvia (2012). "The Design of Fiscal Adjustments", NBER Working Paper 18423. Available at: www.nber.org/papers/w18423.pdf

Alesina, Alberto and Bayoumi, Tamim (1996). "The Costs and Benefits of Fiscal Rules: Evidence from U.S. States", NBER Working Papers 5614. Available at: www.nber.org/papers/w5614

Alesina, Alberto and Giavazzi, Francesco (2012). "The Austerity Question: 'How?' Is as Important as 'How Much?'", Giancarlo Corsetti (ed.), *Austerity: Too Much of a Good Thing?*, A VoxEu.org eCollection of views of leading economists, London: CEPR Press, pp. 11–15.

Alesina, Alberto and Perotti, Roberto (1994). "The Political Economy of Budget Deficits", NBER Working Paper 4637. Available at: www.nber.org/papers/w4637.pdf

Alesina, Alberto and Perotti, Roberto (1995). "Fiscal Expansions and Adjustments in OECD Countries", NBER Working Paper 5214. Available at: www.nber.org/papers/w5214.pdf

Alesina, Alberto and Perotti, Roberto (1996). "Fiscal Adjustments in OECD Countries: Composition and Macroeconomic Effects", NBER Working Paper 5214. Available at: www.nber.org/papers/w5730.pdf

Alesina, Alberto and Tabellini, Guido (1990). "A Positive Theory of Fiscal Deficits and Government Debt", *Review of Economic Studies*, 57, pp. 403–414.

Alesina, Alberto *et al.* (1998). "The Political Economy of Fiscal Adjustments", Brookings Papers on Economic Activity (Spring), pp. 197–266.

Alesina, Alberto *et al.* (2019). *Austerity – When it Works and When It Doesn't*, Princeton: Princeton University Press.

Allen, Franklin *et al.* (2011). *Cross-Border Banking in Europe: Implications for Financial Stability and Macroeconomic Policies*, Brussels: CEPR Press.

Altavilla, Carlo (2004). "Do EMU Members Share the Same Business Cycle?", *Journal of Common Market Studies*, 42(5), pp. 869–896.

Anderson, Karen M. (2015). *Social Policy in the European Union*, New York: Palgrave.

Andrade, Philippe *et al.* (2016). "The ECB's Asset Purchase Programme: An Early Assessment", European Central Banks Working Paper Series, No. 1956, September 2016.

Araújo, Fernando (2005). *Introdução à Economia*, 3rd ed., Coimbra: Almedina.

Araújo, Fernando (2007). *Teoria Económica do Contrato*, Coimbra: Almedina.

Archer, Clive and Butler, Fiona (1996). *The European Union – Structure & Process*, 2nd ed., London: Pinter.

Ardy, Brain (2004). "The Development of the EU Budget and EMU", Mark Baimbridge and Philip Whyman (eds.), *Fiscal Federalism and European Economic Integration*, London and New York: Routledge, pp. 83–100.

Ardy, Brain *et al.* (2003). "How Will EMU Affect Cohesion?", Working Papers in Economics, Universidade de Aveiro, E/n° 6/2003.

Ark, Bart van (2010). "Productivity, Sources of Growth and Potential Output in the Euro Area and the United States", *Intereconomics 2010*, 1, pp. 17–20.

Ascani, Andrea *et al.* (2012). "New Economic Geography and Economic Integration: A Review", Search Economic Series WP1/02.

Asdrubali, Pierfederico *et al.* (1996). "Channels of Intestate Risk Sharing: United States 1963–1990", *The Quarterly Journal of Economics*, 111(4), pp. 1081–1110.

Attinasi, Maria-Grazia *et al.* (2011). "What Explains the Surge in Euro Area Spreads during the Financial Crisis 2007–2008?", Robert W. Kolb (ed.), *Sovereign Debt – From Safety to Default*, Hoboken, New Jersey: Wiley, pp. 407–414.

Baele, Lieven *et al.* (2004). "Measuring Financial Integration in the Euro Area", ECB's Occasional Paper Series, Paper No. 14, April 2004.

Bagehot, Walter (1873). *Lombard Street: A Description of the Money Market*, London.

Bajo-Rubio, Oscar and Díaz-Roldán, Carmen (2003). "Insurance Mechanisms Against Asymmetric Shocks in a Monetary Union: As Application to the European Monetary Union", *Recherches économiques de Louvain*, 69, pp. 73–96.

Baldwin, Richard and Giavazzi, Francesco (eds.) (2015a). *The Eurozone Crisis: A Consensus View of the Causes and a Few Possible Solutions*, A VoxEU.org Book, London: CEPR Press.

Baldwin, Richard and Giavazzi, Francesco (2015b). "Introduction", Richard Baldwin and Francesco Giavazzi (eds.), *The Eurozone Crisis: A Consensus View of the Causes and a Few Possible Solutions*, A VoxEU.org Book, London: CEPR Press, pp. 18–61.

Baldwin, Richard and Giavazzi, Francesco (eds.) (2016). *How to Fix Europe's Monetary Union – Views of Leading Economists*, A VoxEU.org Book, London: CEPR Press.

Baldwin, Richard and Gros, Daniel (2015). "What Caused the Eurozone Crisis", CEPS Commentary. Available at: www.ceps.eu/system/files/What%20caused%20 the%20EZ%20Crisis%20RB%20DG%20CEPS%20Commentary.pdf

Baldwin, Richard and Wyplosz, Charles (2015). *The Economics of European Integration*, 5th ed., London: McGraw Hill Education.

Baldwin, Richard *et al.* (2015). "Rebooting the Eurozone: Step I – Agreeing a Crisis Narrative", CEPR Policy Insight No. 85. Available at: https://voxeu.org/sites/ default/files/file/Policy%20Insight%2085.pdf

Ball, Laurence M. (2014). "Long-Term Damage from the Great Recession in OECD Countries", NBER Working Paper No 20185. Available at: www.nber.org/papers/ w20185.pdf

Ball, Laurence M. *et al.* (2016). *What Else Can Central Banks Do?*, Geneva: International Center for Monetary and Banking Studies.

Balli, Faruk and Sorensen, Ben E. (2007). "Risk Sharing Among OECD and EU Countries: The Role of Capital Gains, Capital Income, Transfers, and Saving", MPRA Paper No. 10223. Available at: https://mpra.ub.uni-muenchen.de/10223/

Balteanu, Irina and Erce, Eitor (2017). "Linking Bank Crises and Sovereign Defaults: Evidence from Emerging Markets". Available at: https://papers.ssrn.com/sol3/papers. cfm?abstract_id=2972818

Banerjee, Ryan and Zampolli, Fabrizio (2016). "What Drives the Short-run Costs of Fiscal Consolidation? Evidence from OECD Countries", BIS Working Papers No. 553. Available at: www.bis.org/publ/work553.htm

Bardutzky, Samo and Fahey, Elaine (2014). "Who Got to Adjudicate the EU's Financial Crisis and Why? Judicial Review of the Legal Instruments of the Eurozone", Maurice Adams *et al.* (eds.), *The Constitutionalization of European Budgetary Constraints*, Oxford and Portland, OR: Hart Publishing, pp. 341–358.

Bargain, Olivier *et al.* (2012). "Fiscal Union in Europe? Redistributive and Stabilising Effects of an EU Taxa-Benefit System", IZA Discussion Paper Series No. 6585.

Bayoumi, Tamim and Eichengreen, Barry (1992). "Shocking Aspects of European Monetary Unification", NBER Working Papers No. 3949. Available at: www. nber.org/papers/w3949 www.nber.org/papers/w3949

Bayoumi, Tamim and Masson, Paul T. (1995). "Fiscal Flows in the United States and Canada: Lessons for Monetary Union in Europe", *European Economic Review*, 39(2), pp. 253–274.

Bayoumi, Tamim and Masson, Paul T. (1998). "Liability-Creating versus Non-Liability-Creating Fiscal Stabilization Policies: Ricardian Equivalence, Fiscal Stabilization, and EMU", IMF Working Paper, WP 98/112.

Beblavý, Miroslav and Maselli, Ilaria (2014). "An Unemployment Insurance Scheme for the Euro Area: A Simulation Exercise of Two Options", CEPS Special Report No 98, Brussels: CEPS.

Beblavý, Miroslav et al. (2015). "A European Unemployment Benefit Scheme: The Rationale and the Challenges Ahead", CEPS. Brussels: European Commission.

Beblavý, Miroslav et al. (2017). "The (Future) European Unemployment Insurance and Its Role as an Automatic Stabilizer", Nazaré da Costa Cabral et al. (eds.), *The Euro and the Crisis – Perspectives for the Eurozone as a Monetary and Budgetary Union*, Switzerland: Springer, pp. 289–301.

Bech, Morten and Malkhozov, Aytek (2016). "How Have Central Banks Implemented Negative Policy Rates?", *BIS Quarterly Review*, March 2016, pp. 31–44.

Beck, Thorsten (ed.) (2012). "Banking Union for Europe – Risks and Challenges", A VoxEU.org Book. Available at: https://voxeu.org/sites/default/files/file/Banking_Union.pdf

Beck, Thorsten (2017). "Looking Back at a Lost Decade; Avoiding a Second One", Agnés Bénassy-Quéré and Francesco Giavazzi (eds.), *Europe's Political Spring – Fixing the Eurozone and Beyond*, A VoxEU.org Book, London: CEPR Press, pp. 17–24.

Beck, Thorsten and Huizinga, Harry (2011). "Taxing Banks – Here We Go Again!", Thorsten Beck (ed.), *The Future of Banking*, A VoxEU.org Book, London: CEPR Press, pp. 65–72.

Beck, Thorsten and Kotz, Hans-Helmut (eds.) (2017). *Ordoliberalism: A German Oddity?*, A VoxEU.org Book, London: CEPR Press.

Beetsma, Roel et al. (2001). "Is Fiscal Policy Coordination in EMU Desirable?", IMF Worjing Paper, WP/01/178.

Begg, Iain (2009). "Fiscal Federalism, Subsidiarity and the EU Budget Review", SIEPS, Swedish Institute for European Policy Studies, Report No 1, Stockholm.

Begg, Iain (2012). "Breaking the Shackles of Austerity? Using the EU Budget to Achieve Macroeconomic Stabilization". Available at: https://library.fes.de/pdf-files/id/09450.pdf

Begg, Iain and Grimwade, Nigel (1998). *Paying for Europe*, Sheffield: Academic Press.

Begg, Iain and Schelkle, Waltraub (2004). "Can Fiscal Policy Co-ordination be Made to Work Effectively?", *Journal of Common Market Studies*, 42(5), pp. 1047–1056.

Belke, Ansgar and Gros, Daniel (2017). "Greece and the Troika – Lessons from International Best Practice Cases of Successful Price (and Wage) Adjustment", *The European Journal of Comparative Economics*, 14(2), pp. 177–195.

Belke, Ansgar and Osowski, Thomas (2016). "Measuring Fiscal Spillovers in EMU and Beyond: A Global VAR Approach", CEPS Working Document, No. 428. Available at: www.ceps.eu/system/files/WD428%20Fiscal%20spillover.pdf

Belke, Ansgar et al. (2016). " Business Cycle Synchronization in the EMU: Core vs. Periphery", CEPS Working Document, No. 427. Available at: www.ceps.eu/publications/business-cycle-synchronization-emu-core-vs-periphery

Bénassy-Quéré, Agnès (2015). "Maastricht Flaws and Remedies", Richard Baldwin and Francesco Giavazzi (eds.), *The Eurozone Crisis: A Consensus View of the*

Causes and a Few Possible Solutions, A VoxEU.org Book, London: CEPR Press, pp. 71–83.

Bénassy-Quéré, Agnès (2016). "A Sovereignless Currency", Richard Baldwin and Francesco Giavazzi (eds.), *How to Fix Europe's Monetary Union – Views of Leading Economists*, A VoxEU.org Book, London: CEPR Press, pp. 62–74.

Bénassy-Quéré, Agnès (2017). "Unequal Imbalances", Thorsten Beck and Hans-Helmut Kotz (eds.), *Ordoliberalism: A German Oddity?*, A VoxEU.org Book, London: CEPR Press, pp. 201–215.

Bénassy-Quéré, Agnès and Giavazzi, Francesco (eds.) (2017). *Europe's Political Spring – Fixing the Eurozone and Beyond*, A VoxEU.org Book, London: CEPR Press.

Bénassy-Quéré, Agnès *et al.* (2014). "Tax Harmonization in Europe: Moving Forward", Les notes du Conseil d' Analyse Économique, no. 14, July 2014.

Bénassy-Quéré, Agnès *et al.* (2016). "Which Fiscal Union for the Euro Area?", Les notes du Conseil d' Analyse Économique, no. 29, February 2016.

Bénassy-Quéré, Agnès *et al.* (2018). "Reconciling Risk Sharing with Market Discipline: A Constructive Approach to Euro Area Reform", CEPR Policy Insight No. 91, January 2018. Available at: https://cepr.org/active/publications/policy_insights/viewpi.php?pino=91

Bento, Vitor (2013). *Euro Forte, Euro Fraco – Duas culturas, uma moeda: um convívio (im)possível?*, bnomics.

Bentoglio, Guilhem *et al.* (2001). "Unité et pluralité du cycle européen", *Problèmes économiques*, N° 2728, pp. 1–16.

Berensmann, Kathrin (2011). "A Code of Conduct for Sovereign Debt Restructuring: An Important Component of the International Financial Architecture?", Robert W. Kolb (ed.), *Sovereign Debt – From Safety to Default*, Hoboken, New Jersey: Wiley, pp. 197–204.

Bergvall, Daniel *et al.* (2006). "Intergovernmental Transfers and Decentralised Public Spending", *OECD Journal on Budgeting*, 5(4), pp. 111–158.

Bernanke, Ben S. (1983). "Non-Monetary Effects of the Financial Crisis in the Propagation of the Great Depression", NBER Working Paper No 1054. Available at: www.nber.org/papers/w1054.pdf

Bernanke, Ben S. (2003). "Some Thoughts on Monetary Policy in Japan", Remarks by Governor Ben S. Bernanke. Available at: www.federalreserve.gov/boarddocs/speeches/2003/20030531/

Bernanke, Ben S. (2005). "The Global Saving Glut and the U.S. Current Account Deficit", Remarks by Governor Ben S. Bernanke. Available at: www.federalreserve.gov/boarddocs/speeches/2005/200503102/

Bernanke, Ben S. and Blinder, Alan (1990). "The Federal Funds Rate and Channels of Monetary Transmission", NBER Working Paper No 3487. Available at: www.nber.org/papers/w3487.pdf

Bernanke, Ben S. and Gertler, Mark (1987). "Financial Fragility and Economic Performance", NBER Working Paper No 2318. Available at: www.nber.org/papers/w2318.pdf

Bernanke, Ben S. and Gertler, Mark (1995). "Inside the Black Box: The Credit Channel of Monetary Policy Transmission", NBER Working Paper No 5146. Available at: www.nber.org/papers/w5146.pdf

REFERENCES

Bernanke, Ben S. *et al.* (1999). "The Financial Accelerator in a Quantitative Business Cycle Framework", J. B. Taylor and M. Woodford (eds.), *Handbook of Macroeconomics*, Vol. 1, Amsterdam: Elsevier Science, pp. 1341–1393.

Betson, David and Haveman, Robert (1984). "The Role of Income Transfers in Reducing Inequality between and within Regions", Marilyn Moon (ed.), *Economic Transfers in the United States*, Chicago: University of Chicago Press, pp. 283–326.

Blanchard, Oliver J. *et al.* (2015). "Inflation and Activity – Two Explanations and Their Monetary Policy Implications", IMF WP/15/230.

Blanchard, Oliver J., and Leigh, Daniel (2013). "Growth Forecast Errors and Fiscal Multipliers", IMF Working Paper, WP/13/1.

Blanchard, Oliver J., and Summers, Lawrence H. (1986). "Hysteresis in Unemployment", NBER Working Paper No 2035. Available at: www.nber.org/papers/w2035.pdf

Blöchliger, Hansjörg and King, David (2006). "Fiscal Autonomy of Sub-central Governments", OECD Working Papers on Fiscal Federalism, No. 2.

Blöchliger, Hansjörg and Nettley, Maurice (2011). " Sub-central Tax Autonomy: 2011 Update", OECD Working Papers on Fiscal Federalism, No. 20.

Blöchliger, Hansjörg and Petzold, Oliver (2009). "Taxes and Grants: On the Revenue Mix of Sub-Central Governments", OECD Working Papers on Fiscal Federalism, No 7.

Blöchliger, Hansjörg and Rabesona, Josette (2009). "The Fiscal Autonomy of Sub-Central Governments: An Update", OECD Working Papers on Fiscal Federalism, No 9.

Blöchliger, Hansjörg *et al.* (2007). "Fiscal Equalisation in OECD Countries", OECD Working Papers on Fiscal Federalism, No 4.

Blyth, Mark (2013). *Austerity – The History of a Dangerous Idea*, Oxford and New York: Oxford University Press.

Boadway, Robin (2007). "Grants in a Federal Economy: A Conceptual Perspective", Robin Boadway and Anwar Shah (eds.), *Intergovernmental Fiscal Transfers – Principles and Practice*, Washington, DC: The World Bank, pp. 55–74.

Boadway, Robin and Shah, Anwar (eds.) (2007). *Intergovernmental Fiscal Transfers – Principles and Practice*, Washington, DC: The World Bank.

Boadway, Robin and Shah, Anwar (2009). *Fiscal Federalism – Principles and Practice of Multiorder Governance*, Cambridge: Cambridge University Press.

Boadway, Robin *et al.* (1994). "Fiscal Federalism – Dimensions of Tax Reform in Developing Countries", Policy Research Working Paper, WPS 1385, The World Bank, Washington, DC.

Bofinger, Peter *et al.* (2011). "A European Redemption Pact", Available at: https://voxeu.org/article/european-redemption-pact

Bolton, Patrick and Jeanne, Olivier (2008). "Structuring and Restructuring Sovereign Debt: The Role of Seniority", NBER Working Paper No. 11071. Available at: www.nber.org/papers/w11071

Bongardt, Annette and Torres, Francisco (2017). "EMU as a Sustainable Currency Area", Nazaré da Costa Cabral *et al.* (eds.), *The Euro and Crisis – Perspectives for the Eurozone as a Monetary and Budgetary Union*, Switzerland: Springer, pp. 17–32.

Bordo, Michael D. and Landon-Lane, John (2013). "Does Expansionary Monetary Policy Cause Asset Price Booms; Some Historical and Empirical Evidence", NBER Working Paper No 19585. Available at: www.nber.org/papers/w19585.pdf

Borio, Claudio and Zabai, Anna (2016). "Unconventional Monetary Policy: A Reappraisal", BIS Working Paper No. 570. Available at: www.bis.org/publ/work570.pdf

Borio, Claudio *et al.* (2016). "Fiscal Sustainability and the Financial Cycle", BIS Working Paper No. 552. Available at: http://financial-stability.org/wp-content/uploads/2016/03/2016-3_bis_fiscal-sustainability-financial-cycle.pdf

Boulhol, Hervé (2002). "Le Pacte the stabilité et the croissance à l' épreuve du ralentissement économique", *Problèmes économiques*, No. 2755, pp. 18–23.

Bouvet, Florence (2004). "Dynamics of Regional Income Inequality in Europe and Impact of EU Regional Policy and EMU". Available at: http://ec.europa.eu/economy_finance/events/2007/researchconf1110/bouvet_en.pdf.pdf

Breton, Albert (1996). *Competitive Governments: An Economic Theory of Politics and Public Finance*, Cambridge: Cambridge University Press.

Breton, Albert (2006). "Modelling Vertical Competition", Ehtisham Ahmad and Giorgio Brosio (eds.), *Handbook of Fiscal Federalism*, Cheltenham, UK: Edward Elgar, pp. 86–105.

Breuss, Fritz (2017). "The Crisis Management of the ECB", Nazaré da Costa Cabral *et al.* (eds.), *The Euro and Crisis – Perspectives for the Eurozone as a Monetary and Budgetary Union*, Switzerland: Springer, pp. 199–221.

Breuss, Fritz *et al.* (2015). "The Stabilizing Properties of a European Banking Union in Case of Financial Shocks in the Euro Area, European Economy", Economic Papers 550. Brussels: European Commission.

Broz, Tanja (2005). "The Theory of Optimum Currency Areas: A Literature Review", *Ekonomska Politika*, 104/2005, pp. 53–77.

Brunnermeier, Markus K. and Schnabel, Isabel (2015). "Bubbles and Central Banks: Historical Perspectives". Available at: https://scholar.princeton.edu/sites/default/files/markus/files/bubbles_centralbanks_historical_0.pdf.

Brunnermeier, Markus K. *et al.* (2012). "European Safe Bonds (ESBies)", The Euro-nomics Group. Available at: https://personal.lse.ac.uk/vayanos/Euronomics/ESBies.pdf

Brunnermeier, Markus K. *et al.* (2016a). *The Euro and the Battle of Ideas*, Princeton and Oxford: Princeton University Press.

Brunnermeier, Markus K. *et al.* (2016b). "ESBIes: Safety in Tranches", ESRB Working Paper Series, No. 21, September 2016.

Buchanan, James M. (1950). "Federalism and Fiscal Equity", *American Economic Review*, 40(4), pp. 583–599.

Buchanan, James M. (1965). "An Economic Theory of Clubs", *Economica*, XXXII(125), pp. 1–14.

Buiter, Willem H. and Rahbari, Ebrahim (2012). "The ECB as a Lender of Last Resort for Sovereigns in the Euro Area", Discussion Paper Series No. 8974, Center for Economic Policy Research.

Bullard, James *et al.* (2009). "Systemic Risk and the Financial Crisis: A Primer", *Federal Reserve Bank of St. Louis Review*, 91(5, Part 1), pp. 403–417.

Bullow, Jeremy and Rogoff, Kenneth (1988). "Sovereign Debt: Is to Forgive or to Forget?", NBER Working Paper No. 2623. Available at: www.nber.org/papers/w2623

Burgess, Michael (2000). *Federalism and European Union: the Building Process of Europe, 1950–2000*, London and New York: Routledge.

Buti, Marco and Carnot, Nicolas (2018). "The Case for a Central Fiscal Capacity in EMU". Available at: https://voxeu.org/article/case-central-fiscal-capacity-emu

Buti, Marco and Pench, Lucio (2012). "Fiscal Austerity and Policy Credibility". Available at: https://voxeu.org/article/fiscal-austerity-and-policy-credibility

Buti, Marco et al. (2001). "'Stabilizing Output and Inflation': Policy Conflicts and Co-Operation under a Stability Pac", Journal of Common Market Studies, 39(5), pp. 801–828.

Caballero, Ricardo and Farhi, Emmanuel (2014). "On the Role of Safe Assets Shortages in Secular Stagnation". Available at: https://voxeu.org/article/role-safe-asset-shortages-secular-stagnation

Cabo, Sérgio Gonçalves (2017). "Sovereign Debt Restructuring in a Monetary Union: The Case of Euro Area Member States", Nazaré da Costa Cabral et al. (eds.), The Euro and Crisis – Perspectives for the Eurozone as a Monetary and Budgetary Union, Cham, Switzerland: Springer, pp. 173–195.

Cabral, Nazaré da Costa (2010). "Breve guia temático e bibliográfico sobre o estudo da actual crise económica e financeira" ("Short Thematic Guide to the Study of Current Financial and Economic Crisis"), MPRA Paper No 20743. Available at: https://mpra.ub.uni-muenchen.de/20743/1/MPRA_paper_20743.pdf

Cabral, Nazaré da Costa (2013). "O Memorando da 'Troika': metalinguagem e construções económicas subjacentes", Eduardo Paz Ferreira (Coord.), Troika – Ano II, Lisboa: Edições 70, pp. 463–475.

Cabral, Nazaré da Costa (2016). "Which Budgetary Union for the E(M)U?", Journal of Common Market Studies, 54(6), pp. 1280–1295.

Cabral, Nazaré da Costa (2017). "The Eurozone's Private and Governmental Shock Absorbers: Current Setup and Future Prospects", Nazaré da Costa Cabral et al. (eds.), The Euro and Crisis – Perspectives for the Eurozone as a Monetary and Budgetary Union, Switzerland: Springer, pp. 249–269.

Cabral, Nazaré da Costa (2018). A Teoria do Federalismo Financeiro, 3rd ed., Coimbra: Almedina.

Cabral, Ricardo et al. (2017). "Heading South: Rethinking the Eurozone, The Ulysses Study". Available at: https://eu.boell.org/sites/default/files/heading_south_rethinking_the_euro_zone.pdf

Caceres, Carlos et al. (2011). "From Financial Crisis to Sovereign Risk", Robert W. Kolb (ed.), Sovereign Debt – From Safety to Default, Hoboken, New Jersey: Wiley, pp. 393–400.

Calvo, Guillermo A. (1998). "Capital Flows and Capital-Market Crises: The Simple Economics of Sudden Stops". Available at: https://ideas.repec.org/a/cem/jaecon/v1y1998n1p35-54.html

Carmona, Magdalena Sepúlveda (2014). "Alternatives to Austerity: A Human Rights Framework for Economic Recovery", Aoife Nolan (ed.), Economic and Social Rights After the Great Financial Crisis, Cambridge: Cambridge University Press, pp. 23–56.

Carnot, Nicolas et al. (2015). "Income Insurance: A Theoretical Exercise with Empirical Application for the Euro Area", European Economy, Economic Papers 546.

Casella, Francesco and Frey, Bruno (1992). "Federalism and Clubs – Towards an Economic Theory of Overlapping Political Jurisdictions", European Economic Review, 36, pp. 639–646.

Caselli, Francesco *et al.* (2016). "The Challenge of European Inequality", Francesco Caselli *et al.* (eds.), *After the Crisis – Reform Recovery and Growth in Europe*, Oxford: Oxford University Press, pp. 171–193.

Catarino, João Ricardo (2012). "O Orçamento da União Europeia", João Ricardo Catarino e José F.F. Tavares (coord.), *Finanças Públicas da União Europeia*, Coimbra: Almedina, pp. 109–147.

Centeno, Mário and Coelho, Miguel Castro (2018). "The Turnaround of the Portuguese Economy: Two Decades of Structural Changes". Available at: https://voxeu.org/article/turnaround-portuguese-economy

Cerra, Valeri and Saxena, Sweta Chaman (2008). "Growth Dynamics: The Myth of Economic Recovery", *American Economic Review*, 98, pp. 439–457.

CESifo (2010). "Fiscal Stimulus – Stabilization of Economic Activity in the EU", CESifo DICE Report 3/2010. Available at: www.cesifo-group.de/DocDL/dicereport310-db1.pdf

CFP (2012). "Portugal's Fiscal Strategy 2012–2016", A Report by the Portuguese Public Finance Council, Report No 1/2012.

CFP (2014). "Analysis of the Fiscal Strategy Document 2014–2018", A Report by the Portuguese Public Finance Council, Report No 3/2014.

Charbit, Claire (2010). "Explaining the Sub-National Tax-Grants Balance in OECD Countries", OECD Working Papers on Fiscal Federalism, No 11.

Chatterjee, Satyajit and Eyigungor, Burcu (2015). "A Seniority Arrangement for Sovereign Debt", *AER*, 105(2), pp. 3740–3765.

Checherita, Cristina *et al.* (2009). "The Role of Fiscal Transfers for Regional Convergence in Europe", European Central Bank Working Paper Series No. 1029, March 2009.

Cimadomo, Jacopo *et al.* (2012). "Risk Sharing in the Euro Area". Available at: www.ecb.europa.eu/pub/pdf/other/ecb.ebart201803_03.en.pdf

Cipriani, Gabriele (2014). *Financing the EU Budget – Moving Forward or Backwards?*, London: CEPS, Center for European Policy Studies.

Cipriani, Gabriele (2016). "Reforming the EU's Budget Revenue – The Case for a Visible VAT-Based Resource", CEPS Special Report, No. 150, 2016. Available at: www.ceps.eu/ceps-publications/reforming-eus-budget-revenue-case-visible-vat-based-resource/

Claessens, Stijn *et al.* (2011). "Crisis Management and Resolution: Early Lessons from the Financial Crisis", IMF Staff Discussion Note, SDN/11/05. Available at: www.imf.org/external/pubs/ft/sdn/2011/sdn1105.pdf

Claveres, Guillaume and Strásky, Jan (2019). "Euro Area Unemployment Insurance at the Time of Zero Nominal Interest Rates". Available at: https://uece2.rc.iseg.ulisboa.pt/events/2019/INFER%20REM%20sessions/Session%20A1_Chair_Martin%20Zagler/1_11_Claveres%20Strasky%20ISEG%20Workshop%2022%20nov%202019.pdf

Claeys, Grégory (2018). "New EMU Stabilization Tool within the MFF Will Have Minimal Impact without Deeper EU Budget Reform". Available at: http://bruegel.org/2018/05/new-emu-stabilisation-tool-within-the-mff-will-have-minimal-impact-without-deeper-eu-budget-reform/

Claeys, Grégory and Leandro, Álvaro (2016). "The European Central Bank's Quantitative Easing Programme: Limits and Risks", Bruegel Policy Contribution Issue 2016/04, February 2016.

REFERENCES

Coenen, Günter *et al.* (2003). "Price Stability and Monetary Policy Effectiveness When Nominal Interest Rates Are Bounded at Zero", European Central Bank Working Paper Series, Working Paper No. 231.

Cogan, John F. *et al.* (2009). "New Keynesian versus Old Keynesian Government Spending Multipliers", NBER Working Paper 14782. Available at: www.nber.org/papers/w14782.pdf

Commission of the European Communities (1993). "Stable Money – Sound Finances", European Economy, No. 53, 1993. Brussels.

Congleton, Roger D. (2006). "Asymmetric Federalism and the Political Economy of Decentralization", Ehtisham Ahmad and Giorgio Brosio (eds.), *Handbook of Fiscal Federalism*, Cheltenham, UK: Edward Elgar, pp. 131–153.

Constâncio, Vítor (2016). "The Challenge of Low Real Interest Rates for Monetary Policy". Available at: www.ecb.europa.eu/press/key/date/2016/html/sp160615.en.html

Constâncio, Vítor (2017). "Synergies Between Banking Union and Capital Markets Union". Available at: www.ecb.europa.eu/press/key/date/2017/html/ecb.sp170519_1.en.html

Cooper, George (2008). *The Origin of Financial Crises – Central Banks, Credit Bubbles, and the Efficient Market Fallacy*, Petersfield, UK: Harriman House Ltd.

Cooper, Richard N. (2017). "Germany and the World Economy", Thorsten Beck and Hans-Helmut Kotz (eds.), *Ordoliberalism: A German Oddity?*, A VoxEU.org Book, London: CEPR Press, pp. 181–186.

Cooper, Russel and Nikolov, Kalin (2013). "Government Debt and Banking Fragility: The Spreading of Strategic Uncertainty", NBER Working Paper No. 19278. Available at: www.nber.org/papers/w19278

Corden, W.M. (1960). "The Geometric Representation of Policies to Attain Internal and External Balance", *The Review of Economic Studies*, 28(1), pp. 1–22.

Corden, W.M. (1972). *Monetary Integration*. Princeton Essays in International Finance No. 93, International Finance Section. Princeton, NJ: Princeton University.

Corsetti, Giancarlo (2008). "A Modern Reconsideration of the Theory of Optimum Currency Areas", Economic Papers 308. Brussels: European Economy.

Corsetti, Giancarlo (2012a). "Introduction", Giancarlo Corsetti (ed.), *Austerity: Too Much of a Good Thing?*, A VoxEU.org eCollection of views of leading economists, London: CEPR Press, pp. 1–10.

Corsetti, Giancarlo (2012b). "Has Austerity Gone Too Far?", Giancarlo Corsetti (ed.), *Austerity: Too Much of a Good Thing?*, A VoxEU.org eCollection of views of leading economists, London: CEPR Press, pp. 103–113.

Corsetti, Giancarlo (2015). "Roots of the Eurozone Crisis: Incomplete Development and Imperfect Credibility of Institutions", Richard Baldwin and Francesco Giavazzi (eds.), *The Eurozone Crisis: A Consensus View of the Causes and a Few Possible Solutions*, A VoxEU.org Book, London: CEPR Press, pp. 86–98.

Corsetti, Giancarlo *et al.* (2016). "Macroeconomic Stabilization, Monetary-Fiscal Interactions, and Europe's Monetary Union", European Central Bank Working Paper Series, No. 1988, December 2016.

Corsetti, Giancarlo *et al.* (2019). "Macroeconomic Stabilization, Monetary-Fiscal Policy Interactions, and Europe's Monetary Union", *European Journal of Political Economy*, 57(2019), pp. 22–33.

Cottarelli, Carlo (2012). "The Austerity Debate: Make Haste Slowly", Giancarlo Corsetti (ed.), *Austerity: Too Much of a Good Thing?*, A VoxEU.org eCollection of views of leading economists, London: CEPR Press, pp. 39–43.

Cottarelli, Carlo and Jaramillo, Laura (2012). "Walking Hand in Hand: Fiscal Policy and Growth in Advanced Economies", IMF Working Paper, WP/12/137.

Courant, Paul *et al.* (1979). "The Stimulative Effects of Intergovernmental Grants: Or Why Money Sticks Where It Hits", P. Mieszkowski and W. H. Oakland (eds.), *Fiscal Federalism and Grants-in-Aid*, Washington, DC: The Urban Institute, pp. 5–10.

Courchene, Thomas J. (2008). "Macro Federalism: An Introduction with Principal Reference to the Canadian Experience", Anwar Shah (ed.), *Macro Federalism and Local Finance*, Public Sector Governance and Accountability Series, Washington: The World Bank, pp. 45–76.

Couré, Benoît (2017). "Monetary Policy, Exchange Rates and Capital Flows". Available at: www.ecb.europa.eu/press/key/date/2017/html/ecb.sp171103.en.html

Craig, Paul and Markakis, Menelaos (2016). "*Gauweiler* and the Legality of Outright Monetary Transactions". Available at: www.law.ox.ac.uk/business-law-blog/blog/2016/03/gauweiler-and-legality-outright-monetary-transactions

Cuaresma, Jesus Crespo and Amador, Octavio Fernandez (2010a). "Business Cycle Convergence in EMU: A First Look at the Second Moment". Available at: https://econpapers.repec.org/paper/innwpaper/2010-22.htm

Cuaresma, Jesus Crespo and Amador, Octavio Fernandez (2010b). "Business Cycle Convergence in EMU: A Second Look at the Second Moment". Available at: www.econstor.eu/handle/10419/73468

Cunha, Paulo de Pitta (2000). "The Flimsiness of the Euro: A Currency without a State", *Revista da Faculdade de Direito da Universidade de Lisboa*, XLI(2), pp. 595–597.

Cunha, Paulo de Pitta (2009). *Da crise internacional às questões europeias – Estudos diversos*, Pólo Europeu da Universidade de Lisboa.

Cunha, Paulo de Pitta (2013). *Sombras sobre a integração europeia*, Coimbra: Coimbra Editora.

Cunha, Paulo de Pitta (2019). *A Europa em tempo de incerteza*, Lisboa: A.A.F.D.L.

Dadush, Uri and Eidelman, Vera (2010). "Germany: Europe's Pride or Europe's Problem?", Uri Dadush and Contributors (eds.), *Paradigm Lost – The Euro in Crisis*, Washington, DC: Carnegie Endowment for International Peace, pp. 17–21.

Dadush, Uri and Stancil, Bennett (2010). "Europe's Debt Crisis: More than a Fiscal Problem", Uri Dadush and Contributors (eds.), *Paradigm Lost – The Euro in Crisis*, Washington, DC: Carnegie Endowment for International Peace, pp. 9–16.

Darvas, Zsolt and von Weisäcker, Jakob (2010). "Financial Transaction Tax: Small Is Beautiful", Directorate-General for Internal Policies, European Parliament.

de Grauwe, Paul (2011a). "The European Central Bank as a Lender of Last Resort". Available at: https://voxeu.org/article/european-central-bank-lender-last-resort

de Grauwe, Paul (2011b). "The Governance of a Fragile Eurozone", CEPS Working Document, No. 346. Available at: www.ceps.eu/system/files/book/2011/05/WD%20346%20De%20Grauwe%20on%20Eurozone%20Governance.pdf

de Grauwe, Paul (2013). "Design Failures in the Eurozone – Can They Be Fixed?", European Economy, Economic Papers 491.

de Grauwe, Paul (2014). *Economics of Monetary Union*, 10th ed., Oxford: Oxford University Press.

de Grauwe, Paul and Ji, Yuemei (2012). "Self-Fulfilling Crises in the Eurozone: An Empirical Test". Available at: https://papers.ssrn.com/sol3/papers.cfm?abstract_id=2091056

de Grauwe, Paul and Ji, Yuemei (2016a). "Crisis Management and Economic Growth in Europe", Francesco Caselli *et al.* (eds.), *After the Crisis – Reform Recovery and Growth in Europe*, Oxford: Oxford University Press, pp. 46–72.

de Grauwe, Paul and Ji, Yuemei (2016b). "How to Reboot the Eurozone and Ensure its Long-term Survival", Richard Baldwin and Francesco Giavazzi (eds.), *How to Fix Europe's Monetary Union – Views of Leading Economists*, A VoxEU.org Book, London: CEPR Press, pp. 137–150.

de Grauwe, Paul and Ji, Yuemei (2018). "How Safe Is a Safe Asset'", CEPS Policy Insights No. 2018–08, February 2018.

de Grauwe, Paul and Moesen, Wim (2009). "Gains for All: Proposal for a Common Eurobond". Available at: www.ceps.eu/ceps-publications/gains-all-proposal-common-eurobond/

de Paoli, Bianca *et al.* (2011). "Output Costs of Sovereign Debt Default", Robert W. Kolb (ed.), *Sovereign Debt – From Safety to Default*, Hoboken, New Jersey: Wiley, pp. 23–31.

de Streel, Alexandre (2014). "EU Fiscal Governance and the Effectiveness of its Reform", Maurice Adams *et al.* (eds.), *The Constitutionalization of European Budgetary Constraints*, Oxford and Portland, OR: Hart Publishing, pp. 85–104.

Debrun, Xavier and Jonung, Lars (2019). "Under Threat: Rules-based Fiscal Policy and How to Preserve It", *European Journal of Political Economy*, 57(2019), pp. 142–157.

Degiannakis, Stavros *et al.* (2014). "Business Cycle Synchronization in EMU: Can Fiscal Policy Bring Member-Countries Closer?", MPRA Paper No. 67892. Available at: https://mpra.ub.uni-muenchen.de/67892/

Delbecque, Bernard (2013). "Proposal for a Stabilization Fund for the EMU", CEPS Working Document, No. 385, October 2013. Available at: www.ceps.eu/wp-content/uploads/2013/10/WD385%20B%20Delbecque%20Stabiliisation%20Fund%20formatted_0.pdf

Delong, J. Bradford and Summers, Lawrence H. (2012). "Fiscal Policy in a Depressed Economy". Available at: http://larrysummers.com/wp-content/uploads/2012/10/2012_spring_BPEA_delongsummers.pdf

Delors, Jacques (1989). "Report on Economic and Monetary Union in the European Community", EU Commission – Working Document, Brussels.

Delpla, Jacques and Weizsäcker, Jakob von (2010). "The Blue Bond Proposal", Bruegel Policy Brief, Issue 2010/03, May 2010.

Demertzis, Maria and Wolff, Guntram B. (2016). "The Effectiveness of the European Central Bank's Asset Purchase Programme", Bruegel Policy Contribution Issue 2016/10, June 2016.

Denton, Geoffrey (1977). "Reflections on Fiscal Federalism in the EEC", *Journal of Common Market Studies*, 16(4), pp. 283–301.

Díaz-Cassou, Javier and Erce, Aitor (2011). "IMF Interventions in Sovereign Debt Restructurings", Robert W. Kolb (ed.), *Sovereign Debt – From Safety to Default*, Hoboken, New Jersey: Wiley, pp. 179–188.

Dimopoulos, Angelos (2014). "The Use of International Law as a Tool for Enhancing Governance in the Eurozone and its Impact on EU Institutional Integrity", Maurice Adams, Federico Fabbrini and Pierre Larouche (eds.), *The Constitutionalization of European Budgetary Constraints*", Oxford and Portland, OR: Hart Publishing, pp. 41–63.

Dobler, Marc *et al.* (2016). "The Lender of Last Resort Function after the Global Financial Crisis", IMF Working Paper, WP/16/10, International Monetary Fund.

Dolls, Mathias *et al.* (2010). "Automatic Stabilizers and Economic Crisis: US vs. Europe", NBER Working Paper 16275. Available at: www.nber.org/papers/w16275

Dolls, Mathias *et al.* (2015a). "An Unemployment Insurance Scheme for the Euro Area? A Comparison of Different Alternatives Using Micro Data", CESifo Working Paper No. 5581, October 2015.

Dolls, Mathias *et al.* (2015b). "Reconciling Insurance with Market Discipline: A Blueprint for a European Fiscal Union", ZEW Discussion Papers, No. 15–044.

Domanski, Dietrich *et al.* (2014). "Central Bank as a Lender of Last Resort: Experiences during the 2007–2010 Crisis and Lessons for the Future", Finance and Statistic Discussion Series, No 2014–10, Washington, DC: Federal Reserve Board.

Dornbusch, Rudiger (1974). "Real and Monetary Aspects of the Effects of Exchange Rate Changes", R.Z. Aliber (ed.), *National Monetary Policies and the International Financial System*, Chicago: University of Chicago Press.

Dornbusch, Rudiger (1980). *Open Economy Macroeconomics*, New York: Basic Books.

Draghi, Mario (2018). "Monetary Policy in the Euro Area". Available at: www.ecb. europa.eu/press/key/date/2018/html/ecb.sp180314_1.en.html

Drèze, Jacques H. and Durré, Alain (2013). "Fiscal Integration and Growth Simulation in Europa", Discussion Paper 2013/13, Louvain-La-Neuve: Center for Operations Research and Econometrics.

Dullien, Sebastian (2007). "Improving Economic Stability in Europe: What the Euro Area Can Learn from the United States' Unemployment Insurance", Working Paper FG 1, SWP, Berlin.

Dullien, Sebastian (2012). "A European Unemployment Insurance as a Stabilization Device – Selected Issues", Brussels: European Commission.

Dullien, Sebastian (2013). "A Euro-area Wide Unemployment Insurance as an Automatic Stabilizer: Who Benefits and Who Pays?", Social Europe, Brussels: European Commission.

Dullien, Sebastian and Schwarzer, Daniela (2009). "Bringing Macroeconomics into the EU Budget: Why and How?", *Journal of Common Market Studies*, 47(1), pp. 153–174.

Dunne, Peter *et al.* (2015). "The Expanded Asset Purchase Programme – What, Why and How of Euro Area QE", *Quarterly Bulletin*, 3, pp. 61–71.

Duttagupta, Rupa *et al.* (2005). "Moving to a Flexible Exchange Rate – How, When, and How Fast?", Economic Issues 38, Washington: International Monetary Fund.

Eaton, Jonathan and Fenandéz, Raquel (1995). "Sovereign Debt", NBER Working Paper No. 5131. Available at: www.nber.org/papers/w5131

ECB (2011). "The Monetary Policy of the ECB", European Central Bank.

ECB (2014). "Guide to Banking Supervision", European Central Bank, November 2014.

REFERENCES

ECB (2016). "Financial Integration in Europe", European Central Bank, April 2016.

ECB (2017). "The International Role of the Euro", Frankfurt: European Central Bank.

Eichengreen, Barry (1991). "Is Europe an Optimum Currency Area?", NBER Working Paper No. 3579. Available at: www.nber.org/papers/w3579

Eichengreen, Barry (1996). "Saving Europe's Automatic Stabilizers", Center for International and Development Economics Research, Berkeley: University of California.

Eichengreen, Barry (1997). *European Monetary Unification – Theory, Practice and Analysis*, Cambridge, MA: The MIT Press.

Eichengreen, Barry (1998). "Saving Europe's Automatic Stabilizers". Available at: https://ideas.repec.org/p/wpa/wuwpma/9805013.html

Eichengreen, Barry and von Hagen, Jürgen (1996). "Fiscal Policy and Monetary Union: Is There a Tradeoff between Federalism and Budgetary Restrictions?", NBER Working Paper 5517. Available at: www.nber.org/papers/w5517

Eichengreen, Barry and Wyplosz, Charles (2016). "Minimal Conditions for the Survival of the Euro", Richard Baldwin and Francesco Giavazzi (eds.), *How to Fix Europe's Monetary Union – Views of Leading Economists*, A VoxEU.org Book, London: CEPR Press, pp. 34–45.

Eichengreen, Barry et al. (1995). "Exchange Market Mayhem: The Antecedents and Aftermath of Speculative Attacks". Available at: http://faculty.haas.berkeley.edu/arose/erw3ep.pdf

Eichnberger, Reiner and Frey, Bruno S. (2006). "Functional, Overlapping and Competing Jurisdictions (FOCJ): A Complement and an Alternative to Today's Federalism", Ehtisham Ahmad and Giorgio Brosio (eds.), *Handbook of Fiscal Federalism*, Cheltenham, UK: Edward Elgar, pp. 154–181.

Emerson, Michael et al. (1990). "One Market, One Money – An Evaluation of the Potential Benefits and Costs of Forming an Economic and Monetary Union", European Economy, No 44, October 1990.

Enderlein, Henrik et al. (2012). "Completing the Euro – A Road Map towards Fiscal Union in Europe", Report of the 'Thommaso Padoa-Schioppa Group, Studies & Reports, 92, Notre Europe.

Enderlein, Henrik et al. (2013). "Blueprint for a Cyclical Shock Insurance in the Euro Area", Studies & Reports, 100, Notre Europe, Jacques Delors Institute.

Enderlein, Henrik et al. (2016). *Repair and Prepare Growth and the Euro after Brexit*, Berlin: Jacques Delors Institute.

ESRB (2018). "Sovereign Bond-backed Securities: A Feasibility Study", Vol. I: Main Findings, ESRB.

Eucken (1952). *Grundsätze der Wirtschaftspolitik*, Bern: Verlag.

European Commission (2010). "The Economic Adjustment Programme for Greece", European Economy, Occasional Papers 61, Directorate-General for Economic and Financial Affairs, Brussels: European Commission.

European Commission (2011). "Green Paper on the Feasibility of Introducing Stability Bonds", COM(2011), 818 Final.

European Commission (2012). "The Second Economic Adjustment Programme for Greece", European Economy, Occasional Papers 94, Directorate-General for Economic and Financial Affairs, Brussels: European Commission.

European Commission (2016). "Study on the Potential of Green Bond Finance for Resource-Efficient Investments". Available at: http://ec.europa.eu/environment/enveco/pdf/potential-green-bond.pdf

European Commission (2017a). "Reflection Paper on the Deepening of the Economic and Monetary Union". Available at: https://ec.europa.eu/commission/sites/beta-political/files/reflection-paper-emu_en.pdf

European Commission (2017b). "Feasibility and Added Value of a European Unemployment Benefit Scheme – Main Findings from a Comprehensive Research Project", Brussels: European Commission.

European Commission (2018a). "Vade Mecum on the Stability & Growth Pact", European Economy, Institutional Paper 075, March 2018, Directorate-General for Economic and Financial Affairs, Brussels: European Commission.

European Commission (2018b). "Commission Staff Working Document Impact Assessment – Accompanying the Document Proposal for a Regulation of the European Parliament and of the Council on the Establishment of a European Investment Stabilization Function", SWD(2018) 297 Final, of 31.05.2018.

European Commission (2018c). "Financing the EU Budget: Report on the Operation of the Own Resources System", Commission Staff Working Document, Accompanying the Document Proposal of a Council Directive on the System of Own Resources of the European Union, SWD (2019) 172 Final.

European Commission (2019). "Vade Mecum on the Stability & Growth Pact", European Economy, Institutional Paper 101/April 2019, Directorate-General for Economic and Financial Affairs, Brussels: European Commission.

Eyraud, Luc and Weber, Anke (2013). "The Challenge of Debt Reduction during Fiscal Consolidation", IMF Working Paper, WP/13/67.

Eyraud, Luc et al. (2018). "Second-Generation Fiscal Rules: Balancing Simplicity, Flexibility, and Enforceability", IMF Staff Discussion Note, SDN/18/04.

Fabbrini, Federico (2014a). "The Euro Crisis and the Courts: Judicial Review and the Political Process in Comparative Perspective", Berkeley Journal of International Law, 32(1), pp. 64–123.

Fabbrini, Federico (2014b). "From Fiscal Constraints to Fiscal Capacity: The Future of EMU and its Challenges", Maurice Adams et al. (eds.), The Constitutionalization of European Budgetary Constraints, Oxford and Portland, OR: Hart Publishing, pp. 399–417.

Fabbrini, Federico (2014c). "Taxing and Spending in the Euro Zone: Legal and Political Challenges Related to the Adoption of the Financial Transaction Tax". Available at: www.sweetandmaxwell.co.uk/catalogue/eDownloadDoc.aspx?filename=501_2014105_9421.pdf&sapmaterialnum=7216&fileserver=EPIC

Fabbrini, Federico (2017). "Brexit and the Reform of Economic and Monetary Union", Nazaré da Costa Cabral et al. (eds.), After Brexit – Consequences for the European Union, Cham, Switzerland: Palgrave Macmillan, pp. 129–146.

Farhi, Emmanuel and Tirole, Jean (2016). "Deadly Embrace: Sovereign and Financial Balance Sheets Doom Loops", NBER Working Paper No. 21843. Available at: www.nber.org/papers/w21843

Farhi, Emmanuel and Werning, Iván (2012). "Fiscal Unions", NBER Working Paper No. 18280. Available at: www.nber.org/papers/w18280

Fatás, Antonio (1997). "EMU: Countries or Regions? Lessons from the EMS Experience", CEPR Discussion Papers 1558.

Fatás, Antonio (1998). "Does EMU Need a Fiscal Federation?", *Economic Policy*, 13(26), pp. 163–203.

Fatás, Antonio (2016). "The Agenda for Structural Reform in Europe", Francesco Caselli *et al.* (eds.), *After the Crisis – Reform Recovery and Growth in Europe*, Oxford: Oxford University Press, pp. 6–45.

Fatás, Antonio and Mihov, Ilian (2002). "On Constraining Fiscal Policy Discretion in EMU". Available at: https://faculty.insead.edu/fatas/oxrep.pdf

Fatás, Antonio and Mihov, Ilian (2008). "The Euro and Fiscal Policy", NBER Working Paper No. 14722. Available at: www.nber.org/papers/w14722

Fatás, Antonio and Mihov, Ilian (2012). "Fiscal Policy as a Stabilization Tool". Available at: https://faculty.insead.edu/fatas/Fiscal_Stabilization.pdf

Fatás, Antonio and Summers, Laurence H. (2016). "The Permanent Effects of Fiscal Consolidations", NBER Working Paper 22374. Available at: www.nber.org/papers/w22374.pdf

Fawley, Brett W. and Neely, Christopher (2013). "Four Stories of Quantitative Easing", *Federal Reserve Bank of St. Louis Review*, 95(1), pp. 51–88.

Fecht, Falko *et al.* (2007). "Welfare Effects of Financial Integration". Available at: https://papers.ssrn.com/sol3/papers.cfm?abstract_id=1136618

The Federal Reserve Bank of Philadelphia (2014). "History of Central Banking – From 1791 to the 21st Century". Available at: www.philadelphiafed.org/-/media/education/teachers/resources/history-of-central-banking/history-of-central-banking.pdf?la=en

Felbermayr, Gabriel *et al.* (2017). "The German Current-Account Surplus: Causes and Consequences", Thorsten Beck and Hans-Helmut Kotz (eds.), *Ordoliberalism: A German oddity?*, A VoxEU.org Book, London: CEPR Press, pp. 187–199.

Feld, Lars P. *et al.* (2017). "The 'Dark Ages of German Macroeconomics' and other Alleged Shortfalls in German Economic Thought", Thorsten Beck and Hans-Helmut Kotz (eds.), *Ordoliberalism: A German oddity?*, A VoxEU.org Book, London: CEPR Press, pp. 41–52.

Fernandes, Catarina *et al.* (2016). "Determinants of European Banks' Bailouts Following the 2007–2008 Financial Crisis", *Journal of International Economic Law*, 19(3), pp. 707–742.

Fernández, Raquel and Martin, Alberto (2015). "The Long and the Short of It: Sovereign Debt Crises and Debt Maturity", NBER Working Papers No. 20786. Available at: www.nber.org/papers/w20786

Ferra, Sergio de (2015). "External Imbalances, Gross Capital Flows and Sovereign Debt Crises". Available at: www.ne.su.se/polopoly_fs/1.264328.1452595258!/menu/standard/file/jobmarket_paper.pdf

Ferreira, Eduardo Paz (2012). "A crise do Euro e o papel das Finanças Públicas", João Ricardo Catarino and José F.F. Tavares (Coord.), *Finanças Públicas da União Europeia*, Coimbra: Almedina, pp. 19–33.

Ferreira, Eduardo Paz (Coord.) (2013). *Troika – Ano II*, Lisboa: Edições 70.

Ferrer, Jorge Núñez and Alcidi, Cinzia (2018). "Should the EU Budget Have a Stabilization Function?", CEPS Commentary. Available at: www.ceps.eu/ceps-publications/should-eu-budget-have-stabilisation-function/

Ferrer, Jorge Núñez *et al.* (2016). "Study on the Potential and Limitations of Reforming the Financing of the EU Budget", Expertise Commissioned by the European Commission on behalf of the High Level Group in Own Resources under Service Contract No. 14/PO/04, Final Version, 3 June 2016.

Fisher, Ronald C. (1982). "Income and Grant Effects on Local Expenditure: The Flypaper Effects and Other Difficulties", Wallace E. Oates (ed.), *The Economics of Fiscal Federalism and Local Finance*, Originally published 1998, Cheltenham, UK: Edward Elgar.

Fleming, Marcus J. (1962). "Domestic Financial Policies under Fixed and under Floating Exchange Rates", *Staff Papers (International Monetary Fund)*, 9(3), pp. 369–380.

Forni, Lorenzo *et al.* (2016). "Sovereign Debt Restructuring and Growth", IMF Working Paper, WP/16/147.

Fossum, John Erik and Jachtenfuchs, Markus (eds.) (2018). *Federal Challenges and Challenges to Federalism*, London and New York: Routledge.

Franco, António L. de Sousa *et al.* (1994). *Finanças Europeias – Introdução e Orçamento*, Volume I, Coimbra: Almedina.

Frankel, Jeffrey A. (1999). "No Single Currency Regime Is Right for All Countries or at All Times", Essays in International Finance, ns. 215, August 1999.

Frankel, Jeffrey A. (2009). "The Estimated Trade Effects of the Euro: Why Are They Below Those from Historical Monetary Unions Among Smaller Countries?", LEQS Paper No. 07/2009, London School of Economics.

Frankel, Jeffrey A. (2012). "Could Eurobonds Be the Answer to the Eurozone Crisis?". Available at: https://voxeu.org/article/could-eurobonds-be-answer-eurozone-crisis

Frankel, Jeffrey A. (2017). "German Ordoliberals vs American Pragmatists: What Did They Get Right or Wrong in the Euro Crisis?", Thorsten Beck and Hans-Helmut Kotz (eds.), *Ordoliberalism: A German Oddity?*, A VoxEU.org Book, London: CEPR Press, pp. 135–143.

Frankel, Jeffrey A. and Rose, Andrew K. (1996). "Currency Crashes in Emerging Markets: An Empirical Treatment", International Finance Discussion Papers 534, Board of Governors of the Federal Reserve System (U.S.).

Frankel, Jeffrey A. and Rose, Andrew K. (1997). "The Endogeneity of the Optimum Currency Area Criteria". Available at: http://cemi.ehess.fr/docannexe/file/2393/2.fraenkel.rose.pdf

Frankel, Jeffrey A. and Rose, Andrew K. (2000). "Estimating the Effect of Currency Unions on Trade and Output", NBER Working Paper 7857. Available at: www.nber.org/papers/w7857.pdf

Freixas, X. *et al.* (1999). "Lender of Last Resort: A Review of the Literature", *Financial Stability Review*, 7, pp. 151–167.

Fuentes, Michael and Saravia, Diego (2011). "Are Sovereign Defaulters Punished?: Evidence from Foreign Direct Investment Flows", Robert W. Kolb (ed.), *Sovereign Debt – From Safety to Default*, Hoboken, New Jersey: Wiley, pp. 149–154.

Furceri, Davide and Mourougane, Annabelle (2009). "The Effect of Financial Crises on Potential Output: New Empirical Evidence from OECD Countries", OECD Economics Department Working Papers, No. 699, Paris: OECD Publishing. Available at: http://dx.doi.org/10.1787/224126122024

Furceri, Davide and Zdzienicka, Aleksandra (2013). "The Euro Area Crisis: Need for a Supranational Fiscal Risk Sharing Mechanism?", IMF Working Paper, WP/13/198.

Gaballo, Gaetano and Zetlin-Jones, Ariel (2016). "Bailouts, Moral Hazard and Bank's Home bias for Sovereign Debt", *Journal of Monetary Economics*, 81(C), pp. 70–85.

Gagnon, Joseph E. (with Marc Hinterschweiger) (2011). *Flexible Exchange Rates for a Stable World Economy*, Washington, DC: Peterson Institute for International Economics.

Galí, Jordi (2020). "Helicopter money: The time is now". Available at: https://voxeu.org/article/helicopter-money-time-now

Gambacorta, Leonard *et al.* (2014). "Has the Transmission of Policy Rates to Lending Rates been Impaired by the Global Financial Crisis?", BIS Working Paper No. 477. Available at: www.bis.org/publ/work477.pdf

Gambetti, Luca and Musso, Alberto (2017). "The Macroeconomic Impact of the ECB's Expanded Asset Purchase Programme (APP)", ECB Working Paper Series No 2075, June 2015. Available at: www.ecb.europa.eu/pub/pdf/scpwps/ecb.wp.2075.en.pdf

Gayer, Christian (2007). "A Fresh Look at Business Cycle Synchronisation in the Euro Area", European Economy, Economic Papers, No 287, September 2007.

Gechert, Sebastian *et al.* (2017). "Long-term Effects of Fiscal Stimulus and Austerity in Europe", IMK Macroeconomic Policy Institute Working Paper Nr. 179.

Geerooms, Hans and Karbownik, Pawel (2014). "A Monetary Union Requires a Banking Union", Bruges European Economic Policy Briefings, 33/2014.

Gerhardt, Maria and Vennet, Rudi Vander (2016). "Bank Bailouts in Europe and Bank Performance", Working Paper No 2016/921, Universiteit Gent.

Gerlach, Stefan and Lewis, John (2010). "ECB Interest Rate Policy and the 'Zero Lower Bound'". Available at: https://voxeu.org/article/ecb-interest-rate-policy-and-zero-lower-bound

Giavazzi, Francesco and Pagano, Marco (1990). "Can Severe Fiscal Contractions Be Expansionary? Tales of Two Small European Countries", NBER Working Paper No. 3372. Available at: www.nber.org/papers/w3372

Gilbert, Niels *et al.* (2013). "Towards a Stable Monetary Union: What Role for Euro-bonds?", DBN Working Paper, No. 379, May 2013.

Gonçalves, José Renato (2010). *O Euro e o Futuro de Portugal e da União Europeia*, Coimbra: Wolters Kluwer/Coimbra Editora.

Gonçalves, José Renato (2019). *O Euro: Balanço e Perspectivas*, Coimbra: Almedina.

Goodhart, Charles and Smith, S. (1993). "Stabilization", The Economics of Community Public Finance, European Economy, Reports and Studies No 5–1993.

Governatori, Matteo and Yim, David (2012). "Fiscal Decentralization and Fiscal Discipline", *Quarterly Report on the Euro Area, Directorate General Economic and Financial Affairs (DG ECFIN), European Commission*, 11(4), pp. 20–24.

Goves, Peter *et al.* (2016). "Regulatory Treatment of Sovereign Risk: Risk Weights vs Large Exposure Limits". Available at: https://voxeu.org/article/regulatory-treatment-sovereign-debt-0

Goyal, Rishi *et al.* (2013). "A Banking Union for the Euro Area", IMF Staff Discussion Note, SDN/13/01.

Gramlich, Edward M. (1977). "Intergovernmental Grants: A Review of Empirical Literature", Wallace E. Oates (Ed.), *The Economics of Fiscal Federalism and Local Finance*, Originally published 1998, Cheltenham, UK: Edward Elgar, pp. 274–294.

Gros, Daniel (2011). "Can Austerity Be Self-Defeating?". Available at: https://voxeu.org/article/can-austerity-be-self-defeating

Gros, Daniel (2014). "A Fiscal Shock Absorber for the Eurozone? Lessons from the Economics of Insurance". Available at: http://voxeu.org/article/ez-fiscal-shock-absorber-lessons-insurance-economics

Gros, Daniel (2015). "Completing the Banking Union: Deposit Insurance", CEPS Policy Brief, No. 335, December 2015.

Gros, Daniel (2016a). "Negative Interest Rates and Seigniorage: Turning the Central Bank Business Model Upside Down? The Special Case of the ECB", CEPS Policy Brief, No. 344, July 2016.

Gros, Daniel (2016b). "Completing the Banking Union", Richard Baldwin and Francesco Giavazzi (eds.), *How to Fix Europe's Monetary Union – Views of Leading Economists*, A VoxEU.org Book, London: CEPR Press, pp. 87–98.

Gros, Daniel (2016c). "The Stabilization Properties of a European Unemployment Benefits Scheme", CEPS Commentary. Available at: www.ceps.eu/ceps-publications/stabilisation-properties-european-unemployment-benefit-scheme/

Gros, Daniel (2017a). "The Single Monetary Policy and Its Decentralized Implementation: An Assessment", CEPS Policy Insights, No. 2017/36, September 2017.

Gros, Daniel (2017b). "Try Again to Complete the Banking Union!", Agnés Bénassy-Quéré and Francesco Giavazzi (eds.), *Europe's Political Spring – Fixing the Eurozone and Beyond*, A VoxEU.org Book, London: CEPR Press, pp. 47–59.

Gros, Daniel (2017c). "The Commission's Views on Strengthening the Euro Area: Barking up the Wrong Tree?", CEPS Commentary, 14 September 2017.

Gros, Daniel (2018a). "Convergence in the European Union: Inside and Outside the Euro", Informal Meeting of Economic and Financial Affairs Ministers, CEPS. Available at: www.ceps.eu/ceps-publications/convergence-european-union-inside-and-outside-euro/

Gros, Daniel (2018b). "Does the Euro Area Need a Safe or Diversified Asset?", CEPS Policy Brief, No. 2018/03. Available at: www.ceps.eu/ceps-publications/does-euro-area-need-safe-or-diversified-asset/

Gros, Daniel and Alcidi, Cinzia (2010). "The Impact of the Financial Crisis on the Real Economy", *Intereconomics 2010*, 1, pp. 4–10.

Gros, Daniel and Belke, Ansgar (2015). *Banking Union as A Shock Absorber – Lesson for the Eurozone from the US*, Brussels: CEPS Press.

Gros, Daniel and Mayer, Thomas (2017). "A European Monetary Fund: Why and How?". Available at: https://papers.ssrn.com/sol3/papers.cfm?abstract_id=3122298

Gros, Daniel *et al.* (2018). "The European Dimension of Regional and Cohesion Policies", CEPS and Laboratorio LUISS Mezzogiorno. Available at: www.ceps.eu/ceps-publications/european-dimension-regional-and-cohesion-policies/

Gruber, Jonathan (2013). *Public Finance and Public Policy*, 4th ed., New York: Worth Publishers.

Guiso, Luigi *et al.* (2013). "The Determinants of Attitudes toward Strategic Default on Mortgages", *Journal of Finance*, LXVIII(4), pp. 1473–1515.

Guzman, Martin and Stiglitz, Joseph (2014). "Creating a Framework for Sovereign Debt Restructuring that Works". Available at: https://www8.gsb.columbia.edu/faculty/jstiglitz/sites/jstiglitz/files/Ch.1%20-%20Guzman-Stiglitz%20UPDATED.pdf

Haan, Jakob de *et al.* (2002). "Do Business Cycles Become More Synchronized", *Journal of Common Market Studies*, 40(1), pp. 23–42.

Haan, Jakob de *et al.* (2012). *Financial Markets and Institutions: A European Perspective*, 2nd ed., Cambridge: Cambridge University Press.

Hale, Galina and Obstfeld, Maurice (2014). "The Euro and the Geography of International Debt Flows", NBER Working Paper No. 20033. Available at: www.nber.org/papers/w20033

Hall, Robert E. (2010). "Why Does Economy Fall to Pieces after a Financial Crisis?", *Journal of Economic Perspectives*, 24(4), pp. 3–20.

Hamilton, Alexander (1778). *The Federalist*, New York: The Independent Journal.

Hammond, Gregory and von Hagen, Jürgen (1995). "Regional Insurance against Asymmetric Shocks: an Empirical Study for the European Community", *The Manchester School of Economic & Social Studies*, 66(3), pp. 331–353.

Hatchondo, Juan Carlos *et al.* (2011). "Understanding Sovereign Default", Robert W. Kolb (ed.), *Sovereign Debt – From Safety to Default*, Hoboken, New Jersey: Wiley, pp. 137–148.

Hayashi, Masayoshi and Boadway, Robin (2000). "An Empirical Analysis of Intergovernmental Tax Interaction: The Case of Business Income Taxes in Canada", *The Canadian Journal of Economics/Revue canadienne d'Economique*, 34(2), pp. 481–503.

Healey, Nigel M. (1999). "The Case for European Monetary Union", M. Baimbridge, B. Burkitt and P. Whyman (eds.), *The Impact of the Euro: Debating Britain's Future*, Palgrave Macmillan, pp. 19–41.

Heening, C. Randall and Kessler, Martin (2012). "Fiscal Federalism: US History for Architects of Europe's Fiscal Union", Peterson Institute for International Economics, Working Paper Series, WP 12–1.

Heipertz, Martin and Verdun, Amy (2005). "The Stability and Growth Pact – Theorizing a Case in European Integration", *Journal of Common Market Studies*, 43(5), pp. 985–1008.

Heipertz, Martin and Verdun, Amy (2010). *Ruling Europe: The Politics of the Stability and Growth Pact*, Cambridge: Cambridge University Press.

Hemerijck, Anton (2013). *Changing Welfare States*, Oxford: Oxford University Press.

Henkel, Marcel *et al.* (2018). "A Germany without Transfers". Available at: https://voxeu.org/article/germany-without-fiscal-transfers

Hepp, Ralf and von Hagen, Jürgen (2010). "Interstate Risk Sharing in Germany: 1970–2006", ZEI-Working Paper, No. B 03–2010.

Herndon, T. *et al.* (2014). "Does High Public Debt Consistently Stifle Economic Growth? A Critique to Reinhart and Rogoff", *Cambridge Journal of Economics*, 38, pp. 257–279.

Hinarejos, Alicia (2014). "Fiscal Federalism in the European Union: Evolution and Future Choices for EMU", Legal Studies Research Paper Series, University of Cambridge, Faculty of Law.

Hinarejos, Alicia (2015). *The Euro Area Crisis in Constitutional Perspective*, Oxford Studies in European Law, Oxford: Oxford University Press.

Hoffmann, Mathias and Sørensen, Bent E. (2012). "Don't Expect Too Much from EZ Fiscal Union – and Complete the Unfinished Integration of European Capital Markets!". Available at: http://voxeu.org/article/hedging-macroeconomic-risk-eurozone-fiscal-union-versus-capital-markets

Hübner, Danuta (2017). "Regroup and Reform – Ideas for a More Responsive and Effective European Union", Report of a CEPS Task Force, CEPS.

Huertas, Thomas (2016). "European Banking Resolution: Making It Work!", Interim Report of the CEPS Task Force on Implementing Financial Sector Resolution, January 2016.

Iara, Anna (2015). "Revenue for EMU: A Contribution to the Debate on Fiscal Union", European Commission Taxation Papers, Working Paper N. 54, 2015.

Illes, Anamaria *et al.* (2015). "Why Did Bank Lending Rates Diverge from Policy Rates after the Financial Crisis?", BIS Working Paper No. 486. Available at: www.bis.org/publ/work486.pdf

IMF (2004). "Sovereign Debt Structure for Crisis Prevention". Available at: www.imf.org/external/np/res/docs/2004/070204.htm

IMF (2009). "Macro Policy Lessons for a Sound Design of Fiscal Decentralization". Available at: www.imf.org/external/np/pp/eng/2009/072709.pdf

IMF (2010). "World Economic Outlook: Recovery, Risk and Rebalancing", Washington, DC: International Monetary Fund, October 2010.

IMF (2012). "World Economic Outlook: Coping with High Debt and Sluggish Growth", Washington, DC: International Monetary Fund, October 2012.

Ingram, J.C. (1962). *Regional Payments Mechanisms: The Case of Puerto Rico*, Chapel Hill: University of North Carolina Press.

Ishfaq, Mohammad (2010). "Overview of Different Exchange Rate Regimes and Preferred Choice for UAE", Economic Paper Series, The Government of Dubai, Economic Paper Series, Paper No. 1.

Italianer, Alexander and Pisiani-Ferry, Jean (1992). "Systèmes budgétaires et amortissement des chocs régionaux: les implications pour l'Union économique et monétaire", *Économie Prospective Internationale*, 51, pp. 49–69.

Italianer, Alexander and Vanheukelen, Marc (1992). "Proposals for Community Stabilization Mechanisms: Some Historical Application", *Economics of Community Public Finance, European Economy*, 5, pp. 493–510.

Jalilvand, Abolhassan and Switzer, Jeannette (2011). "Sovereign Spreads and Perceived Risk of Default Revisited", Robert W. Kolb (ed.), *Sovereign Debt – From Safety to Default*, Hoboken, New Jersey: Wiley, pp. 401–406.

Joumard, Isabelle and Konsgrud, Per Mathis (2003). "Fiscal Relations across Government Levels", *OECD Economic Studies*, 36, pp. 155–215.

Juncker, Jean-Claude *et al.* (2015). "Completing Europe's Economic and Monetary Union". Available at: https://ec.europa.eu/commission/sites/beta-political/files/5-presidents-report_en.pdf

Juncker, Jean-Claude *et al.* (2017). "Roadmap for a More United, Stronger and More Democratic Union". Available at: https://ec.europa.eu/commission/publications/roadmap-more-united-stronger-and-more-democratic-union_en

Kalemli-Ozcan, Sebnem *et al.* (2004). "Asymmetric Shocks and Risk Sharing in a Monetary Union: Updated Evidence and Policy Implications for Europe". Available at: http://econweb.umd.edu/~kalemli/assets/books/KSYforEUFeb042.pdf

Kaminsky, Graciela L. and Reinhart, Carmen M. (1999). "The Twin Crises: The Causes of Banking and Balance-of-Payments Problems", *American Economic Review*, 89(3), pp. 473–500.

Kaminsky, Graciela L. *et al.* (2004). "When It Rains, It Pours: Procyclical Capital Flows and Macroeconomic Policies", NBER Working Paper No. 10780. Available at: www.nber.org/papers/w10780

Kaufmann, Pascal (1997). *L'Éuro*, Paris: Dunod.

Keister, Todd (2010). "Bailouts and Financial Fragility", Federal Reserve Bank of New York Staff Reports, Staff Report No. 473, September 2010. Available at: www.newyorkfed.org/medialibrary/media/research/staff_reports/sr473.pdf

Kelly, Morgan (2010). "Whatever Happened to Ireland?". Available at: https://voxeu.org/article/whatever-happened-ireland

Kenen, Peter (1969). "The Optimum Currency Area: An Eclectic View", R. Mundell and Swoboda (eds.), *Monetary Problems of the International Economy*, Chicago: Chicago University Press.

Kindleberger, Charles P. and Aliber, Robert Z. (2005). *Manias, Panics, and Crashes – A History of Financial Crises*, 5th ed., Hoboken, New Jersey: Wiley.

King, Darryl *et al.* (2017). "Central Bank Emergency Support to Securities Markets", IMF Working Paper, WP/17/152, International Monetary Fund.

Klein, Barbara and Staal, Klaas (2017). "Was the American Recovery and Reinvestment Act an Economic Stimulus?", *International Advances in Economic Research*, 23, pp. 395–404. Available at: https://link.springer.com/content/pdf/10.1007/s11294-017-9655-7.pdf

Klein, Robert W. (2014). "A Primer on The Economics of Insurance". Available at: www.researchgate.net/publication/270500085_A_Primer_on_The_Economics_of_Insurance

Kletzer, Kenneth and von Hagen, Jürgen (2000). "Monetary and Fiscal Federalism", ZEI Working Paper B1 2000.

Kopits, George (2001). "Fiscal Rules: Useful Policy Framework or Unnecessary Ornament", IMF Working Paper, WP/01/145.

Kopits, George and Symansky, Steven (1998). "Fiscal Policy Rules", IMF Occasional Paper, No. 162, Washington, DC: IMF.

Kose, M. Ayan *et al.* (2006). "Financial Globalization: A Reappraisal", IMF Working Paper WP/06/198.

Kouparitsas, Michael A. (1999). "Is the EMU a Viable Common Currency Area? A VAR Analysis of Regional Business Cycles", *Economic Perspectives*, 23(3), pp. 2–20.

Krugman, Paul (1979). "A Model of Balance of Payments Crises", *Journal of Money, Credit and Banking*, 11, pp. 311–325.

Krugman, Paul (1991). "Increasing Returns and Economic Geography", *The Journal of Political Economy*, 99(3), pp. 483–499.

Krugman, Paul (2009). *The Return of Depression Economics and the Crisis of 2008*, New York and London: W.W. Norton & Company.

Krugman, Paul and Venales, Anthony (1990). "Integration and the Competitiveness of Peripheral Industry", CEPR Discussion Papers, No 363. Available at: https://econpapers.repec.org/paper/cprceprdp/363.htm

Krugman, Paul *et al.* (2015). *International Economics – Theory & Policy*, 10th ed., global ed., New York: Pearson.

Kydland, Finn E. and Prescott, Edward C. (1977). "Rules Rather than Discretion: The Inconsistency of Optimal Plans", *Journal of Political Economy*, 85(3), pp. 473–492.

Laeven, Luc and Valencia, Fabián (2008). "Systemic Banking Crises: A New Database", IMF Working Paper, WP/08/224.

Laeven, Luc and Valencia, Fabián (2012). "Systemic Banking Crises Database: An Update", IMF Working Paper, WP/12/163.

Landmann, Oliver (2017). "What's Wrong with the EZ: Conflicting Narratives", Thorsten Beck and Hans-Helmut Kotz (eds.), *Ordoliberalism: A German Oddity?*, A VoxEU.org Book, London: CEPR Press, pp. 123–133.

Lane, Philip R. (2006). "The Real Effects of the European Monetary Union", *Journal of Economic Perspectives*, 20(4), pp. 47–66.

Lane, Philip R. (2013). "Capital Flows in the Euro Area", European Economy, Economic Papers 497, Brussels: European Commission.

Lane, Philip R. (2016). "Macro-Financial Stability under EMU", Francesco Caselli *et al.* (eds.), *After the Crisis – Reform Recovery and Growth in Europe*, Oxford: Oxford University Press, pp. 89–108.

Lane, Philip R. and Langfield, Sam (2019). "The Feasibility of the Sovereign Bond-Backed Securities for the Euro Area", Jean Pisany-Ferry and Jeromin Zettelmeyer (eds.), *Risk-Sharing Plus Market Discipline: A New Paradigm for Euro Area Reform? A Debate*, A VosEU.org Book, London: CEPR Press, pp. 51–61.

Lane, Philip R. and Milesi-Ferretti, Gian Maria (2017). "International Financial Integration in the Aftermath of the Global Financial Crisis", IMF Working Papers, WP/17/115. Available at: www.imf.org/en/Publications/WP/Issues/2017/05/10/International-Financial-Integration-in-the-Aftermath-of-the-Global-Financial-Crisis-44906

Lannoo, Karel (2015a). *The Great Financial Plumbing – From Northern Rock to Banking Union*, Brussels: CEPS – Centre For European Policy Studies.

Lannoo, Karel (2015b). "Which Union for Europe's Capital Markets?", CEPS, ECMI Policy Brief No. 22/2015. Available at: www.ceps.eu/publications/which-union-europe%E2%80%99s-capital-markets

Lannoo, Karel (2019). "The Final PEPP or How to Kill an Important EU Commission Proposal", Nazaré da Costa Cabral and Nuno Cunha Rodrigues (eds.), *The Future of Pension Plans in the EU Internal Market – Coping with Trade-Offs Between Social Rights and Financial Markets*, Switzerland: Springer, pp. 193–196.

Lannoo, Karel and Thomadakis, Apostolos (2019). "Rebranding Capital Markets Union – A Market Finance Action Plan", Report of the CEPS-ECMI Task Force.

Larch, Martin and Turrini, Alessandro (2009). "The Cyclically-adjusted Budget Balance in EU Fiscal Policy Making: A Love at First Sight Turned into a Mature Relationship", European Economy, Economic Papers 364, March 2009, European Commission.

Lavigne, Anne and Villieu, Patrick (1996). "La coordination des politiques économiques", *Problèmes Économiques*, no. 2496, pp. 26–32.

Leandro, Álvaro and Zettelmeyer, Jeromin (2018). "The Search for a Euro Area Safe Asset", PIEE Wotkin Paper Peterson Institute for International Economics.

Le Cacheux, Jacques (2007). "Funding the EU Budget with a Genuine Own Resource: The Case for a European Tax", Notre Europe, Studies & Research, 57.

Lenaerts, Karolien *et al.* (2017). " Unemployment Insurance in America: A Model for Europe?", CEPS Policy Insights No. 2017/23. Available at: www.ceps.eu/system/files/PI2017-23_KL%20et%20al%20EUBS.pdf

Lenarcic, Andreja *et al.* (2016). "Tackling Sovereign Risk in European Banks", ESM Discussion Paper Series/1, March 2016.

Lindseth, Peter L. (2014). "Power and Legitimacy in the Eurozone: Can Integration and Democracy be Reconciled?", Maurice Adams *et al.* (eds.), *The Constitutionalization of European Budgetary Constraints*, Oxford and Portland, OR: Hart Publishing, pp. 379–398.

Liu, Lili and Wailbel, Michael (2008). "Subnational Borrowing, Insolvency and Regulation", Anwar Shah (ed.), *Macro Federalism and Local Finance*, Washington, DC: The World Bank, pp. 215–241.

Lo Schiavo, Gianni (2013). "The Judicial 'Bail Out' of the European Stability Mechanism: Comment on the Pringle Case", Research Paper in Law, 09/2013, Bruges: Collège d'Europe.

Louçã, Francisco (2017). "Has the Euro Any Future under Secular Stagnation?", Nazaré da Costa Cabral *et al.* (eds.), *The Euro and Crisis – Perspectives for the Eurozone as a Monetary and Budgetary Union*, Cham, Switzerland: Springer, pp. 95–107.

Loureiro, João (2008). *Política Orçamental na Área do Euro*, Porto: Vida Económica.

MacDougall, Donald *et al.* (1977). *Report of the Study Group on the Role of Public Finance in European Integration*. Volume I: General Report, Brussels: Commission of the European Communities.

Majocchi, Alberto (1999). "Stabilisation Policy in the European Monetary Union and Fiscal Federalism", Amadeo Fossati and Giorgio Panella (eds.), *Fiscal Federalism in European Union*, London and New York: Routledge, pp. 80–99.

Majocchi, Alberto and Rey, Mario (1993). "A Special Financial Support Scheme in Economic and Monetary Union: Need and Nature", The Economics of Community Public Finance, Luxembourg.

Majone, Giandomenico (2014). *Rethinking the Union of Europe Post-Crisis – Has Integration Gone Too Far?*, Cambridge: Cambridge University Press.

Malleghem, Pieter-Augustijn van (2014). "(Un)Balanced Budget Rules in Europe and America", Maurice Adams *et al.* (eds.), *The Constitutionalization of European Budgetary Constraints*, Oxford and Portland, OR: Hart Publishing, pp. 151–180.

Marjolin, Robert *et al.* (1975). *Report of the Study Group "Economic and Monetary Union 1980"*, Brussels: Commission of the European Communities.

Martin, Philippe (2005). "The Geography of Inequalities in Europe", *Swedish Economic Policy Review*, 12, pp. 83–108.

Martin-Aceña, Pablo (2013). "Savings Banks Crisis in Spain: When and How?". Available at: www.wsbi-esbg.org/SiteCollectionDocuments/Martin-AcenaWeb.pdf

Martins, Guilherme W. d'Oliveira (2014). *Consolidação Orçamental e Política Financeira*, Coimbra: Almedina.

Matthijs, Herman (2010). "The Budget of the European Union", IES/Working Paper 4, 2010.

Matziorinis, Kenneth (2011). "Is the 'Euro Bond? The Answer to the Euro Sovereign Debt Crisis? What Outcome Can Investors Expect Out of Europe?". Available at: https://papers.ssrn.com/sol3/papers.cfm?abstract_id=1999518

McKinnon, Ronald I. (1963). "Optimum Currency Areas", *The American Review*, 53(4), pp. 717–725.

McLeay, Michael *et al.* (2014). "Money Creation in Modern Economy", *Bank of England Quarterly Bulletin*, 2014-Q1, pp. 14–27.

McNamara, Kathleen R. (2015). "The Forgotten Problem of Embeddedness", Matthias Matthijs and Mark Blyth (eds.), *The Future of the Euro*, Oxford: Oxford University Press, pp. 21–45.

Meade, James E. (1951). *The Theory of International Economic Policy, Volume I: The Balance of Payments*, London: Oxford University Press.

Mélitz, Jacques (1997). "Some Cross-country Evidence about Debt, Deficits and the Behavior of Monetary and Fiscal Authorities," CEPR Discussion Paper No. 1653.

Mélitz, Jacques and Vori, Silvia (1993). "National Insurance against Unevenly Distributed Shocks in a European Monetary Union", *Recherches Économiques de Louvain*, 59(1–2), pp. 81–104.

Mendonça, António (2017). "The Unconventional Monetary Policy of the ECB and the International and Economic Financial Crisis: Effectiveness versus Exhaustion", Nazaré da Costa Cabral *et al.* (eds.), *The Euro and Crisis – Perspectives for the Eurozone as a Monetary and Budgetary Union*, Cham, Switzerland: Springer, pp. 223–247.

Merks, Paulus *et al.* (2016). "European Commission Publishes an EU Corporate Tax System for Multinational Companies". Available at: www.dlapiper.com/en/uk/insights/publications/2016/10/european-commission-publishes-an-eu-corporate-tax/

Mertens, Daniel and Thiemann, Matthias (2017). "Building a Hidden Investment State? The European Investment Bank, National Development Banks and European Economic Governance", *Journal of European Public Policy*, 26(3), pp. 1–21.

Micossi, Stefano (2017). "A Blueprint for Completing the Banking Union", CEPS Policy Insights No. 2017/41, November 2017.

Milesi-Ferretti, Gian Maria and Tille, Cedric (2011). "The Great Retrenchment: International Capital Flows during the Global Financial Crisis", *Economic Policy*, 26(66), pp. 285–342.

Minsky, Hyman P. (1986). "Stabilizing an Unstable Economy", Levy Economics Institute of Bard College.

Minsky, Hyman P. (1992). "The Financial Instability Hypothesis", Working Paper No 74, Levy Economics Institute of Bard College.

Mintz, N. (1970). "Monetary Union and Economic Integration", The Bulletin, CJ Devine Institute of Finance. New York: New York University Press.

Mitchener, Kris James and Weidenmier, Marc D. (2011). "Supersanctions and Sovereign Debt Repayment", Robert W. Kolb (ed.), *Sovereign Debt – From Safety to Default*, Hoboken, New Jersey: Wiley, pp. 155–168.

Mongelli, Francesco Paolo (2008). "European Economic and Monetary Integration and the Optimum Currency Area Theory", Economic Papers 302, Brussels: European Economy.

Mongelli, Francesco Paolo *et al.* (2017). "Are Euro Area Economic Structures Changing?", Nazaré da Costa Cabral *et al.* (eds.), *The Euro and Crisis – Perspectives for the Eurozone as a Monetary and Budgetary Union*, Cham, Switzerland: Springer, pp. 47–72.

Montoya, Lourdes Acebo and Haan, Jakob de (2007). "Regional Business Cycle Synchronization in Europe?", BEER Paper no. 11.

Mota, Paulo (2017). *Austeridade Expansionista* – *Como matar uma ideia zombie?*, Coimbra: Almedina.

Mountford, Andrew and Uhlig, Harald (2008). "What Are the Effects of Fiscal Policy Shocks?", NBER Working Paper No 14551. Available at: www.nber.org/papers/w14551

Mourougane, Annabelle (2015). "Crisis, Potential Output and Hysteresis", IPAG Business School Working Paper 2015/631.

Mourre, Gilles *et al.* (2013). "The Cyclically-adjusted Budget Balance in the EU Fiscal Framework: An Update", European Economy, Economic Papers 478, March 2013, European Commission.

Mourre, Gilles *et al.* (2014). "Adjusting the Budget Balance for the Business Cycle: The EU Methodology", European Economy, Economic Papers 536, November 2014, European Commission.

Muet, Pierre-Alain (1996). "Union monétaire: l'importance de la politique budgetaire", *Problèmes économiques*, N° 2461, pp. 1–4.

Mundell, Robert A. (1960). "The Monetary Dynamics of International Adjustment under Fixed and Flexible Exchange Rates", *The Quarterly Journal of Economics*, 74(2), pp. 227–257.

Mundell, Robert A. (1961). "A Theory of Optimum Currency Areas", *The American Economic Review*, 51(4), pp. 657–665.

Mundell, Robert A. (1963). "Capital Mobility and Stabilization under Fixed and Flexible Exchange Rates", *Canadian Journal of Economics and Political Science*, XXIX(4), pp. 475–485.

Musgrave, Richard A. (1959). *The Theory of Public Finance: A Study in Public Economy*, New York: Mc Graw Hill.

Musgrave, Richard A. (1983). "Who Should Tax, Where, and What?", Wallace E. Oates (ed.), *The Economics of Fiscal Federalism and Local Finance*, Originally published 1998, Cheltenham, UK: Edward Elgar, pp. 63–80.

Nakamura, Emi and Steinsson, Jón (2011). "Fiscal Stimulus in a Monetary Union: Evidence from U.S. Regions", NBER Working Paper No 17391. Available at: www.nber.org/papers/w17391.pdf

Neal, Larry and Barbezat, Daniel (1998). *The Economics of the European Union and the Economics of Europe*, New York and Oxford: Oxford University Press.

Nugent, Neill (1999). *The Government and Politics of the European Union*, 4th ed., Palgrave Macmillan.

O'Cinneide, Colm (2014). "Austerity and the Faded Dream of a 'Social Europe'", Aoife Nolan (ed.), *Economic and Social Rights After the Great Financial Crisis*, Cambridge: Cambridge University Press, pp. 169–201.

O'Leary, Christopher J. and Barnow, Burt S. (2016). "Lesson from the American Federal-State Unemployment Insurance System for a European Unemployment Benefits System", Upjohn Institute Working Papers, 16–264. Available at: www.econstor.eu/bitstream/10419/172226/1/16-264.pdf

Oates, Wallace E. (1965). *Fiscal Federalism*, New York: Harcourt Brace Jovanovitch.

Oates, Wallace E. (1968). "The Theory of Public Finance in a Federal System", *Canadian Journal of Economics*, I, pp. 37–54.

Oates, Wallace E. (ed.) (1998). *The Economics of Fiscal Federalism and Local Finance*, Cheltenham, UK: Edward Elgar.

Oates, Wallace E. (2004). "An Essay on Fiscal Federalism", Mark Baimbridge and Philip Whyman (eds.), *Fiscal Federalism and European Economic Integration*, London and New York: Routledge, pp. 13–47.

Oates, Wallace E. (2005). "Toward a Second-generation Theory of Fiscal Federalism", *International Tax and Public Finance*, 12, pp. 349–373.

OECD (2012). "Going for Growth", Economic Policy Reforms 2012.

Oganesyan, Gayane (2013). "The Changed Role of the Lender of Last Resort: Crisis Responses of the Federal Reserve, European Central Bank and Bank of England", Workins Paper No. 19/2013, Institute for International Political Economy Berlin.

Oliveira, Ana Perestrelo de (2018). *Manual de Corporate Finance*, 2nd ed., Coimbra: Almedina.

Ollivaud, Patrice and Turner, David (2015). "The Effect of the Global Financial Crisis on OECD Potential Output", *OECD Journal: Economic Studies*, vol. 2014.

Olson, Mancur (1969). "Strategic Theory and Its Applications. The Principle of 'Fiscal Equivalence': The Division of Responsibilities among Different Levels of Government", *The American Economic Review*, 59(2), pp. 479–487.

Ozkan, Gulcin F. and Unsal, Filiz D. (2012). "Global Financial Crisis, Financial Contagion, and Emerging Markets", IMF Working Paper, WP/12/293.

Pacheco, Luís Miguel (2000). "Fiscal Federalism, and Shock-Absorption Mechanisms: A Guide to the Literature". Available at: https://papers.ssrn.com/sol3/papers.cfm?abstract_id=302753

Padoa-Schioppa, Tommaso *et al.* (1987). *Efficiency, Stability and Equity – A Strategy for the Evolution of the Economic System of the European Community*, Oxford: Oxford University Press.

Paoli, Bianca De *et al.* (2011). "Output Costs of Sovereign Default", Robert W. Kolb (ed.), *Sovereign Debt – From Safety to Default*, Hoboken, New Jersey: Wiley, pp. 23–32.

Pardal, Paulo Alves (2015). *A Redistribuição das Competências Orçamentais no Seio da União Europeia*, Coimbra: Almedina.

Pâris, Pierre and Wyplosz, Charles (2014). "The PADRE Plan: Politically Acceptable Debt Restructuring in the Eurozone". Available at: https://voxeu.org/article/padre-plan-politically-acceptable-debt-restructuring-eurozone

Patrício, José Simões (1998). *Regime Jurídico do Euro*, Coimbra: Coimbra Editora.

Perotti, Roberto (1998). "Fiscal Policy in Good Times and Bad". Available at: ftp://ftp.igier.unibocconi.it/homepages/perotti/BADTIMES.pdf

Perotti, Roberto (2002). "Estimating the Effects of Fiscal Policy in OECD Countries", European Central Bank Working Paper Series, Working Paper No. 168.

Perotti, Roberto (2007). "In Search of the Transmission Mechanism of Fiscal Policy", NBER Working Paper No 13143. Available at: www.nber.org/papers/w13143

Perotti, Roberto (2011). "The 'Austerity Myth': Gain without Pain?", NBER Working Paper No 17571. Available at: www.nber.org/papers/w17571.pdf

Persson, Torsten and Tabellini, Guido (1992). "Federal Fiscal Constitutions – Part I: Risk Sharing and Moral Hazard", Discussion Paper 72. Available at: https://ideas.repec.org/p/fip/fedmem/72.html

Persson, Torsten and Tabellini, Guido (1996). "Federal Fiscal Constitutions: Risk Sharing and Redistribution", *The Journal of Political Economy*, 104(5), pp. 979–1009.

Philip, Alan Butt (2002). "The Coordination of Budgetary Policy in the Context of the Stability and Growth Pact", Paulo de Pitta e Cunha and Manuel Porto (eds.), *The Euro and the World*, Coimbra, Portugal: Almedina, pp. 37–44.

Pisani-Ferry, Jean (2011). *The Euro Crisis and Its Aftermath*, Oxford and New York: Oxford University Press.

Pisani-Ferry, Jean *et al.* (1993). *Stabilization Properties of Budgetary Systems: A Simulation Analysis*, Brussels: European Economy.

283

Pisani-Ferry, Jean *et al.* (2008). "A European Recovery Programme", Bruegel Policy Brief, Issue 2008/09. Available at: http://bruegel.org/wp-content/uploads/imported/publications/PBf_17112008_European_Recovery_Programme.pdf

Pisani-Ferry, Jean *et al.* (2013). "Options for a Euro-Area Fiscal Capacity", Bruegel Policy Contribution, Issue 2013/01, January 2013. Available at: http://bruegel.org/2013/01/options-for-a-euro-area-fiscal-capacity/

Pisauro, Giuseppe (2001). "Intergovernmental Relations and Fiscal Discipline: Between Commons and Soft Budget Constraints", IMF Working Paper, WP/01/65.

Poghosyan, Tigran *et al.* (2015). "The Role of Fiscal Transfers in Smoothing Regional Shocks". Available at: www.imf.org/en/Publications/WP/Issues/2016/12/31/The-Role-of-Fiscal-Transfers-in-Smoothing-Regional-Shocks-Evidence-from-Existing-Federations-44111

Pola, Giancarlo (1999). "A Comparative View of Local Finances in EU Member Countries: Are There Any Lessons to be Drawn?", Amadeo Fossati and Giorgio Panella (eds.), *Fiscal Federalism in European Union*, London and New York: Routledge, pp. 15–56.

Porto, Manuel (2006). *O Orçamento da União Europeia – As Perspetivas Financeiras para 2007–2013*, Coimbra: Almedina.

Porto, Manuel (2012). "O sistema financeiro atual e futuro da União Europeia", João Ricardo Catarino e José F.F. Tavares (coord.), *Finanças Públicas da União Europeia*, Coimbra: Almedina, pp. 87–108.

Porto, Manuel Carlos Lopes (2017). *Teoria da Integração e Políticas da União Europeia – Face aos Desafios da Globalização*, 5th ed., Coimbra: Almedina.

Praet, Peter (2016a). "The ECB and Its Role as a Lender of Last Resort". Available at: www.ecb.europa.eu/press/key/date/2016/html/sp160210.en.html

Praet, Peter (2016b). "Financial Cycles and Monetary Policy". Available at: www.ecb.europa.eu/press/key/date/2016/html/sp160831.en.html

Praet, Peter (2016c). "Monetary Policy Transmission in the Euro Area". Available at: www.ecb.europa.eu/press/key/date/2016/html/sp161006.en.html

Praet, Peter (2017a). "Calibrating Unconventional Monetary Policy". Available at: www.ecb.europa.eu/press/key/date/2017/html/sp170406_1.en.html

Praet, Peter (2017b). "Maintaining Price Stability with Unconventional Monetary Policy Measures". Available at: www.ecb.europa.eu/press/key/date/2017/html/ecb.sp171002.en.html

Praet, Peter (2017c). "The ECB's Monetary Policy: Past and Present". Available at: www.ecb.europa.eu/press/key/date/2017/html/sp170316.en.html

Praet, Peter (2017d). "Unconventional Measures – A Case of Realpolitik", Beck, Thorsten Beck and Hans-Helmut Kotz (eds.), *Ordoliberalism: A German Oddity?*, A VoxEU.org Book, London: CEPR Press, pp. 79–89.

Praet, Peter (2017e). "We Need to Complete the Banking Union". Available at: www.ecb.europa.eu/press/key/date/2017/html/sp170406_3.en.html

Praet, Peter (2018a). "Economic Developments in the Euro Area". Available at: www.ecb.europa.eu/press/key/date/2018/html/ecb.sp180507.en.html

Praet, Peter (2018b). "Assessment of Quantitative Easing and Challenges of Policy Normalization". Available at: www.ecb.europa.eu/press/key/date/2018/html/ecb.sp180314_2.en.html

Praet, Peter (2018c). "Improving the Functioning of the Economic and Monetary Union: Lessons and Challenges for Economic Policies". Available at: www.ecb.europa.eu/press/key/date/2018/html/ecb.sp180416.en.html

Prud'Homme, Remy (1995). "The Dangers of Decentralization", *The World Bank Observer*, 10(2), pp. 201–220.

Puga, Diego and Venales, Anthony (1996). "The Spread of Industry: Spatial Agglomeration in Economic Development", *Journal of Japanese and International Economies*, 10(4), pp. 440–464.

Quadros, Fausto and Sidjanski, Dusan (eds.) (2017). *The Future of Europe – The Reform of the Eurozone and the Deepening of the Political Union*, Lisboa: A.A.F.D.L.

Quaresma, Jesús Crespo and Amador, Octavio Fernández (2010a). "Business Cycle Convergence in EMU: A First Look at the Second Moment". Available at: https://econpapers.repec.org/paper/innwpaper/2010-22.htm

Quaresma, Jesús Crespo and Amador, Octavio Fernández (2010b). "Business Cycle Convergence in EMU: A Second Look at the Second Moment". Available at: www.sciencedirect.com/science/article/pii/S0261560613000752

Quelhas, José Manuel (2013). *Sobre as Crises Financeiras, o Risco Sistémico e a Incerteza Sistemática*, Coimbra: Almedina.

Ravn, Morten O. and Sola, Martin (2004). "Asymmetric Effects of Monetary Policy in the United States", *Federal Reserve Bank of St. Louis Review*, 86(5), pp. 41–60.

Razin, Assaf (2014). *Understanding Global Crises: An Emerging Paradigm*, Cambridge, MA: MIT Press.

Reinhart, Carmen M. (2012). "The Return of Financial Repression", CEPR Discussion Paper No. DP8947. Available at: https://ssrn.com/abstract=2066320

Reinhart, Carmen M. and Kirkegaard, Jacob (2012). "Financial Repression: Then and Now". Available at: https://voxeu.org/article/financial-repression-then-and-now

Reinhart, Carmen M. and Rogoff, Kenneth S. (2009a). "The Aftermath of Financial Crisis", NBER Working Paper No 14656. Available at: www.nber.org/papers/w14656.pdf

Reinhart, Carmen M. and Rogoff, Kenneth S. (2009b). *This Time Is Different – Eight Centuries of Financial Folly*, Princeton and Oxford: Princeton University Press.

Reinhart, Carmen M. and Rogoff, Kenneth S. (2010). "Growth in a Time of Debt", *American Economic Review: Papers and Proceedings*, 100, pp. 573–578.

Reinhart, Carmen M. and Rogoff, Kenneth S. (2013). "Financial and Sovereign Debt Crises: Some Lessons Learned and Those Forgotten", IMF Working Paper, WP/13/266.

Reinhart, Carmen M. and Sbrancia, M. Belen (2011). "The Liquidation of Government Debt", NBER Working Paper No 16893. Available at: www.imf.org/external/np/seminars/eng/2011/res2/pdf/crbs.pdf

Reinhart, Carmen M. and Trebesch, Christoph (2016). "Sovereign Debt Relief and Its Aftermath", *Journal of the European Economic Association*, 14(1), pp. 251–251.

Reinhart, Carmen M. *et al.* (2017). "Capital Flow Cycles: A Long, Global View". Available at: file:///Users/nazarecostacabral/Downloads/CapitalFlowCyclesA-LongGlobalView_preview.pdf

Repasi, René (2017). "Legal Options and Limits for the Establishment of a European Unemployment Benefit Scheme", Social Europe, Brussels: European Commission.

Riet, Ad van (2017). "Addressing the Safety Dilemma: A Safe Sovereign Asset for the Eurozone", ESRB Working Paper Series No. 35, February 2017.

Rinaldi, David and Ferrer, Jorge Núñez (2017). "The European Fund for Strategic Investments as a New Type of Budgetary Instrument", CEPS Research Report, No 2017/07.

Rixtel, Adrian van and Gasperini, Gabriele (2013). "Financial Crises and Bank Funding: Recent Experience in the Euro Area", BIS Working Papers No 406. Available at: www.bis.org/publ/work406.pdf

Rodden, Jonathan A. (2006). *Hamilton's Paradox – The Promise and Peril of Fiscal Federalism*, Cambridge: Cambridge University Press.

Rodrigues, Nuno Cunha (2019). "The Pan-European Pension Product and the Capital Markets Union: A Way to Enhance and Complete the Economic and Monetary Union?", Nazaré da Costa Cabral and Nuno Cunha Rodrigues (eds.), *The Future of Pension Plans in the EU Internal Market – Coping with Trade-Offs Between Social Rights and Financial Markets*, Switzerland: Springer, pp. 179–191.

Rodrigues, Nuno Cunha and Gonçalves, José Renato (2017). "The European Banking Union and the Economic and Monetary Union: The Puzzle Is Yet to Be Completed", Nazaré da Costa Cabral *et al.* (eds.), *The Euro and Crisis – Perspectives for the Eurozone as a Monetary and Budgetary Union*, Switzerland: Springer, pp. 271–288.

Romer, Christina D. and Bernstein, Jared (2009). "The Job Impact of the American Recovery and Reinvestment Plan". Available at: www.economy.com/markzandi/documents/The_Job_Impact_of_the_American_Recovery_and_Reinvestment_Plan.pdf

Romer, Christina D. and Romer, David H. (2010). "The Macroeconomic Effects of Tax Changes: Estimates Based on a New Measure of Fiscal Shocks", *American Economic Review*, 100(3), pp. 763–801.

Rose, Andrew K. (1999). "One Money, One Market: Estimating the Effect of Common Currencies on Trade", NBER Working Paper 7443. Available at: www.nber.org/papers/w7432.pdf

Rossi, Sergio (2017). "A Structural-Reform Proposal for a Two-Speed European Monetary Union", Nazaré da Costa Cabral *et al.* (eds.), *The Euro and Crisis – Perspectives for the Eurozone as a Monetary and Budgetary Union*, Switzerland: Springer, pp. 33–46.

Rossi, Sergio and Dafflon, Bernard (2012). "Repairing the Original Sin of the European Monetary Union", *International Journal of Monetary Economics and Finance*, 5.

Rule, Garreth (2015). "Understanding the Central Bank Balance Sheet", Centre for the Central Banking Studies, Bank of England.

Sala-I-Martin, Xavier, and Sachs, Jeffrey (1991). "Fiscal Federalism and Optimum Currency Areas: Evidence for Europe from the United States", National Bureau of Economic Research Working Paper, Cambridge, MA.

Salmon, Pierre (2006). "Horizontal Competition among Governments", Ehtisham Ahmad and Giorgio Brosio (eds.), *Handbook of Fiscal Federalism*, Cheltenham, UK: Edward Elgar, pp. 61–85.

Salter, W.E.G. (1959). "Internal and External Balance: The Role of Price and Expenditure Effects", *Economic Record*, 35(71), pp. 226–238.

Sapir, André (2016). "Dealing with EMU Heterogeneity – National versus European Institutional Reforms", Francesco Caselli *et al.* (eds.), *After the Crisis – Reform Recovery and Growth in Europe*, Oxford: Oxford University Press, pp. 73–88.

Sapir, André and Schoenmaker, Dirk (2017). "We Need a European Monetary Fund, But How Should It Work?". Available at: https://bruegel.org/2017/05/we-need-a-european-monetary-fund-but-how-should-it-work/

Schaechter *et al.* (2012). "Fiscal Rules in Response to the Crisis – Toward the 'Next-Generation' Rules. A New Dataset", IMF Working Paper, WP/12/187.

Schelkle, Waltraud (2005). "The Political Economy of Fiscal Policy Coordination in EMU: From Disciplinarian Device to Insurance Arrangement", *Journal of Common Market Studies*, 43(2), pp. 371–391.

Schelkle, Waltraud (2017). *The Political Economy of Monetary Solidarity – Understanding the Euro Experiment*, Oxford: Oxford University Press.

Schimmelfennig, Frank (2014). "European Integration in the Euro Crisis: The Limits of Postfunctionalism", *Journal of European Integration*, 36(3), pp. 321–337.

Schimmelfennig, Frank (2015). "Liberal Intergovernmentalism and the Euro Area Crisis", *Journal of European Public Policy*, 22(2), pp. 177–195.

Schoenmaker, Dirk (2011). "The Financial Trilemma", *Economics Letters*, 111, pp. 57–59.

Schoenmaker, Dirk (2015). "Firmer Foundations for a Stronger European Banking Union", Bruegel Working Paper 2015/13.

Schoenmaker, Dirk (2017). *From Risk to Opportunity: A Framework for Sustainable Finance*, Rotterdam: Rotterdam School of Management, Erasmus University.

Schoenmaker, Dirk and Wolff, Guntram B. (2015). "What Options for the European Deposit Insurance?". Available at: https://bruegel.org/2015/10/what-options-for-european-deposit-insurance/

Schratzenstaller, Margit (2014). "Reform Options for the EU's System of Own Resources", *Revue de l' OFCE*, 1/2014(N° 132), pp. 327–355.

Sepulveda, Cristian F. and Martinez-Vasquez, Jorge (2011). "The Consequences of Fiscal Decentralization on Poverty and Income Inequality", Paper Series, International Center for Public Policy Working, George State University.

Sgherri, Silvia and Zoli, Edda (2011). "Euro Area Sovereign Risk during the Crisis", Robert W. Kolb (ed.), *Sovereign Debt – From Safety to Default*, Hoboken, New Jersey: Wiley, pp. 415–421.

Shah, Anwar (1991). "Perspectives on the Design of Intergovernmental Fiscal Relations", Policy Research Working Paper, WPS 726, Washington, DC: The World Bank.

Shah, Anwar (2006). "A Practitioner's Guide to Intergovernmental Fiscal Transfers", The World Bank Policy Research Working Paper, 4039, Washington, DC: The World Bank.

Shah, Anwar (ed.) (2007a). *The Practice of Fiscal Federalism: Comparative Perspectives*, A Global Dialogue on Federalism, Vol. 4, Montreal and Kingston: McGill-Queen's University Press.

Shah, Anwar (2007b). "Introduction: Principles of Fiscal Federalism", Anwar Shah (ed.), *The Practice of Fiscal Federalism: Comparative Perspectives*, A Global Dialogue on Federalism, Vol. 4, Montreal and Kingston: McGill-Queen's University Press.

Shah, Anwar (2007c). "A Practitioner's Guide to Intergovernmental Fiscal Transfers", Robin Boadway and Anwar Shah (eds.), *Intergovernmental Fiscal Transfers – Principles and Practice*, Washington, DC: The World Bank, pp. 1–53.

Shah, Anwar (ed.) (2008). *Macro Federalism and Local Finance*, Washington, DC: The World Bank.

Shah, Anwar (2012). "Public Services and Expenditure Need Equalization – Reflections on Principles and Worldwide Comparative Practices", Policy Research Working Paper, WPS 6006, Washington, DC: The World Bank.

Shankar, Raja and Shah, Anwar (2008). "Regional Income Disparities and Convergence: Measurement and Policy Impact Evaluation", Anwar Shah (ed.), *Macro Federalism and Local Finance*, Washington, DC: The World Bank, pp. 143–191.

Shankar, Raja and Shah, Anwar (2009). "Lessons from European Union Policies for Regional Development", Policy Research Working Paper 4977, The World Bank, June 2009.

Shiller, Robert J. (1993). *Macro Markets: Creating Institutions for Managing Society's Largest Economic Risks*, New York: Oxford University Press.

Simões, Marta C.N. *et al.* (2017). "Differences in Human Capital and Openness to Trade as Barriers to Growth and Convergence in the EU", Nazaré da Costa Cabral *et al.* (eds.), *The Euro and Crisis – Perspectives for the Eurozone as a Monetary and Budgetary Union*, Switzerland: Springer, pp. 73–93.

Sinn, Hans-Werner (2012). "The European Balance of Payment Crisis: An Introduction", *CESifo Forum*, 13, pp. 3–10.

Sluis, Marijn Van Der (2014). "Maastricht Revisited: Economic Constitutionalism, the ECB and the Bundesbank", Maurice Adams *et al.* (eds.), *The Constitutionalization of European Budgetary Constraints*, Oxford and Portland, OR: Hart Publishing, pp. 105–123.

Smaghi, Lorenzo Bini (2009). "Conventional and Unconventional Monetary Policy". Available at: www.bis.org/review/r090429e.pdf

Smaghi, Lorenzo Bini and Marcussen, Michala (2019). "Delivering a Safe Asset for the Euro Area: A Proposal for a Purple Bond Transition", Jean Pisany-Ferry and Jeromin Zettelmeyer (eds.), *Risk-Sharing Plus Market Discipline: A New Paradigm for Euro Area Reform? A Debate*, A VosEU.org Book, London: CEPR Press, pp. 68–73.

Smets, Frank and Wouters, Raf (2007). "Shocks and Frictions in US Business Cycles: A Bayesian DSGE Approach", *American Economic Review*, 97(3), pp. 506–606.

Snoddon, Tracy R. (2004). "Fiscal Institutions, Regional Adjustment and Convergence in Canada's Currency Union", Mark Baimbridge and Philip Whyman (eds.), *Fiscal Federalism and European Economic Integration*, London and New York: Routledge, pp. 172–194.

Soares, António Goucha (2016). "Euro – E se a Alemanha Sair Primeiro?", Temas e Debates, Círculo de Leitores.

Sørensen, Bent E. and Yosha, Oved (1998). "International Risk Sharing and European Monetary Unification", *Journal of International Economics*, 45(1998), pp. 211–238.

Spahn, Paul Bernd (1997). "Decentralized Government and Macroeconomic Control", The World Bank, Urban No. FM-12.

Spahn, Paul Bernd (2006). "Contract Federalism", Ehtisham Ahmad and Giorgio Brosio (eds.), *Handbook of Fiscal Federalism*, Cheltenham, UK: Edward Elgar, pp. 182–197.

Spence, Michael (1973). "Job Market Signaling", *The Quarterly Journal of Economics*, 87, pp. 355–374.

Stancil, Bennett (2010a). "Why Greece Has to Restructure Its Debt?", Uri Dadush and Contributors (eds.), *Paradigm Lost – The Euro in Crisis*, Washington, DC: Carnegie Endowment for International Peace, pp. 25–29.

Stancil, Bennett (2010b). "Ireland: From Bubble to Broke". Available at: https://carnegieendowment.org/2010/05/13/ireland-from-bubble-to-broke-pub-40799

Steinbach, Armin (2012). "Towards a European Recovery Programme for the Crisis Countries", *Intereconomics*, 2012/6.

Steinberg, Philipp (2017). "Global Imbalances – Coordinating with Different Script Books", Thorsten Beck and Hans-Helmut Kotz (eds.), *Ordoliberalism: A German Oddity?*, A VoxEU.org Book, London: CEPR Press, pp. 167–180.

Stigler, George J. (1957). "The Tenable Range of Functions of Local Government", Joint Economic Committee, Subcommittee on Fiscal Policy, U.S. Congress, Federal Expenditure Policy for Economic Growth and Stability, Washington, DC: U.S.

Stiglitz, Joseph (2000). "Capital Market Liberalization, Economic Growth, and Instability", *World Development*, 28(6), pp. 1075–1086.

Stiglitz, Joseph (2016). *The Euro – How a Common Currency Threatens de Future of Europe*, New York and London: W.W. Norton & Company.

Stiglitz, Joseph (2017). "The Fundamental Flaws in the Euro Zone Framework", Nazaré da Costa Cabral *et al.* (eds.), *The Euro and Crisis – Perspectives for the Eurozone as a Monetary and Budgetary Union*, Switzerland: Springer, pp. 11–16.

Stockman, Alan C. (1999). "Choosing an Exchange-rate System", *Journal of Banking & Finance*, 23, pp. 1483–1498.

Stossberg, Sibylle *et al.* (2016). "Fiscal Decentralisation and Income Inequality: Empirical Evidence from OECD Countries", OECD Working Papers on Fiscal Federalism, No. 1331.

Strásky, Jan and Claveres, Guillaume (2019). "A European Fiscal Capacity Can Avoid Permanent Transfers and Improve Stabilization". Available at: https://voxeu.org/article/european-fiscal-capacity-can-avoid-permanent-transfers-and-improve-stabilisation

Strasser, Daniel (1975). *Les finances de l'Éurope*, Paris: PUF.

Strauss, Robert (2016). "The History and Debate in Europe on a European Unemployment Benefits Scheme". Available at: www.upjohn.org/sites/default/files/inline-files/strauss.pdf

Summers, Lawrence H. (2016). "The Age of Secular Stagnation". Available at: http://larrysummers.com/2016/02/17/the-age-of-secular-stagnation/

Sutherland, Douglas *et al.* (2005). "Sub-central Government Fiscal Rules", *OECD Economic Studies*, 41, pp. 141–181.

Swann, Dennis (1995). *The Economics of the Common Market – Integration in the European Union*, 8th ed., London: Penguin Books.

Tabellini, Guido (2016). "Building Common Fiscal Policy in the Eurozone", Richard Baldwin and Francesco Giavazzi (eds.), *How to Fix Europe's Monetary Union – Views of Leading Economists*, A VoxEU.org Book, London: CEPR Press, pp. 119–131.

Tanzi, Vito (1996). "Fiscal Federalism and Decentralization: A Review of Some Efficiency and Macroeconomic Aspects", In *Proceedings of the Annual World Bank Conference on Development Economics*, Washington, DC: World Bank, pp. 295–316.

Tanzi, Vito (2005). "The Stability and Growth Pact: Its Role and Future", *Revista da Faculdade de Direito da Universidade de Lisboa*, XLVI(1), pp. 109–119.

Tavares, José F.F. (2012). "Linhas de evolução das finanças públicas europeias", João Ricardo Catarino e José F.F. Tavares (coord.), *Finanças Públicas da União Europeia*, Coimbra: Almedina, pp. 35–60.

Taylor, Alan M. (2013). "External Imbalances and Financial Crises", IMF Working Paper, WP/13/260.

Ter-Minassian, Teresa (ed.) (1997). *Fiscal Federalism in Theory and Practice*, Washington DC: International Monetary Fund.

Ter-Minassian, Teresa (2006). "Fiscal Rules for Subnational Governments: Can They Promote Fiscal Discipline?", *OECD Journal on Budgeting*, 6(3), pp. 111–121.

Ter-Minassian, Teresa and Craig, Jon (1997). "Control of Subnational Government Borrowing", Teresa Ter-Minassian (ed.), *Fiscal Federalism in Theory and Practice*, Washington, DC: International Monetary Fund, pp. 156–172.

Thirion, Gilles (2017). "European Fiscal Union: Economic Rationale and Design Challenges", CEPS Working Paper, No. 2017/01. Available at: www.ceps.eu/publications/european-fiscal-union-economic-rationale-and-design-challenges

Thomadakis, Apostolos (2017). "Developing EU Capital Markets for SMEs: Mission Impossible?", ECMI Commentary No. 46/4, September 2017.

Tiebout, Charles M. (1956). "A Pure Theory of Local Expenditures", *Journal of Political Economy*, LXIV(5), pp. 416–424.

Tirole, Jean (2006). *The Theory of Corporate Finance*, Princeton and Oxford: Princeton University Press.

Tondl, Gabriele (2000). "Fiscal Federalism and the Reality of the European Union Budget", Colin Crouch (ed.), *After the Euro – Shaping Institutions for Governance in the Wake of European Monetary Union*, Oxford: Oxford University Press, pp. 227–256.

Treichel, Volker (2012). "The Euro Crisis – What Role Did the Common Currency Play?". Available at: http://blogs.worldbank.org/developmenttalk/the-euro-crisis-what-role-did-the-common-currency-play

Trein, Philipp (2017). "Federal Dynamics and European Union Crisis Politics". Available at: www.researchgate.net/publication/318379241_Federal_Dynamics_Solidarity_and_European_Union_Crisis_Politics

Tridimas, Takis and Xanthoulis, Napoleon (2016). "A Legal Analysis of the *Gauweiler* Case – Between Monetary Policy and Constitutional Conflict", Federico Fabbrini (ed.), *The European Court of Justice, the European Central Bank and the Supremacy of EU Law*, Special Issue (2016), 23 *Maastricht Journal of European & Comparative Law* 1, pp. 17–39.

Turrini, Alessandro (2011). "EPL Reforms in Europe: A Portuguese Way to Single Contract Outcomes?". Available at: https://voxeu.org/article/labour-market-reforms-lessons-portugal

Ubide, Ángel (2015). "Stability Bonds for the Euro Area", PIIE Policy Brief, Number 15–19, October 2015.

Ugolini, Stefano (2018). "The Historical Evolution of Central Banking", Stefano Battilossi *et al.* (eds.), *Handbook of the History of Money and Currency*, Switzerland: Springer.

Uhlig, Harald (2013). "Sovereign Default Risk and Banks in a Monetary Union", *German Economic Review*, 15(1), pp. 23–41.

Valiante, Diego (2016). "Europe's Untapped Capital Market – Rethinking Financial Integration After the Crisis", Final Report of the European Capital Markets Expert Group Chaired by Francesco Papadia, Brussels: Centre for European Policy Studies European Capital Markets Institute Brussels.

Van Rompuy, Herman *et al.* (2012). "Towards a Genuine Economic and Monetary Union". Available at: www.consilium.europa.eu/media/23818/134069.pdf

Vandendroucke, Frank *et al.* (2017). "Institutional Moral Hazard in the Multi-tiered Regulation of Unemployment and Social Assistance Benefits and Activation", Social Europe, Brussels: European Commission.

Varoufakis, Yanis (2016). *And the Weak Suffer What They Must?: Europe's Crisis and America's Economic Future*, New York: Nation Books.

Verdun, Amy (2010). "Ten Years EMU: An Assessment of Ten Critical Claims", *International Journal of Economics and Business Research*, 2(1/2), pp. 144–163.

Véron, Nicolas (2011). "Testimony on the European Debt and Financial Crisis", Bruegel Policy Brief Issue 2011/11. Available at: www.infoeuropa.eurocid.pt/files/database/000047001-000048000/000047508.pdf

Véron, Nicolas (2015). "Europe's Radical Banking Union", Bruegel Essay and Lectures Series.

Vigneault, Marianne (2007). "Grants and Soft Budget Constraints", Robin Boadway and Anwar Shah (eds.), *Intergovernmental Fiscal Transfers – Principles and Practice*, Washington DC: The World Bank, pp. 133–171.

von Hagen, Jürgen (1992). "Fiscal Arrangements in a Monetary Union – Some Evidence for the US", Don Fair and Christian de Boissieux (eds.), *Fiscal Policy, Taxes, and the Financial System in an Increasingly Integrated Europe*, Deventer: Kluwer Academic Publishers.

von Hagen, Jürgen (1998). "Fiscal Policy and Intranational Risk-sharing", ZEI Working Paper, B 13, 1998.

von Hagen, Jürgen (2007). "Achieving Economic Stabilisation by Sharing Risk within Countries", Robin Boadway and Anwar Shah (ed.), *Intergovernmental Fiscal Transfers – Principles and Practice*, Public Sector Governance and Accountability Series, Washington, DC: The World Bank, pp. 107–132.

von Hagen, Jürgen and Hepp, Ralf (2001). "Regional Risk Sharing and Redistribution in the German Federation". Available at: https://econpapers.repec.org/paper/cprceprdp/2662.htm

von Hagen, Jürgen and Mundschenk, Susanne (2002). "Fiscal and Monetary Policy Coordination in EMU", Central Bank of Chile Working Papers, No. 194, December 2002.

von Hagen, Jürgen and Wyplosz, Charles (2008). "EMU's Decentralized System of Fiscal Policy", European Economy Economic Papers 306, February 2008.

Wasserfallen, Fabio (2013). "Political and Economic Integration in the EU: The Case of Failed Tax Harmonization", *Journal of Common Market Studies*, 52(2), pp. 420–435. https://doi.org/10.1111/jcms.12099

Watt, Andrew (2009). "A Quantum of Solace? An Assessment of Fiscal Stimulus Packages by EU Members States in Response to the Economic Crisis", Etui, Working Paper 2009.05. Available at: www.etui.org/Publications2/Working-Papers/A-quantum-of-solace-An-assessment-of-fiscal-stimulus-packages-by-EU-Member-States-in-response-to-the-economic-crisis

Watts, Ronald L. (2008). *Comparing Federal Systems*, 3rd ed., Montreal, Kingston and London: Institute of Intergovernmental Relations, McGill-Queen's University Press.

Weber, Max (1930). *The Protestant Ethic and the Spirit of Capitalism*, Abingdon: Routledge.

Whelan, Karl (2013). "Ireland's Economic Crisis – The Good, the Bad and the Ugly", Conference Paper. Available at: www.karlwhelan.com/Papers/Whelan-IrelandPaper-June2013.pdf

Wieland, Volker (2009a). "Eurozone Stimulus: A Myth, Some Facts, and Impact Estimates". Available at: http://econ.tu.ac.th/archan/rangsun/ec%20460/ec%20460%20readings/global%20issues/Global%20Financial%20Crisis%202007-2009/Academic%20Works%20By%20Instituion/VoxEU/Eurozone%20Stimulus-%20Myth,%20facts,%20Impact.pdf

Wieland, Volker (2009b). "The Fiscal Stimulus Debate: 'Bone-headed' and 'Neanderthal'?". Available at: https://voxeu.org/article/will-stimulus-work-reasons-doubt-romer-bernstein-spending-multiplier-estimates

Wildasin, D.E. (1997). "Externalities and Bailouts – Hard and Soft Budget Constraints in Intergovernmental Fiscal Relations", Policy Research Working Paper No 1843, Washington, DC: The World Bank.

Winkler, Adalbert (2014). "The Lender of Last Resort in Court", Frankfurt School – Working Paper Series, No. 207, Frankfurt School of Finance & Management.

Winkler, Adalbert (2017). "Ordoliberalism, Post-Crisis, Monetary Policy and the German 'Angst'", Thorsten Beck and Hans-Helmut Kotz (eds.), *Ordoliberalism: A German oddity?*, A VoxEU.org Book, London: CEPR Press, pp. 91–105.

Wolf, Martin (2014). *The Shifts and the Shocks – What We've Learned – and Have Still to Learn – From the Financial Crisis*, New York: Penguin Books.

Wolff, Guntram B. (2012). "A Budget for Europe's Monetary Union", Bruegel Policy Contribution, Issue 2012/22. Available at: http://bruegel.org/2012/12/a-budget-for-europes-monetary-union/

Wonders, Grant (2010). *The Imminent Crisis – Greek Debt and the Collapse of the European Monetary Union*, Cambridge: Create Space.

Wymeersch, Eddy (2014). "The Single Supervisory Mechanism or 'SSM', Part One of the Banking Union", Law Working Paper No. 240/2014, University of Gent.

Wyplosz, Charles (1999). "Economic Policy Coordination in EMU: Strategies and Institutions", Mimeo.

Wyplosz, Charles (2012). "The Impossible Hope of an End to Austerity", Giancarlo Corsetti (ed.), *Austerity: Too Much of a Good Thing?*, A VoxEU.org eCollection of views of leading economists, London: CEPR Press, pp. 71–78.

Wyplosz, Charles and Pisani-Ferry, Jean (1990). "Les implications budgetaires de l'union monétaire", *Observations et diagnostics économiques: Revue de l'OFCE*, 33, pp. 155–173.

Xafa, Miranda (2014). "Lessons from the 2012 Greek Debt Restructuring". Available at: https://voxeu.org/article/greek-debt-restructuring-lessons-learned

Xafa, Miranda (2015). "European Banking Union, Three Years On", CIGI Papers, No. 73, Ontario: Center for International Governance Innovation.

Young, Brgitte (2017). "Ordoliberalism as an 'Irritating German Idea'", Thorsten Beck and Hans-Helmut Kotz (eds.), *Ordoliberalism: A German Oddity?*, A VoxEU.org Book, London: CEPR Press, pp. 31–40.

Zettelmeyer, Jeromin (2017). "German Ordo and Eurozone Reform: A View from Trenches", Thorsten Beck and Hans-Helmut Kotz (eds.), *Ordoliberalism: A German oddity?*, A VoxEU.org Book, London: CEPR Press, pp. 155–164.

Zettelmeyer, Jeromin and Leandro, Álvaro (2019). "Beyond ESBies. Safety without Tranching", Jean Pisany-Ferry and Jeromin Zettelmeyer (eds.), *Risk-Sharing Plus Market Discipline: A New Paradigm for Euro Area Reform? A Debate*, A VosEU. org Book, London: CEPR Press, pp. 63–67.

Zettelmeyer, Jeromin *et al.* (2013). "The Greek Debt Restructuring: An Autopsy". Available at: https://scholarship.law.duke.edu/cgi/viewcontent.cgi?article=5343& context=faculty_scholarship

INDEX

Note: Numbers in *italics* indicate figures and numbers in **bold** indicate tables on the corresponding page.